Exploring VICTORIA'S *Architecture*

TEXT
Martin Segger

PHOTOGRAPHY
Douglas Franklin

VICTORIA • BRITISH COLUMBIA • CANADA

Copyright © 1996 by Martin Segger (text) and Douglas Franklin (photography)
ALL RIGHTS RESERVED.

Canadian Cataloguing in Publication Data

Segger, Martin, 1946-
  Exploring Victoria's architecture

  Includes bibliographical references and index.
  ISBN 1-55039-066-x

  1. Architecture—British Columbia—Victoria—History. 2.
Victoria (B.C.)—Buildings, structures, etc. 3. Historic
buildings—British Columbia—Victoria. I. Franklin, Douglas,
1947- II. Title.
FC3846.7.S43 1996   971.1'28   C96-910405-7
F1089.5.V6S43 1996

Publication of this book has been financially
assisted by the Canada Council Block Grant Program.

Published by
SONO NIS PRESS
1725 Blanshard Street
Victoria, British Columbia v8w 2j8

Designed, printed and bound in Canada by
MORRISS PRINTING COMPANY LTD.
Victoria, British Columbia

Dedicated in memory of
Gerald Joseph *and* Francis Joseph
encouraging us to study and seek

ACKNOWLEDGEMENTS

The impetus to write this book came mainly from two long-time friends, book seller Jim Munro and publisher Dick Morriss. I am delighted it will at last grace the shelves of Munro's Books, but I am saddened Dick will not see it in finished form. I hope that its publication by the Morriss family's Sono Nis Press, as originally envisioned, will serve as a fitting tribute to Dick's memory as a dedicated supporter of the visual and literary arts.

Many other friends and colleagues came together to support what has turned out to be an exciting but arduous project. Ann West, as editor and now manager of Sono Nis, has worked skillfully with my material for nearly two decades. Designer Jim Bennett has made graphic sense of a stream of brochures, catalogues, books—even political electioneering pamphlets—for over 20 years. Don Pierce's keen eye in the lab at UVic's Photographic Services has patiently rescued so many of my own amateur fumblings at the difficult art. But in particular I must acknowledge the constant assistance, which has included editorial, artistic—indeed almost the entire management of this volume's visual presentation—of my friend and colleague, Doug Franklin.

The content of this book depends mightily on the work of others. I am deeply grateful that the City of Victoria has kept in print two publications, *This Old Town* and *This Old House*, both originally the collective efforts of this province's first Heritage Advisory Committee on which I had the privilege to serve with early supporters of Victoria's heritage movement such as Sam Bawlf, Bob Broadland, Frank Carson, Peter Cotton and Carolyn Smyly. More recently the pioneering research and thorough inventory work in Victoria's adjacent communities must be recognized: Jennifer Barr in Saanich, Stuart Stark and Helen Edwards in Oak Bay, Nancy Oliver and Lt. Col. Nelson's work on the military heritage of Victoria, also Dr. Oliver's research into the industrial heritage of Greater Victoria; Dr. Elida Peers' in Sooke, Dorothy Field's Esquimalt and Western Communities inventory, Dr. David Lai's exhaustive studies of Victoria's Chinese community, John Adam's studies of local cemeteries, Dr. Peter Smith's documentation of the development of the University of Victoria and Geof Castle's *Times-Colonist* historical building features. Donald Luxton has brought Greater Victoria's Art Deco and Moderne heritage into focus, and in partnership with Valda Vidners carried out the extensive update of the Old Town inventory.

For the modern work, which might be the singular ultimate contribution here, I acknowledge the patience and enthusiasm of the many designers, architects, planners and developers whom I faced (or who helped me) during intense committee sessions and public hearings throughout my six years on Victoria's City Council. There were also many private conversations with long-time architectural practitioners, in particular Rod Clack, Bob Baxter, John Di Castri, Barry Downes, Don Emmons, Chris Gower, David Hambleton, Alan Hodgson, Neil Jackson, Claude Maurice, John Wade, Don Wagg, and Terry Williams. John Bovey at the B.C. Archives, Jim Burroughs at the City of Victoria Archives, Chris Petter and Jane Turner at Special Collections, UVic, Doug Koch and Steve Barber at the City of Victoria Planning Department, Helen Edwards at Hallmark—all have been exceptionally cooperative throughout. My field researchers and photographic crew, Nick De Caro, Al Fry, Ian Baird, and Eva Campbell worked with good humour under trying conditions and tight deadlines. Many building owners and residents have been most generous, helpful and co-operative. Sandra Uhl skillfully compiled the bibliography and index. Barbara Jackson and Cheryl Robinson assisted with the typescript.

On the reader's behalf I acknowledge a debt of gratitude for the contributions of all these people who have given generously of their time, skills and knowledge; and of course I admit full and sole ownership of any mistakes made by transmittal herein. And last, but certainly not least, I thank my wife Angèle who for so long now has kindly accepted the role so many authors demand and expect—that of paper widow throughout the many projects that have resulted in *Exploring Victoria's Architecture*.

Preface

This approach to the architectural history of the Victoria region constitutes a very thin slice through a large subject. Our earlier 1979 volume, *Victoria: A Primer for Regional History in Architecture*, was essentially a series of discursive monographs each of which addressed a single building. *Exploring Victoria's Architecture* is intended as a field guide, its geographical range wider, its subject matter more focussed. The essays and building entries examine the various roles of owner, builder and designer in the creation of built forms which now constitute the cultural landscape of this region. The first organizational thrust is geographical, on the basis that there is some logic to a comparative thematic order which demonstrates how Greater Victoria developed. The second level of organization is chronological, but I have not hesitated to interrupt chronologies where I feel a more descriptive approach to a series of buildings, or a landscape, elucidates an interesting architectural subplot. I have indulged in what sometimes may seem odd choices for departures from the text; in particular I have been fascinated by what we, as a society, have consciously chosen to preserve, and what the development community has done to creatively utilize and recontextualize our built historic fabric for new uses. This is often as telling and interesting as first construction.

Where possible I have tried to select in favour of geographical affinities, so to assist those who wish to experience architecture properly—"in the flesh." *The reader should, however, remember always to respect the privacy of building owners and residents.* There are now numerous good maps and a myriad of printed walking tours, each with their special focus, should readers wish to supplement our generic location guides and the reference place-name and street gazetteer. As the bibliography and in-text endnotes illustrate, there is now a range of specialized regional inventories and some excellent biographical studies which have begun to sketch out the details of our rich architectural history. This text has benefitted greatly from these and might be used to put them in the context of wider and more general scholarship. The very complete index will assist that reading approach. *Exploring Victoria's Architecture* can be used as a backgrounder, reference tool, or in-hand guide. It is my earnest hope that it will prompt further investigations into what continues to unfold as a most fascinating subject.

Martin Segger, Victoria, May 1996

Contents

Acknowledgements 4
Preface 6
Map: Downtown Victoria 8
Building Victoria: Trade and Technology 9
Victoria: The Town 26
FEATURES
A *The Parliamentary Precinct* 46
B *Centennial Square* 85
C *Bastion Square* 88
D *Market Square* 93
E *Eaton Centre* 102
F *Chinatown* 109

Conservation Planning 121
Greater Victoria: The Urban Approaches 126
The Residential Approaches 139
FEATURES
G *Prospect Place, Oak Bay* 160
H *Uplands Development* 177
I *Songhees, Victoria West* 211

University of Victoria: The Gordon Head Campus 220
Esquimalt: The Military Mind 234
Dockyard, Naden and Cole Island 236
Work Point, Esquimalt 242
Map: Saanich Peninsula 244
Saanich Peninsula: Rural Landscape 245
FEATURE
J *Sidney-by-the-Sea* 246

Saanich Peninsula 252
Western Communities 271
Green Ways and Green Spaces 288
Biographies 291
Glossary 312
Selected Bibliography 315
Street and Place-Name Gazetteer 320
Index 322

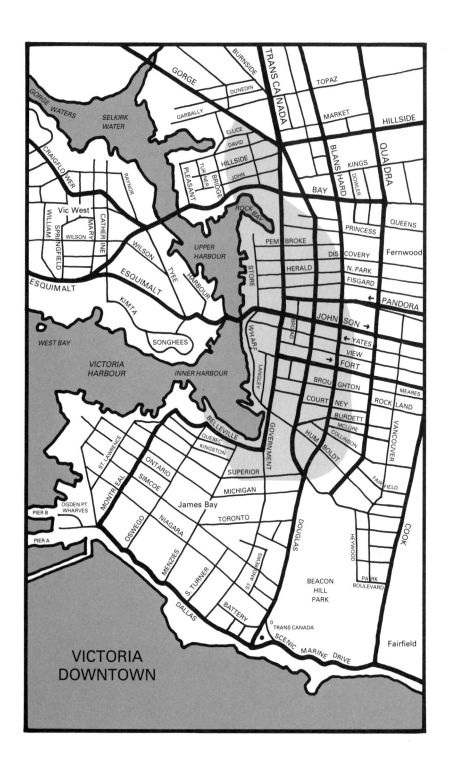

Building Victoria

Trade and Technology

Victoria's lines of migration, communication, transportation, and trade have traditionally been north-south. For thousands of years aboriginal tribes raided and traded along the coastline of the Pacific Northwest. By the 1770s the Spanish explorations pushed north from Mexico and reached the Charlottes. But nineteenth century fur traders and sealers, including the sailing steamers of the Hudson's Bay Company, followed the ancient native trade routes. Only briefly during the early years when the Hudson's Bay Company brought men and materials west did a real east-west axis exist in material form until the completion of the Canadian Pacific Railway. So when HBC chief factor James Douglas landed at Cattle Point he was introduced to the local Coast Salish whose main village site was at Kamosak on the protected harbour side of what is now James Bay. Douglas established the fort adjacent to the native settlement. In 1850 the HBC purchased the entire townsite, and assisted the Songhees in dismantling their huge distinctive cedar plank long houses to relocate on the west side of the harbour.

From that time Victoria's social and economic history is one of migrations. Population movements on a large scale ebbed and flowed with the discovery and depletion of gold from 1858 on and from harvests from the seal, whale, and fish industries from the early 1850s. Mainly born or "processed" Americans formed both the entrepreneurial fibre and skilled trades for the early English colony during these years. Then, with the coming of the Royal Engineers and some of the early colonial administrative staff, English ideas began to filter directly into the area.

The major mode of transportation remained maritime well into this century. By 1869 San Francisco was connected to the eastern states by railroad, thus opening up the entire American continent and its products to Victoria. These patterns of trade died slowly, even after the completion of the Canadian Pacific Railway in 1885. Robert Dunsmuir's coal fortune, many a local lumber baron's prosperity, and even the livelihood of some market gardeners, were directly tied to resource-hungry San Francisco. And along these lines of communication travelled the popular press and magazines such as Portland's *West Shore*—a taste maker and mixer—which featured coastal urban progress through engravings and lithographs of new buildings. Only later did steam power, both marine and on land, change the face of British Columbia's capital city.

Catalogue-ordered ornament, hardware, cast-iron fronts, and decorative millwork were imported by Victorians along these routes. Many early local architects such as John Wright, John Teague, and A. Maxwell Muir came to Victoria via California. Commissions going to outsiders also followed the north-south axis. Portland architect W. H. Williams provided the designs for the first Bank of British Columbia in 1886. As the bank was instrumental in the Dunsmuirs' coal-based financial empire, cultural interests followed commercial trade routes to such American manufacturing centres as Portland and San Francisco. This tradition persisted. During the 1906-1912 real estate boom, much of the speculative building took the form of the California Bungalow. Built from mail-order plans originating in California, many of these sturdy little chalet-adobe hybrid structures have survived. Among individual commissions during these years are the H. G. Wilson house of 1905 designed by California architect Charles King and the Union Club of 1912 by Loring P. Rexford of San Francisco.

About the same time as the first groups of settlers disembarked on "Vancouver's Island" Benjamin William Pearse arrived overland from California. Pearse was second Surveyor General to the Crown colony. Under his direction came such projects as the erection of government buildings, the laying out of road systems on Vancouver Island, the settlement of the Cowichan area, the building of lighthouses, and later, on the mainland, the construction of the Cariboo Road. One of Pearse's first tasks was to assist J. D. Pemberton, then Surveyor General, in laying out Victoria. One of the first important roads was Wharf Street, flanked by the Hudson's Bay Company warehouses on the harbour side, and provisioning stores, some of the earliest brick buildings, on the other wood block sheet pavers muffled the sound of horses hooves. Some of these block pavers are still evident in Waddington Alley off lower Yates Street. Metal curbstones protecting street corners from the steel carriage wheels, and concrete hitching posts, remain on Rockland Avenue as evidence of the days of horse-drawn vehicles.

The inception of various utilities indicated technological stages in Victoria's growth from a ramshackle boom-town to a more permanent settlement. Gas services commenced in 1862; piped water was available from 1873, and electricity from 1884. Sewers were installed beginning in 1890; it was B. W. Pearse who headed the planning commission to oversee their introduction. In July of 1877, one year after Alexander Graham Bell patented the telephone, a short line was strung between Jeffrey's Clothing store, Yates Street and Pendray's Soap Works on Humbolt Street.

The coming of age of iron technology can be read from a number of monuments that have over the years dominated Victoria's skyline. One early structure of particular significance was the famous "Iron Church," prefabricated in England and shipped to the colony of Vancouver Island in 1860. During its life in Victoria, as St. John's Anglican Church (demolished in 1912), it was regarded as a temporary structure although the large nave and full bell tower made it a substantial looking building. It stood on the northeast corner of Fisgard and Douglas, where The Bay department store now stands.

The iron front of the Rithet Building (1861-1885) on Wharf Street is a good example of the structural and decorative capabilities of cast iron. The units for this front were mass-produced in the San Francisco foundries of J. P. Donahue, and remain among the earliest surviving examples of prefabricated iron construction on the west coast. A different use of cast iron is illustrated by the Bank of British Columbia building (at the southwest corner of Government and Fort Streets) which was designed by W. H. Williams of Portland, Oregon in 1866. Here decorative cast iron elements are pinned to a brick structure. Entirely ornamental, the iron has no load-bearing function. The decorative and structural use of cast iron is well married in the Oriental Hotel (now the Goodwill Building, lower Yates Street) built in 1883, designed by architect and sometime Victoria mayor John Teague. Prefabricated structural and decorative components available through American foundry catalogues introduced the economies of mass production and allowed facades to be opened up far beyond the limits of traditional brick construction.

A number of other buildings pioneering cast iron have not survived, amongst them the Agricultural Exhibition Hall at Willows Park in Oak Bay, and the City Market which was demolished to make way for Centennial Square. Both were designed by the Scottish immigrant A. Maxwell Muir. They made extensive use of glass but were not true iron and glass structures in the Victorian London Crystal Palace exhibition hall tradition. A Botanical Gardens, proposed as the centrepiece for Beacon Hill

Victoria Harbour from the Songhees Reserve, *ca.* 1860. CVA

View of Fort Victoria. BCARS A-9088

St. John's Anglican "Iron Church." BCARS B-7346

Windsor Hotel, Government Street.   BCARS A-2716

Victoria Bird's Eye View, 1889.   BCARS 62209

Yates Street, 1860s. BCARS 3712

The Maclure central plan hall house.
Alexis Martin House, Rockland, 1904
as published in
The Craftsman (March 1908).

Publicity Sketch for proposed CPR Hotel, James Bay Causeway, F. M. Rattenbury.
Published *Daily Colonist*, May 23, 1903. COURTESY VICTORIA PUBLIC LIBRARY.

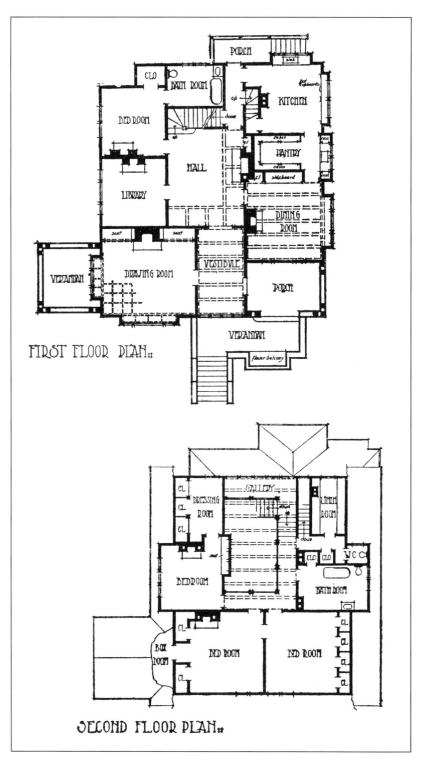

Floor plans for the Alexis Martin House, Rockland, 1908. Architect Samuel Maclure. Note the focus on the "hall."

Imperial Oil Building, 1931. BCARS. CHAPMAN COLL. 93670

park by its landscape architect, John Blair, was never built. The greenhouses at Hatley Park, Colwood, prefabricated by Lord and Burnham Company Limited of St. Catharines, Ontario, suppliers of the Crystal Garden roof, were destroyed in 1956 after having been unsuccessfully offered to the City of Victoria for Beacon Hill Park. Glass and iron structures which remain in the Victoria area include the Empress Hotel ballroom roof and conservatory which, appropriately located on the east side of the hotel, face the Crystal Gardens and constitute a unique visual riposte to the generous spread of their larger cousin on the east side of Douglas Street—the Crystal Gardens. The Crystal (designed by Rattenbury and James, 1925) is Victoria's monument to iron truss building technology, and a true descendant of its London namesake. By this time structural steel frame had become the preferred construction method for the Chicago style office buildings that lined the streets of downtown Victoria following the erection of the Belmont Building in 1912.

A barometer which indicated Victoria's growth in industrial self-sufficiency can be found in one sector closely allied to the building trades. The manufacture of bricks was directly tied to economic growth and mechanization with the industry itself. The *Victoria Gazette* of 1859 contains numerous advertisements for bricks, in lots ranging from 9,000 to 100,000. Their origins are listed variously as England, California, and in particular, San Francisco. Local brickmaking may have begun as early as

1860 to accommodate the construction of Fisgard Lighthouse. By 1863 there was a brickworks on Saanich Road under the direction of Arthur Porter. The brick industry was no doubt encouraged in 1860 by the passage of a bill in the Colonial Assembly which rendered brick chimneys compulsory within the limits of the town of Victoria. Brick production in Victoria peaked with the construction boom of 1912. One of the largest companies growing with increasing demand during those years was the Victoria Brick and Tile Company, founded in 1885. In 1912 its output amounted to 40,000 bricks and 12,000 feet of drain tiles a day.

The 1905 Empress Hotel was built on piles driven deep into the soft clay subsoils. The Crystal Gardens' 1925 gossamer roof of steel and glass is, however, supported by massive concrete substructures. Built on the former tidal mud flat of James Bay, the swimming pool foundation actually floats, suspended within a giant reinforced concrete raft. The first building to really demonstrate the possibilities of reinforced concrete construction was the 1912 Belmont Building, although its final cladding is glazed terracotta expressing an Edwardian Classical vocabulary. True expressions of reinforced and form work concrete construction had to await the Bay Street Electric Substation for the B.C. Electric Company in 1928. This was quasi-industrial architecture and the brief Deco detailing caused it to masquerade as a Nile Valley Egyptian temple. On the Inner Harbour, and perhaps slightly more honest, if heroic, is the concrete tower of the 1931 Imperial Oil gas station. Rather more severe, and modern, the abstract forms of the B.C. Power Commission Building terminating the vista south on Blanshard Street 20 years later are still within this same tradition. World War II provided significant opportunity for developments in concrete construction technology, particularly the need in Germany and England to span huge spaces for aircraft maintenance. These advances can be witnessed in post-war Victoria in the massive compressed concrete arches and roof membrane of the 1947 Memorial Arena. That the gravity-defying structural capabilities of the technology loosened up the architectural vocabulary can be found today in the 1950s and 1960s work of architects such as John Di Castri (CNIB Building, 1951) and Alan Hodgson (new entrance to the McPherson Theatre, 1965).

Form, Function and "Architecture"

The first permanent structures to rise in the Victoria area were those initiated by the Hudson's Bay Company. These were the Fort and ancillary structures, then later the HBC farms at Craigflower, Langford, and Esquimalt, most of them built according to the standard plans or instructions which characterize all the surviving HBC buildings in the West. Hudson's Bay Company domination fast diminished with the influx of the first gold seekers in 1858, and official colonial status was enhanced with

H. O. Tiedemann's Colonial Administration Building familiarly known as the "Birdcages." Despite the decorative trappings, the form derives from British Colonial vernacular architecture of the Pacific Rim colonies. The single-storey elevation nestling under wide expanses of a gently sloping hipped roof, and surrounded by long open verandahs, is a hallmark of the colonial bungalow type. There are endless domestic variations on this theme still standing in the Beacon Hill area and in Esquimalt. The decorative fretwork dressed the building up in the "Swiss" idiom as popularized by A. J. Downing in the 1840s. This was intended to accommodate the building to its majestic setting, silhouetted against the backdrop of the Olympic Mountains.

Tiedemann's official capacity was that of chief engineer to the Colonial Government. In 1859 he was joined by architect John Wright, a Scot who came to Victoria from San Francisco. As Victoria's population was to expand, mainly by the northward trek of California gold seekers, so the architecture was to adopt a decidedly American flavour. Wright's domestic idiom was drawn from Victorian versions of the rural Italianate Villa, a style popular in San Francisco during the 1850s and successfully adapted to the enduring qualities of timber construction. In 1862 another architectural practice opened in Victoria. John Teague, an Englishman and mining engineer, followed the California gold seekers to San Francisco, then to the Fraser, and settled in Victoria to open a construction and architectural business. In 1866 his practice was joined by a third, that of another Englishman and California gold seeker, Edward Mallandaine. Thomas Trounce operated a construction business and also "did plans." Teague's first work was for the British Admiralty at Esquimalt where he worked on the construction of dry-dock and harbour installations. It was no doubt Navy patronage that won him his first domestic commission, a storekeeper's house now called "The Admiral's House" at CFB Esquimalt.

More than any other person it is Teague who sets the tone for Victoria's commercial architecture of the late 1870s, the 1880s and the early 1890s—a period of rapid growth. It is still evident in the buildings now lining lower Johnson, Yates, Fort, Pandora including Government, Bastion, and Broad Streets. Teague's commercial structures are for the most part no-nonsense brick structures with an economical use of Victoria Italianate applied ornament. Again the influences seem to be Californian.

During the 1880s a number of new practices opened in Victoria. Among them were those of A. Maxwell Muir and Thomas Sorby. Muir was a Scot who came to Victoria in 1891 after having worked for some time in Kansas and California. He practised briefly under Teague before setting up his own office. Thomas Sorby, an English-trained architect, arrived in Victoria in 1888, having designed the first generation of stations and hotels along the western Canadian Pacific Railway route. The few of his structures still standing demonstrate, despite his background, a marked sympathy for the prevailing American commercial styles of the 1880s and 1890s.

In 1890 the elders of the Metropolitan Methodist Church engaged Thomas Hooper to plan the expansion of their Wright-designed 1859 Gothic Revival structure. Hooper, an Englishman who had learned architecture with his brother in Winnipeg, first opened a practice in Vancouver in the early 1880s. Hooper was an admirer of the Eastern American architect, Henry Hobson Richardson (1838-1886). Hooper's two commissions for the Methodists—Metropolitan and Centennial Churches—show the marked influence of Richardson. A subsequent commission —the Protestant Orphanage—is on first sight an almost literal quotation of Richardson's Sever Hall at Harvard (1880). Hooper's buildings are marked by a Richardsonian use of rusticated stonework and ample arcuated bays introducing a note of what must have been modernity into the Teague-dominated cityscape. It was Hooper who introduced the delicate flavour of Art Nouveau to the Victoria scene. Both his domestic and commercial interiors, especially those designed in collaboration with his Victoria partner, E. C. Watkins, were both sensitive and fashionable. Roger's Chocolate Shop and the Carnegie Library are examples of this.

In 1891 the architectural community was quietly closing ranks and cementing its professional positions with the formation of the British Columbia Institute of Architects. In 1894 the Ontario journal *Canadian Builder* published a picture of the executive committee which then included Victoria architects Mallandaine, Tiarks, and Hooper. On November 5, 1892 (coincidentally the day set aside to celebrate the Guy Fawkes gunpowder plot), that calm was suddenly shattered. A youthful unknown architect—25 years old—had won the international competition to design the Parliament Buildings. There had been 65 entries from all over the world for this, the biggest building contract in the history of the Province.

Francis Mawson Rattenbury had trained in his uncle's Yorkshire firm of Lockwood and Mawson before coming to Vancouver in 1892. Rattenbury wasted no time in moving to Victoria and setting up a very lucrative practice. Whatever else may be said of Rattenbury, he was a brilliant architect and an astute businessman of boundless energy and ambition. In the 1890s his vision superseded that of his local contemporaries: huge mining projects; vast real estate developments (Uplands); steamers for Atlin Lake; unitized prefabricated housing for the British West Indies. To Rattenbury, an inveterate and extensive traveller, Victoria was only an operational base for the far-ranging horizons of his many schemes. From the beginning he moved in the highest circles, over the next 20 years netting the largest commissions in the province with a practice that he ran only as a sideline to his many interests. In 1893 work began on the Parliament Buildings. In 1900 he teamed up with Maclure to design the

Lieutenant Governor's new residence; in 1905 he designed the Empress Hotel—thus joining the big league architects of the Canadian Pacific Railway and the powerful Bank of Montreal for whom he handled many more commissions throughout the province.

The reason so many public commissions flowed his way was that Rattenbury understood what corporate or public architecture was all about. He knew how to use buildings as visual propaganda. For the Bank of Montreal he used an aggressive version of the Chateau style, thereby relating the building to its origins in French Canada, underlining its close relationship with the financing of the CPR, and emphatically distinguishing it from the Italianate Bank of British Columbia two blocks away on Government Street. As for his larger commissions, we have the Parliament Buildings with their magnificent siting, brooding symbolic domes and related elements, complex sculptural program and curiously attractive mixture of eighteenth century English plan and massing with nineteenth century American Romanesque Revival details. Yet he knew how to use the architectural vocabulary playfully: the CPR steamboat terminal (designed in conjunction with P. L. James) in the Inner Harbour masquerades as a Temple of Neptune. Rattenbury was behind Victoria's first convention centre (the Crystal Gardens) and collaborated in Victoria's first garden city residential suburb (Uplands).

Samuel Maclure arrived in Victoria in 1892 from New Westminster. Within ten years he had built Victoria's most successful practice specializing in domestic architecture. By 1890 Victoria had made the cultural transition from British colony to Dominion province on an east-west railway connector. A new type of architecture was required to suit the taste of a domestically oriented upper-class whose taste was set by a wave of wealthy remittance men from England. The arbiter of taste was the society wife; Maclure was a highly sensitive architect and a family man. He was a designer with an infinite concern for detail.

For nearly 20 years Maclure and Rattenbury dominated the local architectural scene. The style promoted by Rattenbury and Maclure was a consciously fashionable idiom. It typified a society concerned with demonstrating a certain kind of social aloofness or "superiority" through ostentatious cultural refinement and modishness. The preference for the products of the European and American Aesthetic Movement, houses and furniture in the Arts & Crafts style, and domestic wares exhibiting the curvilinear forms of Art Nouveau, indicated a sensitive awareness for a certain prevailing international fashion. Victoria's social life mirrored that promoted by such contemporary periodicals as *Country Life, Studio, Homes and Gardens,* and *The Craftsman.* The tenor of these publications found their echo in such local establishments as the prestigious Weiler Bros. Department Store. Their 1905 catalogue devotes a special section to "hall furnishings":

> We should strongly advise those who can afford to go to the expense to indulge in the luxury of a fairly spacious Hall, even though this should involve some limitation of the area of other rooms on the ground.... For the walls there is nothing so suitable as wood panelling, or at least a wainscot of wood, and the valance of wall covered with some heavy relief-stamped paper in imitation of old leather, or Japanese paper in rich bronze effect, many of which are highly artistic and permanent, and not very costly.... The most suitable kind of furniture for a Hall is Oak or Mahogany, and there are admirable reproductions of old Mission styles that may be safety employed.

The spare lines of Mission furniture, Japanese art wallpapers, and luxurious use of native wood wainscoting, are the hallmarks of the Arts & Crafts approach to interior decoration. By this time a spacious hall had become the distinctive feature of Maclure's highly successful house-type. Shingle style bungalows built during this period are still commonplace in Victoria's residential districts. The English vernacular styles (particularly the Tudor) were popularized in Britain by George Devey (1820-1886), William Butterfield (1814-1900), Richard Norman Shaw (1831-1912), Philip Webb (1831-1915) and Edwin Lutyens (1869-1944). Magazines such as *Studio* and *The Builder* spread the word at home and abroad and reached Victoria as one "option" in the High Victorian vocabulary of ornament in the local work of Leonard Buttress Triman and Thomas Sorby.

But it was Samuel Maclure and Francis Mawson Rattenbury who really popularized the Elizabethan Vernacular Revival in Victoria as an outgrowth of their own unique Arts & Crafts interests, one particularly adapted to the tastes, materials, and climatic conditions of the northwest. Maclure and Rattenbury defined a style, then gathered around them a group of architects and designers who were to dominate the domestic scene in Victoria for some 30 years. During the years 1900 to 1914, the last great expansion period before the middle 1950s, the character of Victoria was substantially created and fixed.

Two giants tower above twentieth century domestic architecture: in America, the brilliant and eloquent rebel, Frank Lloyd Wright (1869-1959); in England, more reticent but equally a pioneer, Charles Francis Annesley Voysey (1857-1941). From Wright, North America would inherit low horizontal forms and flat floating roof-planes which typify architecture of our times, from suburban builders' homes to rural country residences. In England Voysey was to purify the Victorian Queen Anne into a distinctive vertical but clean-lined, brick-and-stucco building type. Few perceptive architects of the early twentieth century could entirely escape the influence of at least one of these men. Maclure was to enjoy contact with both and subsume their influences into his own work, subtly but completely.

In April 1903, the same year Maclure opened a Vancouver office, the young Englishman in charge had come straight from Voysey's London office. Maclure's Vancouver partner was Cecil Croker Fox. Maclure remained the senior design partner, supervising and approving the final designs. However, the Voysey/Fox influence soon began to creep into Maclure's own Victoria commissions, progressively taking a firmer hold over the various stylistic threads that dictated the form and character of his work. For instance after 1903 the low-rise, hip-roof, Colonial bungalow undergoes a transformation into a larger roofed building of more simplified form. Another Voyseyesque detail which appears at this time is the vestigial buttress. By 1912 Maclure was not adverse to producing residences which must be almost literal interpretations of the Voysey manner. One example is the R. D. Finlayson house (1914). Obvious Voysey elements in the scheme are the rough-cast wall treatment relieved at the second storey by rectilinear half-timbering, battered corner buttresses, the massive, slightly flared, hipped roof, and banks of leaded casement windows. The Robert Hall house is excellently proportioned if slightly vertical; roof dormers are plain and unobtrusive while the plain stucco chimneys which rise through the roof act as stabilizing units in the composition.

In 1914 Fox left for the front lines in France and the Vancouver office was closed. He was killed in action the following year. Only occasionally in the post-war years would Maclure return to the Arts & Crafts for design and inspiration, and even then it was usually only a literal quotation of earlier work produced at a client's specific request.

Arts & Crafts influence waned in the post-World War I years and the popularity of Neo-Georgian and Eastern Colonial housetypes is indicative of an age struggling to find security and identity by reaffirming the historical roots of Western society as a civilization with dignity and traditions. Economic recession coupled with grim memories of the war years no doubt fostered a new appreciation of traditional values. Both Maclure and Rattenbury returned to Classical building forms. Only in the late 1920s did the English Vernacular Revival resurface in Victoria with the work of H. Savage, Percy Fox, and Ross A. Lort. But by this time the style had lost its local flavour and the domestic work of those years consists almost entirely of direct quotations from earlier English precedents such as the work of M. H. Baillie Scott (1865-1945) whose work was constantly published in *Studio* magazine.

Maclure's architecture was much emulated in his own time. Within the profession he had numerous imitators; those who worked for him went on to apply his style in their own independent practices. Throughout the 1920s and 1930s the Tudor Revival aspects of his work survived, and although adapted and changed to suit contemporary tastes, were carried on by his younger colleagues. During the pre-World War I years in Victoria the Maclure Chalet style became a popular developer's housetype throughout the rapidly expanding middle-class suburbs of Fairfield and Oak Bay. Percy Leonard James and Douglas James, his brother, opened their architectural practice in Victoria in 1910. A number of prestigious commissions went to the firm including the design for Oak Bay Municipal Hall (1912) and some large houses in Rockland. All are heavy with quotations from Maclure including wide-spreading hipped roofs, balconies and porches enclosed within the body of the building, half-timbering balanced against shingle or rubble masonry wall surfaces. This vein can be detected in the work of Hubert Savage who in the late 1920s had on occasion worked in partnership with Maclure. In The Thatch, a 1939 tea and dance room built amid the rolling farmlands of Saanich, Savage used the Tudor hall house as a design source to achieve the effect of "old-country charm" with some dignity. Savage assumed Maclure's place in Victoria during the 1930s and 1940s with numerous commissions throughout Oak Bay and in particular the prestigious Uplands Estates. With good sense for both functional space and detailing, Savage adapted Maclure's formula to modern times: fewer servants, central heating, more economical building practices. He carried into his designs the exposed timberwork, iron casement windows, intimate "cottagey" detailing—even hand stencilling which this late variant of the English Arts & Crafts popularized. Savage also continued but adjusted Maclure's hall to modern times. Instead of the draughty galleried stairwell, Savage's halls are hammer beamed or cruck timbered living rooms, set off as a public entertainment area from the main body of the house.

Victoria's economic stagnation was not kind to architects of the 1930s and 1940s. The net result was a retrenchment to direct international influences in architectural design. The spirit of Maclure really had to await the modernism of the 1950s when a new group of enthusiastic practitioners such as Arthur Erickson, Doug Shadbolt and Barry Downs in Vancouver, John Di Castri, John Wade, and Alan Hodgson in Victoria were to bring indigenous design back to the Northwest.

In the meantime local building traditions began to fade, new commercial construction favoured more pedestrian versions of the current international styles. Art Deco, itself symbolic of the new alliance between art and technology, was introduced along with local branches of the major international corporations. Both "Art Deco" and "Moderne" were terms applied to the manner of building popularized at the 1925 Paris exhibition, *L'Exposition Internationale des Arts Decoratifs et Industriels Modernes*. The Kresge Department Store (1930, architect G. A. McElroy of Windsor) and Imperial Oil Automobile Service Station (1931, architects Townley and Matheson of Vancouver—both Victoria-born but Pennsylvania University-trained) were symbols of this new era which also saw Victoria briefly enjoy the reputation of "Hollywood North." British film content laws prompted several film studios to use Victoria as a location for a number of "B" movies. There were, however, very competent local practitioners who adopted the style: Johnson and Spurgin produced the Gibsons shop on View Street (1931); Eric C. Clarkson designed the Coronet Theatre (1936); and in 1938 Patrick Birley designed the much-lauded Sussex Hotel, the facade of which has now been incorporated into Paul Merrick's Sussex Place for Princeton Developments (1995). James and James' Main Post Office on Government Street (1948-1952) was a late Art Deco variant, hovering between Classicism and International Modernism, and a far cry from their English and American vernacularism when they worked in the shadow of Rattenbury and Maclure.

Wartime saw Art Deco give way to Moderne, often with a strident enthusiasm. Architect W. J. Seymen had pioneered the spare lines, white streamlined surfaces and rhythmic massing of Moderne in the Tweedsmuir Mansions overlooking Beacon Hill Park in 1936. Scarce and substandard building materials during the war years may have further popularized the stucco finished look among the local contractors. The Gordon Head Camp Communications Building (1941-1942) which survives at the University of Victoria is a small but sophisticated essay in the idiom. Patrick Birley's Athlone Apartments (1940), and as Birley, Wade & Stockdill the Salvation Army Building (1946-1947), as well as a series of houses designed by S. N. Hill for the A. H. F. Stelck family 1214, 1218, 1221 Old Esquimalt Road (1941-1945), are of very high calibre. However these additions to the townscape with their smooth lines, surfaces and sparse flat ornamentation typify a period which experienced massive inroads into the local economy and popular culture by foreign interests While some of these structures are significant monuments in their respective idioms, and were hailed "progressive" in their day, they are still foreign and estranged from the traditional residential character of Victoria which even to this time maintains a love affair with the Picturesque.

Historian and critic Chris Gower has written on the role of "centennialism" in ushering in to Victoria the Progressive architectural movement. Certainly the economic boom and heady nationalism that accompanied various celebrations associated with 100 years since something (1858 Crown Colony of British Columbia established; 1866, colonial union of British Columbia and Vancouver Island; 1871 British Columbia enters Canadian Confederation) provided some opportunity for monument building. Victoria marked 1958 with construction of Beacon Hill "Mile Zero" monument designed by Rod Clack. A pivotal figure was Victoria Mayor Richard Biggerstaff Wilson. It was Wilson who kick started urban renewal of Victoria's downtown with the city's own Centennial Square Project in 1963. It was also Wilson who spearheaded the campaign to relocate the University of Victoria to Gordon Head in 1959 and who sought out one of America's foremost planning firms to oversee the development of the garden campus. And just as the University Campus was to grow within the tensions of a bifurcated aesthetic, the heroic grey

Brutalism of Abstract Expressionist architecture blurring into the green folds of its sylvan setting, so "Old Town" Victoria set off in search of a compromise blend of romantic historicism (paint-up and preservation) with International modernity (shopping centres, highrises and freeways). The seminal document of Wilson mayoralty, *Over All Plan for Victoria* (1965), established the terms and language of the debate which would carry forward some 30 years. So the monuments and personalities of this period were to dominate Victoria for a generation: architects Nicholas Bawlf, Rod Clack, Peter Cotton, Clive Campbell and Alan Hodgson (variously at work restoring Bastion Square, conserving Old Town, and reconstructing burned-out Government House) and the powerhouse firms: Birley, Wade, Stockdill; R. W. Siddall Associates; Wagg & Hambleton; John Di Castri—inserting parkades and institutional monuments into the downtown core or the green fields of suburbanite Saanich (which itself was building a Corbusier-inspired Municipal Hall and defining its urban containment boundaries at this time).

And it is interesting that these same themes continue to play out their roles in Post-Modern Victoria of the 1990s, particularly in the crucible of comprehensive development: Songhees—high density urban renewal on the edge of Old Town Victoria; the later parts of Broadmead—Romantic Eclectic Revivalism in the Royal Oak subdivision which pushes the edge of Saanich's containment envelope; Selkirk Waters—environmental reclamation for live-work mixed use; and outright defensive historicism in the traditional neighbourhoods of Oak Bay, Fairfield, Esquimalt and High Quadra. And variously suited to such causes these opportunities have given rise to a new breed of designers. John Keay and Bas Smith specialize in social housing as sensitive infill. de Hoog, D'Ambrosio Rowe postulate a restrained High-Tech to mark urban edge developments. Eric Barker and Doug Campbell playfully re-introduce the Classical vocabulary to soften institutional monumentalism with varying degrees of success. These are all themes that can be traced in the rich history of urban design in Victoria.

NOTE

Ref. Barrett, Anthony A. & Liscombe, Rhodri Windsor. "Francis Rattenbury and British Columbia:Architecture and Challenge in the Imperial Age." 1983. Baskerville, Peter A. "Beyond the Island: An Illustrated History of Victoria." 1986. Hora, Z. D. & Miller, L. B. "Dimension Stone in Victoria, B.C." 1994. Parker, Douglas V. "No Horsecars in Paradise: A History of the Street Railways and Publick Utilities in Victoria, British Columbia before 1897." 1981. Pethick, Derek. "Victoria: the Fort." 1968. Reksten, Terry. "More English than the English: A Very Social History of Victoria." 1982. Segger, Martin & Douglas Franklin. "Victoria A Primer for Regional History in Architecture 1843-1929." 1974.

Victoria: The Town

Quadra Street Cemetery
ca. 1855
Quadra Street, Church Hill, Fairfield (Pioneer Square)

The Quadra Street Cemetery, when it was laid out in the 1850s, was Victoria's second burial site. The first, at the corner of present day Johnson and Douglas streets, leaves no trace today. The location is strategic, being adjacent to the Victoria District Church which later became Christ Church Cathedral. Although the cemetery was interdenominational, its proximity to the Anglican Church has always made it seem like a traditional church yard.

The cemetery was closed for burials in 1873 when Ross Bay Cemetery was opened. In the early 1930s the City of Victoria Parks Department cleaned up the site and it officially became a park. The largest monuments were left in place but the smaller ones were all either relocated to the eastern edge of the park or put into storage. The surviving stone monuments are the earliest examples of locally produced stone sculpture in Victoria. Some are architecturally significant, such as the Medana family monument in sandstone and white marble, the obelisk to the sailors who had died at the Esquimalt Station and the many other benches, tables, ledger caps, and tablets which provide examples of the Rococo Revival, Gothic Revival and Classical Revival styles popular mid-nineteenth century architecture and design. Most of the monuments are made of BC sandstone and have suffered severe damage over the years. The cemetery is now known as Pioneer Square.

Victoria Hotel
1858
901-905 Government Street
Archt. Addition: A. Maxwell Muir, 1903

Behind the mock Tudor façade survives Victoria's oldest brick structure (p. 13). The two-and-one-half-gable structure was originally fronted by a handsome arched masonry single story shop front (originally containing a tobacco shop and saloon). Above this the hotel rooms opened out onto a balustraded balcony. The hotel became the Windsor in the 1890s and acquired its Tudor Revival dress in the 1930s when Victoria began promoting itself as a tourist destination under the slogan "a little bit of old England." In 1903 Muir designed the Courtenay Street addition, a yellow brick restrained essay in the Edwardian Classical style.

James Yates Building
ca. 1860
1218 Wharf Street

Originally a three-storey random rubble structure, this may be Victoria's oldest surviving masonry building. It was certainly in place by 1860 and was the city's first use of cast iron for the street front columns; it also housed Victoria's first saloon and liquor warehouse. An unfortunate renovation in the 1970s demolished the very fine trabbiated stonework of the harbour front façade, and also added a fourth attic storey. An example of this original detailing survives further along Wharf Street at 1314 and 1316/1318, both very early structures that predate the assessment roles.

"Wentworth Villa" for Capt. Henry Ella
1862
1156 Fort Street, Rockland

One of Victoria's most fastidious examples of Victorian Gothic "Gingerbread" architecture, the house was built for one of Victoria's foremost pioneer families. Essentially a central-plan house with symmetrically organized façades, the dominant feature is the elaborate fretted barge boards in the gables. Originally a walk-out decorated balcony ran the length of the façade atop the verandah, no doubt to take advantage of the fine views from this dominant location on the Fort Street rise.

Dickson Campbell & Co. Building
1862, 1889-1891
Store Street, Victoria
Archts. Wright & Sanders, L. B. Triman
Addition and Restoration:
Claude Maurice, 1985

Designed originally as a wharfside import/export establishment for Dickson Campbell, a firm of commission merchants, the building was two storeys: warehouse below street level retail. The street façade was one of the city's earliest examples of the full-blown Renaissance Revival style executed in large quarried sandstone blocks. The two-floor Tudor Revival expansion occurred in 1889-1891 along with the more somber neighbouring structure for the Victoria Roller Flour and Rice Mill. Designs were from the office of L. B. Triman. The sympathetic modern addition and careful restoration of the two older buildings were done during the 1980s under the direction of local architect Claude Maurice.

Temple Emanuel
1863

1461 Blanshard at Pandora
Archts. Wright & Sanders
Restoration: Peter Cotton,
Bawlf Cooper Associates, 1979

The cornerstone for the Jewish Synagogue, the oldest in Western Canada, was laid in 1863, and Victorians were quick to point out their liberal mindedness in this respect. As there were only 35 members of the Jewish local community, the construction of the building was based on something more than just religious tolerance. Other organizations, individual gentiles, and even religious denominations donated toward the costs of the building. For their Jewish clients, the firm of John Wright produced a small but highly successful little brick building in the Romanesque Revival style. From the exterior there appears a subtle suggestion of a four-square spatial arrangement, each corner defined by slightly projecting blocks and roof elements as if to signify truncated towers perhaps a sleight-of-hand suggestion of those great Lombard four-towered eleventh century prototypes. At the gabled east end protrudes a diminutive but well-scaled apse. The west façade contains a large rose window and triple-arched doorway. Round-headed windows and a course of blind arcading carried round the building under the eaves assert the Romanesque Revival character although rather out of place are the additional Italianate brackets tucked between the arcading and the eaves. The southern lean-to is a later addition. The synagogue still serves its original function and by some accounts is the oldest in continual use in North America.

Starting in 1979 the building has been completely and meticulously restored to its original condition under the direction of the provincial Heritage Conservation Branch and architects, Peter Cotton and also Bawlf Cooper Associates.

Bridgeman Building
1863, 1886, 1890, 1905

1007 Government Street
Archts. Dennis Harris, Thomas Hooper

The cast iron shopfront surmounted by arched windows on the second floor and capped by a bracketted cornice— this was a typical Government Street commercial frontage of the 1860s, 1870s and 1880s. These elements were the hallmark of the Italianate commercial style familiar throughout the boom-towns of the Pacific coast. The second floor was added in 1886 for realtors Lowenberg & Harris to designs by engineering partner Dennis Harris. The neighbouring building, 1009-1013, is also a similar Harris design executed two years earlier. The present storefront (1905) with its delicate Art Nouveau feel is the work of Thomas Hooper.

Southgate and Lascelles Block
1869, 1880

1102 Government Street
Archts. Restoration:
Bawlf Cooper Associates, 1986

Originally built as a one-storey brick general merchandising building with street-level verandahs, the structure was

larger by two bays along Government Street. The second floor was a later addition above the cast iron shop frontage, reutilizing the elaborate Italianate cornice and inserting the equally elaborate pedimented windows. Purchased as a ticket and administrative office by the Canadian Pacific Steamship Co., it remained in their hands as the Victoria base for CNCP Communications. In 1978 Bawlf Cooper designed the 140-foot microwave tower which was added to the rear and disguised as a campanile. Later it was discovered that this was the location of the old HBC Fort bell tower.

St. Ann's Academy
1871, 1886, 1910

835 Humboldt Street
Archts. Fr. Joseph Michaud,
John Teague, Thomas Hooper
Restoration: Paul Merrick Architects,
1995

St. Ann's began as a modest wooden Hudson's Bay Company house purchased by Bishop Modeste Demers in 1858 for the newly arrived contingent of teachers, Sisters of St. Ann from Vaudreuil, Quebec. Architect-cleric Father Joseph Michaud, who had accompanied the Sisters, prepared the plans for the new convent which was built in two phases. The first four-storey west wing was supervised by local architect Charles Vereydhen. Michaud had already built the first Cathedral on a site, now facing St. Ann's, in 1858. Eastern convents of French Canadian teaching orders provided the model for this brick structure articulated by low relief pilasters and surmounted by a steep pitched

dormered roof. This first block forms the central unit of the present structure. In 1886 architect John Teague, following Michaud's original scheme, completed the building by adding the central pedimented entrance block and matching eastern wing. At the same time, the old cathedral was put on skids and moved to the rear of the building as the convent chapel. Michaud's chapel with its low flat barrel-vault bears considerable resemblance to baroque Quebecois Recollet churches of the eighteenth century which were probably its inspiration.

The Hooper-designed addition of 1910 became the girls boarding school proper, with dormitories, classrooms, and an auditorium. In style it is rather unsympathetic to the Teague block. This seems to result from some confusion at the time between the French Baroque (as evident in Teague's convent) and the Chateau/Mansard styles, which by this time was known to Victorians from Rattenbury's nearby Empress Hotel. The landscaping was laid out by Father Adrian Joseph Vullinghs about 1913. The grounds combined a contemplative novitiate garden in the southeast quadrant, a formal parterred arboretum in the northwest, an orchard and graveyard in the northeast quadrant. The Baroque bi-axial stairway entrance was approached along an avenue lined with tall poplars. The final effect is quite dramatic, this Baroque symbol of French Canada facing the equally Classical, but English Queen Anne. St. Joseph's Hospital was also designed by Hooper's firm in 1908.

After passing into the hands of the government in 1974, then abandoned in 1982, the structure was restored and recycled as an office building commenced under the Provincial Capital Commission in 1995. The scheme, devised by Paul Merrick Architects, called for the restoration of the chapel and central entrance block as an interpretation centre, the east and west wings including the Hooper addition to be recycled as government offices and cultural uses.

Church of Our Lord
1874
626 Blanshard at Humboldt
Archt. John Teague

This attractive little church was the direct result of a theological dispute between the Reverend Edward Cridge, Dean of Christ Church Cathedral, and the Rt. Reverend Bishop George Hills of the Cathedral. In 1874 Rev. Cridge seceded and formed the Reformed Episcopal Church around the nucleus of about 250 followers, including a number of the more prominent men of Victoria. There seems little doubt that this Carpenter Gothic building in many ways suited the near fundamentalist beliefs of the dissenting congregation. The simple board-and-batten construction carrying with it implications of indigenous rustic piety was very much in contrast to the ornate and pretentious brick and stone ecclesiastical edifices which were later built "up the hill." Such an approach to construction was popularized by the writings in the 1850s of A. J. Downing and the architect A. J. Davis. The little church itself is a fine example of Victorian rural Picturesqueness. The plan is a symmetrical T-shape with a nave, two side aisles, and transept and apse. "Gothic" is introduced by the vertical siding, the vestigial buttresses, and the turrets flanking the façade. The interior is finished in Douglas Fir; windows of English stained glass are dedicated to prominent members of the congregation.

The Cridge Memorial Hall next door was originally conceived as a tribute to Bishop Cridge who died in 1913. It was finally erected in 1930 according to plans by the late Samuel Maclure, whose design was sympathetic in style and materials to the 1874 church.

The designs originated from the Ottawa office of Thomas Seaton Scott (1826-1895), the (Federal) Department of Works Chief Architect at this time. Scott endowed Canada with a number of Second Empire style buildings during the 1870s, of which one of the best examples was the old post office (destroyed in the 1904 fire) in Ottawa itself.

The Customs House was therefore a symbolic keystone of Confederation and tangible evidence to the people of British Columbia of their new status within the Dominion of Canada. Overlooking the harbour, the House was erected on a granite promontory next to the Hudson's Bay Co. warehouses. The Mansard roofline evoked the style of the Canadian presence and law amid the turbulent events accompanying the massive immigration of goldrush miners, merchant adventurers, and land speculators of the boom-and-bust early economy of the province.

Dominion Customs House
1876

1002 Wharf Street
Archt. T. S. Scott, Department of Public Works, Ottawa

Deluge Fire Company Hall
1877

636 Yates Street
Archt. John Teague
Restoration:
Bawlf Keay Associates, 1995

Victoria's volunteer fire brigades competed not only in speedy fire suppression but also in architectural splendour. Boasting names such as the Tiger Engine Company and Union Hook and Ladder Company, their once-proud firehalls are well commemorated in the bold and fastidious detailing of this Italianate structure. Only the once tall and proud bell and hose tower is missing from the exemplary restoration by architects Bawlf Keay Associates in 1995.

Masonic Temple
1878, 1903
650 Fisgard at Douglas
Archt. John Teague

Plans for a Temple to house the Lodge for British Columbia Freemasonry went out to competition although it seems there were only two competitors, John Teague and Thomas Trounce—both lodge members. Teague's plans were accepted and the initial capital was raised through subscription to a joint stock company, the remainder being borrowed against anticipated revenue from two shopfronts.

The exterior by itself is unimpressive, but as an integral part of the surrounding city, it harmonizes with the Second Empire City Hall, also by Teague. A simple but Picturesque composition, the main entrance is set at 45° to the southeast corner and emphasized by the vertical thrust of the tower. The contract to decorate the interior of the Temple was given to Eli Harrison who was also the Grand Master of British Columbia. The *Daily British Colonist* described it: "The ceiling or canopy is a masterpiece of work. It assumes the form of a dome and has first been tinted with a sky-blue shade and then studded with golden stars, fringed with clouds, in representation of the firmament. At the eastern end of the room the rising sun is very faithfully depicted." The building was solemnly consecrated by the Grand Lodge of British Columbia on October 28, 1878.

Anderson Building
1879
565 Johnson Street

Little changed over the years, this small shop retail structure for Elijah Howe Anderson defines the eastern edge of Oriental Alley. As a corner building like Maclure's later Temple Building, the façade is not treated merely as a false front but is wrapped around the alley frontage to the depth of one bay. The shamfered stone piers, quoined second storey and bracketted cornice make this a fine essey in the Italianate style. The inset central entrance using cast iron columns is also a traditional Victoria feature.

Fell & Co. Building
1879
655-671 Fort Street at Broad

Originally a no-nonsense two-storey brick building with the characteristic splayed corner entrance, the overall form has survived numerous alterations. The original wooden arcade at street level is gone and the retail level has been opened up for large shop windows; the bricks are covered with a stucco finish. However, recent restoration and cleanup has revealed a fine late 1930s look, the second floor largely untouched from original. Sometime mayor of Victoria James Fell operated his grocery business from here; the upper floor was leased to Weiler Bros. until they built their furniture factory next door.

John Weiler's Furniture Factory
1879-1884

636 Broughton Street at Broad
Archt. Thomas Trounce
Restoration: P. Cotton, 1969

This red brick structure is a representative example of the Pioneer commercial building that lined Victoria's streets from the late 1860s to the early 1890s. There is nothing pretentious in the three-storey red brick façade with its regular fenestration pattern carried evenly and geometrically across the street frontage. Likewise a nondescript pattern-book ornament is used to articulate the window casements. A human scale is evoked by the warm red brick masonry and the logical delineation of floor levels through the use of coloured string courses. These elements relate the structure to human proportion in a way which the bland grey walls of modern ferro-concrete structures cannot.

Mr. Trounce was a building contractor who "did plans" as a sideline to his regular business. With the guidance of local restoration architect Peter Cotton, the interior has been renovated into a commercially viable series of spaces, utilizing the Maclure-designed staircase rescued during the demolition of the Robin Dunsmuir house. At the same time, the architect has preserved the structure and character of a significant, once-popular, building type that is now becoming progressively more rare.

Amelia Street Houses
1880s-1890s

1517, 1519, 1521, 1525, 1527, 1529 Amelia Street

These houses are significant primarily because they constitute a period grouping. Homes such as these were once common in this part of the city, providing working class accommodation close to the city centre. Although none of the houses is identical, each is a variation of the Victorian Italianate theme. Porches with decorated columns survive on some of the buildings but otherwise they are simple two storey structures featuring bay windows and low-pitched roofs. Most of the houses appear to have been built by one man, a Mr. S. T. Styles (who actually lived at 1519 Amelia Street) during the 1880s and 1890s. Other residents included a locksmith, contractor, bricklayer carpenter, engineer and shoemaker.

Finlayson Building
1882

1202-1214 Wharf Street
Archt. H. O. Tiedemann
Rehabilitation: Wayne Wenstob, 1975

This building, a speculative venture by Roderick Finlayson, an ex-HBC chief factor, is the northern surviving neighbour of the now gone Hudson's Bay Company Warehouse. In arrangement it is similar to the earlier

Turner, Beeton and Company Ltd., a pioneer firm established in 1863 by John H. Turner in affiliation with the London House of Beeton, dealers in drygoods. Turner later became Mayor of Victoria, and from 1895 to 1898 was Premier of British Columbia. The present structure is the result of two construction stages. This explains the asymmetrical elevation and the rather awkward attempt to emphasize the rather handsome entrance by springing a blind arch over the third-storey central window. Early photographs show the building to have been finished with an ornamental cornice and an ornate balcony over the main entrance. From its bedrock foundation the 1882 building rose two storeys to street level. These lower storeys were used as a bonded warehouse. The street level floor contained the offices and vaults and the upper floor was given over to sales displays. The structure was also equipped with a Spratt's hydraulic elevator, manufactured by Victoria's Albion Iron Works. The steel shutters that protected the lower windows of the rear elevation are still in place. The most appealing feature is the entrance alcove behind the heavy stone arched entry.

HBC structure. Goods were offloaded from ships to wharves, then moved into the bonded warehouse first floor for unpacking, before being raised to the second for storage. Retailing was done at street level. The building has been renovated numerous times in recent years including the addition of a fourth floor and heavy timbered galleries. The first renovation by architect Wayne Weinstapp hollowed out a centre bay so that the entire building can be read through the floors, a daring and revealing use of that space.

Yates Block
1882, 1896

1252 Wharf Street
Archt. John Teague

For nearly 40 years, this building served as the offices and warehouse of

Pitts and Hall Buildings
1882, 1899

516-518 Yates Street
Archt. A. Maxwell Muir, 1899
Restoration: Darrel Jensen, 1990

These two buildings, both subject to masterful exterior restorations, now form a single unit as Victoria's Youth Hostel. In both cases imposing Victorian Italianate façades have been recovered. The 1882 structure was built as a warehouse for Sidney Pitts. The later block replaced the Albion Saloon and was commissioned by Dr. F. Hall.

Oriental Hotel
1883-1888

560 Yates Street
Archt. John Teague

The Oriental Hotel is Victoria's best surviving example of the effect of iron technology. Precast structural components available through catalogues from San Francisco or eastern foundries introduced the first cheap unitized type of construction and allowed the façades of structures to be opened up to an extent far beyond the limits of brick technology. The spectacular cantilevered corner bay seems to hang precariously over the old entrance to Oriental Alley. Early cast iron lent itself to mass produced ornament, at first the forms merely carrying on stone and plaster traditions. The Oriental's High Victorian Italianate design with its Picturesque array of pediments, brackets, floriated capitals, spindly columns, cable moulding, and swag-decorated cornices was once completed at the eastern corner by an ornate tower and spire.

The tower of the Oriental with its observation deck was a well-known Victoria landmark; the street balcony and verandah for "taking the view" was likewise a common feature of hotels before the age of in-room television.

Morley's Soda Water Factory
1884

1315-1317 Waddington Alley

Christopher Morley specialized in the production of soda water, lemonade, medicinal lake water, essences of peppermint and ginger, "all kinds of syrups." His finely detailed brick building fronts Waddington Alley and is one of the best preserved of its era and type in Victoria. Two pedestrian doorways are arranged adjacent to a carriage entrance which allowed access to the rear courtyard and stables. Morley delivered! Waddington Alley has recently been restored by the City of

Victoria with creosote impregnated wooden paving blocks—illustrating the original finish of many of Victoria's main streets at the turn of the century.

Galpin Block
1884

1017-1021 Government Street
Archts. Harris and Hargreaves

A three-storey variant of Victoria's standard Italianate commercial style, this brick structure illustrates how architects varied a common stock of elements: bracketted cornice, shallow and round arched windows, wide bayed shopfronts at street level. Above the cornice a gently curved false-front parapet caps the building. From 1900 to 1911 the second floor housed the ladies Alexandria Club.

The Bank of British Columbia
1886

1022 Government at Fort
Archt. W. H. Williams, Portland
Restoration: Bawlf Cooper Associates, 1985

The Bank of British Columbia is one of the largest, oldest, and finest of Victoria's temple-style banks. It is a lesson in nineteenth century construction technology and applied decoration. A heavy wooden frame integrated with the brick walls formed the structural core of the building. The ornament—dressed stone slabs, moulded cement, cast iron—was then applied to the building. Moulded cement was used to effect the rusticated base while cast-iron corbels, cornices,

and pilasters were pinned to the walls. The dimensions of the frontages (50 feet on Fort Street and 90 feet on Government) allowed Williams to divide the façade into three bays unified by the triple repetition of the doorway section. The decorative scheme is centralized within each bay by a segmental arched pediment beneath the frieze. To counter the excessive verticality of the windows and their flanking pilasters, a bold string course divides the two storeys. At the roofline a relatively plain frieze punctuated with sunflower motifs is capped with a cornice in high relief. In 1985 the building was sensitively restored, and the interior renovated for retail use.

Wille's Bakery
1887

537 Johnson Street
Archt. Elmer H. Fisher

Louis Wille trained as a miller and baker in his native Saxone, departing for Canada during the Franco-Prussian War. After operating a successful business in New Westminster, he moved to Victoria and commissioned this building for his new bakery. Until recently the elaborate Victorian façade

with its Eastlake scrollwork window copings was capped with a metalwork baker's sign as a finial.

Boucherat Building
1887
533 Yates Street

Built as a warehouse and retail outlet for Boucherat & Co., Liquor Merchants, the building later housed a Turkish sulpher baths emporium. The façade features very high quality though simple decorative brick detailing, especially at the cornice level, and this is carried around through the alley frontage on the west side. Boucherat & Co. was taken over by Luke Pither, eventually to become Pither and Leiser—erecting the adjacent structure for their expanding business.

Victoria Gas Building
ca. 1888
502 Pembroke Street

Developed as part of the Victoria Gas Company's Rock Bay complex, this building housed a company that had begun with a distribution service as early as 1862. As a utilitarian building, however, it demonstrates both design and craft skill as the handling of the pilaster and corbel details indicates.

Albion Iron Works Building
ca. 1888
622 Pembroke Street

Given the nature of their long use, these wooden industrial structures are among Victoria's most historic and most significant. Vancouver Iron Works was first established on this site in 1882; in 1893 this became Victoria Iron Works and in 1896 was taken over by Albion Iron Works, a main competitor founded in 1861 by Joseph Spratt. In 1882 Albion had become the largest such operation, its board of directors including such local luminaries as Robert Dunsmuir, R. P. Rithet, Robert Ward, and Joseph Trutch. These buildings, still operating

as a foundry which for many years made the famous Albion wood stoves, are among the few left from what was one of Victoria's largest industrial complexes.

Cameron Building
1888

579-581 Johnson Street
Archts. Fisher and Wilson

Scrolled brackets support a heavy Italianate false front cornice and constitute the most impressive design element. Cast iron columns open up the retail front and flank the inset central entrance. From here W. G. Cameron, city alderman and later land commissioner, operated his "Mechanic's Cash Clothing Store" until 1911.

Green Building
1889

1210-1216 Broad Street at Trounce Alley
Archt. Thomas Trounce
Restoration: John Keay, 1995

Known for many years as the Exchange Building because it briefly housed the Victoria Stock Exchange at the time of the 1929 crash, this elaborate Victorian structure was built for A. A. Green, partner in the Garesche, Green and Co. private bank. Originally this and a mirror image flanked the entrance to Trounce Alley almost like diminutive versions of John Nash's work for Regent Street, London. This matching block burned down in 1910. From the collapse of Green's bank in 1889 to 1909 the surviving northern block was also home to the YMCA. In recent years the entire building has been meticulously restored by architect John Keay.

Metropolitan Methodist (United) Church
1890

1411 Quadra at Pandora Avenue
Archt. Thomas Hooper

The First Methodist Church on Pandora at Broad dates from 1859 and was designed by architects Wright & Sanders. Twenty years later, Thomas Hooper was engaged to formulate plans for a new and larger church. There was good reason why the Elders took pains to send Hooper east to study church designs and why he subsequently adopted Richardsonian Romanesque. The style of the church was to emphasize the Nonconformist standing of the Methodist Church with its theological and ritualistic distinction from the "Gothic" Church of England and the Church of Rome. At this time, Henry Hobson Richardson was receiving much publicity as the first "all American" architect in the United States. Using Richardson's architectural idiom of massive forms composed from the juxtaposition of rough cast stone, cyclopean archways, and heavy tower elements, Hooper created a unique and highly attractive building which was also quite acceptable to those who were used to Victorian rusticated arches, thirteenth century French Chateau roofs, and Scottish Baronial hanging turrets. Koksilah Island stone

was used in the exterior walls. When the education centre was added in the 1960s the builders were able to match the stone. The interior, with its expansive gallery sloping gently down from under the rose window, has an excellent reputation for its acoustics. The iron work was carried out by Albion Iron Works and the coloured glass of the rose window came from the studios of Lewis & Co. of London, Ontario.

Dominion Hotel
1890-1913

755-765 Yates Street

A gradualist approach to business development saw the Jones family extend and then replace the original wooden structure that Stephen Jones built in 1876 as the Dominion Hotel. Clues in the slight variation of window and cornice treatment indicate that the first three-storey brick block was added west of the wooden building in 1890, with further additions in 1898 and a fourth storey in 1907. The late Victorian Italianate scheme was continued throughout the entire project.

St. Andrew's Presbyterian Church
1890

900 Douglas at Broughton
Archt. L. Butress Triman

H. O. Tiedemann had won the competition to design the church which had first housed the St. Andrew's congregation in 1869. In 1888, plans were completed by L. B. Trimen for the construction of a new church. Given the Scottish heritage of Presbyterianism, it is not surprising that the design for the new St. Andrew's would try to incorporate elements of the Scottish Baronial such as the "crow's step" gable and the baronial turrets. The only stained glass in the original design were the façade windows which were installed by the Dunsmuir family at a cost of $4,000. The plan follows a typical Nonconformist amphitheatre scheme with a semicircular seating arrangement and a sloped floor.

Interior structural members are of cast iron, although the effect of this is softened by the brown, curved, hardwood ceiling. The organ was built by the Warren Company of Toronto and was installed in the old church in 1881. The church has recently been sensitively restored under the supervision of R. Baxter, Architect.

Pinchon & Lenfesty Building
1890
567-569 Johnson Street

From 1904 to 1918 these two partners operated a well-known gunsmith shop from here. The building was actually built for Elijah Howe Anderson's "London House Gents Furnishings" as an addition to his earlier adjacent investment property. Cast iron columns allow for a generous shopfront at street level and also support a strident essay in Victorian Italianate above. The three bays are framed with Corinthian pilasters, the windows feature detailed head mouldings and entire ensemble is capped with a Classical entablature and pediment.

Maynard Building
1891
723-725 Pandora Avenue

The ground floor features a cast iron open shopfront and an arched side entrance to the second floor. Upstairs the expansive windows beneath the corbelled brick cornice are unusual although the central doorways indicate the original presence of a cantilevered balcony. This configuration was purpose-built for the Maynards' two enterprises: a shoe store on the main floor and photographic studio above. Hanah Maynard was noted both for her portrait studies of contemporary townsfolk and also for artistic montage compositions, some of a most macabre nature.

Doane Building
1891
1314-1324 Douglas Street
Archt. John Teague

The three cantilevered bays define this building which provided residential accommodation above the retail level. To achieve this effect, cast iron components were used extensively in façade construction and detailing. The verticality of the composition and the Italianate cornice are thoroughly Victorian. In 1891 the Doane, along with the Oriental Hotel and the New England Hotel, constituted Victoria's new look.

Centennial Methodist Church
1891
549 Gorge Road, North Douglas
Archt. Thomas Hooper

Hooper's scheme incorporated the earlier small brick Gothic Revival church designed by John Wright (1864) as a church hall for his more imposing 850-seat Romanesque Revival structure. For the Methodists Hooper adapted features of Henry Hobson Richardson's Trinity Church (1873-1886) in Boston, Mass. which had been widely published when built. The façade, featuring the gable, arched clerestory, and triple-arched portals, and the east side with its round-headed lancets and octagon lantern capping the roof, are obvious references to the Boston prototype. An education centre was added on the southwest in 1962.

Colonial Metropole Hotel
1890, 1892
541-559 Johnson Street
Archt. John Teague

A much more conservative design than the Teague's later Driard, the Colonial was nevertheless a large commission. To give a business a streetfront presence for proprietor Thomas Tugwell, Teague produced an Italian Villa false front. The centre block, comparatively plain brick with a bracketted cornice, was flanked by two "pavilions," these slightly larger scaled and executed in a more robust fashion with quoined corners, squared second-storey windows contained separate leased retail on the ground floor. The centre block is still evident but only the eastern "pavilion" survives. The western pavilion was replaced by the surviving brick Romanesque structure in 1892 when the hotel was renamed the "Colonial Metropole." The design was also by Teague although the diaper brick work and brick panelled parapet give a decidedly more eclectic Picturesque effect. The building now forms part of a range of structures that have undergone a program of façade restoration and adaptive reuse as housing by developer Michael Williams.

London Block
1892
1315-1327 Broad Street

An understated piece of urbanism, this red brick arched structure actually defines a major corner and two street fronts. The splayed entrance and oriel window bay mark the corner block, the arched windows mark a pleasant rhythm as these recede from it along each frontage. The London Hotel replaced the former wooden London Harmony Hotel and at the ground floor housed the London Saloon.

Duck Building
1892
1314-1322 Broad Street
Archt. W. T. Whiteway

This rather aggressive and boldly detailed Victorian structure constitutes a dominating presence within the narrow confines of Broad Street. Simeon Duck rose from city tax collector to provincial minister of finance and this building housed his other enterprises including Duck's carriageworks and the meeting rooms of the Knights of Pythias. Rusticated masonry piers provide a solid podium of the two floors of brick and stone lintels, arches, and corbelled cornices, a truly Picturesque eclectic mix of details.

E. A. Morris, Tobacconist
1892
1116 Government Street
Archt. Thomas Hooper

The building Luney Brothers erected from the plans of Thomas Hooper was one specifically suited to the taste of the masculine smoking public. It is not surprising then, that the Georgian Revival façade should be continued as a dominating motif into the interior, which not unconsciously emulates the atmosphere of one of those high Victorian masculine institutions, the gentleman's club. The arch motif is established in the shopfront. The doorway is cut from Mexican onyx and the dome-shaped leaded window above it culminates in a large segmental arch supported on rusticated columns. The interior continues the spatial illusion through the use of leaded mirror domes in the ceiling and large wall mirrors built into the walls. Mahogany is used for the wall panelling, and a high standard of craftsmanship is exhibited in the Classical carved columns and pediment which decorate the "humidor," a walk-in cabinet used for the dry storage of cigars. At the centre, and providing a focal point for the interior space, is a large electrolier, a column on a pedestal with two extending gas jets, for the convenience of customers intent on consuming their purchases before leaving.

St. Andrew's Roman Catholic Cathedral
1892

740 View at Blanshard
Archts. Perrault & Mesnard, Montreal
Restoration: Bawlf Cooper Associates
1980-1996

The Daily Colonist announced February 11, 1890 that working plans had been received by Bishop Lemmens for the new St. Andrew's Cathedral. The style is High Victorian Gothic Revival, inspired by European Cathedrals of the fourteenth and fifteenth centuries. The 72-foot façade is dominated by a main tower terminating in a 175-foot spire. The north side tower seems to be left unfinished, in fact to emulate the random asymmetry which was so dear to the High Victorian tradition of the Picturesque. The nave, crossed by a transept and terminating at the west end in a narrow sanctuary, was designed so that an uninterrupted view of the altar could be had from almost any part of the church. At the back, over the entrance vestibule, are located two galleries: the lower originally for the Sisters and school children, the upper for the choir. The Cathedral was finally dedicated at a Pontifical High Mass by Bishop Lemmens on October 30, 1892. Figurative stained glass has been added over the years, the windows sourced mainly from Munich, Portland, Oregon, and Toronto.

In 1980 an extensive restoration program was commenced under the direction of architects Bawlf Cooper Associates. Over a period of 15 years the building was upgraded and a late nineteenth century decor was reintroduced. However, the circulation and furnishings were re-arranged to accommodate the new liturgies of the Second Vatican Council. The overall scheme was developed by ecclesiastical design consultants, Rambusch Co., NY. Also new items of liturgical furniture were introduced, commissioned from major northwest coast aboriginal artists—the main altar, for instance, is the work of Salish artist, Charles Elliott; the ambo is by Roy Vickers. The insertion of an extended entrance narthex was also part of this program.

The New England Hotel
1892

1312 Government Street
Archt. John Teague

Tenders were issued on May 1, 1892, and in October Bavarian immigrants Henry and Louis Young opened the new New England Hotel. Forty guest rooms were supplied with hot water and electric lighting, and the high ceilings were complemented by full-length windows hung with red plush drapes. In addition, there was a restaurant on the main floor, a sumptuously decorated dining room, and several rooms for private parties. The basement contained wine cellars and the bakery's great stone ovens. Based on the idea of a family hotel, there was no bar, although liquor was available with meals.

Construction consists of iron structural piers throughout. On the ground floor façade they reinforce red-brick columns; on the first floor they are encased in rusticated stone and capped with terracotta floral panels; from the second floor up they are within brick pilasters. The cast iron bay windows emphasize the building's narrow verticality.

COURTESY CITY OF VICTORIA PLANNING DEPARTMENT.

Aerial view, from James Bay over the Inner Harbour, *ca.* 1960.

The Parliamentary Precinct 1893-1996

In addition to Parliament Building range, notable high points of the precinct are the giant redwood (*Sequoia sempervirens*, planted about 1863) in front of the buildings to the right of the main path and the nearby obelisk, 27 feet high, made of BC marble from Beaver Cover by Mortimer & Reid. This was erected in 1879 to the memory of Sir James Douglas, KCB, Governor and Commander-in-Chief from November 1851 to October 1864. Further along the path just below the terrace is an ornate fountain manufactured in New York by J. W. Fiske in 1905. The statue of Queen Victoria is by the English sculptor Allen Bruce Joy. The World War I memorial erected in 1925 is by sculptor Vernon Marech of Farnborough, Kent. The sunken rose gardens behind the west wing of the buildings were developed 1935-1936 as a depression relief-work project. The Provincial Library portico, south side, overlooks the Centennial Fountain (architect Robert Savory, 1958) celebrating the union of the four territories—the Crown Colony of Vancouver Island, the Dependency of the Queen Charlotte Islands, the Crown Colony of British Columbia, and the Stikine Territory—which in 1862 were formed into the Colony of British Columbia. Programmed water and lights produces a night-time spectacle. The four bronze allegorical animals are Indian society totems and function also as regional symbols: the eagle for Vancouver Island, raven for the Queen Charlottes, wolf for the Stikine, and bear for BC. The centrepiece of otters and gulls symbolizes the fur trade and the sea: the early economy base of BC. To the west is a large red brick

Colonial Administrative Buildings "Birdcages," n.d.   BCARS 44759

building: the Menzies Street Drill Hall erected in 1892, and beyond that Rattenbury's garage structure for the official limousine.

Immediately west of the buildings (Menzies Street) is Confederation Square and Fountain (architects: B.C. Public Works, 1967). The coats of arms of the Canadian provinces are displayed. Balancing this on the east side, across Government Street can be seen the curatorial tower of the Royal British Columbia Museum (B.C. Public Works, 1967) and immediately south of it the imposing late Deco style Douglas Building of 1949-1950 (B.C. Public Works, Chief Architect H. Whittaker, design architects Dawson & Hall, Vancouver); also the Douglas Building Annex on Superior Street, a modern severe Brutalist structure (architect Wade Williams, 1983).

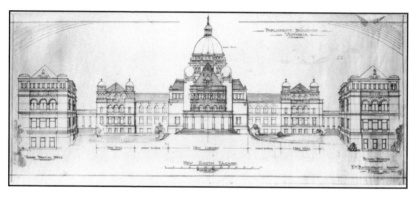

Proposed Connaught Library Addition, Parliament Buildings.
F. M. Rattenbury, 1911. BCARS

Maquette for Connaught Library Addition, Parliament Buldings. As built.
BCARS 8215

Parliament Buildings
1893-1897, 1912-1916
501 Belleville at Government
Archt. F. M. Rattenbury

The first Colonial Administration Buildings had been designed in 1859 by H. O. Tiedemann, a German civil engineer then working in the Lands

47

Office. Popularly known as The Birdcages, they were the butt of local humour: "the latest fashion," reported one journalist, "of Chinese pagoda, Swiss-cottage, Italian-villa, fancy birdcages." The competition of 1892 drew 65 entries from 62 competitors in various countries. A government committee selected the winner: Francis Mawson Rattenbury, a 25-year-old Yorkshireman who had arrived in Vancouver just before the competition was announced. The 500-foot frontage on an east-west axis faced the harbour and skillfully managed to squeeze itself between the two rows of "Birdcage Buildings." The tripartite plan, English eighteenth century in conception, allowed a huge central block to contain Legislative Hall and administrative departments with the two flanking blocks located at the ends of 40-foot colonnades. The blocks were to contain the Land Registry and the Printing Office. The central block consisted of three wings in a T-cross-axial formation with a 42-foot diameter dome covering a large waiting hall at the crossing. According to Rattenbury, the scheme followed fashionable Victorian "free Classical style." The monolithic, multi-tiered, Richardsonian-arched entrance surmounting a long flight of steps was conceived as a ceremonial approach to the great Domical Hall that serves as an antechamber to the Legislature. The huge dome on its octagonal drum dominates the skyline and subordinates the symmetrically arranged ancillary domes of the related administrative blocks. All possible effort was made to utilize local resources: the foundations were of Nelson Island granite; Haddington Island andesite was chosen for the sun-starved north façade because of the light gray colour; the bricks and lime were produced in Victoria; the roof slates were quarried and split at Jervis Inlet; Douglas Fir was used for the construction work; and the interior finishing is remembered in such names as Maple Committee Room and Cedar Committee Room. Contracts for the foundations were let on May 30, 1893 and on November 7, 1895 the last stone in the great dome was placed by the Provincial Secretary. The old 1859 Legislative Hall was preserved and served as the Department of Mines until 1957 when it was destroyed by

Provincial Library and Centennial Fountain

fire. The brick from the others, which were pulled down as the various departments occupied their new quarters, was used to pave the front carriageway. The entire cost finally came to $923,882.30. The buildings were first illuminated on June 21, 1897 to celebrate Queen Victoria's Diamond Jubilee. Between 1912 and 1915, Rattenbury designed additions to the structure, the main one being the south wing to accommodate the Provincial Library which was named after H.R.H. the Duke of Connaught. Like the Legislative Hall, the library with its rotunda was the focal point of the design though the concentration of ornament was within the interior. The walls are panelled with Italian marble; eight scagliola columns support the dome, and the floor is paved with coloured-marble inlay. Defining the upper corners of the cruciform plan, a series of 14 statues commemorates famous figures from the history of British Columbia; among others Cook, Fraser, McLaughlin, and Moody are represented.

An extensive restoration program under the direction of architect Alan Hodgson commenced in 1973. Along with structural reinforcing the project also included an almost complete resurfacing of the interior, carried out with meticulous attention to the feeling and detail of the Rattenbury original construction drawings.

Royal British Columbia Museum.

Royal British Columbia Museum
1967, 1996

Belleville Street at Government
Archts. Department of Public Works
Foyer addition: John Di Castri

The Museum originated with a collection of natural history artifacts which in 1886 was housed in a 15-foot by 20-foot room next to the Provincial Secretary's Office at the central Administration Building of the "Birdcages." Three years later, on completion of a new Supreme Court Building (in Bastion Square), the "Provincial Museum of Natural History" was moved to the old Court Building, slightly to the southwest of the Administration building. The Museum was officially opened on May 24, 1890.

49

Douglas Building
Government Street

Queen's Printer
Superior Street

In 1897, the new Parliament Buildings neared completion and over the protestations of F. M. Rattenbury, the architect, it was decided to locate a new Provincial Museum in the west wing. In 1898 the old legislative assembly hall was renovated to accommodate laboratories, assaying facilities for students, and a permanent mineral exhibit. The building was used as such until its destruction by fire in 1957. Rattenbury himself tried again to have a purpose-built museum, and presented a proposal when he was asked to design additions to the Parliament Buildings in 1911. His sketch, "New Facade of the Parliament Building facing Superior Street" (or south façade), which now hangs in the speaker's corridor, shows two separate buildings extending south from the east and west blocks: "Proposed Departmental Wing or Printing Office" and "Proposed Museum." These were never built.

The Royal British Columbia Museum is now housed in two structures (exhibition building and multi-storey curatorial tower) facing Heritage Court. These were designed by B.C. Department of Public Works (design architect Andrew Cochrane) according to a strict functional program which differentiated curatorial functions and collections in a tower structure and public exhibits in a freestanding exhibition hall. The Provincial Archives Building balances these large blocks with negative space, literally a two-storey sunken garden and reflecting pool. Construction began in 1967 as a Provincial Centennial project. Cladding materials, marble and sandstone, respected the nearby

Helmcken House.

Parliament Buildings. Apparently Cochrane had recently returned from a trip to Venice and this might account for the vaguely Gothic arch and pier references. More directly the functional relationship is with Minoru Yamasaski's work for the Seattle World's Fair, the soaring free-standing arches of the Fair site re-rendered in abstract Gothic by Cochrane for the Carillon Tower. The exhibit hall contains numerous items of public art by local artists of the period: for instance, murals by Herbert Siebner, light fixtures by Jack Wilkinson. The four-storey glazed foyer linking to the structures was completed in 1996 according to designs by architect John Di Castri. The Carillon Tower is a focal point of the precinct, a gift of the Dutch people who settled in British Columbia. (HM Queen Juliana of the Netherlands unveiled the carillon cornerstone on May 23, 1967.) In 1971, to commemorate the British Columbia Confederation centennial, an additional 13 bells were donated. The chimes can be heard on the quarter hour with recitals as posted throughout the year. Adjacent to the Heritage Court and to the east is Thunderbird Park. The park was established in 1940 and features the work of British Columbia aboriginal artists. As well as the demonstration workshop where new poles are created and older poles replicated, there are several exhibition poles of interest. The replication program was begun in 1952 and from then until 1962, the chief carver was the now famous Mungo Martin, a Kwakiutl chief from Fort Rupert. The long house is named in Chief Martin's honour. This and the adjacent carving shed demonstrate traditional West Coast big house construction technologies: massive post-and-beam structures, walls and roof clad with wide vertical boards.

Adjoining Thunderbird Park to the south is the 1852 residence of Dr. J. S. Helmcken, first speaker of the Vancouver Island Legislative Assembly. The furnishings have been preserved and the house is open to the public. The landscaped enclave also includes the first school building of the Sisters of St. Ann. It is of a similar type of construction, Hudson's Bay Company squared timber, but is believed to date from 1848.

Parliament Buildings.

Parliament Buildings, Provincial Museum, *ca.* 1920. BCARS 8124

Roger's Chocolate Shop
1893

913 Government Street
Archts. Thomas Hooper, John Teague

The first tenant of the shop was Wilkerson's Jewelry. In 1894 a twin block was added (now 909 Government) to house Brown & Cooper's grocery shop. The central store was added soon after and contained an electrical supplies retailer. Roger's Chocolate shop and factory moved into 913 in 1918. The design demonstrates an awareness of the commonly ignored nature of two styles: Georgian with a Queen Anne flavour, and Art Nouveau. While Classical serves well for imposing and attractive façades, Art Nouveau, a style of ornament and intimacy, suits interiors where it can show off the intricacies of its linear designs. The Classical elements of the façade use galvanized iron, terracotta, and plaster. The shopfront and interior are composed of leaded art glass set in golden oak panelling and frames, Art Nouveau light fixtures, mosaic floor tile, and brown and marble detailing.

Temple Building
1893

535 Fort Street
Archt. Samuel Maclure

Robert Ward and Company's office on lower Fort Street was the first commercial building designed by Samuel Maclure in Victoria. The Temple Building is of more than passing interest to architectural historians as it is a high-quality, provincial variation of American architect, Louis H. Sullivan's (1856-1924) approach to handling structural materials and architectural ornament. It accords with the Chicago School's precepts of organic design. The building rests on a substantial rusticated sandstone base carried to the height of the ground floor where an ashlar sill articulates the division of the storeys. The pressed-brick second floor is integrated with the first by the vertical thrusts of the arches rising through both stories. The warmth of red pressed-brick with its smooth face rounded at the corners lends a tactile as well as visual effect of massiveness

tempered with plasticity; the skillful handling of the terracotta ornament alleviates any potential blandness in the expanses of masonry. Hoary faces peering out of the terracotta floral forms decorating the façade spandrels introduce a note of levity. The façade is handled as a three-dimensional unit carried to a depth of one bay along the west wall. The "business hall" behind is treated in a more simplified manner. It contained the open entrance foyer and offices of the firm's principal partners.

Leiser Building
1896
524 Yates and Waddington Alley
Archt: A. C. Ewart

The conservative nature of the Leiser's eclectic Frontier false front fails to reveal the advanced degree of nineteenth century inventive functionalism behind. The structure was built as a warehouse for Mr. Simon Leiser who had invested the profit from his contract to construct the Overland trail, from Telegraph Bay to Dease Lake, in a chain of grocery stores. Convenience and efficiency determined the internal plan. It was equipped with an electric freight elevator as well as a staircase; and to facilitate the handling of goods, two lines of track were laid on every floor. These tracks crossed on the elevator itself, which was fitted with a turntable so that a loaded truck could be run out in four directions. The façade is embellished with a rich variety of historical elements: the red brick walls are articulated with hammer-dressed granite transoms; the three-bay façade is divided by brick pilasters which are terminated at the top in the iron cornice with Gothic style finials. In this cornice, the pediment serves to define the central bay which contains, in the first floor, the rather handsome Assyrian arch with its granite voussoirs resting on imposts of carved stone. The Greater Victoria Regional District has recycled the building for its head offices and connected it to the adjacent Thomas Earle warehouse built in 1900. Its sophisticated brickwork and massive façade arch are recognizable design features of its architect, Thomas Hooper.

Bank of Montreal
1896
1200 Government Street
Archt. F. M. Rattenbury

It is not by accident that the Chateau style was stipulated by the Bank of Montreal. As the financial backer of the Canadian Pacific Railway, it was the first of the major eastern banking houses to establish a western office on the completion of the railroad (Vancouver in 1887). For this reason the stylistic affinity of the bank with Rattenbury's later Empress Hotel in particular, and the CPR's official Chateau style in general, was appropriate. This building's rusticated granite base gives the appearance of a strong foundation and this manner of stonework is used to emphasize the surrounds of the ground floor windows and the Bastion Street entrance. Above the main floor, the masonry is articulated with alternating bands of rusticated and ashlar Haddington Island stone. The corner doorway, now filled in, with second floor oriel window above, carries the eye into the Gothic roofline. Here an eclectic assemblage of medieval motifs breaks the skyline in a Picturesque interplay of lines, planes, volumes, and voids—a prelude to Rattenbury's later design for the Empress Hotel. Similar to the Parliament Buildings, the exterior is sheathed in Haddington Island stone, the base with ashlar granite from Nelson Island. In 1988 the interior was refurbished to accommodate retail use, necessitating dropping the main windowsills for street retail display—a sensitive adaptation to the design of Wagg & Hambleton, Architects.

Hall Building
1897

727-729 Yates Street
Archt. John Teague

In an ambitious design for a small structure, Teague here works in the Victorian Romanesque Revival style. Large-scale masonry elements including the large stone lintels and massive diapered parapet are organized about a central arched bay, suppressing to some degree the verticality of the tall windows.

Weiler Building
1899

1921 Government at Broughton Street
Archt. Thomas C. Sorby

The diversified interests of Otto Weiler's manufacturing firm propelled it quickly to the summit of success as Victoria developed at a dramatic pace during the 1890s. The business quickly expanded into every branch of the drygoods field. It was Weiler's who held the Liberty of London franchise for the famous art glass, silverware, and textiles. At a cost of $31,000, Sorby supplied Weiler with 109,162 square feet of well-lit display and storage space. This was housed within a five-storey structure some 82 feet high. Sorby's main problem was to provide a series of spaces within so tall a structure that would be illuminated sufficiently to show off the many high-quality exotic wares in which the firm specialized. The solution was a post-and-beam structure within an arcuated brick exterior. Massive clear grain 2-foot by 2-foot fir timbers were used to construct the interior frame while the brick shell, opened up to the limits of its structural endurance, is slightly battered to compress and reinforce the other free-standing internal structure. The gravity-defying arcuated bays which amaze the innocent spectator carry only their own weight while they exert lateral compression on the loadbearing structure within. The heavy corbelled cornice above the fifth floor serves to weigh down the shell, directing the explosive tension of the splaying arches downward and inward.

Hooper's design for D. E. Campbell and A. G. McCandless produced a remarkably well detailed brick building which was a hallmark of Hooper's work at the time. Although the inspiration is American, Richardsonian Romanesque, here style gives way to good masonry using pressed and moulded brick which is diapered and corbelled for decorative effect.

Vernon Building
1899

1000-1002 Government Street
Archt. Thomas Hooper

The heavy rusticated stone plinths of the first storey provide a solid footing for the open arched bays of the two upper floors. The rich articulation, carved stone and terracotta against a warm buff brick, was probably intended as a streetfront promotion for owner Charles A. Vernon's other business interest, the B.C. Pottery and Terra Cotta Company.

Earle Building
1900

530-534 Yates Street
Archt. Thomas Hooper

Built as a warehouse for grocer and provisioning merchant Thomas Earle, this pressed brick façade marks Hooper's skill in using the more advanced engineering principles of his day to open up street front, so admitting greater quantities of light in the depth of the three-storey interior. The sweep of the single arch is, however, somewhat restrained by the Picturesque treatment of the gable parapet.

Campbell & McCandless Building
1899

574-580 Johnson Street
Archt. Thomas Hooper

Pither & Leiser Building
1900

535 Yates Street
Archt. Thomas Hooper

The heavy stonework of the first storey provides a supporting podium

for the three-storey arches of the upper floors. Brick spandrels are hung from the columns opening up the façade to gain maximum interior illumination for this enclosed centre-block warehouse. Moulded and pressed buff brick is used for a restrained decorative effect although the loss of the Classical cornice and nameplate finial is unfortunate.

Porter Block
1900

1402-1406 Douglas Street
Archt. W. R. Wilson

For butcher, alderman, mayor and developer Robert J. Porter, Wilson produced a conservative masonry building. The plain brick second storey rests securely on a rusticated sandstone first floor. But at the roof line a terracotta balustrade, providing a note of decorative whimsy, is unique to the skylines of Victoria.

B.C. Electric Railway Co. Depot
1901, 1907

502-508 Discovery Street
Archt. F. M. Rattenbury

Victoria's tramways were founded in 1890 and after a series of financial setbacks were consolidated into the BCER in 1897. In 1960 the company became B.C. Hydro, one of the continent's largest hydro-electric power companies. These car sheds accommodated the rolling stock for the expanding network of streetcar lines. They are large brick utilitarian structures attractive in their scale and largely functional expression of interior spaces and construction materials. The massive timber trusswork required for the span of the sheds is particularly impressive.

Carnegie Library
1904

794 Yates at Blanshard
Archts. Hooper & Watkins
Rehabilitation: SDW Architects, 1981

In their winning scheme for the design competition, Hooper & Watkins produced a variation on a theme which is handled with equal success in many of their other buildings, such as the Roman Catholic Bishop's Palace, and Roger's Chocolate Shop—that is, the combination of a formal style exterior with an intimate Arts & Crafts interior. This magnificently proportioned little building (in 1996 the subject of a Canadian postage stamp), its Richardsonian Romanesque exterior complete with generous Assyrian arched portico, Ionic peristyle upper balcony, and Classical cornice, boasted a complementary interior finished in Art Nouveau joinery and stained art

glass. The result was a prominent public façade with a decorative and humanly scaled interior accommodation. In 1981 the exterior was restored, and the interior sympathetically remodelled, and the northern modern addition renovated for commercial use.

Promise Block
1905

1006-1010 Government Street
Archts. Hooper & Watkins

This very finely detailed building, a Hooper trademark, has a second four-storey frontage with the distinctive recessed bay windows on Langley Street. The two-storey Government Street façade with its glazed brick, delicately moulded terracotta cornice, and equally well executed cast iron columns, gives the building a mark of refined distinction. The developer was Oscar Promise of San Jose, California.

Hanna's Undertaking Parlour
1905

738-740 Yates Street
Archt. Hooper & Watkins

This small commercial commission for W. J. Hanna exhibits the tight, very competent design work in the Edwardian Classical style which was coming out of Hooper's office at this time. With a consistent attention to scale, arrangement of the building elements, and handling of construction detail, the work of these years had a consistent look to it. As a result, commercial Edwardian Victoria was very much a product of this architectural office.

B.C. Electric Railway Company Offices
1906-1907, 1911-1912

517 Fort Street, 1016 Langley Street
Archt. F. M. Rattenbury

Rattenbury's original 1904 designs called for a stone-faced structure. As built two years later, it was a two-storey pressed brick and stone trim Classical Temple building. The splayed corner entrance is traditional in Victoria. The attic storey was added later, probably also to Rattenbury's designs. The building makes a good streetscape fit with Maclure's earlier Temple Building across the street.

Pither and Leiser Warehouse
1905

1019 Wharf Street
Archts. Hooper & Watkins

Defined by its corner entrance monopod column, this towering utilitarian brick structure seems to rise through its arches to challenge the compression of its heavy corbelled cornice line. Rather than the Chicago influences of this period, the ultimate inspiration for this structure seems to come from the much earlier, and very famous, Port of London's St. Catharine's Docks warehouses designed in 1825 by the engineer Thomas Telford. And in fact this was built as the headquarters of Pither and Leiser's thriving import and distribution business for wines and liquors.

Roman Catholic Bishop's Palace
1907

740 View Street
Archts. Hooper & Watkins

The function of the palace was to serve as the official residence of the Bishop and to house several priests, the "Veritas" library and archives, and the Chancellor's and Bishop's offices. The cost was $12,000. Working within the Classical style, the architectural team of Hooper & Watkins designed a simple but handsome Queen Anne Revival building, symmetrical in both plan and elevation. Brick pilasters with Ionic capitals frame the entire front elevation and a similar pair of pilasters topped by a broken pediment define the slightly projecting central block. Inside a central stairwell with landings allows convenient access to the three floors and also interior lighting from a skylight in the roof above.

Mahon Building
1907

1110-1112 Government Street
Archt. W. R. Wilson

This building reaches through the block to Langley Street. Both façades illustrate Wilson's fastidious attention to detail in his use of white glazed brick along with cast and pressed tin. Edward Mahon, real estate agent and developer, was a partner in the firm of Mahon, McFarland & Proctor.

Merchants Bank
1907, 1945

1225 Douglas at Yates Street
Archt. F. M. Rattenbury
Addition: C. J. Thompson, 1945

When Francis Mawson Rattenbury submitted his plans for the "Merchants Bank" in May 1907, it was Victoria's most expensive building in proportion to its size. At a contract price of $40,000.00 exclusive of fittings, the bank cost 32¢ for every square foot of space; in comparison, the Parliament Buildings cost only 22¢ per square foot. The contract called for five-foot-thick walls, against which was to stand a peristyle of free-standing Ionic columns flanked by massive piers with richly carved headings. The building was heralded as "pure Renaissance" in style, what we now call "Beaux Arts." The floors and roof are reinforced concrete. Limestone was brought from Newcastle Island, and marble was imported for the 17-foot-high banking room floors, walls, and also the counters which were ornamented with bronze grill work.

A Moderne Classical addition to the north elevation was designed by the Vancouver firm of C. J. Thompson in 1945 for the Bank of Montreal. A contemporary renovation has sympathetically reinterpreted the original interior scheme for modern use.

Empress Hotel
1907-1929

721 Government Street
Archt. F. M. Rattenbury
Addition and Renovations:
Poon, Billington, Gardner, 1988

The Empress is one of a long line of Chateau style railroad hotels

originating in William Van Horne's dream of a chain of Picturesque hotels commanding the choicest views in the Rocky and Selkirk mountains of British Columbia. Stylistically it is directly related to a series of predecessors designed for the CPR by Bruce Price: the original Banff Springs Hotel (1886-1888), the Chateau Frontenac in Quebec City (1892), and the Place Viger Hotel and Station in Montreal (1896-1898). Rattenbury's design is a development of Price's work (which itself remained very close to Richardsonian influences) and the original archaeological sources, namely the medieval Loire chateaux. Flat wall surfaces, a Picturesque broken roofline, the concentration of detail in the roof architecture, Neo-Gothic dormers and the overall emphasis on verticality recall Price's work in the Chateau Frontenac. Many elements, however, evidence Rattenbury's personal signature. The stylized Tudor arches of the porch introducing the Elizabethan flavour of the lobby and the quatrefoils along the cornice appear in local domestic buildings. Domed polygon turrets relate the structure to Rattenbury's Parliament Buildings facing the Empress on the south side of the harbour. Together they associate the structure with the cultures of English and French Canada and their union within the Dominion. Rattenbury's original unit, comprising the central block of the present-day structure, contained 160 rooms. North and south wings of 74 and 100 rooms respectively were added in 1910 and 1913. In 1912 the Ballroom and Library were added by W. S. Painter, who also supplied the designs for later CPR Hotels (the Banff Springs Hotel [1912-1913] and Chateau Lake Louise [1912-1913]). In 1929, 273 new guest rooms and suites were completed under the direction of J. W. Orrock, Engineer of Buildings for the CPR. The conservatory was added to the Ballroom in the same year. In 1988 the Empress underwent a complete refurbishment. A Chateau style roofed elevator tower and forward guest entrance and lobby were added to the northern wing. This contained a galleried retail concourse, swimming pool, and also underground parking entry. At the same time the Empress gardens were completely recreated in the old tradition: a drystone "natural landscape" featuring native plants on the north side, formal beds for annuals on the west front, and a pergola feature and formal rose garden at the south front. At the same time the Victoria Conference Centre was added to the east side with new kitchens and underground parking integrated to serve both facilities.

61

Hafer Machine Co. Building
1908, 1911, 1941

1720 Store Street
Archt. D. C. Frame
Renovations: Bawlf Cooper Associates

Ludwig Hafer moved his mechanical industrial workshop into the building in 1912 where it remained until a recent renovation by architect Bawlf Cooper Associates recycled the structure for drygoods retail. Additions were made over the years but the large brick gabled warehouse dominated the complex in Victoria's old industrial district.

St. Joseph's Hospital
1908

800 Humboldt Street
Archts. Hooper & Watkins

A work of social mercy by the Sisters of St. Ann, the first hospital opened on this site in 1876. The present heritage structure, now bracketted by modern additions, was built in 1908 in an Edwardian variant of the Queen Anne style much used throughout the province for public school architecture. The Ionic columned portico and pedimented upper floor balconies provide an imposing entrance to the hipped roof block behind. The recessed bay window wall surfaces are grey brick relieved with courses of white stone. Across the intervening green space of the St. Ann's gardens

Mable Carriage Works
1908

713-715 Johnson Street
Archts. Hooper & Watkins

The advertising sign for W. J. Mable's business is still evident on the eastern brick wall. The street frontage, more Victorian in feeling because of the individual windows set within the brick panelled bays, is conservative and restrained, certainly an industrial rather than flamboyant commercial structure.

this gable and spire echo similar elements of the earlier St. Ann's convent school. At the rear of the entrance wing is a charming architectural conceit, a small chapel, inspired by the well-known Pazzi Chapel of Sta. Croce, Florence, by the early Renaissance architect, Filippo Brunelleschi.

Lee Cheong Building
1909

618-624 Johnson at Broad Street
Archt. Hooper & Watkins

Three partners, Lee Cheong, Lee Woy and Lee Yan Yow, developed this prominent corner location. The architects provided a plain but handsome Edwardian Classical block with cast iron opening up the shopfronts for maximum light, while above, the panelled brickwork is protected by a Classical cornice and parapet—all surviving substantially unaltered to the present day.

**Royal Bank Building
Munro's Books**
1909

1108 Government Street
Archt. Thomas Hooper

A second storey has been removed, but this is still one of Victoria's finest small Temple bank designs. The deep relief of the design elements, boldness of the detailing and solidity of the cut stone give a Beaux Arts feeling that reinforces the building's presence on the street. In 1985 the bank was acquired by book retailer James Munro, who has restored the grand interior banking hall. A major feature is a set of colourfully expressive wall hangings, "The Four Seasons" by well-known fabric artist, Carol Sabiston.

Bridgman Building
1885,

604 Broughton Street
Archts. James and James, 1910

Although built in 1885 for C. E. Redfern, the building is recognized today by its unusual 1910 façade. The thin framing columns, simplified rectilinear window elements, and the mosaic spandrel utilizing Art Nouveau motifs recall then-current English work of C. F. A. Voysey and Charles Rennie MacIntosh. This façade was unique in its day and remains so to the present, a pleasant surprise amid the more ponderous and pretentious structures of Old Town.

commercial use and the building has survived being integrated into the British Columbia Building Corporation's adjoining development (Architects Hawthorn, Mansfield Towers, 1979) containing government offices and the Victoria Public Library.

Sweeney McConnel Building
1910

1010-1012 Langley Street
Archt. H. S. Griffith

For many years the home of one of Victoria's better known printing and stationery supply companies, this ornate Edwardian Classical façade was a fixture on the block. Unfortunately the very generous dentillated cornice is gone but the pressed tin spandrel panels and side pier escutcheons give some idea of the original splendour of the design.

Alexandria Club
1911

716 Courtenay Street
Archt. David C. Frame

As a female response to the all-male Union Club, the building featured a ballroom, lounges, dining room and accommodation. The façade was given a restrained Edwardian Classical treatment with a central entrance columned portico, second-floor recessed balcony and double hung windows at the residential level above.

The handsomely appointed former clubroom has remained in its new

Saward Building
1911

1202-1213 Douglas at View Street
Archts. G. C. Mesher & Co.

J. A. Saward, a principal investor in the project, was also the managing director of the Esquimalt Waterworks. The six-storey building, although a clean lined Chicago School essay, still retains the basic elements of the Classical vocabulary. The retail first floor provides a podium for the body of the building where the window grid expresses its steel skeleton and opens the structure for maximum natural light. Above the fifth storey an attic storey is capped by a generous Classical cornice. The mix of retail and professional offices survives to this day.

Pemberton Block
1911
637-649 Fort Street
Archt. George C. Mesher

Pemberton and Son, an old Hudson's Bay Company family, were one of the largest realtors and developers in Victoria. Edwardian both in its Victoria. Edwardian both in its restrained Classical references and in the Chicago School open treatment of the window bays, the brick upper floors rest firmly on heavy rusticated granite piers at street level. The Pacific Club had the top floor and Victoria's Stock Exchange occupied the basement along with a gentleman's barber shop in the early years.

Hotel Douglas
1911
1450 Douglas Street at Pandora
Archt. L. W. Hargreaves

Developed by local businessman and Saanich market gardener Lim Bang, the hotel was first successful as the Prince George. It closed and re-opened in 1918 as the Douglas. Essentially a Chicago School design in tan brick with generous window bays expressing the structural grid, this fact is handsomely disguised by quite lavish Classical detailing in cream coloured terracotta.

Strathcona Hotel
1911
919 Douglas Street
Archt. H. S. Griffith
Addition: SDW Architects, 1993

Originally built as the Empress office block, this six-storey very handsome Edwardian building actually opened as the Strathcona Hotel. The high point of the building is its glazed terracotta façade capped by a very ornate Classical cornice. In 1993 a two-storey restaurant pavilion with rooftop garden cafe and tennis court was added to fill in the southern end of the block. The terracotta finish and detailing was carried through the new façade with an unusually high degree of sensitivity for the original design; it is therefore very successful.

Congregational Church
1912
1600 Quadra Street
Archts. Breseman & Durfee, Seattle

The cornerstone for the Congregational Church was laid on October 28, 1912 and construction was completed for consecration on April 3, 1913. The consecration address was given by the Rev. W. J. Hindley, mayor of Spokane, Washington and betrays the American origin of the Congregational movement. Similarly, the architects were an American firm who exported to Victoria an Eastern American Classical Revival church-type. With the amalgamation of the Congregationalists, the Methodists, and Presbyterians to form the United Church in 1925, its congregation merged with the Metropolitan Church. The building is plainer than originally conceived. The large blank upper zones of brick flanking the portico were to have carried a handsome entablature and balustrades. A domed bell tower would likewise have capped the Classical gable. The appeal to American Adamesque architectural taste is not out of place here. The Congregational Church, as evidenced by those attending the consecration, was an American progeny in Victoria.

Church of St. John the Divine
1912
1611 Quadra Street
Archt. W. R. Wilson

The history of St. John's is one of the most fascinating ecclesiastical episodes in BC's history. The present church boasts an ancestry back to the first Anglican church established under the auspices of the Hudson's Bay Company in Victoria between 1853 and 1856. An ongoing informal relationship no doubt prompted the Hudson's Bay Company to sell the lot at the northeast corner of Fisgard and Douglas to the Episcopalian Church. On this site was erected the famous St. John's "Iron Church" in 1860. George Hills, Bishop of Columbia, arrived in Victoria in January 1860, and his church building, prefabricated from sheet and cast iron, soon followed him. This was a founding gift to the diocese from its patron, banking heiress, Baroness Angela Burdett-Coutts. The church was consecrated on September 30, 1860. The structure itself may have originated from the designs of W. Slater, being one of a series which were manufactured in England and shipped out to many parts of the British Empire during the late 1850s and 1860s. Although at that time considered a marvel, the church was soon outgrown and outdated. In 1912, and not without some controversy, the Hudson's Bay Company bought back the property for the construction of its department store. The generous purchase price of $140,000 was no small help in financing construction of the new brick Gothic Revival church. The sensitively scaled seniors' housing infill, creating a garden precinct on the north side (1973, architect Alan Hodgson), draws its form and style from the 1912 manse.

Kaiserhof Hotel
1912

1320 Blanshard Street
Archt. Thomas Hooper

With the anti-German riots of 1915 the hotel was damaged and underwent a name change to the Blanshard, the Cecil Hotel and, most recently, Kent Apartments. Hooper's design utilizes extensive cream glazed terracotta to articulate a tan brick structure. Alternating bands of brick and terracotta are used at street level, in the arched entrance voussoirs, and then to detail the brick pilasters at the cornice line. The effect is dramatic if somewhat discordant.

W. & J. Wilson Building
1912

1221 Government Street at Trounce Alley
Archt. W. R. Wilson

Wilson's Clothiers was founded in 1863 and the present building resulted from extensive alterations to their earlier structure. Utilizing cast and structural steel, the architect provided an open shopfront which featured an island window display inset into the frontage; the display floor was flooded with natural light from a faceted glass

clerestory which though now overpainted can still be seen above the street-level canopy. A recent very sensitive renovation utilized the original brass and hardwood millwork in reconfiguring the shopfront and also highlighting the cast iron Edwardian Italianate detailing.

Belmont Block
1912

600-620 Humboldt Street
Archts. Hoult Horton

Dominating the entrance to the commercial core of Old Town, the Belmont was originally intended to be a hotel.

It was designed as one of the first reinforced concrete buildings in Victoria. The smooth multi-bayed design with its corner tower elements and matte-glazed cream terracotta cladding owes much to the earlier pioneering work of Holabird and Roche in Chicago where the modern multi-storey office building was invented. And in fact the economic collapse and war of 1914 halted

67

construction, causing it to be finished post-war as an office building. The overall effect is of a rich but restrained Edwardian elegance with just the lightest of the requisite Classical touches.

Fairfield Block
1912
1601-1609 Douglas Street at Cormorant
Archt. H. S. Griffith

By the late first decade of the twentieth century, Victoria's commercial centre had graduated from the verandah-fronted Italianate wood and brick of a western boom-town to the Edwardian presumption of a Renaissance city. Hotels, clubs, institutional structures and even commercial buildings sported the new style beneath generous Classical cornice lines and sculptural details in creamy white terracotta. The three-storey Fairfield, built for partners Grant and Lineham, is very much of this period as Victoria's perception of itself and its prospects expressed the optimism of that rapid growth decade.

The Union Club of British Columbia
1912
805 Gordon at Humboldt Street
Archt. Loring P. Rexford

The Victoria Union Club was organized in 1879 with Sir Matthew Baillie Begbie as its first President. For this building a design competition attracted 17 entries and San Francisco architect Loring P. Rexford with his Beaux Arts Renaissance Palazzo design was judged the winner. The Renaissance façade is

finished in glazed, dark-brown brick accented with light-yellow glazed terracotta trim. The main floor, housing the various club rooms, rests above the ashlar-faced ground floor. A shallow portico with low relief pilasters emphasizes the centralized entrance approached by a flight of stairs and a balustraded main floor balcony. To emphasize its Classical horizontality and integrate the portico into the façade, the arcuated fenestration with its terracotta surrounds is continued on all sides of the main floor, as is the rectangular window treatment of the third and fourth floors. On the southern side a ladies lounge and entrance were added in 1962-1963 (architect Peter Cotton).

Yorkshire Trust Co.
1912
737 Fort Street
Archt. A. Arthur Cox

A pair of free-standing Corinthian columns defines the portico for the arched entrance and these are flanked by two massive pylons which support the Classical entablature above. The composition is a small but very competent essay in Edwardian Beaux Arts classicism. The Yorkshire Trust played a major role of funnelling investment funds from the cotton manufacturers of northern England to British Columbia and it is probably the same route of contacts that businessmen and professionals such as F. M. Rattenbury followed.

Union Bank Building
1912
1205 Government Street
Archt. A. Arthur Cox

and

Central Building
1912
614-622 View Street
Archt. Jesse M. Warren

At seven storeys this ranks as one of Victoria's best surviving "skyscrapers." Others such as the Royal Bank and Campbell Building, both on Douglas, are gone; also Maclure's Jones Building on Fort Street. This Beaux Arts extravaganza of brick and white glazed terracotta Renaissance detailing is a fitting riposte to the Bank of Montreal (opposite) and the James Brothers' federal Post Office which it also faces. Adjacent, on View Street, is the Central Building, a more restrained version of the Bank. The Central's View Street lobby has been restored along with the main staircase. This leads to the upper floors which have been for the most part maintained with their original tenant fitments.

The Saint James Hotel
1912
642 Johnson Street
Archts. Breseman & Durfee
Addition: Wagg & Hambleton, 1981

Called the Carlton Hotel on its building plans, this was developed by Victoria entrepreneur and mayor Charles Hayward. Tan brick and white terracotta, with a finely detailed attic storey and cornice, constitute the design elements which are repeated (although the terracotta is fibreglass) in the western 1981 addition by architect David Hambleton.

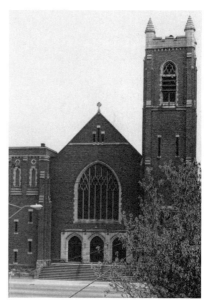

First Presbyterian Church
1912
1411 Quadra at Fisgard Street
Archt. J. C. M. Keith

The Presbyterian community on Vancouver Island dates from the early missionary work of the Rev. John Hall, sent out under the sponsorship of the Dublin Presbytery of the Irish Presbyterian Church. The first church was built on the corner of Blanshard and Pandora, according to plans by the firm of Wright and Sanders. In August 1911, the Presbyterians commissioned Keith to plan and supervise construction of what was to be a multi-stage building program for a Gothic Revival style concrete, brick and stone church. On May 11, 1913, the inaugural services were held in the hall and Mr. Keith was authorized to proceed with the main church structure. The entire project was to cost $130,000. Luney Brothers contracted to excavate the site and the erection of the new building was carried out by Steven's Brothers. The new church was opened on Sunday, May 2, 1915.

Scott and Peden Warehouse Complex
1913, 1987

1601 Store at Johnson Street
Archts. M. S. Farewell, Percy Fox

The look of the Swan's Hotel complex as it is now known is very much the result of a restoration and recycling program undertaken by owner Michael Williams and designed by William Patterson. For Scott and Peden, wholesalers of grain, feed and related products, Farewell produced a heavy timber structure with a plain brick envelope; an E&N rail spur entered from Store Street. The 1987 renovation produced the current Edwardian Classical scheme. The adjacent Store Street storefront, also by Farewell, has however been restored. On the Pandora frontage an adjoining earlier building (1887) was renovated by Percy Fox in 1913 and given a more Classical look, including this abstract, almost Deco variation of a Classical cornice in pressed tin.

Kinemacolour Theatre
1913

1600 Government Street at Pandora
Archts. Rochfort & Sankey

The Royal Theatre was also in the architects' office while design work for the Island Amusement Company's movie house was underway. It is not surprising, therefore, that both share a similar Edwardian Italianate arrangement of decorative elements. However, in this smaller private commission the use of ornament, both in the handling of the brickwork and the pressed tin, almost abstract Classical ornamentation is much more restrained. Inside, some of the original ornate cast plaster work has survived the building's varied uses over the years.

Royal Victoria Theatre
1913

805 Broughton at Blanshard Street
Archts. Rochfort & Sankey
Renovations: Wagg & Hambleton Architects, 1991

The Royal Victoria Theatre functioned as an opera house and theatre until it was closed during the 1930s and was bought for a cinema by Famous Players. Even as it stands today, "The Royal" is an impressive structure. It is a steel-framed block with brick infill. As a fire precaution the interior is lined with asbestos brick under the plaster finish. The magnificent façade is achieved with a surprising economy of glazed white terracotta ornament, which is used to highlight the complicated patterning of brick diaper-work. The Beaux Arts ornament is carried through to the interior, which boasts an impressive Baroque Revival decorative scheme executed in plaster by two Parisian craftsman, Henri Gotter and C. E. Dorisy. Extensive wall and ceiling murals are now gone. Architects Wagg & Hambleton undertook the restoration of the building after it was acquired for reuse as a civic concert hall. The new east and west lobbies, sympathetic in style and Classical detailing, set off the original building and also provide seismic reinforcing.

Hudson's Bay Co. Department Store
1914-1921, 1948-1949

1701 Douglas at Fisgard Street
Archts. Horwood & White, Toronto
Addition: Moore & Moody, Winnipeg

An Edwardian Classical Temple, "The Bay" is now Victoria's only architectural monument to the institution which had such a profound influence on the establishment and early development of Victoria and the Canadian West. Construction was halted in 1914 by World War I; the building was dedicated in 1920 during the 250th anniversary of the HBC Charter and completed the following year. An imposing block, the design by Toronto architects gives the impression of stylistic purity while it is in fact a mixture of many Classical ingredients. A vaguely Classical first floor with generous fenestration for display provides the podium for Temple-type peristyles of engaged columns with tobacco-leaf capitals. These articulate and frame what would otherwise be a modern-looking office block. The columns are capped by a bracketted Classical entablature with a roofline balustrade. The economy of detail, the smooth terracotta surfaces, and crisply defined volumes give the structure an air of luxury and grandeur without ostentation. Probably for this reason the design proved successful and explains why the Victoria store is one of many nearly identical ones in Vancouver, Calgary and Winnipeg. The eastern addition of 1948-1949, three bays deep, was designed by Moore & Moody, Architects, of Winnipeg.

Bay Street Armories
1915
713 Bay at Blanshard Street
Archt. W. R. Wilson

Dominion Custom House
1914
811 Wharf at Government Street
Archts. Thomas Fuller, Department of Public Works, Ottawa
Renovations: Irvin Kew, 1994

This was built as an addition to the 1894 Second Empire Post Office which stood at the Government Street corner.

Demolition of the Post Office in 1965 and replacement with a bland modern structure constituted a major loss to Victoria's grand processional entrance as seen from the Inner Harbour. The surviving addition utilized the Edwardian palazzo form but quoted many of the Classical elements from the wall surfaces of the old Post Office. Interestingly the Federal Government recognized its symbolic faux pas and in time for Victoria's hosting the Commonwealth Games in 1994 had the modern building reclad. The Post-Modern design by architect Irving Kew referenced the design vocabulary of the surviving 1914 customs block.

The castle image was common to armories under construction throughout Canada during this period as the country mustered troops for the European theatre of war. In fact this Neoclassical plan, a centre block flanked by two wings, expresses the dominant interior feature, a huge galleried drill hall. The basement contained a gymnasium, two rifle ranges and a swimming pool. Access to the various campaign rooms, mess rooms and armories was off the central hall. The crenalated tower, containing a caretaker suite, marks the entrance with its symbolic portcullis. The brick buttressed walls relieved by the corner oriel turrets and stone copings lend further to the martial imagery.

First Church of Christ Scientist
1919
1205 Pandora Avenue
Archts. George Foote Dunhan & C. H. Wallwork, Portland

To the spectator who stands at the corner of Quadra Street and Pandora Avenue and looks eastward up Pandora, a Picturesque view features this handsome Neoclassical structure rising over the green lawn and copse of trees in the divide between the two forks of Blanshard. The building is indirectly but obviously derived from the Roman Pantheon via Palladio's "Villa Rotunda" and follows the design of the mother church of Christian Science in Boston, Massachusetts (ca. 1890). Approaching the church one can appreciate the heavy, monumental, yet rational proportions. Concrete steps lead up to the base of the towering Ionic columns within the two-storey façade, a motif which is carried through the sides in pilasters of the same height. Above the entablature rises the huge drum which supports the roof of the dome.

Bank of Nova Scotia
1923, 1963

702 Yates Street
Archt. A. Arthur Cox

This stone-faced Temple style bank anchors the corner of Yates and Douglas. Subdued but delicate Classical detailing, pilaster columns with ornate capitals define the banking hall and an attic storey provides offices above. The northern three bays are a later addition faithful to the style of the original design.

CPR Steamship Terminal
1924

468 Belleville Street
Archts. F. M. Rattenbury, P. L. James

There is more than a suggestion of humour in this building designed by

the same team later responsible for the Crystal Gardens. In obvious mimicry of a Greek temple, the shipping terminal is Victoria's most pure example of the Neoclassical revival and may have been inspired by some of the Beaux Arts "follies" popular in the heyday of the great exhibitions in the early 1900s. Rattenbury was probably familiar with those of architect Bernard Maybeck at the San Francisco Panama-Pacific International Exhibition in 1915. The structural columns represented the first attempt in Victoria of on-site precast concrete techniques. The north and south façades are lined with a massive Ionic peristyle. Decorating the main piers at the corners and flanking the entrances just below the entablature appear a series of hoary heads with a crown and crossed tridents, attributes of Poseidon, the Greek god of the sea—identifying the building's maritime function. The Terminal is a monumental introduction for the ceremonial tone of the Inner Harbour, a tone echoed here but previously sounded by Rattenbury in his earlier buildings, the Parliament Buildings and the Empress Hotel.

Johnson Street Bridge
1924

Johnson at Wharf Street
Engineer: Strauss Bascule Bridge Co.

This double lifting span bridge serves both vehicular and rail traffic and guards the entrance to the Upper Harbour. It cost the substantial sum of $918,00 to construct. The bridge is electric powered although most of the work is done by the massive counterweights

on the east side of the bridge. The principal of the San Francisco company that designed the bridge was Joseph Strauss, designer also of the Golden Gate suspension bridge. The spans manufactured from 1000 tons of steel were prefabricated by the Canadian Bridge Co. in Walkerville, Ontario.

Crystal Gardens
1925

701 Douglas at Belleville Street
Archts. F. M. Rattenbury, P. L. James
Rehabilitation: Wagg & Hambleton, 1978

An extensive promotional campaign ended December 29, 1923, when Victoria's citizens voted approval to underwrite the construction of a combination swimming pool-convention centre. Intended to make Victoria the convention centre of the West, it was built by the CPR on reclaimed James Bay land leased for 21 years from the city with revenues accruing to the builders. F. M. Rattenbury was commissioned to design the building as a matter of course; he had already completed large projects for the company in Vancouver and Victoria. His associate was P. L. James, a man who had worked with Saxon & Snell, an English firm noted for hospitals and public baths. The problem of supporting a building holding 232,000 gallons of water on a filled-in bog was solved by "floating" it on a massive, 30-inch thick, steel-reinforced, concrete raft. The pool is "suspended" in the middle, the shallow end of the 150-foot by 40-foot basin rides above the general grade, and the deep end below. The actual weight of the roof is carried by heavy iron piers springing from the pool deck inside the building. Although most of the materials were locally obtained, the glass was imported from Belgium by the Lord and Burnham Company of Ontario who manufactured the iron-and-glass superstructure. As well as the pool, the building housed three large ballrooms, a mezzanine, tearoom, Turkish baths, offices, and clubrooms. The pool originally featured heated salt sea water, at the time believed to be particularly healthful.

Operated since 1978 by the Provincial Capital Commission as a public botanical gardens, the restoration conversion was carried out by architects Wagg & Hambleton. At this time the south and west perimeter walls were breached to allow for the insertion of retail and restaurant use at street level, a sympathetic treatment of new economic uses for one of Victoria's major civic monuments.

Christ Church Cathedral
1926

951 Quadra at Rockland Street
Archt. J. C. Malcolm Keith
Completion archts.: Wade Williams
Design: J. Wade, R. Baxter, 1983-1994

The spate of church building among the Nonconformists in the late 1880s and early 1890s no doubt encouraged the Anglicans to consider erecting a more substantial cathedral of their own. The winner of the 1891 international competition was an English-born architect who moved to Victoria from Seattle specifically to work on his entry. The design of John Charles Malcolm Keith under the *nom de plume* "Fides" was selected as the

winner by Sir Arthur Blomfield, one of the great English ecclesiastical architects of the day. It was no doubt a disappointment to Keith that he had to wait some 30 years before seeing his building started, and then never completed. A start was made in 1926. Keith acknowledged a debt to Grace Episcopal Cathedral in San Francisco (1910) and to many cathedrals of thirteenth century France and England, including obvious references to Notre Dame in the floor plan and west end, and to Lincoln in the great crossing tower that was not built. The contract was awarded to the Parfitt Brothers of Victoria. The structure itself is of reinforced concrete faced with rusticated sandstone from Newcastle Island near Nanaimo. Granite was used to dress the base, while Canmos moulded "art stone" was used to articulate the doors, windows, and arches. Two square towers flank the west wall and 85-foot Gothic arch. Within the arch, set into the end of the nave, is a rose window. The towers themselves, 33 feet square, rise to a height of 135 feet, and the unbuilt central crossing tower was to have risen 185 feet above the cathedral floor. Along the side elevations runs a clerestory consisting of six groups of three pointed windows, and from the wall between these groups to the outer walls of the side aisles spring the flying buttresses. Just behind the west tower is the small, though attractive, semioctagonal baptistery. Next to this is an outdoor pulpit. One enters the Cathedral through either of the tower doors or the massive central double-doors which lead into the narthex. From there one proceeds through any one of the six sets of doors to the nave. Five pairs of free-standing Doric columns made of steel-reinforced Canmos stone support soaring sandstone pilasters which take the eye up through the clerestory into the brick Gothic rib vaulting 80 feet above the floor. The floor of the nave is finished in a warm red tile which harmonizes with the vault above and the stained glass in the west end. The baptistry, lit by three glowing lancet windows, is floored with Texada Island marble. The Cathedral is one of Victoria's most impressive churches. This has been acknowledged, for, although Keith never saw the completion of the church, its design brought him worldwide acclaim which included being elected a Fellow of the Royal Institute of British Architects. In 1924, Rev. E. P. Laycock was appointed Archdeacon with the duty of supervising construction. Four south aisle windows came from the studios of J. E. Nuttgens, and 12 in the north aisle from James Ballantine of Edinburgh; those in the western lancets and the rose window are by Percy Bacon of London. The northwest tower was raised in 1936 so that the peal of bells by Mears and Stainbank could be hung; the twin towers were at last dedicated in 1954. The final treatment of the east end was to truncate the proposed larger sanctuary and move it forward to the location of the proposed crossing tower of the original scheme. This arrangement finally completed the building in 1994 according to plans prepared by architect Robert Baxter.

Causeway Garage Building for Imperial Oil
1931

812 Wharf Street
Archts. Townley & Matheson

The Garage was opened on June 19, 1931. Cars were then becoming very evident on the Victoria scene. The Garage signaled another dominant aspect of the late 1920s and 1930s, that enthusiasm for flying which had been sparked by Col. Charles A. Lindbergh's solo flight from New York to Paris in 1927. Three years later, in Chicago, Elmer A. Sperry, the inventor of the Sperry Beacon, had dedicated to Lindbergh the 2,000,000,000 candlepower Lindbergh Beacon atop the Palmolive (now Playboy) Building. The beacon's original purpose had

been to guide aviators at night. On an obviously smaller scale, the Causeway Garage, with its 10,000,000 CANDLEPOWER SPERRY BEACON, COULD BE SEEN 60 miles away.

The original gas station featured California style pantiled roofs on the main building and the canopied pump islands, fitting Victoria's tourist image as a Palm Springs type "land-of-the-sun" resort (p. 16). The gas station was one of Victoria's first designated heritage buildings.

St. Louis College
1931
1002 Pandora Avenue

This three-storey poured concrete building provides an Art Deco interpretation of the Collegiate Gothic style. St. Louis himself guards the approach from his niche above the entrance. Banks of tall windows articulate the east and west façades, lending the building a sense of airy verticality.

Sand's Memorial Chapel
1932
1803 Quadra Street
Archt. C. Elwood Watkins

Another phase in Victoria's history is registered in the popularity of the California Mission style, revived here for a mortuary chapel. During the 1930s Victoria briefly saw itself as Hollywood north as it became the location for a series of British Empire "B rated" movie specials. A masterful composition in white stucco, battered walls and pantiled roofs, the original design was by T. Hooper's former

partner, C. E. Watkins, with sympathetic 1953 additions by D. C. Frame (a former partner of F. M. Rattenbury).

The Atlas Theatre
1936
836-838 Yates Street
Archt. Eric C. Clarkson
Addition: Vic Davies, 1994

A vaguely Mayan feeling is carried through the massing and Deco motifs of this very Moderne cast concrete façade. The central pillar once supported a monumental marquee sign in the figure of Atlas supporting the globe. The Atlas was the first airconditioned movie theatre in Victoria. Closed in 1987, its designated façade was used to generate the design of the new building, a Post-Modern interpretation of the popular 1930s style, inserted behind it in 1994.

Army and Navy Veterans Club
1936
1001 Wharf Street at Johnson
Archt. Eric C. Clarkson

An imposing façade on two frontages, this is a design that hovers between the streamlined Moderne and Art Deco styles. Windows are enlarged from the original at street level but the outline detailing of the buttress piers and cornice survives as a curious zig-zag Deco motif. The club function was retired in 1984 but the stylized logo over the entrance announces its former use.

National Trust Building
1938
1280 Douglas Street
Archt. Douglas L. Kertland, Toronto

Originally built as the Dominion Bank, the traditional Classical elements of the Temple bank have been suppressed or abstracted in favour of a late Art Deco, almost Moderne effect. The tone-panelled walls rest securely on a heavy black marble base, the requisite bankers' institutional image thus preserved. The engaged columns, however, carry the popular Deco Egyptian references with their papyrus-styled capitals. The original lavish silver and black Formica banking hall unfortunately disappeared in the renovations carried out for National Trust by Wade, Stockdill and Armour in 1964.

British Columbia Power Commission Building
1939-1940
780 Blanshard Street
Archt. H. Whittaker, Provincial Department of Public Works

A stridently modern building in its day, it was also sited to make a dramatic

statement on these steep slopes facing the harbour. The concrete construction has allowed for cast-in-place low relief Deco ornament. The interior is also remarkably intact, including a three-storey aluminum stairwell screen, a design feature of which are the initials BCP.

Bartlet Gibson Building
1941

960 Yates Street
Archts. Birley and Frame

The storefront is contained within a one-storey poured concrete building. The Moderne style is indicated by the flat roof, vitrolit tiling and horizontal band details. The building is remarkably intact, well illustrating this transitional period in the city's architectural history.

Rainbow Mansion Apartments
1947-1948

805, 11 Academy Close
Archt. W. J. Semeyn

The grey broken glass stucco façade is relieved by the horizontal metal banding; an octagon motif is repeated in a series of windows and balustrade ironwork. This is a transitional design from the Streamlined Moderne to the Abstract Expressionism of the early 1950s.

Imperial Bank of Commerce
1946

1301 Government Street at Yates
Archts. D. C. Frame and
Douglas James

As a match to the Federal Post Office across the street, Classical references have been suppressed, or abstracted, in favour of a more Moderne feel to the building. It is still, however, a temple bank, the fluted pilasters of the stone facing rising from the black marble base. To accommodate a more recent change to street retail use, the first floor window sills were dropped; however, these alterations have been executed with a sensitivity that does not compromise the original design.

Salvation Army Citadel
1946-1947

757 Pandora Avenue
Archts. Birley, Wade & Stockdill

International Style with a distinctive English flavour, the Salvation Army building is more reminiscent of the suburban London tube stations designed by Charles Holden in 1930s than ecclesiastical buildings of any period. Similar to Birley's other building for the Army in Nanaimo, these structures, progressive for Victoria at the time, nevertheless symbolized the Salvation Army's no-nonsense business/martial approach to Christianity where community service comes first. Even so, the Classical formula (or Venetian after the country villas of Andrea Palladio) a central main block flanked by pavilions betrays the Edwardian Neoclassical tradition of architectural training still evident at this point in the modern period. An earlier attempt at "nightscaping" incorporated into the original design is evident from the built-in flood lamps at the base of the brick piers—obviously intended to render them as dramatic shafts of light. At the time of publication, the future of the building is unsure.

Athlone Apartments
1947-1948

895 Academy Close
Archt. S. Patrick Birley

This is one of the most sophisticated pieces of Moderne design in Victoria. The two-and-one-half-storey stucco apartment block features a range of three stair towers establishing a powerful design rhythm for the entrance front, which is further reinforced by the repetition of the tall leaded glass stairwell windows. Each stair provides access to four suites. Those on the ground floor open out onto the park side of the building.

Odeon Theatre
1947-1948

780 Yates Street
Archt. H. H. Simmonds, Vancouver

The Vancouver-based Simmonds specialized in theatre and exhibition hall design for the Odeon Theatre chain in Victoria; he provided one of Victoria's best examples of the Moderne streamline style. The constricted Yates Street frontage is cleverly dramatized by an asymmetrical scooped false-front and projecting curved canopy—both transfixed by the vertical Odeon neon signpost which signals the foyer entrance. The curved and sweeping lines carry you through the entrance lobby into the foyer by means of a clever ceiling feature. On the Johnson Street front, the cast concrete is detailed with streamline motifs, the letters ODEON rising out of the central panel—a very filmic effect.

Memorial Arena
1948

1925 Blanshard Street
Archts. Hubert Savage, D. C. Frame, and Douglas James Associated Architects

Although first mooted in 1940, the Arena had to await the end of World War II when it was built as a memorial to those who gave their lives. The original 1940 proposal called for a large gable roof structure, more in the traditional of a military drill hall. As finally built in 1948, the form was dictated by a construction technology based on large-scale reinforced concrete structures pioneered in the European airship hangars of the 1930s, then perfected on wartime airfields and coastal defence installations. Even so, the construction was fraught with technical problems and cost overruns. The 76-foot-high concrete load-bearing arches were poured in place using travelling false-work supports. Exterior dimensions are 280 feet by 165 feet with a seating capacity of 7,200. One can discern brief low-relief decorative gestures, obviously built into the concrete form-work, vaguely Classical references to the then-retardetaire Art Deco style. At the time of publication, there are plans to replace the present structure.

Main Post Office and Federal Building
1948-52

1230 Government Street
Archts. James & James
Renovations: Irvin Kew, 1994

Brothers Percy and Douglas James worked together on this, Victoria's largest single piece of immediate post-war construction. Originally envisaged as a depression years make-work project in 1936, site preparation finally began in 1948. The minimalist Moderne effect dominates this monumental structure, given a symmetrical Classical treatment on the Government Street façade—the columns recognizable as such only to the most discerning eye. This was P. L. James' last major project and he claimed it as one of his best. Recent renovations by architect Irving Kew have replaced the postal station hall with a series of streetfront shops under a sidewalk canopy. This makes the original structure even more difficult to read, though perhaps more friendly at street level.

Bank of Toronto
1950

630 Yates Street
Archt. William Frederick K. Gardiner

This is Victoria's best example of a Moderne bank. The structure has been cleaned of all Classical references and although plain, the design remains solid and conservative—looking forward to the International style. Cast-stone panels face the building above its black marble base; the same

marble defines the two-storey inset window panels. The splayed corner entrance is a traditional Victoria banking-hall feature. Though the building is now put to other uses, the Toronto Bank's corporate crest is still proudly displayed above the door, a low relief sculpture with the incised motto "Industry, Intelligence and Integrity."

Canadian National Institute for the Blind Building
1951

1609 Blanshard Street
Archts. Nichols and Di Castri

One of the first Victoria commissions by Di Castri, the CNIB building demonstrates his interest in the modernism of Frank Lloyd Wright. The curvilinear forms united by the strong horizontality of the roof planes are intersected by window and brickwork courses. This commission introduced an architect to Victoria whose work remains distinctive for its West Coast expression: a rich mixture of materials and complex, eccentric forms.

Ballantyne's Florists
1954

900 Douglas Street
Archt. John Di Castri

Possibly now threatened by their comparatively low density, these shopfronts deserve preservation. The angular entrance bays and complex geometry of the constructivist canopies are illustrative of the sophisticated abstract designs with which Di Castri broke Victoria's tradition of Romantic Historicism.

British Columbia Electric Building
1954

1515 Blanshard Street at Pandora
Archt. original: Sharp Thompson Berwick and Pratt
Design archt. Ron Thom
Addition: Siddall, Dennis Warner Architects, 1974

B.C. Electric, shortly before public expropriation, was undergoing a massive expansion as part of the general post-war resource industries boom. The Victoria regional head

office was the first of two major building commissions awarded to STBP; the second was the Vancouver office tower on Burrard. Ron Thom devised the siting and design scheme. A sheer narrow building was located to save the mature Blanshard side trees providing a park-like entrance. The concrete structure supports a glass curtainwall. The cross motif in the roofline concrete frieze is a Deco style holdover, but strikingly innovative was the use of die-cast aluminum sun louvers, marking the curtainwalls with strong horizontal bands. Unfortunately the original colour scheme by B. C. Binning has not survived renovations by the British Columbia Building Corporation, part of which has been the 1974 Neo-Brutalist 200,000-square-foot addition (Richard Blanshard Building) by SDW architects, for the Ministry of Health. The lobby features various pieces from the Provincial Art Collection, including a large mobile, "Intersection," by Joseph Caveno and a mosaic wall mural by Margaret Peterson.

Toronto Dominion Bank Building
1963

1080 Douglas Street
Archt. Frank Musson with Dominion Construction

After the 1952 construction of Lever House in New York by Progressive architects Skidmore Owings and Merril, every city had to have a version of the this classic International style design which placed a soaring glass curtainwall tower over a horizontal podium. Victoria received its scaled-down version ten years later. The design is remarkably well-scaled for the town; the extruded aluminum and glass detailing well conveys the intended mass production/machine technology look.

Royal Trust Building
1963

1061 Fort Street
Archt. John Di Castri
Muralist: Andres Salgo

This was the only serious attempt to create an office block version of

Victoria's residential walk-up, a popular apartment and motel building form of the 1950s. On the east and west sides the offices open onto external balustraded galleries at each level. Also unusual, and the subject of some debate when built, were the north and south windowless slab walls. These were decorated with mosaic tile murals depicting the historic and modern industries of British Columbia, by Mexican artist Andres Salgo.

Centennial Square, 1963

Model for Bastion Square Revitalization, 1963.

The creation of the Centennial Square project marked the 100th birthday of Victoria. Rod Clack (city planner) worked with a group of architects including John Di Castri, Alan Hodgson, Bob Siddall, Clive Campbell, Don Wagg and John Wade under the leadership of mayor R. B. Wilson. It marked the beginning of a vast scheme to preserve, restore and revive downtown Victoria. Street realignments and the demolition of an old public market allowed for grouping the McPherson Playhouse (Hodgson), renovated police station (Wagg), parkade and specialty shops (Di Castri), Senior Citizens' Centre (Campbell) and sunken "Knot Garden" around a public space. The focal point is a fountain, its balustraded rim reminiscent of elements from Oscar Niemeyer's Government complex at Brazilia (1958), and the mosaic concrete totems by local artist J. C. S. Wilkinson. The fountain was a centennial gift to the city from neighbouring municipalities. The scheme successfully re-established City Hall as a downtown focal set piece, the square its major public recreational amenity. It was also the first part of the downtown revitalization program which called for a general paint-up modelled on the "Norwich Plan," and pedestrian malls linking City Hall to a redeveloped and restored Bastion Square.

Victoria City Hall
1878, 1881, 1891

1 Centennial Square
Archt. John Teague
Addition: Wade, Stockdill, Armour,
R. W. Siddall, R. Clack, 1963

Mayor Roderick Finlayson's first objective after his election to office in January of 1878 was to erect a city hall. Overriding the sentiments of the townsfolk who considered the whole idea an unnecessary extravagance, $10,000 were allocated and a competition announced for plans. The winner was John Teague. It was to contain a corn market, surveyors' quarters, apartments for the assessor, a jail, police court, council chamber, committee rooms, and a museum room. The final form was a rectangular block, now comprising the south wing of the present City Hall. A good example of the Second Empire style, it is built in red brick with a tin mansard roof.

The 1881 addition consisted of a small wing on the southwest corner for the Fire Department. In 1891 City Council approved a bylaw for the borrowing of $35,000 for the completion of the northeast addition. The new wing as added to the existing building constitutes the present City Hall, as it is seen today. At this time, the main entrance was moved to the base of the tower block at the centre of the Douglas elevation. The façade is divided into three bays, the projecting centre bay carrying the thrust of the brick and stone tower block, 140 feet in height. The entrance is further accented by a balustrade over the indented porch. On May 6, 1891, C. E. Redfern was awarded the contract for the installation of the clock which

Pantages Theatre (McPherson Theatre)
1914

3 Centennial Square
Archt. Jesse M. Warren
Renovation: A. Hodgson, 1963

Alexander Pantages, a West Coast theatrical promoter who operated a chain of playhouses, including ones at Seattle and Spokane, leased this theatre from Messrs. McPherson, Fuller, and Elliot. Structural materials are steel and concrete with a local red-brick facing. The exterior features a modest Renaissance Revival façade with five bays outlined in brick. The high point of what is now The McPherson is its Baroque Revival interior: marble half-columns dividing the foyer from the auditorium, balcony boxes grouped under wide segmental arches topped with full relief plaster cherubs. After a somewhat irregular career, it was willed by Thomas McPherson along with a substantial part of his estate to the city. In 1964-1965 the playhouse was restored and the Pandora addition constructed by local architect Alan Hodgson. A new wing is successfully related to the original structure through the sympathetic use of similar materials.

had been manufactured by Messrs. Gillet & Johnson of Croydon, Surrey, England. Four 500-pound dials each 7 feet 6 inches in diameter and the 2,170-pound bell had to be lifted into place. The clock requires winding once a week.

Since 1891 there have been no major alternations, except those connected with the Centennial Square project in 1963. At this time the interior was completely renovated and an International style addition was constructed at the west end. This was carried out by the architectural firms of Wade, Stockdill, Armour & Partners and R. W. Siddall & Associates, with Rod Clack, city architectural consultant and director of special planning projects.

Bastion Square, 1963

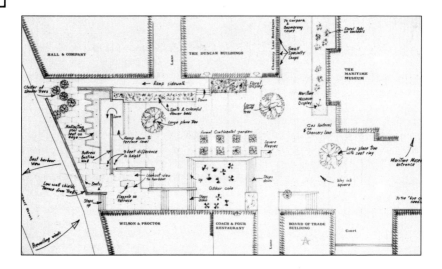

In 1963, under the direction of city planner Rod Clack, Bastion Square was developed as a heritage book-end to the modern scheme for Centennial Square. View Street was closed off and a pedestrian sanctuary was created, set off by restored historic buildings on three sides, a magnificent view across the harbour on the fourth. It was to feature a major public amenity, the old Provincial Supreme Court building recycled as the Maritime Museum of British Columbia. The museum has come and stayed, but over time the edge buildings cycled through various uses of restaurant, retail and office. Problems with design of the square itself compromised vigorous success as an attractive urban space until renovations (architect M. Lam, City of Victoria) in 1994 reworked the pedestrian amenities, particularly by establishing a "ceremonial" entry arch on View at Government Street, and a grand staircase linking the Square with Wharf Street. On the Wharf Street side at the foot of the steps is a floorscape mosaic, Compass Rose, by local artist J. C. Scott.

MacDonald Block
1863

1205-1213 Wharf Street
Archt. John Wright?
Renovation: Bawlf & Cooper
Associates, 1979

Framing the northwest edge of Bastion Square, the building was built by Captain James Murray Reid and was subsequently owned by his son-in-law W. J. MacDonald, twice mayor of Victoria, provincial MLA and pioneer British Columbia senator. The arched second-storey windows and restrained ornaments, still discernible under the modern stucco, are hallmarks of the Italianate style introduced to Victoria by pioneer architect John Wright. Walk-in commercial spaces were occupied by smithies, dry-goods merchants and wheelwrights when this was the original commercial core of this growing colonial city.

In 1979 the block was renovated under the direction of Architects Bawlf & Cooper—the final effect sympathetic to but not a restoration of the original structure.

Rithet Building
1861, 1865, 1885, 1889

1117-1125 Wharf Street
Archts. Restoration: B.C. Public Works

The south flank of the Bastion Square Wharf Street entrance is marked by the Rithet Building, Victoria's finest example of West Coast iron fronts. An early k.d. construction technology, the marks on the base of the cast iron columns tell the story of the structure. The two northern bays are dated 1861 (nine columns) and indicate they were made at the San Francisco Foundry of Peter Donahue's Union Iron Works. The southern bays were cast later in 1888 by Victoria's own Albion Iron Works (in which Robert Patterson Rithet had an interest)—obviously using the earlier one as a mould pattern. Upper storeys in the Italianate style introduced by the iron fronts were added over the years, the most northerly in 1865. In 1978 the Province of British Columbia bought and restored the buildings for office use (architect Mark Bautenheimer) and in the process uncovered the original Fort water well, complete with mechanical pump. This has been made into a lobby fountain feature.

Two adjacent early structures now form part of this restored complex. At 1109 is the 1861 brick warehouse built for Philip M. Bachus, auctioneer, the second floor added in 1873 but has lost its bold Italianate cornice. Further south, at 1107, is the 1862 single-storey showroom of wholesaler and commission agent Richard Carr, father of the famed West Coast artist Emily Carr.

Burnes House
1886
Beaver Building
1882

516 Bastion Square
Archt. John Teague
Restoration: Peterson & Lester

This handsome three-storey brick building and the adjoining old Beaver Building, built earlier in 1882, were both the property of hotelier Thomas J. Burnes. Burnes erected one of Victoria's earliest luxury hotels to serve successful gold miners and English remittance men.

A very typical High Victorian building with its strong verticality emphasized by the paired narrow ground floor windows and the second- and third-storey oriels overlooking the square—it stands rather uncomfortably beneath a bold bracketted Italianate cornice. The building cost Burnes $20,000 and served as a fashionable hotel close to such public amenities as the Court House, Customs House, HBC warehouses, and waterfront. In 1967 under the direction of architects Peterson and Lester, the exterior of Burnes House was restored and the interior was redeveloped into the rather charming series of multi-level specialty shops, now offices.

Supreme Court Building
(Now Maritime Museum of British Columbia)
1889, 1901

28 Bastion Square
Archts. H. O. Tiedemann,
F. M. Rattenbury

In 1887 the Chief Commissioner of Lands and Works authorized the erection of a new Court House, a brick building on a stone foundation on the site of the old police barracks and jail. Tiedemann's design was supposedly based on a court building in the architect's native Munich. Local tradition has it that this was the first building in the city to make extensive use of reinforced concrete. The brick facing was stuccoed and rendered to resemble the grouting of huge granite blocks. S. G. Burris was architect-in-charge. The building was completed in 1889 at a total cost of $35,075.

In its day, the Court House presented an impressive spectacle towering over other buildings in the immediate area. It is an eclectic assemblage of motifs, Richardsonian-Romanesque in the massing, arch-and-window grouping, and turreted roofline.

In 1900-1901 architect F. M. Rattenbury carried out alterations. Steel beams from the Carnegie Foundry were installed to accommodate an ornate open-cage elevator for the convenience of The Honourable Theodore Davie, Chief Justice, who was advised by his doctor not to climb stairs. The elevator remains a high point of the interior and is the oldest operational lift in BC. Also during the 1900-1901 remodelling, many of the windows were filled in, the main arches in the east portico were converted into windows and the interior space utilized as an office. The last hearing was held in February 1962, just before the courts moved to the new buildings on Courtenay Street. During 1963-1964 the old Court House served as a temporary City Hall and in 1965 the Maritime Museum was relocated there.

Board of Trade occupied its new premises. The façade's decorative elements illustrate architect A. M. Muir's familiarity with both the High Victorian eclectic style and Richardsonian Romanesque. It is divided symmetrically into two tighter bays flanking a broad central bay. The bays are defined by four composite pilasters. The window treatment, with diaper work transoms, differs at each level. Within the rusticated Saturna granite base is housed the basement and first floor. The entrance, let into the left bay by means of a superb Richardsonian archway, is flanked by two squat Doric columns and a band of organic ornament. Another horizontal band of granite floral ornament runs midway across the façade elevation at the third floor. The cornice, a heavier and more elaborate repetition of fourth floor string course, is executed in brick and galvanized iron.

In 1971 architects Peterson and Lester renovated the building and modernized the interior for reoccupation by commercial businesses.

Board of Trade Building
1892

31 Bastion Square
Archt. A. Maxwell Muir
Restoration: Peterson & Lester, 1971

The Victoria Chamber of Commerce was founded February 9, 1863, its first duty being to organize an armed escort to accompany gold shipments from the Cariboo. In 1878 the name was changed to the British Columbia Board of Trade. In February of 1893 the

Law Chambers
1899

45 Bastion Square
Archt. F. M. Rattenbury
Restoration: Peter Cotton, 1970

Rattenbury not only carried out extensive renovations to the Supreme Court building itself (creating a new Langley Street entrance) but also bracketted the Courts with two of his own designs. The overall scheme is a restrained version of Italianate featuring very fine brick detailing and the form is conceived as a renaissance palazzo facing the square. This was one of the first restorations as part of the Bastion Square revitalization scheme.

Chancery Chambers
1905

1218 Langley Street
Archt. F. M. Rattenbury

Unfortunately window renovations mar this otherwise well proportioned Edwardian Classical structure. It was developed by J. H. McGregor and its proximity to the Courts adjacent provided good marketable office space for the legal fraternity. Now it anchors the northeast approach into Bastion Square.

Market Square, 1975

Fort Victoria Properties under the direction of local businessman Sam Bawlf has been a major player in the restoration of major private sector landmarks of Old Town. Rattenbury's Law Chambers in Bastion Square and the Belmont Building were earlier projects, also redeveloped in association with Sam's brother, restoration architect Nicholas Bawlf. Market Square consists of eight heritage buildings facing three streets and the development focussed on a two-level galleried interior courtyard to create Victoria's first open air urban retail mall. Partial covering of the east end of the mall was accomplished by re-utilizing salvaged heavy timber trusses from the Victoria Machinery Depot's Ogden Point shipyard. The streetfront façades were restored and the Johnson Street main entrance features an old city horse and dog watering trough recycled as a fountain. A focal point of the interior courtyard is a contemporary 18-foot colourful steel sculpture by Victoria artist Luis Merino. In 1976, the scheme earned a regional award of honour from the Heritage Canada Foundation.

Market Square, Store Street view.

Grand Pacific Hotel
1879, 1883, 1887

530-540 Johnson at Wharf Street

In the 1870s harbour proximity prompted this area to become Victoria's hotel district; one block over on Yates, warehouses dominated the street frontages. The Bossi family, brothers Giacomo and Carlo, were major players in this early boom. The Grand Pacific had pretentions in name but was a frugal no-nonsense Italianate block which developed with the business through a series of in-style additions.

Tye Chong Building
1884

529 Pandora Avenue

Built on a lot leased from Carlo Bossi, this was for many years a Chinese wholesale grocery outlet. The bold bracketted cornice and round arched ground floor windows distinguish this building on the block. The second-floor central doorway provides evidence for the original verandah frontage.

Bossi Building
1884

505-511 Pandora Avenue

A spec development by Carlo Bossi in the same spare Italianate style as the Grand Pacific Hotel, these retail shopfronts were once sheltered by a continuous streetfront verandah and boardwalk. Utilitarian in nature, such structures provide the backdrop to the Victorian flavour of Old Town Victoria.

Carey Building
1888

515-527 Pandora Avenue
Archt. John Teague

Joseph Westrope Carey, 1858 gold seeker, businessman and sometime mayor of Victoria, developed this handsome Victorian block, a retail and tenement mix. The second-storey doors which opened out onto the

balustraded balconies of the original streetfront verandah are still evident, a reference to the now-lost western boom-town look of early Victoria. The minimal iron balconies are a later substitution, reflecting concern for the rapid spread of fires which plagued Victoria during the 1880s and 1890s.

Milne Building
1891

546-548 Johnson Street
Archt. Thomas Hooper

Gold miner, customs agent, freemason and Knight Templar Alexander Roland Milne built this as the Empire Hotel and Restaurant. Victorian, but American in feeling, the heavy diapered brickwork and arched features are the signatures of Richardsonian Romanesque style. Street level features a very fine cast iron front.

Scott & Peden Building
ca. 1896

1415-1425 Store Street

The painted sign of these early occupants has been conserved in the Market Square restoration project. The simple Italianate scheme which maximizes the window area for street retail is typical of Victoria commercial building at this time and works well today.

Station Hotel
1913

501 Pandora, 1441 Store Street
Archt. Jesse M. Warren

95

Feature D

The prominent location, facing the Esquimalt and Nanaimo Railway terminus, gave the building both its function and name. The Victoria Phoenix Brewing Company developed the hotel on the site of the old Light House Saloon. The 30 rooms were housed within a spare brick building, almost Moderne in feeling.

Strand Hotel
1892
550-554 Johnson Street

An early speculative venture of the B.C. Land & Investment Company, the Strand now constitutes an anchor building for the Market Square complex. Open cast iron shopfronts support this Italianate façade dominated by the two-storey central bay window. Such bays or street verandahs were an essential element for early urban hotels as they provided an opportunity for guests to relax and watch the street life.

Bank of Commerce Building
1967-1968

1175 Douglas at View Street
Archts. McCarter Nairne Architects

This massively scaled concrete tower, perhaps designed for a corporate presence on Douglas Street (then planned for urban freeway status), nevertheless suffocates View Street and masks out from numerous directions one of Victoria's major skyline features, the diaphanous polychrome spire of St. Andrew's Cathedral.

Maynard Court
1967

731-733 Johnson Street
Archt. Peter Cotton

The building was originally known as Grimm's Carriage Factory. It was built in 1889. At a construction cost of $16,000 William Grimm got a substantial building well-suited to the nature of his business. Flanking a carriage entrance at street level were offices and production shops. The second floor was given over to a large showroom, and above that an extensive storage area.

One of Cotton's first commercial restoration projects, the final scheme required total rebuilding of the façades and the insertion of new structures adjacent to the mid-block walkway. Cotton's treatment is whimsical, drawing on the traditional forms of boom-town false fronts with their wooden galleries, and a Johnson Street frontage inspired by the previous Italianate commercial character Grimm's orginal block.

North Park Manor
1975

875 North Park Street
Archts. Wade Stockill Armour & Blewett

The unusual angled siting, rarely economical for land use, was chosen here to protect an old arboretum, an amenity useful to this senior citizens' housing society. The formal solution for the tower, class curtainwall contained between soaring concrete end walls recalls Geo Ponti's well-published 1956-1960 Pirelli Building, Milan.

First Baptist Church
1976

877 North Park Street
Archts. Wade Stockdill Armour & Blewett

The original pipe organ from the old Quadra Street church was incorporated into the fabric. Otherwise, the interior is pure modern Expressionism. The natural surface finishes of brick and wood provide for the simplicity of the sanctuary space to be defined by powerful timber trusses.

Nootka Court
1976

634-688 Humboldt at Douglas Street
Archt. Wayne Wenstob

This half-block of turn-of-the-century structures fronting on three streets represents the early adaptive use approach to urban conservation in Victoria. Skillfully inserted into the old fabric are new buildings and elements; the exterior is finished in brick with historicist detailing. Accessed via three retail galleries, the open interior courtyard focusses on aboriginal totem carvings in a West Coast Contemporary style building and native landscape setting. Numerous alterations have taken place since its construction but the original innovative scheme is still discernible. On completion Nootka Court was awarded the prestigious Park and Tilford Award for innovative architectural design.

Rohani Building
1977

747 Fort Street
Archts. Siddall, Dennis Warner Architects

One of the more elegant of Victoria's early skyscrapers, the ten-floor textured concreted and glass curtainwall tower is cleverly set back so as not to crowd the streetscape. The developers provided a through-block retail walkway at street level. The two-storey banking hall respects the scale of the extant Fort Street frontages.

Greater Victoria Public Library Waddington Building
1979

735 Broughton Street
Archts. Hawthorn, Mansfield Towers
Fit-out Wade Williams
Renovations: Wagg & Hambleton 1991

The building encompasses the better part of a city block, incorporating two previous structures; one of them on Courtney, D. C. Frame's Alexandria Club, can still be discerned. Three levels of parking are provided for the Victoria Public Library Main Branch and government offices contained in four storeys above. Entrances from the Blanshard Street plaza or a portal from Broughton lead into a skylit atrium featuring the "Dynamic Mobile Steel Sculpture" by artist George Norris. The brick façades cant back from the second storey on the street frontages in an attempt to better fit the massive scale to Old Town frontage heights.

Salvation Army Building
1980

521 Johnson at Wharf Street
Archts. Wagg & Hambleton

The building anchors a key corner and a major gateway to Old Town. The set-back form, brick finish, and arched elements, particularly the streetfront gallery, reference the Richardsonian Romanesque character of the old warehouse district.

Hongkong Bank of Canada
1985

752 Fort Street
Archt. Wade Williams Corp.

The design legacy of modern British architect James Stirling must infuse this facetted-mirror jewel of a building, whose geometry reflects the Beaux Arts Classicism of the adjacent Edwardian Temple style bank (Yorkshire Trust Building, 1912, by A. A. Cox).

Victoria VIA Rail Station
1985

Johnson and Store Streets
Archt. Irvin Kew Architecture Inc.

The steep-pitched roof and symmetrical plan of this station pavilion intentionally recalls the turn-of-the-century Rocky Mountain CPR stations of F. M. Rattenbury, elements of which he was to insert into the institutional and domestic commissions in his hometown.

Ministry of Forests Building
1987

595 Pandora Avenue
Archt. John Neilson Associates

One of Victoria's most sophisticated pieces of architectural contextualism, the form, detailing and brick treatment is generated by the adjacent architectural vocabulary of Chinatown. And the structure is three-dimensional, viewable from the street and via the mid-block access to Market Square.

Victoria Conference Centre
1988

720 Douglas Street
Archts. Bawlf Cooper Associates with Marshall Goldsworthy & Associates

The City of Victoria undertook the construction of the Victoria Conference Centre in conjunction with the CPR's complete renovation of the Empress Hotel. The new building, two storeys of conference meeting spaces above a parkade, is an inspired piece of urbanism. At a cost of $17 million, the building program features a 1,500-capacity assembly hall, a 400-seat theatre, 300 stalls of underground parking, a galleria of street retail on Douglas Street, and a four-storey interior water feature on the main

concourse, of which the central axial focus is a powerful Kwagiulth totem pole by Tony Hunt. The glazed foyer pavilion functionally links the new building to the Hotel through the old Empress conservatory, but also responds to the Crystal Gardens which it faces across Douglas Street. The Classical vocabulary of the Crystal is reiterated in the arcaded shop fronts at street level. However, the south-facing forecourt, with its fountain, processional stairway, flanking chitras and wisteria-covered colonnaded pergolas is a masterpiece of architectural metaphor—with its obvious references to Edwin Lutyen's Viceroy's House at Delhi and the intimations of the British Raj, and thus Queen Victoria, Empress of India.

Eaton's Centre, 1990

Douglas, Fort, Government and View Streets. Archts: IBI Group

The Driard Hotel, 1892

The Driard Hotel Façade,
Eaton's Centre, 1996

One of Victoria's most controversial heritage "appropriation" projects, Cadillac-Fairview's proposal to raze these two city blocks of historic buildings for an enclosed mall prompted the largest public outcry in recent history. The final scheme worked through a series of compromises. A four-storey atrium mall, redolent with Neo-Edwardian trappings, but probably more directly influenced by architect Maurice Sunderland's highly successful West Edmonton Mall (1981-1986), is wrapped with reconstructed (or fancifully "in the spirit of") heritage façades. These are scant memories of a former era.

The View Street part of the façade of the Driard Hotel has been reconstructed utilizing elements from the original 1892 historic fabric. The Driard was a Victoria institution. It began existence as a Mansarded four-storey brick building, the St. George's Hotel, designed by John Wright in

1862. In 1871, after it had passed through the hands of a number of unsuccessful owners, the hotel was brought by a "genial Frenchman" from Lachapelle by way of San Francisco, Sosthenes Driard. In 1872, after extensive renovation which increased the hotel's capacity to 100 rooms, Driard re-opened the hotel under his own name. In 1886, the hotel was renovated and extended over the Victoria Theatre, which had been constructed in 1883. The Douglas Street façade of Eaton's Centre may be said to recall the severe classicism of the earlier Theatre building, identifiable by its dentillated string courses and Greek pediments. A similar treatment is afforded the block facing Government Street.

The primitive brick Chateau style block now facing Broad at View is a shell reconstruction based on the original Driard design by John Teague completed for the grand opening on November 1, 1892, at a cost of $275,000. Teague's design was perhaps not wholly original, as the structure bore a striking resemblance to Portland's then-new Opera House and office complex, "The Marquam," completed in 1889. Teague's block added another 225 guest rooms. An early description paints the following picture:

> A giant banana tree rears its huge leaves proudly over the surrounding palms which gives them an air of insignificance. The drawing room artistically frescoed and beautifully draped was furnished by Weiler Bros. Winding his way up the spacious stairway carpeted in rich velvet pile the visitor was instinctively prompted to look over the banisters of polished hardwood and take in the view below.

Times Building Façade, Eaton's Centre, 1996

On the Fort Street side of Eaton's Centre are reconstructed façades of the Times Building, the Winch Building and the Lettice and Sears Building. The Times Building (architect A. Maxwell Muir) was originally built in 1910 for the *Times* newspaper. It demonstrated early use of reinforced concrete, a fact expressed in the generous opening up of the façade in contrast to the traditional treatment of the roofline with a Classical attic and entablature. The Winch Building (Thomas Hooper, 1912) was built for businessman R. V. Winch. The cut and moulded stone façade composes a richly detailed Classical Temple form, an artistic setpiece which holds its own on the street. The Lettice and Sears Building façade reconstruction, although less accurate than the others, memorializes a fine piece of late Victorian brickwork, particularly evident in the corbelled cornice. Robert Sears and John Lettice, painters and decorators, provided many of the fine interiors for Victoria banks and hotels.

Macdonald's Building, Douglas and View. The Post-Modern scheme reutilized handsome Deco mosaic panels salvaged from Kresge Department Store (architect G. A. McElroy, Windsor, 1930) which previously stood on this site. The 1991 redevelopment was part of the Eaton's Centre package.

Broad Street Square
1988

1290 Broad at Yates Street
Archt. Eric Barker Architects

Broad Street, a major pedestrian heritage spine of Old Town, required a building which at once complemented the masonry Italianate retail character but also revealed its contemporary age. The Post-Modern treatment of a Jazz Deco theme, in brick with glazed reveals, does this with sensitivity for the street.

Municipal Affairs Building
1989

800 Johnson at Blanshard Street
Archts. IBI Group
Design: David Thom

As a six-storey building located on the edge of Old Town, the design had to be particularly sensitive to the adjoining national and provincial historic site, the small Romanesque Revival 1863 Temple Emanuel. Its quiet architectural expression, in colour, facetted detailing, and traditional treatment of the structural envelope, make this a model for emulation elsewhere.

Hotel Grand Pacific
1989

450 Quebec Street
Archts. Campbell Moore Group Architects

Victoria's Inner Harbour is an institutional stage set. As an architectonic symbol, and major presence in the viewscape, the choice of a Post-Modern treatment of Second Empire complements the Romanesque domes, Chateauesque roofs, and Edwardian Classical cornices that constitute this skyline, and perhaps provides a gestural bow to the Mansardic 1876 old Customs House on Wharf Street.

Regents Park
1991

1010-20 View Street
Archts. Neale Staniszkis Doll

A height transfer variance allowed these two towers a more Picturesque profile on the skyline and the massed densities have given back to the public a richly landscaped urban park. One of the more elegant of the City's recent condominium developments, the star shaped floor plans allow for four identical fronts, articulated by the inset balconies and strips of corner curtain wall.

First Island Financial Building
1992

727 Fisgard at Douglas Street
Archt. Jones Design Corp.

Jack Davis Building for the Ministry of Mines
1992

1810 Blanshard Street
Archts. Chandler Kaston Kennedy

A gateway building to Victoria, and visual riposte to the Moderne Memorial Arena opposite, the High-Tech design treatment was nevertheless intended to express the interests of its client ministry in the environmental techno-fix. State-of-the-art passive heating, all ener-save computerized lighting, air-conditioning controls and floor-plate-use efficiency techniques were utilized. The vertical bay extruded from the south-face streamlined curtainwall (treated as if unwrapping from the ends) and the playful aluminum sculpture (artist: Eric Ranft) engaging the cut-away corner entrance enliven this otherwise serious essay in structural rationalism.

Polished granite faced shear-walls seem to only just contain the soaring greenhouse structure behind. The strident Beaux Arts terracotta classicism of the Hudson's Bay Store and aggressive Post-Modernism of Centra Gas, its immediate neighbours, make this background tower block a well-mannered foil to adjacent, more robust urbanism.

CRD Housing Corporation Building
1906, 1992

616 Yates Street
Archt. Renovation: Bas Smith

After a disastrous fire which gutted the building, a new façade decorative treatment was applied. Smith uses the Eclectic Victorian vocabulary as a source for his Post-Modern scheme, playfully re-arranging and adjusting comparative scales to achieve a whimsical, ostentatiously clever effect.

Centra Gas Building
1992

1675 Douglas at Fisgard Street
Archts. Musson Catell Mackay

Corporate head offices require a flagship urban presence, and this was obtained in spite of resorting to Post-Modern contexturalism which popular sensitivities to Victoria architectural tradition require. The surface treatments step back from Douglas Street, each generated out of the adjacent buildings, brick Edwardian commercial to the south, the terracotta classicism of the Horwood & White's HBC to the north, the gardens of Centennial Square to the west, and a glazed modern core culminating in a cornice-sheltered attic storey. When built, Centra Gas provided a new benchmark for design and material quality in the downtown area.

Vefra Building
1993

908 Pandora Avenue
Archt. Alan Lowe

For this four-storey concrete and steel office building, a site sensitive approach was required as the location was in Victoria's Quadra Street "church row." So borrowing forms (a copper-clad tower element) and materials (brick, split-faced concrete block, and large glazed panels set back from columns) from its immediate surroundings, the building fits well at the gateway to Harris Green.

McDonald's Restaurant
1995

980 Pandora Avenue at Vancouver
Archt. G. D. Willie

The golden arches are suppressed in this third-generation design, indicating this ubiquitous multinational has now settled down to a comfortable urban presence in the service of the auto generation. A quiet Post-Modernism belies a highly efficient service production package including parking, short-term seating, and drive-in pick-up.

The Metropolitan
1995

835 View Street
Archt. Eric Barker Architects

Intended to address an emerging market for small condominium suites, the Metropolitan also attempted to soften its scale by referencing the Classical vocabulary and masonry materials of the Edwardian downtown fringe.

Sussex Building
1938, 1995

1001 Douglas Street
Archt. S. Patrick Birley, 1938
Revitalization: Paul Merrick Associates, 1995

Built as the Sussex Apartment Hotel, this was one of the early downtown hotels designed to cater to the automobile traveller and "seasonal visitor." Its compact apartment units featured kitchenettes, dining nooks, and bed-sitting rooms with fold-out Murphy beds. Birley was one of Victoria's architects most comfortable with the Art Deco style, here utilizing ceramic tiles and vertical brick piers to accent the abstract formalism of the Deco feel. This façade, along with features of ornate corner lobby, has been preserved in the Post-Modern tower block project of Princeton Developments. The envelope of the old hotel now forms a courtyard entrance to the office tower where architect Paul Merrick has provided a building of landmark status, combining almost playfully many elements of the Sussex with the American skyscraper 1920s' idiom in which Art Deco found its supreme expression.

NOTE

Ref. Cotton, Peter. "The Stately Capitol," *Royal Architectural Institute Journal.* 35 (April 1958). Edwards, Gregory. "Hidden Cities: Art & Design in Architectural Details of Vancouver & Victoria." 1991. Foundation Group Designs. "City of Victoria Downtown Heritage Inventory." 1990. Insight, Consultants. "Heritage Inventory of Industrial Buildings Victoria." Victoria, B.C. 1982. Segger, Martin & Douglas Franklin. "Victoria A Primer for Regional History in Architecture 1843-1929." 1974. "This Old Town: City of Victoria Central Area Heritage Conservation Report." 1983.

Chinatown Victoria

Chinese Arch on Store Street erected for the visit of the Governor General of Canada, the Marquis of Lorne and Princess Louise in 1882. BCARS 15351

The migration of Chinese to Canada began in 1858 with the goldrush to British Columbia's lower Fraser River. The Chinese living in California arrived first, followed by others coming directly from Hong Kong. Here they obtained licences and equipped themselves with supplies setting out for the gold fields. Chinese merchants and labour contractors from San Francisco set out acquiring and building shacks to provide accommodation for their workers. Cormorant Street between Store and Douglas Streets soon became the embryo of Victoria's Chinatown — the first Chinatown in Canada.

At the time of Victoria's incorporation in 1862, the Chinese population numbered about 300, or 6% of the city's population. By 1881, Victoria's Chinese population had risen to 690. Then between 1881 and 1884 nearly 16,000 Chinese entered Victoria on their way to the mainland to help build the Canadian Pacific Railway. Victoria was the gateway to Canada from China and Chinatown prospered. By 1900 it covered about six city blocks, housing most of the city's 3,000 Chinese. All of the Chinese clan, county and other associations headquartered in Chinatown, as did most of the Chinese import and export companies, retail stores and other business concerns. During these years Chinatown boasted two theatres, three Chinese schools, two churches, a hospital, several temples and shrines, many opium dens and more than ten opium factories, gambling dens, brothels and other amenities. An entire city block encompassed the "Forbidden City" of Chinatown. Here were to be found a large theatre, a temple, opium and gambling dens, restaurants, and numerous closely packed tenement buildings and shacks. Fan Tan Alley and Theatre Alley crossing between Pandora Avenue and Fisgard Street provided access to the core which was closed to the outside world by heavy wooden doors or gates. Fan Tan Alley was at one time a busy, boisterous street with numerous gambling dens on both sides, and the main entry to the labyrinth of the "Forbidden City." Geographer David Lai has noted that Chinatown functioned as the training base for numerous first generations of mainly bachelor Chinese immigrants. Here they were first exposed to Western culture, learned English, and often acquired a trade before moving on. When unemployed or ill, they returned to Chinatown for help.

After the turn of the century, Vancouver gradually replaced Victoria as the major seaport on the Pacific coast, and its Chinatown outstripped Victoria's in population and importance. Today, Chinatown covers less than three city blocks; many properties and business concerns are no longer owned by Canadians of Chinese descent. Still a great variety of retailers which include art galleries, antiques, souvenir shops, Chinese grocery stores, a barbecue shop and restaurants serving genuine Chinese food support its historic character, and many buildings remain. The intricate networks of picturesque arcades, narrow alleys and enclosed courtyards are still found behind the commercial façades of the old buildings. They are characterized by their Oriental features such as recessed balconies, upturned eaves and roof corners, baroque parapets, extended eaves covering the balconies, and tiled roofs. These are typical architectural features of Chinatown buildings. Imperial gold, mandarin red, emerald green, golden yellow and other brilliant colours are used to highlight the decorative details. In July 1979, the City Council embarked on the restoration and rehabilitation program of Chinatown, which included the painting or cleaning of old buildings, installation of Oriental-styled lamp posts and bilingual street signs, sidewalk improvements, ornamental planting, and the construction of a decorative arch called the "Gate of Harmonious Interest." It symbolizes the joint efforts of both the Chinese and non-Chinese communities to preserve the oldest Chinatown in Canada.

NOTE

Ref. "A Plan for the Rehabilitation of Chinatown." City of Victoria. Victoria, B.C. August 1979. "Chinatown Victoria," Heritage Conservation Branch, 1977. Kerr, Alastair W., "The Architecture of Victoria's Chinatown." *Datum*, Vol. 4, Summer, 1979. Lai, Chuen-yan David. "Socioeconomic Structures and Viability of Chinatown," in C. N. Forward, ed., *Residential and Neighbourhood Studies in Victoria*, Western Geographic Series, Vol, 5, 1973. Lai, Chuen-yan David. "The Future of Victoria's Chinatown: A Survey of Views and Opinions," City of Victoria, 1979. Lai, Chuen-yan David. *The Forbidden City within Victoria*, 1991. Lai, Chuen-yan David. *Arches in British Columbia*, 1982.

Finlayson Building
1882

528-532 Pandora Avenue

This type of building, once very common to Old Town Victoria, well represents the look of Chinatown from this period. The detailing is typical of the work of architect John Teague at this time. Along the west side is Theatre Alley which originally connected to the Chinese Theatre in the centre of the block, at a meeting point of the network of alleys which honeycombed this part of town.

On Hing and Brothers Store
1882, 1914

546-552 Fisgard Street

Tong Ork On Hing & Brothers had been merchants in Victoria since 1867 when they constructed the eastern three bays of what was then a very utilitarian brick three-storey structure with a street level verandah. In 1914 the western half was added and a Classical style cornice was added to unify the entire frontage.

Loo Chew Fan Building
1884

536-544 Pandora Avenue

The building, built *ca.* 1884, was purchased by Loo Chew Fan who was the owner of Kwong Lee & Co., the largest Chinese import and export company in Canada during the Gold Rush. In 1904 it became the Ning Young Yee Hing Tong, renamed Hoy Sun Ning Young Benevolent Association in 1914. The Association was formed by the Chinese people who

Lum Look and Lew Chew Fan Buildings.

had emigrated from Hoy Sun County in South China. A residential tenement house, the Fan Tan Alley ground floor was occupied by gambling clubs.

The building's wooden balcony was removed during the renovation in the 1950s. Major entrances and windows were also altered. However the original decorative brickwork at the cornice and the Italianate heads of the windows on the top storey can still be identified.

Lum Look Building
1884

534 Pandora Avenue

Two businessmen, Lum Sam and Look Dom, leased the lot from Roderick Finlayson to develop the handsome retail structure. The corbelled arcade at the cornice level draws attention to the very fine brickwork and the second-storey door denotes the one-time existence of a streetfront verandah.

Hart Building Livery Stables
1890

529-539 Herald Street

The building has two prominent carriage entrances because it was originally used as a carriage repair shop and livery stables. During the early twentieth century, the second floor contained a well-known brothel. Although believed to have been constructed as a unit, the building is curiously asymmetrical. The two carriage bays and a central doorway mark have their symmetry upset by the addition of an extra doorway to the left. Furthermore, there is no apparent logic to the placement of the second floor windows. By 1910 ownership was in hands of two Chinese businessmen and it is probably from this date that a common internal passageway connects through a series of tenement structures in the rear to Fisgard Street.

Chinese Benevolent Association Building
1885

554-562 Fisgard Street
Archt. John Teague

The Chinese Consolidated Benevolent Association has long been an umbrella organization governing all the Chinese societies and associations in Victoria. The Association engaged John Teague to design this three-storey building. During the nineteenth century the ground floor was rented to stores, the second floor housed the Association's office, and the third floor was occupied by Lok Kwun Free School and All Saints' Temple. Originally the present simple iron balconies were elaborate wood balconies masking the entire façade. Nevertheless, still retained are

Italianate cornices, original windows, hood mouldings and other details. Behind the building is the Chinese hospital which has been rebuilt as a modern care facility.

Lim Dat/Wong Soon Lim Building
1898

505 Fisgard Street
Archt. Thomas Hooper

The corner portion of the building, to the arched bay entrance, was built in 1898 for Lim Dat and Wong Soon Lim; the southern bay was added later in the same style. The ground floor was used for stores and the upper floor as tenements. In December 1909, the building was sold to architect F. M. Rattenbury. The building originally had a wooden balcony which was removed in the 1930s. The Romanesque style recalls the popular "Chicago School" mode of the period. Its sophisticated façade design, a studiously applied series of wide arched bays interspersed with banks of rectangular windows, makes this one of the most handsome versions of this style which was being introduced to Victoria at this time by architects Samuel Maclure and Thomas Hooper.

Loo Tai Cho Building
1893

549-555 Fisgard Street
Archt. W. R. Wilson

Built as a series of small shops with living accommodation above, this building is typical of Chinatown development during the nineteenth century. Early in the building's life, street level arched openings were squared to allow for the insertion of a mezzanine or "cheater storey," so-called because it was not assessable for taxes. The Yue Shan Society, owner since 1941, is another county association which was formed by those who had emigrated from Pan-you County in South China.

The building is an Edwardian Italianate structure forming part of the entrance to Fan Tan Alley. An interesting feature is a bay window built out from the corner of the building over an arched entrance.

Tip, Low and Lee Building
1888, 1901

539-545 Fisgard Street

This Italianate building was built in two sections, the eastern two bays first in 1888 for two business partners, then the two western bays for Lee Mong Kaw in 1901. The lower floor is occupied by retail stores and the second floor is tenements. During the nineteenth century, the rear section of the building

was used as an opium factory. Arched windows on the second floor are open to a wrought iron balcony which formerly extended the length of the building.

Lee Cheong and Lee Weong Building
1901

533-537 Pandora Avenue

The two Chinese developers sold the building to the city in 1933 for tax in arrears but in 1954 it passed back into the hands of ethnic Chinese. Situated here is the Chinese Canadian Friendship Association, which is a community organization. It is the first Chinese association in Victoria which recognized the People's Republic as the government of China. The original second-storey tenement balcony for which the elaborate arched doorway was constructed has been replaced by these iron cantilevered grates; the corbelled brickwork of the window heads and cornice is very fine.

Gee Tuck Tong Benevolent Association
1903

622-626 Fisgard Street

Two buildings here share a common façade. The western two bays originally belonged to the Gee Tuck Tong and the eastern bay became the Yee Fung Toy Tong. Curiously the entrance door to the second floor is sandwiched between two pilasters marking the division between the blocks. At the upper level are recessed balconies, with a tripartite arcade, and a bracketted Italianate cornice capped by a semi-circular pediment plaque. Behind this structure is a sensitively scaled tenement complex built in 1913 to designs by architects Fox & Berrill.

to a clan association for peoples named Low, Kwan, Cheung and Chiu.

On Hing Company Store
ca. 1905

1710-1714 Government Street
Archt. Thomas Hooper

Built for the Chan Tong Ork of On Hing Company, this two-storey structure also contains a "cheater storey" which is another common feature of Chinatown buildings. A "cheater floor" is an extra floor created within a floor and may be regarded as a mezzanine. It is called a "cheater floor" because it avoided higher building assessment rates. This cheater floor is lit by a glazed clerestory identifiable in the arrangement of the windows of the shopfront.

Chinese Empire Reform Society / Lung Kong Kung Shaw Society Buildings
1905

1715-1717 Government Street

Essentially Edwardian Classical structures, the buildings are marked by their open balconied façades above the retail shop fronts. Lion's head finials top the framing pilasters and the northern block is capped by an ornate parapet. The Empire Reform Society, a Mainland China protest movement of the Ching Dynasty, built the entire building. After the Republic of China was formed, the northern half was sold

Chinese Consolidated Benevolent Association School
1908

636 Fisgard Street
Archt. D. C. Frame

Exotic commissions provided the nineteenth and early twentieth century architect with an opportunity to indulge his fancy. Frame did this within the western architectural tradition of "chinoiserie" which includes such

well-known monuments as William Chamber's pagoda-like follies in Kew Gardens and John Nash's Brighton Pavilion in the "Indic" style. The Chinese School echoes the pagoda form to which is added a host of decorative elements: the Gothic trefoil fretwork in the second-floor balcony; the Classical brackets under the eaves orientalized at the corners; the Moorish first-floor window frames and stock Italianate window heads—in other words an eclectic array of element design to invoke the exotic effect of orientalism for the western eye. The school, however, struck a series of chords in the minds of many Chinese, as it was built in response to the Victoria School Board ruling in 1908 restricting access to the public schools, in particular denying entry to those children born in China.

Lim Dat Building
1910

1802-1826 Government Street
Archts. Hooper & Watkins

One of the most prominent structures in Chinatown, the block-long building stretches from Herald to Chatham Street. The sloping site requires the plan to step down in three sections. Two residential storeys are contained

above the street retail, the second floor features a band of large multi-light windows contained within the bays, the top floor arched windows with long recessed balconies. The bricks were supplied at the Bazan brickyard in North Saanich owned by Lim Dat's brother Lim Bang who built the Douglas Hotel. Recently, the current owners have completed a very sensitive recycling of the building into innovatively designed rental suites.

Lee Block
1910

565 Fisgard Street at Government
Archt. C. Elwood Watkins

Partners Lee Chung, Lee Wong and Lee Yanyou financed this large Edwardian Classical structure, a mix of retail, office and residential uses. Structural steel was used for the shopfronts on the first floor. Above, a

more conservative treatment of the façade has windows inserted into recessed masonry bays rather than a full opening up of the building envelope such as with J. Warren's designs for the Saward Building the same year.

tripartite columned balcony on the top floor capped by a pantiled cornice and decorative parapet. In 1935 the Shon Yee Benevolent Association purchased the smaller building as a headquarters for those people from Chung-shan county without the surname Lee. This takes the form of an Edwardian office block with an orientalized pantiled cornice replacing the more usual dentilated Classical entablature.

Lee Benevolent Association Building
1911

612-614 Fisgard Street
Archt. C. Elwood Watkins

These two structures share a common party wall and were designed "as a piece" by Watkins. The smaller western building was rental offices; the taller structure contains the administration and meeting rooms of the Lee Benevolent Association, a clan organization for those with the surname Lee. It is an imposing edifice, the

Hook Sin Tong Building
1911

658-666 Herald Street
Archt. C. Elwood Watkins

Hook Sin Tong is a county association which was formed by emigrants from Chung Shan County in South China. The ground floor was rented to stores and the upper floors used as the Society's office and tenements. Dr. Sun Yat Sen stayed here during his fundraising tour through North America in 1911. This is one of the best examples of Chinatown architecture. The recessed balcony, which is a very common feature of the Chinatown association buildings, provides open space for worshipping the heavens during religious or festival occasions. The third storey is divided into a triple opening by two columns supported by brackets. Above the Classical cornice is a parapet capped by large pine cone finials. A magnificent stained glass dome lights the association assembly room on the top floor.

Fan Tan Alley
1912-1913
Archts. C. Elwood Watkins, Thomas Hooper

The buildings which form the core, and ambiance, of Fan Tan Alley are actually a series of very typical Edwardian commercial blocks. The narrowness of the street and the scaled-down first floor contribute to the density of the constricted space. However, apart from some missing pressed tin cornices, the shopfronts and brickwork upper storeys are in remarkably good condition, and the quality of the detailing is excellent. The name "Fan Tan" derives from that of a popular Chinese gambling game.

Yen Wo Society Building
1912
1713 Government Street
Archt. L. W. Hargreaves

Yen Wo Society is an association formed by the Hakka people. The ground floor of the building is occupied by stores, the second by a Chinese women's club and the third floor by Tam Kung Temple, so called after Tam Kung, a patron saint of the Hakkas as well as seafarers. Two cornices define the Temple storey. The building is essentially Edwardian Classical, with Renaissance pilasters and cornices.

Lim and Wong Building
1913
542-556 Herald Street

In its day a building of striking modernity, this three-storey Edwardian Classical commercial frontage contained stores at street level, 40 tenement rooms above, and a rice mill at the rear. Lim Bang and Wong Jan Way were original partners in the venture. In

1983 this was one of the first successful rehabilitation projects in Chinatown for retail and commercial use; it is now known as the Herald Building.

New Victoria Police Station (architects Carl Peterson with Rebanks Assoc.), 1996, Caledonia at Quadra Street.

City of Victoria Police Station
1914

625 Fisgard Street
Archt. J. C. M. Keith, 1914

Retardetaire by comparison with the Chicago style commercial buildings going up in Victoria at this time, the Police Station is built as an almost literal essay in the manner of a Florentine palazzo. The rusticated stone first floor with its arched entrance and windows, then above three brick storeys detailed with stone quoined corners and window surrounds, are capped by a generous Italianate cornice. No doubt the city wanted, and got from Keith, an imposing institutional statement rather than commercial modernity.

Foo Hong Building
1946

564-572 Fisgard at Government Street
Archt. D. C. Frame

One of the few commercial buildings in Chinatown to actually present a distinctive Chinese character, the one-storey series of retail shopfronts is capped by a series of pagoda-like parapets. The key is perhaps the architect who had designed the new Chinese Benevolent Association building 30 years earlier as a conscious attempt at orientalization.

The Gate of Harmonious Interest
1981

Fisgard at Government Street
Archt. M. Lam, City of Victoria Planning Department

The Gate of Harmonious Interest memorializes six impressive temporary ceremonial gates erected by the Chinese community over the years to celebrate important visitors to Victoria. The first series of celebration arches greeted the visiting Governor General, the Earl of Dufferin, in 1876. The present gate was intended to focus public and private resources on the restoration of Victoria's Chinatown and constitute a major tourist attraction in its own right. The glazed ceramic cladding materials were obtained in Taiwan. The People's Government of Suzhou, Victoria's China Mainland sister city, donated the stone lions. According to author David Lai, the 38-foot-high structure is modelled on the entrance gateway to the Dun Huang Caves in Cansu Province and the gate of Ping Shan Hall in Yangzhou. On the eaves of the stupa are Chinese supernatural creatures; beneath is an array of square panels containing gilded dragons. On the Government Street side the centre panel reads "To work together with one heart"; on the opposite the translation reads "To help each other achieve harmony."

Fisgard at Government Street before the Gate of Harmonious Interest, looking west.

Conservation Planning:
The Management of Urban Design

In January 1963, Mayor R. B. Wilson, acting on a Council resolution, requested that the Capital Region Planning Board undertake an *Overall Plan for Victoria*. Victoria was facing drastic changes. That year BC Ferries opened their Swartz Bay-Tsawwassen service; the Provincial Museum was under construction; and spot zoning for high-rise office and apartment development—challenging the 1956 comprehensive zoning bylaw—was becoming commonplace. Council noted it was facing major decisions relating to land use, plans for Centennial Victoria Square, the Cathedral Hill Precinct, Harbour-Causeway Improvement, Urban Renewal, Downtown Improvement, park development, traffic, and waterways.

The resulting document, tabled in early 1965, set the terms for 30 years of debate regarding the future of the city. On the one hand, it noted "a measure of a city's maturity is the extent to which it will on the one hand encourage in the proper setting well-planned modern office buildings or high-rise apartments and on the other hand, preserve a building constructed in the last century." The reference was in particular to the city's plan for Centennial Square. The document's recommendations were both specific and sweeping. "Retention of the ingredients of genuine character" was encouraged but dramatic increases in density were recommended to spur economic renewal. Chinatown should be rehabilitated. Bastion Square should be rejuvenated. Revitalization of the Inner Harbour and downtown by means of recreational use, reducing through traffic, improving pedestrian use and providing parking were all laudable objectives. However, also on the order paper were a major 250,000-square-foot shopping mall in the vicinity of Johnson and Pandora, a sweeping reordering of traffic circulation via a major urban "high-speed truck route" (West Victoria Freeway) that would slice through the heart of Victoria West, leap the Inner Harbour Narrows at Laurel Point, then feed Ogden Point Terminal or snake around the Parliament Buildings on Superior and return out on Douglas Street. This would also provide for the densification of James Bay with high-rise residential towers.

The story of heritage conservation in Victoria is one of gradually, neighbourhood by neighbourhood, taming these parts of the plan. Neighbourhood groups coalesced, James Bay being the earliest. Preservation societies such as the Victoria Hallmark (founded 1973) formed to

Victoria Brewing Co., Government Street, n.d. BCARS 68480

Award-winning restoration before demolition. Conservation successes can be ephermeral without an active heritage management program.

Early 1960 renovations often attempted "modernization" at the expense of now highly valuable historic fabric.

defend heritage by intensive casework and building-by-building protest. Finally, a group of UBC architecture students published a seminal document, *The Old Town Report*, in 1971 which argued for a comprehensive conservation program for the civic core. In 1972, Mayor Peter Pollen

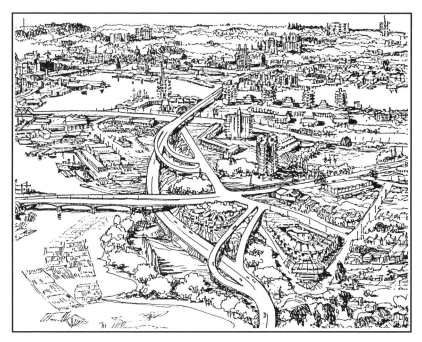

Proposed "Victoria West, 1990," from the *Overall Plan for The City of Victoria*, 1965.

appointed a Heritage Advisory Committee under the chair of Alderman Sam Bawlf. Their recommendations for an amendment to the Municipal Act for heritage protection via designation became provincial law in 1973. Early in 1975, the first designation in the oldest part of Old Town was enacted, the Wharf Street commercial frontages. Simultaneously the Department of Public Works was undertaking an in-depth study of the Parliamentary Precinct. Among its various recommendations were to refurbish St. Ann's Academy, refocus public marine transit in the CP Steamship Building, shift new office buildings into downtown, repair the heritage character in the Parliament Buildings vicinity and infill with contextual housing. In 1977 the Crystal Gardens Preservation Society was formed under the chair of Peter Cotton to lobby for the public re-use of this major Victoria monument. By the 1970s Victoria's conservation programs were attracting national attention. In 1976, for instance, Fort Victoria Properties Ltd. won a Heritage Canada Foundation Award of Honour for its revitalization of Market Square.

In September 1977, Section 71 4A of the Municipal Act was replaced by the Heritage Conservation Act. The new Act enabled City Council to designate by bylaw, lands, structures or buildings, in whole or in part, as municipal heritage sites. Public notice and hearings were required before a heritage bylaw could be adopted. It also empowered Council to withhold a demolition or building permit for a period of up to 90 days where a non-designated property may have possible heritage significance. Finally, the Act required municipalities to compensate an owner where economic loss was suffered through designation. Also in 1977, the Provincial Act was revised. A Heritage Conservation Branch was established to assist local government with heritage stewardship in an expert advisory role. The British Columbia Heritage Trust was founded to assist with financial incentives and collaborative projects.

Since 1975 the Heritage Program of the City of Victoria has been founded on education and popularization of heritage conservation values. Foremost has been the inventory process and resulting publications. The Heritage Advisory Committee membership was constituted to reflect community values rather than merely professional or academic concerns. The Downtown Inventory was first published as a popular book, *This Old Town*, in March 1975. *This Old House*, covering the residential neighbourhoods, followed in 1979. In 1990 the Foundation Group completed a comprehensive building-by-building inventory of Old Town. By 1980 some 136 buildings had been voluntarily designated in the City of Victoria. A second aspect has been the provision of incentives. The Victoria Heritage Foundation was established in 1983; it receives an annual subvention from the City to award grants to owners of designated homes to assist with restoration and maintenance. In 1990 the Victoria Civic Heritage Trust was established to similarly assist owners of commercial buildings through grants, interpretive and education programs. Designated buildings are recognizable by a distinctive bronze plaque.

Evaluation of the heritage merit of buildings in Victoria is one based on community discussion and debate. Every designation requires a public hearing and vote of Council. The Heritage Advisory Committee's primary task is to maintain a Heritage Registry consisting of those buildings designated, and those deemed worthy of designation. A first consideration is the concept of "Conservation Areas": a group of buildings having special architectural or historic interest giving an area a distinctive character. Streetscapes, viewscapes and identifiable groups of buildings provide for the application of a range of protective measures to ensure the long-term health of buildings. Beyond this, buildings demonstrating various styles and forms, representing different ethnic or income groups, are considered. Final selection criteria then consider the specifics of historical significance, architectural and environmental integrity; restoration or rehabilitation potential. The election of a building to the Heritage Registry means that it is flagged in the planning and building department files for special attention in the event of proposed rezoning, alterations or demolition.

The Heritage Advisory Committee has articulated criteria for evaluating and selecting heritage buildings. Buildings and sites of historical value are defined as those which are representative of a significant era in the evolution of the community; a milestone signifying an important turn of events locally or nationally; or reflective of particular cultural or social values of the community. Structures of architectural value are those which exhibit richness in details reflective of the times or which are pieces of artwork in themselves, representative work of generally recognized masters, an overall aesthetic pleasure to the public eye, important influence on the character of the surrounding environment, unique style or technique. Buildings of practical value for restoration are those buildings which are structurally sound, have the potential for functional adaptability for future use, contain adequate essential services and safety provisions, retain a high degree of design integrity, are compatible with the surrounding land use.

The ultimate success of heritage conservation has, however, been the result of embedding conservation values, practices and management mechanisms in the official Community Plan. Controlling densities and height restrictions to favour the retention of extant building stock, bonusing to reward designation or conservation investment, articulating design guidelines and controls to retain and enhance the heritage character of an area, permitting special uses in exchange for rehabilitation, rerouting traffic, public beautification projects and encouraging pedestrian use to assist the health of retail uses, undertaking interpretation and animation programs from guided tours to street vending—all result from policy objectives articulated in the downtown and individual neighbourhood plans. The city has published general Advisory Design Guidelines for new development throughout the city and more specific guidelines for the city's Chinatown area. Special guidelines have also been published to assist owners of heritage buildings in carrying out renovations or adding signs to commercial buildings.

In 1995, after extensive consultation with municipalities and the heritage community, the Government of British Columbia enacted a revised Heritage Act. As well as formally enabling a number of the initiatives already underway in Victoria, the Act expanded both the range of preservation tools and the applicability of heritage designation to areas (i.e., landscapes, neighbourhoods) to building interiors and even objects (i.e., marine vessels, industrial machinery).

NOTE

Ref. "British Columbia, Designated Heritage Sites Registry." 1993. "City of Victoria Downtown Heritage Management Plan." 1989. "City of Victoria: Official Community Plan." 1986. "Inner City Neighbourhoods." 1976. Mazer, L. D. and M. Segger "City of Victoria Central Area Heritage Conservation Report." 1975. "Overall Plan for The City of Victoria." 1965. "Wharf Street: City of Victoria: Heritage Designation Report." 1974.

View to James Bay, Litho. From *The West Shore Magazine*, 1885.

The Urban Approaches

JAMES BAY   The business of Fort Victoria was provisioning the fur trade. So the environs of Victoria were the farms of the Hudson's Bay Company's subsidiary, the Puget Sound Agricultural Company. James Bay started out as a 160-acre HBC farm in 1843; in 1850 the farm was leased out and renamed Beckley Farm; within another ten years the Colonial Government was building its headquarters and the subdivision of James Bay into ten-acre small holdings was underway. The construction of the James Bay Bridge across the mudflats of the Bay and the erection of the "Birdcages," (the Colonial Administration Buildings) was completed by 1859. It became fashionable to locate near the Province's first house of government and many of Victoria's early social and political elite took up residence on lands surrounding the Legislative Buildings until the prestigious Rockland District was developed.

Surrounded by water on three sides, James Bay also became a nat-

House for architect Thomas Hooper. Corner of Belleville and Menzies.
COURTESY RON A. GREENE

ural location for industrial activity and much of the waterfront land stretching from the Inner Harbour to the Outer Harbour was consigned to industrial interests. Nearby residential dwellings become the working-class neighbourhoods of the 1880s and 1890s. Many of these residences were so called "widow's cottages," rental housing built for investment annuities. The infill of James Bay during these years was very much a function of the Victoria Electric Lighting and Railway Company's lines linking downtown with the Outer Wharf at Ogden Point along a route following Government and Superior, and later also Beacon Hill Park via Menzies and Niagara Streets. By the turn of the century virtually all large tracts of land had been subdivided except for an area west of Holland Point which remained undeveloped until the 1940s.

Rapid growth of Greater Victoria in the 1950s and 1960s created enormous pressures for redevelopment in James Bay and many of its landmark residences were demolished in favour of higher density developments.

CATHEDRAL HILL AND ROCKLAND The forerunner of today's Christ Church Cathedral began in 1853 as the Victoria District Church, under the direction of Rev. Edward Cridge. From here a series of ecclesiastical buildings over the years marked Victoria as a cathedral town. Cridge's early wooden structure was Victoria's first church building. It stood across Quadra Street from the present church (on the Law Courts site) where it commanded a panoramic view over the Fort and the harbour below. Today's buildings have now almost totally obscured the sea views, but the cathedral on the hill still stands out from many vantage points in the city as a landmark.

The Cathedral Hill Precinct shared the dominant ecclesiastical function with the quiet residential streets built up during the 1880s. The character of this area is expressed in the Victorian Italianate and Queen Anne style residences. However, it was on this early City edge that Victoria's residential amenities also developed: schools, hospitals, the YM/YWCA, parks, churches —even the cemetery and more recently the Law Courts.

The Rockland area was carved out of the 500-acre Douglas Estate, "Fairfield Farm," in the early 1880s and was intended as a prestige subdivi-

Christ Church Cathedral, *ca.* 1890. BCARS 26001

sion. Architect Charles Vereydhen planned the layout of the five- to seven-acre estates between Fort Street and Belcher Avenue (now Rockland). These estates dominated the Victoria skyline and commanded superb views over the lush farmlands of Fairfield and across the Juan de Fuca Strait to the Olympic Mountains. During this period, *Colonist* editor D. W. Higgins built "Regents Park," banker A. A. Green, "Gyppeswyk," biscuit baron Samuel Nesbitt built a lavish home, Premier and later Lieutenant-Governor E. G. Prior, "The Priory" and above them all towered Robert Dunsmuir's "Craigdarroch Castle."

As further subdivisions encroached on the original estates during the 1890s and the turn of the century, Rockland's unique character as a prestige residential area for the province's influential and wealthy families continued to develop. At the request of this select clientele, Rockland quickly became a competitive laboratory for the city's major society architects and designers. John Wright's Italianate style "Pentrelew" and Portland architect W. H. William's Scottish Baronial style "Craigdarroch Castle" remain major monuments. In 1890 Leonard Buttress Trimen introduced the Tudor Revival to Victoria in "Ellesmere" for James Angus, brother of the CPR president. William Ridgeway Wilson designed the largest Tudor Revival commission "Schuhuum" for the Bostock family

"The Laurels" for Robert Ward, Rockland. Architect T. C. Sorby, 1889.

(1894). T. C. Sorby designed the eclectic style "Laurels" for Robert Ward (1889). F. M. Rattenbury built his most impressive and innovative residential commissions in Rockland: The Chateauesque Lyman Duff house in 1898 and the Chalet style Alice Galletley residence in 1902. The Rattenbury influence is discernible in the later work of Rattenbury's associate, P. L. James; the Helmcken House on Moss Street (1912) and the Gallicher home on Rockland (1912). More unusual and foreign is the H. G. Wilson home (1912) on lower St. Charles in the California Arts & Crafts manner by San Francisco architect Charles King. Rockland was, however, more than anything else, the preserve of British Columbia's premier architect, Samuel Maclure. Maclure and Rattenbury shared the massive Government House commission (1902) and the exterior result in the American Shingle style was mainly Rattenbury. The 1899 Judge A. E. McPhillips' house was Maclure's first experiment in the Chalet form—so successfully perfected in the A. A. Munn house in the following year. Maclure introduced his own unique version of the Tudor Revival in the J. Wilson house of 1901, improving it through a series of commissions, including the impressive Biggerstaff Wilson house of 1906 and the Picturesque C. F. Todd house of 1907. Many other residences in Rockland are evidence of Maclure's genius and talent, representing infill on the streetscapes and compromises within his extensive stylistic vocabulary. For some 50 years Rockland remained the preserve of the province's bankers, senior bureaucrats, politicians, successful realtors, businessmen and industrialists. For them, the city's foremost architects created the architectural image of their age and lifestyle.

By the 1920s, however, Rockland had been eclipsed by Uplands Estates as the place for Victoria's wealthy to build. At first the infill was sympathetic as, for instance, the Craigdarroch estate was subdivided for Arts & Crafts shingle and half-timbered residences. And during the 1930s many of the larger mansions were sympathetically revitalized to accommodate rental units. Post-war development, however, has been somewhat more brutal with plain stucco bungalows shoehorned into smaller lots. In the 1980s a new Rockland Plan established a zoning category with subdivision guidelines to preserve viewscapes to the old character residences. The insertion of condominium units into what had been garden tennis courts, orchards and croquet lawns was therefore continued, but under tighter design controls.

FAIRFIELD AND OAK BAY   From a patchwork of medium to large farm holdings, most of them held by such prominent men as James Douglas, Joseph Trutch, J. D. Pemberton and John Todd, the swath of rolling meadows which describes a large arc east of the city core developed into an Edwardian, middle-class neighbourhood during the great land boom of 1905-1912. A major factor was the Victoria Electric Railway and Lighting Company's 1891 line extensions to Windsor Park and Willows in Oak Bay. The basic gridiron patterns of boulevarded streets, compromised occasionally to accommodate the geography, afford the residents scenic views northward toward the oak-clad estate homes of Rockland, westward toward Beacon Hill and the looming towers of Christ Church Cathedral and southward across the Strait of Juan de Fuca and the spectacular views of the Olympic Mountains. The land boom resulted in a competitive building industry that produced many spec-built bungalow style residences in the neighbourhood. The California Bungalow type can be identified by its display of structural wooden supports in the porch, gabled roof and an array of cladding materials such as shingles, half-timbering, fieldstone and stucco. The Colonial Bungalow is a simpler form with a generous bellcast or hipped roof, sheltering an entrance verandah and extensive eaves shading one-and-one-half storeys of clapboard and shingle siding. The eastern side of the peninsular, from Foul Bay Point to Cadboro Bay, was incorporated as a separate municipality in 1906 (coincidentally with the Municipality of Saanich) and was soon noted for its recreational amenities, the Oak Bay Golf Course and the very upmarket Olmsted-planned garden-city suburb, Uplands. The latter was developed from what had been an HBC cattle farm.

Jubilee Street Car Shelter
PHOTO AL FRY, 1985

Mount Baker Hotel, Oak Bay, *ca.* 1890. BCARS 63837

Indicative of the residential nature of Victoria's neighbourhoods are the very fine red brick schools which dominate the skyline; the churches for the most part serve neighbourhood parishes and are small scale. The "red brick" schools following the precedent of architect R. Ridgeway Wilson's South Ward Elementary of 1894 include George Jay Elementary (1909, architect C. E. Watkins), Sir James Douglas (1910, architect J. C. M. Keith), Bank Street School (1912, architect D. C. Frame), Tolmie School (1912, architect H. J. R. Cullin), Margaret Jenkins (1913, architect J. C. M. Keith), Oaklands (1912-1913, architects C. E. Watkins; annex 1920), Burnside Elementary (1913, architect C. E. Watkins), Monterey Elementary (1914, architect C. E. Watkins), Quadra School (1914, architect C. E. Watkins), Willows School (1919, architect C. E. Watkins). More integrated in their residential suburban settings are the Shingle style schools: for example, Cedar Hill School (1912), Cloverdale School (1917-1921, architect Hubert Savage) and a replica of Cloverdale, Tillicum (1918), also Sundance Elementary (1921, architect C. E. Watkins). Woodframe Oak Bay Secondary is a formal stucco-clad building well proportioned but with Art Deco pretentions hinting at its Queen Anne red-brick ancestry (1929, architects Spurgin & Semeyn). More modern major monuments, stridently Progressive in their style, are S. J. Willis High (1950) and Central Junior High (1952), both by Birley, Wade Stockdill, architects. These latter paved the way for the new form of modernist suburban school: Lansdowne (1953, Wade Stockdill, architects) in Mount Tolmie and Mount Douglas (1960, R. W. Siddall, architects) in Gordon Head.

The eastern boundary between Victoria and Oak Bay is characterized by its significant land forms. A rugged granite escarpment rises gradually from the Fairfield Valley floor, peaks slightly to the east of Foul Bay then falls off sharply, affording dramatic sites commanding extensive vistas.

The development of Foul Bay Road coincided with a climax in the career of architect, Samuel Maclure. A master of sensitive siting, Maclure, almost single-handedly built the Foul Bay residential district. He developed a series of sophisticated house designs featuring complex spatial plans and exterior styles to take advantage of the magnificent view.

SPRING RIDGE/FERNWOOD Development began in the 1860s when a series of springs was discovered in what is now the area of Spring Road and Princess Street, Ridge Road and Pembroke. The Spring Ridge/Fernwood neighbourhood rises from the plainlands east of the central city district to a ridge running along its northern boundary and Belmont Hill delineating the eastern boundary. In keeping with traditional class stratification, residences located on the ridge were lavish dwellings built for the middle-class shortly after the turn of the century. Houses located on the flats closer to the city centre date from the 1880s and 1890s and were generally simple, unadorned, working-class residences. Those on the brow of the hill along Belmont are highstyle Arts & Crafts residences of some substance. Again development responded, in particular, to the opening up of these areas by streetcar lines in the 1890s. Fernwood is dominated by the massive bulk of Victoria High School designed by C. E. Watkins in 1914.

SAANICH AND NORTHERN VICTORIA NEIGHBOURHOODS

The northern neighbourhoods encompass a vast swath of land stretching from the Gorge watercourse along the northern boundary of the City to the Jubilee area. Heritage residences in this district rely heavily on their individual merits for recognition as large tracts of land in this district were developed after 1940. A major influence on land development patterns was the decision by Saanich Municipality in 1963 to relocate its municipal hall to its urban edge. Saanich had not adopted any formal zoning bylaws until 1939 when it began to recognize its emerging bedroom community status. By then it was clear that if its rural (or distinct) identity was to be maintained, some attempt at rural conservation would have to be undertaken. The municipal hall relocation was therefore done in conjunction with the adoption of a set of planning principles heavily influenced by the Progressive schools of urban design, their main objective being the containment of urban sprawl. The elder statesman of the Progressive movement was the Swiss-French architect Le Corbusier whose *Ville Radieuse*, a 1930s conceptual project, gained popularity in North America during the 1950s and 1960s. The essence of radial planning was the preservation of open (agricultural) green spaces by creating very high density population nodes (skyscapers on stilts) linked by linear communication conduits (for vehicular express ways, electrical, sewage and water

Saanich Municipal Hall, *ca.* 1980.

services, etc.). The subsequent planning process in Saanich has been dominated by repeated attempts to preserve rural character, define urban containment boundaries, identify nodes for commercial or residential densification, and provide connectors through and between these elements. The recent development history of Saanich, and indeed the entire Peninsula has therefore been very much tied to the increasing sophistication of land management tools such as the provincial act to establish the Agricultural Land Reserve, development cost charges to feed landbanking and parks acquisition funds, and partnerships with amenity agencies such as the Provincial Capital Commission. The decision by Saanich, therefore, to locate its modernistic Le Corbusier-inspired Municipal Hall facing a nature sanctuary (the front line of green belt on the "*radieuse*") almost inaccessible to pedestrians, and with its back to a proposed shopping centre (since built), was appropriately symbolic. Symbol also must have been paramount in the plan for two adjacent 20-storey landmark apartment towers (not built) intended to supply a distinct nucleus population and gateway marking the transition from Victoria to Saanich. Although Le Corbusier's idealized image of tower block nodes dotting the verdant landscape has not materialized for Saanich, in fact pockets of medium density tied to commercial or institutional uses have become a recognizable feature at Royal Oak, Camosun's Interurban Campus, Broadmead and University Heights. The University of Victoria might be seen as a garden version of the *Ville Radieuse* reconfigured for the industries of academe.

VICTORIA WEST AND ESQUIMALT   Isolated from the rest of Victoria by the Gorge watercourse, Victoria West has played a curious but important role in the development of the city. Shortly after Fort Victoria

View of Esquimalt, Litho. From *The West Shore Magazine*, 1885.

was constructed in 1843, the Songhees Indian Reserve was set up and encompassed all lands from Alston Street to the waterfront. The Indian band congregated its activities generally between Songhees Point and the bridgehead at Esquimalt Road. At an early stage, the Indian band gave permission for sealing and lumber interests to locate on the waterfront, thus setting the stage for the establishment of an industrial precinct after the reserve was relocated in 1911.

A portion of Victoria West formed the Hudson's Bay Company Constance Cove Farm (located between Pine Street and Craigflower Road). Little residential development occurred in Victoria West until the construction of the first Point Ellice Bridge in 1861. The Gorge Inlet was an attractive recreational amenity and much of the residential waterfront land was bought by wealthy Victoria families such as the Grays (Albion Iron Works), Muirheads (lumber and milling interest), Troups (shipping interest), and James Dunsmuir (the coal magnate who built a large rambling estate named "Burleith" in 1891, overlooking the Gorge). Lands peripheral to these large estates were generally subdivided and subsequently built upon after 1891 when Victoria and Esquimalt were linked by streetcar. Prior to 1891, the area's orientation was more to Esquimalt, with its naval base (established in 1865) and the terminus of the Esquimalt & Nanaimo Railway. Esquimalt itself was formally incorporated as a municipality in 1912.

THE CITY OF GARDENS

Gorge Waterway, the picturesque escarpment topography, and the fertile hay farms often broken by stretches of rocky Gary Oak meadowlands, provided the substructure for Victoria's residential expansion into what rapidly became ornamental landscaped suburbs. Given this advantageous fact of geography combined with a core essentially British land-owning population, it is not surprising that the dominant feature of the city's expanding residential development should be its gardens. Since the early days of the Fort, residents responded to both climate and landscape with a passion for gardens. Chief Factor James Douglas recorded in his journal regarding selection of the site on the western-

View to Point Ellice House from the Gorge, *ca.* 1875.

most peninsula of Vancouver Island, "The place itself appears a perfect Eden in the midst of the dreary wilderness of the North West Coast. . . . one might be pardoned for supposing it had dropped from the clouds. . . ." Open parklands sloping back from a series of inlets and harbours transected by small streams and rocky escarpments afforded extensive farmlands for the Company and later building sites with dramatic prospects to the mainland Olympic Coast Range mountains. The notion of Victoria as a garden city was born.

Colonial period mid-Victorian gardens have been restored at the HBC Craigflower Farm (1856), the Judge Peter O'Reilly House (1861) and the Richard Carr House (1863). After confederation in 1871 and goldrush settlement expansion, civic improvements followed A. J. Downing's Picturesque formulae. Certainly Downing's writing influenced the 1873 Ross Bay Cemetery designed by Edward Mallandaine—who also designed other cemeteries: Jewish Cemetery, 1859; Naval Cemetery, 1873; South Saanich, 1880; and Metchosin, 1884. And the Picturesque formulae can be seen carried out in the 500-acre Rockland Estates subdivision (planned by architect Charles Vereydhen) in the early 1880s, and Victoria's High Victorian public park, Beacon Hill (designed by architect John Blair in 1889). Rockland was dominated by Robert Dunsmuir's Craigdarroch Castle and its 18-acre estate (designed by Warren Williams, 1887; landscaping by Hugh Campbell, 1889). The gardens of W. J. Pendray's house of 1895 featuring elaborate topiary work survive as typical of domestic ornamental gardens of the period. During this time the residential architecture of Victoria developed features which became traditional in responding to social and aesthetic aspects of garden life: conservatories, breakfast balconies, sleeping porches, *porte-cocheres*, and elaborate tea houses. Public parks such as Windsor in Oak Bay and the Gorge at Esquimalt were developed in the early 1890s as destination points by the National Electric Tramway and Light Company.

With the turn of the century the Arts & Crafts movement became a powerful means of architectural expression under the leadership of architects such as Samuel Maclure, Francis Mawson Rattenbury and Thomas Hooper. This was a watershed period for Victoria in landscape design. Between 1900 and 1914 great gardens such as those at James Dunsmuir's Hatley Park, Government House, and Jenny Foster Butchart's "Benvenuto" at Tod Inlet were started. Private gardens were regularly thrown open to the public. Large-scale nursery operations flourished,

B.C. Electric observation car "Seeing Victoria" at Gorge Park, *ca.* 1910.

View from the Japanese Gardens, Hatley Park, n.d.

James Layritz published annual planting guides and catalogues. Layritz imported and bred a wide range of plant materials which were marketed not only throughout British Columbia but also to California, Japan and China. With similar purposes in mind the Butcharts founded the Benvenuto Seed Company.

During this period society architect Samuel Maclure formalized the classic Victoria garden in the English manner after the influential planter and writer Gertrude Jekyll. Usually the house dominated an informal park-like frontage of lawns and herbacious borders containing a driveway approach. One side of the garden contained either alpine rockery, oriental style arrangement, or native plant garden; the other side, a formal trellised rose garden often accessed from the house through an attached conservatory. The rear often featured a fruit orchard, vegetable plot and cutting garden arranged to screen tennis courts or croquet lawn. Surviving examples of Maclure include the Biggerstaff Wilson House in Rockland (1905), Hatley Park (with Brett & Hall of Boston, 1913), the R. Sutherland House (1913), Maclure's most published Arts & Crafts expression, the Hon. W. C. Nichol house, "Miraloma" at Sidney (1925). Between 1911 and 1925 Maclure was consulting architect to the Butchart Gardens where he worked with planter William Westby and landscape architect Raoul Robillard (the latter having articled with Maclure). One example of a popular feature, the native plant garden containing indigenous British Columbia flora, survives from Maclure's R. H. Beaven commission (1902) as the Oak Bay Native Plant Garden.

Under the influence of the American City Beautiful movement, the Victoria Parks Board was established in 1901 and charged with implementing a street boulevarding system with flowering trees throughout the city. In 1908 Olmsted Bros. designed the prestigious Uplands Estates in Oak Bay and in 1913 Thomas Mawson planned a similar development

"Meadlands," a garden city suburb at Pat Bay (unbuilt). Serious attention was also paid to period gardens: the Italian garden terrace at Hatley Park (1913-1916), and Italian gardens of the Victoria Normal School (designed by W. C. F. Gillam, 1913). Japanese landscape gardener and architect Isaburo Kishata laid out oriental gardens for Hatley Park (still the largest in Victoria), the Butcharts, Frank Barnard, and also at Gorge Park for B.C. Electric Railway Co. (At Gorge Samuel Maclure provided designs for the architectural elements.) The St. Ann's Academy ornamental gardens were laid out in 1913 to designs by the Dutchman Fr. Adrian Joseph Vullinghs, whose Saanich Our Lady of the Assumption church gardens were already well known.

The Island Arts & Crafts Society, founded in 1909, was a major influence in civic beautification; its members were fashion leaders in residential garden design. Species propagation became a special interest of such groups as the Vancouver Island Agriculture and Horticulture Society (founded in 1865), the British Columbia Agricultural Society (organized 1876), the Victoria Horticulture Society (first show, 1902) and the Vancouver Island Rock and Alpine Garden Society (founded in 1921).

The 1920s saw Victoria's gardens becoming the major attraction in the city's burgeoning tourist industry. The Empress conservatory and rose gardens were equal billed with Butchart's (already hosting 18,000 people per year by 1915). The famous hanging baskets were first installed throughout Victoria's commercial core in 1937. The complete summer

Prince and Princess Abkazi Rhododendron Garden, Fairfield.

basket complement now numbers about 650. Public spaces were continually improved, such as the construction of the Parliament Buildings sunken rose garden, a Depression-era project (1935-1936). In the postwar years Victoria has felt the impact of Robert Hubert Savery, who served as the Provincial Government's senior landscape designer from 1959 to 1967. Under Savery's control fell numerous major projects such as the south face of the Parliament Buildings, nearby Confederation Square (1968), the Law Courts (1962), the alpine and rose gardens at Government House, and the extensive native plant gardens in the Royal British Columbia Museum complex (these latter in consultation with Provincial Botanist Dr. Chris Brayshaw).

Contemporary private gardens have developed international reputations for specialization such as the Prince and Princess Abkhazi Rhododendron gardens. The largest modern public landscape scheme is the University of Victoria Gorden Head Campus started in 1962. It includes natural forest and native flora, a major rhododendron collection, and general landscaping (overall consulting architect: Wurster, Bernardi, Emmons, San Fransisco with Lawrence Halprin & Associates, John Lantzius, Muirhead & Justice, and Don Vaughan Associates).

Oak Bay Native Garden.

NOTE

Ref. Adams, John. "Historic Guide to Ross Bay Cemetery: Victoria, B.C. Canada." 1983. Barr, Jennifer, Nell. "Saanich Heritage Structures: An Inventory." 1991. "A Brief History of Beacon Hill Park 1882-1982." 1981. Stark, Stuart. "Oak Bay's Heritage Buildings: More than just Bricks and Boards." 1995. Field, Dorothy. "Built Heritage in Esquimalt." 1984. Franklin, Douglas & Fleming, John. "Early School Architecture in British Columbia: An Architectural History and Inventory of Buildings to 1930." 1980. Luxton, Donald. "C.R.D. Art Deco and Moderne." n.d. Segger, Martin & Douglas Franklin. "Victoria A Primer for Regional History in Architecture 1843-1929." 1979. "This Old House: An Inventory of Residential Heritage." 1991.

The Residential Approaches

John Todd House
1850-1851

2564 Heron Street, Oak Bay

Todd's house is believed to be the oldest standing residential building on its original site in western Canada. John Todd, a former HBC factor at Fort Kamloops, settled a 200-acre farm which became the core of present-day Oak Bay. The house is built in the HBC manner of squared logs, *piece sur piece*, morticed into grooved corner uprights, then covered with horizontal drop siding. The tall 12-light casement windows, chimneys bracketting the long saddle roof with slightly flaired eaves, and full-length side verandah are all hallmarks of the vernacular Georgian idiom which was common to the HBC structures through the Canadian trading post system.

Helmcken House
1852

St. Ann's School House
ca. 1845

Heritage Court, adjacent to the Royal British Columbia Museum

These two buildings, now *tête-à-tête*, next to the Museum, are uniquely compatible for a number of reasons.

Both are surviving Hudson's Bay Company trading post structures. Both are resonant with local cultural and historical associations. Dr. John Sebastian Helmcken was the first surgeon and doctor at Fort Victoria. He was a founding member of the colony's first Legislative Assembly. The little school house was bought by Bishop Demers in 1856 to accommodate the first contingent of the Sisters of St. Ann from Quebec. They subsequently built up one of the largest and most prestigious girls' schools in western Canada. The two buildings are particularly interesting as surviving examples of typical HBC construction technology. Helmcken wrote of its construction:

To build a house now is a very easy matter, but a very different matter then. How we studied over the design, i.e. interior divisions of the building 30×25 ! ! Then to get it done for there were no contractors, everything had to be done piecemeal. There being no lumber, it had to be built with logs squared on two sides and six inches thick. The sill and uprights were very heavy and morticed. The supports of the floor likewise the logs had to be let into grooves in the uprights. Well the timber had to be taken from the forest squared there and brought down to the water. All this had to be contracted for by French Canadians.
(Taken from a transcription by Tudith Zack of *Reminiscences of John Sebastion Helmcken.* Five Volumes. 1892. Provincial Archives.)

The school house originally stood on the north shore of James Bay where

it was built by Jacques Laquechier *ca.* 1845. In 1853 it was purchased from the HBC by another French Canadian, Leon Morrell, who sold it to Bishop Demers for $500. It was moved in 1973 to its present site. Both buildings constitute a provincial heritage site, open to the public.

Capt. Charles and Grace Dodd House
ca. 1859

4139 Lambrick Way, Gordon Head, Saanich

In 1978 the house was salvaged and moved from a development site on Kenmore Road. Dodd served as master of the HBC coastal steamers *Beaver* and *Labourchere* and later became a chief factor. The shingled Georgian cottage was built as the family's country home and demonstrates the influence and sophistication of HBC vernacular building types. The exterior comprises a symmetrical arrangement of building elements, roof soffits articulated with mouldings and a continuous drip-course at sill level. The interior features 12-foot ceilings, the walls lined with redwood.

"Woodlands" for James Bissett
1861

140 Government Street, James Bay
Archt. Wright & Sanders

Probably the earliest standing architect-designed house in Victoria, "Woodlands" is also a very good example of the Italian Villa style which can also still be seen in Wright's house for Richard Carr. A "villa," says Andrew Jackson Downing in his 1850 book *Architecture for Country Houses*, signifies only "'a country house or abode' [but] ... more strictly speaking, what we mean by a villa ... is the country house of a person of competence or wealth sufficient to build and maintain it with some taste and elegance." Given this rationale it is not difficult to imagine why James Bay's first houses were constructed in this style. Bissett was a prominent Hudson's Bay official. The house is a finely detailed structure with its Italian Villa decorative scheme carried through the real and blind Venetian "triptych" windows tucked neatly under the gables, its "tacked on" corner pilasters culminating in neatly curved brackets, fretwork trim, and miniature consoles under the eaves.

Point Ellice House Residence for The Hon. Peter O'Reilly
1861

2616 Pleasant Street, Victoria
Archt. John Wright
(Additions: John Teague, W. R. Wilson)

The original house, a cottage overlooking the Gorge Waterway, was designed by John Wright for W. A. Wentworth in 1861. Peter O'Reilly, the colony's first gold commissioner, who also served on the early Legislative Council, purchased the property in 1868. Substantial additions and modifications were designed by Teague and Wilson. O'Reilly became a County Court judge and was one of the early advocates of British Columbia's

rocky rise in the middle of a ten-acre estate, carved out of James Douglas' extensive Fairfield Farm. Trutch, Surveyor General for British Columbia, was appointed the Province's first Lieutenant-Governor in 1871. The well-preserved house is an almost literal example of the "Swiss Chalet Cottage" house-type as propounded in the books of popular Victorian arbiter of architectural taste, Andrew Jackson

confederation with Canada. Mrs. O'Reilly, Caroline Agnes, was the sister of Sir Joseph Trutch, the first Lieutenant-Governor of British Columbia. Built only 18 years after the founding of Fort Victoria, the house must have been one of the first in Victoria to set style to domestic living. A simplified version of an Italianate cottage, the house still preserves its decorative trim which has a modest elegance even to the modern eye. The interior and original furnishings have been preserved along with costumes and memorabilia from many noted Victoria families. Among the more interesting points to notice is the original wallpaper in many of the rooms, the ornate marble fireplaces, and the many pieces of high-quality Victorian furniture. Now an historic site, the house and restored period gardens are open to the public.

Downing. The cross-axial plan features widespreading bracketed eaves and is dominated by a central gable wing which commands the vista down Collinson Street, originally the driveway approach. The subdivision of the Trutch estate in 1906 spearheaded the development of Fairfield as a major residential suburb of Victoria.

"Duvals" for Mrs. Elizabeth Miles
1862
1462 Rockland Avenue, Rockland

This house is reputed to have been built for Mrs. Elizabeth Miles, former owner of Cary Castle. From 1865, "Duvals" was occupied by the Hon. Sir Joseph Needham, Chief Justice of the Colony of Vancouver Island, and in 1870 the house was bought by Francis Jones Barnard who owned an express stage line to the Cariboo. He was first elected to the House of Commons for

"Fairfield" House for Hon. Joseph Trutch
1861
601 Trutch Street, Fairfield
Archts. Wright & Sanders

The historic focus of Fairfield is Trutch Street. Here is found one of the best preserved Arts & Crafts streetscapes in Victoria. Wright sited the house on a

Yale in 1879, although earlier (1867-1868) he had been a member of the Legislative Assembly of the Crown Colony of British Columbia. During the early years of the Barnard occupancy, the house acquired its general outline, which can still be recognized by high pitched gables of the "Country Gothic." Part of the porch which extended around the house on all sides is still extant. Balustrades and brackets ornamented with Victorian gingerbread have survived in excellent condition. Architects James and James enlarged the cottage in 1911.

The Richard Carr Home
1863

207 Government Street, James Bay
Archt. Wright & Sanders
Restoration: Peter Cotton, archt., 1969

In her *The Book of Small*, famous British Columbia painter Emily Carr wrote of her childhood reminiscences concerning this house:

When my father came from England he bought ten acres of fine land adjoining Beacon Hill Park. It cost father a lot of money to clear the land. He left every fine tree he could, because he loved trees, but he cleared away the scrub to make meadows for the cows and a beautiful garden. Then he built what was considered in 1863 a big,

fine house. It was all made of California redwood. The chimneys were of California brick, and the mantlepieces of black marble . . . I have heard my mother tell how she cried at the lonesomeness of going to live in the forest. Yet father's land was only one mile out of town.

The Italianate style was usually distinguished, as is illustrated here, by the proliferation of balconies, verandahs, ornamental porches, round headed windows, and the boldness of its abstract, low-relief ornament. It was a style which A. J. Downing promised would awaken "more strong the emotions of the beautiful and the picturesque."

The house was first restored under the direction of architect Peter Cotton and today is a provincial historic site open to the public.

Angela College
1865

923 Burdett Street, Fairfield
Archts. Wright & Sanders

Designed in the Picturesque Gothic Revival style, this building was Victoria's first "Girls' Collegiate School." Operated by the Anglican Church, Angela College was named after the patroness of the diocese, Lady Angela Burdett-Coutts. Wright's original proposal was almost triple the size of the present building. What was finally built was merely the west wing of this

scheme. Even so, both in design and construction detail it is an impressive structure for its time.

Red-brick Gothic was the dominant building idiom for the Church of England's massive building program both at home and overseas during the latter half of the nineteenth century. In 1908, the building became a residential hotel. In 1959, it was bought by the Sisters of St. Ann and remains a cornerstone for the ecclesiastical character of the Cathedral Precinct.

"Highwood" for William Ward
ca. 1869
1021 Gillespie Place, Rockland

"Highwood" played an important role in the social life of Victoria for many years. As the official residence of the powerful Bank of British Columbia, it housed the first manager, William C. Ward. The street acquired its name from a succeeding manager, George Gillespie. The solid masonry house, built in the then-popular Italianate style, was probably designed by John Teague as the house bears remarkable similarities to the so-called "Admiral's House" built by Teague at the Naval Dockyard some 16 years later. Extensive improvements were carried out in 1890 which may have included the addition of front window bays.

Ross Bay Cemetery
1873
Fairfield Road at Memorial Crescent, Fairfield
Archt. Edward Mallandaine

Thomas Gray's famous *Elegy Written in a Country Churchyard*, and its evocation of the poet's contemplation on the futility of anonymous life and the finality of death, required a peaceful rural setting where one could be alone with one's thoughts. Thus, despite practical considerations for the choice of the Ross Bay Cemetery site in 1873, its then-isolated location deep in the farmland belt to the east of Victoria must have come as no surprise. Here one could ponder the sublimity of death amid the beauty of nature. The landscape plan of Ross Bay Cemetery was skillfully designed to enhance such an effect.

A radial plan, centred roughly at the midpoint of the original 12 acres, features axial avenues linked on the periphery by a gently curving carriage-way. From the intersection of the avenues, accented by its oval round-about, one looks down the treed avenue vistas out across the Strait of Juan de Fuca to the snow-capped Olympic Mountains on the distant mainland shore. At close hand, however, this majestic view is softened by the contrived pastoral landscape. According to the original plan one would have looked seaward over a gently sloping meadow, across formal flowerbeds, through copses of trees, and on the eastern border, over the banks of a meandering stream.

In the arrangement of the plots, Victorian utility comes to the fore. These are laid out in a functional grid. Access from the main driveway is provided by 5-foot- and 2-foot-wide paths. No doubt the architect depended on diversity in size and style of headstones as well as the irregular progress of infill to complete that late Victorian sense of the Picturesque.

The significance of Ross Bay Cemetery in the history of Victoria's growth and development is important. It is certainly the oldest surviving landscape design in Victoria and may have been among the first to be commissioned and executed. By comparison, the Beacon Hill Park plan by John Blair dates from only 1889.

Ross Bay Cemetery was intended by its planners to be a place of repose for both living and dead, but for the living in particular, a place of contemplation and meditation. The success of those intentions is evident today: that even as urban sprawl now crowds the landward periphery, a person so inclined can amble down the entrance driveway, stop at the midpoint intersection of the avenues, gaze seaward over the lichen-covered monuments and ponder the brevity of life, as did Thomas Gray at Stoke Poges in 1742: "The paths of glory lead but to the grave."

Residence for Alexander Blair Gray
1877
327 Belleville Street, James Bay
Archt. James Syme

A. B. Gray was a Scottish-born merchant who first passed through

Victoria on his way to find Cariboo gold and later returned to establish a thriving business in drygoods, tobacco and liquor importing. The house is Italianate in style, with symmetrical façade and side elevations, a shallow hipped roof, and two sentinel chimneys flanking the Classical gable. As well as the usual household apartments, the house contained an impressive array of "social" spaces: drawing room, dining room, sitting room, and second-storey billiard room, as well as a large entrance hall, all sumptuously panelled in exotic woods and ornately decorated in Neo-Georgian fashion.

Residence for Hon. John Robson
1885

506 Government Street, James Bay
Archt. John Teague

British Columbia Premier John Robson, and his son-in-law, Joseph Hunter, each built houses on Birdcage Walk, now Government Street, in the same year. The house is a particularly good example of the Victorian Italianate, now missing only the front entrance cornice and the ornate balustrades over the porch. This style was particularly important among the farmers and grape growers in and around San Francisco during the 1870s and 1880s. The detailing of the pilasters and the cornice brackets is very fine.

Beacon Hill Park
1872, 1889

Bounded by Douglas, Cook, Superior and Dallas Roads, Fairfield/James Bay
Archt. John Blair

Beacon Hill itself (called by the Indians Mee-a-can, "the belly," because it resembled a reclining fat man) featured a native burial ground on its south slope, the graves marked with rock cairns. According to native tradition these were the graves of an entire village which once stood on Finlayson Point until eradicated by an epidemic.

Officers of the HBC renamed the hill from there being two marine navigational beacons, so aligned as to mark the existence of the treacherous Brotchie Ledge some distance off shore.

When control of Vancouver Island reverted back to the Crown from the Hudson's Bay Company, Colonial Governor James Douglas, made provisions for the establishment of a public park at Beacon Hill. The final confirmation of the land grant to the City did not occur until February 21, 1882. In the 1860s this hill formed the centre of a horse racing oval with stands erected by the Jockey Club. In

1872 the Government had deeded over to the City the foreshore from Ross Bay to Ogden Point and in 1879 the Province deeded over the park itself although complete municipal control only came under the Public Parks Act of 1882. In 1889 Beacon Hill Park was extended through a gift of land from the Government which included a block in the area of what is now Superior Street, James Bay. Permission was later granted to sell this block in order to purchase other park space in the City.

Over years Beacon Hill Park has been the subject of extensive public debate, especially concerning the nature of its public use. In 1883 the Agricultural Association built stables and an exhibition hall at the head of Pendergast Street. The resulting massive public protest resulted in such structures being declared *ultra vires* to the original intention of the Trust.

A landscape architect of Scottish origin, John Blair, won the prize for the best plan in an 1888 City-sponsored competition. With a loan of $25,000 the project was begun. Blair developed Goodacre and Fountain lakes, both artificial, and some 2,000 trees and shrubs were acquired from the Thos. Meehan Nurseries, Philidelphia. These formed the base planting of the present park. Except for an ornamental lake scheme for the southeast quadrant the Blair plan has been largely followed.

The Robert Burns Memorial was erected in 1900, a "childrens' outdoor gymnasium" in 1911. For some years, from 1890, a zoo also operated within the park complete with bear pits and cages. The present animal enclosure is a 1975 addition. The bowling green and clubhouse were installed in 1910; the present structure is a 1981 replacement. The cricket pitch was established in 1866 and a clubhouse built in 1908-1909; the present Cottage style pavilion dates from 1980 (architects Bawlf Cooper). On the seafront at Douglas Street stands the Centennial "Mile Zero" monument marking the western terminus of the Trans Canada Highway (architect Rod Clack, 1958). The park is noted for its native Garry Oak groves, its fields of camas and naturalized daffodils, and extensive collections of exotic species.

**"Regents Park"
for David W. Higgins**
1885
1501 Fort Street, Rockland
Archt. H. H. Leslie

"Regents Park" was constructed for an energetic businessman who desired a leisurely retreat in the image of a country manse. At a cost of $8,000 D. W. Higgins built a large Victorian Italianate Villa set amid the orchards,

gardens, and meadows of a ten-acre estate. It was therefore a trendsetter for the new Rockland subdivision. In 1866 Higgins bought *The British Colonist* from fellow Haligonian Amor De Cosmos. "Regents Park" provided a fitting setting for Higgins' influential role in the economic, political, and cultural life of the community. The two-and-one-half-storey house is a fine example of the Picturesque Italianate, with vertical volumes receding behind a pedimented façade facing Fort Street.

Their luxurious residences still highlight Victoria's landscape. A coal mining overseer for the Hudson's Bay Company, Robert Dunsmuir was able to amass one of the largest fortunes on the West Coast with profits from the rich coal veins which he discovered at Nanaimo and Wellington. He built a conglomerate of related companies that included a steamship line, a railway, and a range of enterprises from the Albion Iron Works to *The Daily British Colonist* newspaper.

Craigdarroch was set among 27 acres of formal terraced gardens, orchards, and groves of oak trees developed by landscape gardener Hugh Campbell. Lodges guarded the entrances to a long curving driveway which led up to the main entrance. There were stables, barns and extensive kitchen gardens. The castle itself carried evocations of the Dunsmuir's ancestral homeland through a mixture of Jacobean, Scottish Baronial and castellated elements. The heavy stonework rises

**Craigdarroch Castle
for Joan and Robert Dunsmuir**
1885-1890

1050 Joan Crescent, Rockland
Archts. Smith and Williams, Portland

The keystone of Victoria's social aristocracy was the Dunsmuir family.

Craigdarroch Castle Estate, Rockland.
COURTESY CRAIGDARROCH CASTLE
HISTORICAL MUSEUM SOCIETY

through a Picturesque French Gothic ("Chateauesque") roofline, culminating the treed skyline. The numerous iron-braced chimneys serve a total of 35 fireplaces. The stone for the "Scotch Granite" columns and the building granite was quarried in British Columbia. Tile was brought from San Francisco, the leaded glass is believed to have come from Philadelphia, and the stately oak staircase and interior wood detailing were prefabricated in Chicago by the firm of A. H. Andrews. The castle is reputed to have cost more than $500,000. The first floor interior is lavishly finished in a fashion befitting the baronial scope of the exterior elevations. The huge mahogany fireplace in the library with its eclectic Elizabethan cum-Georgian mantle boasts the Baconian motto: "Reading maketh a full man" and complements the equally ornate entrance hall mantle with its quotation from Shakespeare's Troilus and Cressida, "Welcome ever smiles and Farewell goes out sighing." The dining room features a sumptuously decorated built-in oak sideboard and a fireplace which, like that in the library, is designed with split chimney flues to permit the insertion of an oval stained-glass window immediately above the mantle. Originally the ceilings on the main floor were frescoed: cupids, roses, birds and bees in the drawing room, fish and game in the dining room. These were done by a German artist, William Schaefer. Robert Dunsmuir died in 1889, the year that Craigdarroch was ready for occupancy. His widow, Joan Olive, took up residency in 1890, and from there kept a firm hold on the reins of the vast Dunsmuir financial empire until her own demise in 1908. Sold by the family for real estate subdivision after Joan Dunsmuir's death, Craigdarroch has served variously as a convalescent home for soldiers (1914-1918), as Victoria College (1920-1946), as headquarters for the Victoria School Board, and home of the Victoria Conservatory of Music. In 1959, when the building was threatened with demolition, a group of local citizens formed the "Society for the Maintenance and Preservation of Craigdarroch Castle" to preserve the building as an historic landmark. Today, restored and refurnished to period, it is open to the public for complete tours.

Charles Hayward House
1885

1003, 1005 Vancouver Street, Fairfield
Archt. John Teague

This is one of the most imposing versions of the Italianate townhouse in Victoria. Hayward, a member of the well-known undertaking firm, was Mayor of Victoria from 1900 to 1902. The detailing at the roofline, particularly the segmented pediment gable and eave brackets, are particularly bold when compared with other Victoria variants of the style.

House for Maurice Humber
1885

610 Gorge Road, Victoria
Archt. John Teague

Humber's elaborate Italianate home was no doubt intended as a display of his business wares. Humber owned one of the more successful brickyards in

in a series of Roman arches, attenuated corbelled turrets, Jacobean dormers, balconies, oriels, and tall, soaring Elizabethan chimneys. Above the granite walls, and juxtaposed against rough-hewn stone chimneys, the smooth planes of the slate roof provide a sharp contrast of texture and colour which enhances the overall vertical massing of this aggressively Victorian structure. Magnificently set in its grounds on one of the highest sites in the area, the structure is defined by the finial roof ornament as it rises above Victoria; he was also a contractor. The quoined corners, moulded brick window hoods, and ornamental chimneys are complemented by the boldly detailed eave brackets, a striking essay in the Victorian Italianate style.

The Davie home on Rockland Hill is a good example of the Italianate style as it was popularized throughout the West Coast during the 1880s. The house was constructed at a cost of $7,000 by the contractors Messrs. Hill and Conley. The two-storey bay window, balconied porch and bracketted, low-pitched roof are features which were shared by many houses built in a style which enjoyed immense popularity among Victoria's professional class during the 1870s and 1880s.

"Trebatha" for T. J. Jones
1886

1124 Fort Street, Rockland
Archt. (Restoration: John Keay)

Jones spent $8,000 to build the house in 1886 and for many years it was considered one of the city's finer examples of prestige housing. The fine panelled chimneys, Renaissance Revival dormer windows, and a mansarded roof along with wall siding and bands of patterned roof shingling are the major features distributed over symmetrical façade. As restored by architect John Keay this is one of the best examples of this once very popular commercial and domestic style known to Victorians as "Mansarded" or "Second Empire" (after its French Renaissance predecessors).

"Fairhome" for Dr. J. C. Davie
1886

630 Rockland Avenue, Rockland

St. Luke's Anglican Church
1888
3821 Cedar Hill Cross Road,
Cedar Hill, Saanich
Archt. Edward Mallandaine

St. Luke's Anglican Parish was formed in 1860 and their first Church opened on October 25, 1862. As the population in the Cedar Hill region expanded, so did the congregation. The foundation stone of the present church was laid in October 1887. St. Luke's was one of many rural churches built about this time for the ever-growing number of settlers who came out from England to farm the Saanich Peninsula. There is a series of interesting watercolours in the north aisle which shows how the little church nestled in among the rolling hills of the surrounding farmland. When built, it was a simple cross plan church with an east end side steeple at the rear. The north aisle was added in 1942 and the nave was extended to its present length in 1951. Both these extensions have been carried out in sympathy with the original scheme and materials.

"Gyppeswyk" for A. A. Green
1889
1040 Moss Street, Rockland
Archt. William Ridgeway Wilson

Art Gallery of Greater Victoria
1958
Archts. Clack, Clayton & Pickstone

Mrs. A. A. Green, a member of the Rainer family of Ipswich, England, named the house "Gyppeswyk," this being the old English name of her Suffolk County home town. Mr. Green was the manager of one of the early private banks, Garesche, Green & Co. The house was well sited in the centre of the estate amid extensive gardens and orchards, two tennis courts, coach house and stables. The exterior, a rather simple

composition of plane surfaces, was highlighted with fretwork applied to the clapboard facing. The house was approached via a sweeping driveway which directed the visitor to a *porte-cochere* which stood where the glazed breezeway to the art gallery addition now is. The generally symmetrical and not overly vertical massing culminated in a glazed lantern. Inside the two-storey entrance hall is finished in various imported woods polished to a high gloss which brings out the rich textures of the grains. The dramatic sweeping staircase is highlighted by the intricately ornate balustrading and the coffered Jacobean-type ceiling. "Gyppeswyck" became the Art Gallery of Greater Victoria in 1951. The striking Expressionist exhibit wing with it glazed breezeway connection to the old building was added in 1958 and a delightful garden feature is the authentic Japanese Shinto Shrine *ca.* 1900 (Meiji period). Made for the Hayashi family near Kobe, Japan it was sold for export in 1973.

"Ellesmere" for James Angus
1889
1321 Rockland Avenue, Rockland
Archt. L. B. Trimen

L. B. Trimen introduced the Tudor Revival to Victoria in houses like "Ellesmere," one of the few examples to survive. Built for Scottish merchant James Angus at a cost of $10,000, the handling of the stone and timber decorative elements make this an excellent example of a style reminiscent of its Jacobean ancestry. The attenuated Victorian proportioning of the windows in the façade bay is repeated in the slender chimney and in the general massing that is defined by the gables and the applied vertical black trim. To this is added a castellated stucco block protruding from the east elevation where two bands of rectangular windows complement the verticality of the Tudor entrance arch. These elements carry the eye upwards over the surface of the oriel crowded into the Jacobean gable.

Andrew Schnoter House
1890
116 South Turner Street, James Bay

The cubical Italianate house type was a favourite of the Victorian developers because of its simple construction requirements. The discriminating purchaser could, of course, order optional extras such as more, or less, decorated porches, bay windows, summer kitchens, eaves brackets, etc. A streetscape could then be varied, while the basic pattern repeated. 116 South Turner is one of a series of residences on South Turner so treated. Schnoter, from Mexico, operated cigar factories in Victoria and Vancouver.

"Roslyn" for Andrew Gray
1890
1135 Catherine Street, Victoria West

One of Victoria's most ornate renditions of the Victorian Queen Anne, the house is magnificently sited overlooking the Gorge waterway. It was built at a time when the Gorge was Victoria's playground. Patterned shingles, turrets, fretted brackets and finials (much of it probably pattern book ordered) contribute to this fanciful early industrialist's creation. The surrounding shoreline is now public park land. The restorations of the house in the early 1970s was one of Victoria's first public/private partnerships to conserve a heritage residential building.

"Pinehurst"
for William James Macaulay
1890

617 Battery Street, James Bay
Archt. Thomas Hooper
Restoration & Infill: Eric Barker, 1981

Although only the turret spire of "Pinehurst" can now be seen over the densely packed houses of what used to be an all but deserted coastline, the grounds of "Pinehurst" at one time opened out onto Dallas Road and the sea. Irish born W. J. Macaulay, a US lumber baron and banker, chose Victoria as his retirement home in 1890. Two congenial families occupied the house Macaulay built: William, his brother Alexander, and their wives who were sisters. Pinehurst was a substantial home in its day, costing about $25,000 to build. There were 18 rooms leading off the huge baronial entrance hall panelled in dark-stained local woods. Of the 18 fireplaces some featured tiles illustrated with scenes from the tales of Sir Walter Scott. The drawing room, which extended into the tower, adjoined a library, music room, billiard room, and large dining room. The house and part of the original extensive grounds were used as a focal point for a CRD mixed housing development. A full external restoration is complemented by three blocks of condominium units designed in sympathy to the scale and style of the original house.

Five Houses
1890-1897
1012 Richardson Street;
725, 731, 737, 743 Vancouver Street, Fairfield
Archt. John Teague

These Victorian Queen Anne style houses are virtually identical and were built from about 1890 to 1897 from designs by Victoria architect-mayor, John Teague. The mix of exterior textures and forms—double front gables, gable porches with bracket and spindle details, scalloped shingles and panel inserts which articulate the drop siding wall surfaces—constitutes the effect which the Picturesque aesthetic required. The row, restored in the 1980s, forms one of Victoria's finest Victorian streetscapes.

St. Saviour's Anglican Church
1891
310 Henry Street, Victoria West

Dominating the crest of a prominent rocky rise on Catherine Street, this cruciform plan Gothic Revival church is a Picturesque additive composition of elements. Vestigial buttresses tie the frame structure to its site. Pointed arch windows, many displaying fine stained glass, are tucked under the eaves and extended gables of the chancel and crossing. In scale and character it provides a good fit for this Late Victorian residential suburb.

Cuyler A. Holland House
1891
1564 Rockland Avenue, Rockland

Holland was a director of the British Columbia Land Investment Agency. The house is a traditional eastern Georgian Revival house type with a hint of the Victorian Italianate in its eave brackets and attached verandah. The unusual style for Victoria at this time, emphasized by the prominent siting, make the house a feature in Rockland.

Spring Ridge Emmanuel Baptist Church
1892

1900 Fernwood Road, Fernwood
Restoration and Conversion architect: John Keay

The 1892 church at the corner of Fernwood and Gladstone was attached to the earlier (1887) Baptist Church. Originally a Shingle style building, it features a corner tower and expansive banks of art glass windows on the two flanking gable façades. These light the raked galleries inside where the natural stained wood-work finishes have been retained for its new use. Over a period of some 15 years the church has been restored and adapted for use as a community theatre, aptly named The Belfry. The section of Gladstone Street in front is now a neighbourhood square featuring a pergola (architects Bawlf Cooper Associates).

British Columbia Protestant Orphanage
1892

1190 Kings Road, Hillside/Quadra, Victoria
Archt. Thomas Hooper

Originally sited on a large hilltop acreage with a magnificent view of the city, the Protestant Orphan's Home remains to this day one of the most significant architectural set-pieces in Victoria. It is a memorial to the charity of John George Taylor, who died in 1891 leaving $31,000 for child welfare work in the city. The managers of the bequest, Mr. A. A. Green and Mr. P. R. Brown, decided that the sum should be used to erect a new orphanage and immediate steps were taken to effect the purchase of a site. A local realtor, Mr. Owen Alsop (a founder of B.C. Land and Investment Agency), visited several orphanages while on a trip to England and presented the results of his enquiries in the form of a set of plans drawn up by a relative, London architect Mr. Thomas Alsop. The building Hooper produced, however, shows little English influence in its elevation and massing. It is one of those many variations deriving from the popular designs for Sever Hall at Harvard, Mass. (1878-1880), by the American architect, H. H. Richardson. Hooper was a keen admirer of Richardson's American vernacular style. The Victoria architect's Queen Anne shingled houses and aggressively rusticated churches such as the Metropolitan Methodist, all betray his early sympathy for Richardson. Familiar Richardsonian features here are the ample entrance arch flanked by towers, the general horizontal effect lent by the continuous bands of windows, the economical use of incised ornamental detailing, and the smooth planes of the slate roof. The warm red brickwork rising from a low granite base is now further softened by a covering of ivy, a sight the architect must have envisaged when he set the Orphanage among copses of oak and Oregon grape on the gentle rise of the slope. Equally interesting is the view from the rear, where the play of roof planes demonstrates an element of strength and massiveness very much lacking in most of Hooper's other buildings. To the detriment of the aesthetics of the site (although perhaps in sympathy to Taylor's original intentions) recent years have seen redevelopment of the grounds for low-cost community housing. The Orphanage now serves as a community centre.

"Hochelaga" for A. J. C. Galletly
1892
1715 Rockland Avenue, Rockland

The name (an old native Indian word for the present site of Montreal) belies the building's original function as the residence of a manager of the Bank of Montreal. As F. M. Rattenbury designed Galletly's town bank at the corner of Government and View, his name has long been associated with the design of the house, built in the Jacobean Tudor Revival idiom. There has been a significant loss of exterior detailing over the years although the interior is to a large degree intact.

Residence for Charles Robert Nairne
1893
642 Battery Street, James Bay
Archt. A. Maxwell Muir

Charles Nairne's house is a fine example of an architect-planned small Victorian bungalow. Its most interesting feature, however, is the balcony extension with a very low-pitched roof

which picks up and repeats the motif of the bay window roof planes. The curious attached "pergola-like" balcony extension was a common feature of the Picturesque housetypes of the Late Victorian period. They were intended to extend the living space of the house out into the landscape and give what were called "fine prospects" of the gardens. In this location another function would be to sample health-giving sea breezes especially at breakfast or afternoon tea.

"Schuhuum" for Hewitt Bostock
1894
1322 Rockland Avenue, Rockland
Archt. W. R. Wilson

"Schuhuum" is an Indian word meaning "windy spot." This was the name chosen by Mr. Bostock for the house that he built at a cost of $15,000 on the heights above what was then Belcher Avenue. The hallmark of Wilson's designs is the free-floating quality of the many only tenuously related architectural elements. It seems he had no more reservation concerning the mixing of style, than discipline in the massing or grouping of elements. In a very modern fashion his often ungainly exteriors express the interior spaces, which are imbued with the dramatic fluidity that was so popular among his early clients. Maclure designed the *porte-cochere* as a later addition ca. 1900.

House for Captain Jacobsen
1893
507 Head Street, Esquimalt

Often cited as Victoria's example of "steamboat Gothic," mainly because of the lavish application of decorative iron, fretwork, finials and shingles, the actual form is that of a Picturesque Second Empire or Mansard style. Dominant features of the design are the three-storey mansard tower and rooftop "widow's walk"—appropriate for this Finnish mariner's family.

South Ward School
(now South Park)
1894

508 Douglas at Beacon Hill Park, James Bay
Archt. W. R. Wilson

155

South Ward School derives its style from the early London Education Authority Schools built in response to the Elementary Education Act of 1870. Although Gothic Revival had been the official style for educational institutions, the red-brick Queen Anne style with origins among vernacular buildings of the seventeenth and early eighteenth centuries was thought more appropriate to the new mission of non-sectarian learning. Two hundred and sixty such schools were erected in London over the next 11 years. The Queen Anne style can easily be distinguished by the Picturesque charm of warm red brick rising to a height of three or four storeys, terminating in Dutch stepped gables which screen the steep, black-slate roofs. The chimneys are tall and economically detailed; large sash windows open up the walls and further the vertical emphasis of the structure. The external woodwork, gable brackets and trim, is painted white. South Park was a model for the red-brick schools that are fast disappearing from British Columbia's urban landscape which they at one time dominated. In this case, however, the school and adjacent industrial education wing have been meticulously restored by the Greater Victoria School Board.

By 1881 William Pendray's nearby factory was producing 9,000 pounds of soap per day. Later he branched into the production of Roman Meal. With the resultant fortune Pendray erected this Picturesque version of the American Queen Anne which had been popularized by the Eastern architect Henry Hobson Richardson. Shingles are used to create contrasting textural displays while the various structural elements rise gradually through a complex series of planes and voids, roof planes and gables to the peak of the tower. German artisans Muller & Sturn executed ceiling frescoes for the main rooms and the gardens feature the results of one of Pendray's recreational passions, a taste for late Victorian topiary display.

Alfred Briggs House
1896

154 South Turner Street, James Bay
Archt. George Mesher

The house was designed by George Mesher, a local architect who, in partnership with his son, built up one of the largest building and contracting firms in the region. The building is an

W. J. Pendray House
1895

309 Belleville Street, James Bay

example of the Queen Anne style complete with turret and magnificent stained glass windows.

Pemberton Memorial Operating Theatre
1896

Royal Jubilee Hospital
1900 Fort Street, Victoria

The hospital was founded in 1887, the jubilee year of Queen Victoria; thus its name. The foundation stone was finally laid in 1889. The octagonal operating theatre building, donated by J. D. Pemberton, is a small brick building capped by a hipped roof and lantern ventilator. Large windows admitted maximum light; the patient was placed in the centre of the room.

In the current scheme to expand the Royal Jubilee, the restored operating theatre and Pemberton chapel will be preserved within an historic precinct.

"Inglehurst" for P. Attwood-Wilson
1896
1023 St. Charles Street, Rockland

Built at a cost of $3,000 for Mrs. P. Wilson, this was one of the earliest Chalet style houses in Victoria. Only the tall ornamented chimneys and constricted bay window indicate a lingering Victorian influence. A brief suggestion of half-timbering in the gable, bracketed eaves and second-storey balcony and corner porch were later to become hallmarks of Maclure's work in this style. And although no records have come to light that prove Maclure's hand, this may be the case. Attwood-Wilson was employed by the E&N Railroad.

"Warburton" for Robert Verrinder
1896

1032 McGregor Avenue, Rockland

Dr. Rober Verrinder, medical doctor and dental surgeon, built the house on his arrival in Victoria. The various shingle patterns were requisite for the popular Victorian Queen Anne style, as is the domed corner tower, constructed to command a view across the city.

T. G. Mitchel House
ca. 1896

102 South Turner Street, James Bay

Built originally for Robert Dunn, the house was occupied by T. G. Mitchel, Chief Engineer with the Canadian Pacific Navigation Co. (forerunner of B.C. Coast Steamships). Built in the Italianate style and sited on a corner lot, the house anchors the South Turner group of heritage residences.

Robert J. Porter House
1896
649 Superior Street, James Bay
Archt. Samuel Maclure

Maclure designed this house and one for himself on adjoining lots. The Maclure family house still stands although it is unrecognizable, subsumed into a larger structure. Its neighbour, the Porter House, has been very well preserved. The Maclure home was a Shingle style bungalow and created something of a sensation when built because of its centralized plan of rooms around an open core. The Porter House is a less adventurous design, but incorporates many elements which were later to be developed into the hallmarks of Maclure's highly personal idiom. Two hipped roof bays project from the side elevations, betraying an interior cross-axial arrangement of interior spaces arranged around a central hall lit by a skylight. The symmetrical façade, centralized cross-axial plan, and extremely refined and articulated proportioning were to become the very personal signature of Maclure's later work. Here one can see its origins in a combination of the Classical cottage and Colonial Bungalow.

Irwin Browne Farm Houses
1896-1897
915, 929 Island Road, Oak Bay
Archt. J. G. Tiarks (?)

These two houses bear marks indicative of Tiarks: panelled chimneys, attached verandahs, one-and-half-storey gable Cottage design. 929 was used by the Browne family; the other was a speculative development. 929 survived in near original condition while 915 has been meticulously restored. Both represent good examples of rural farm houses in the region during this time.

Skene Lowe House
1897-1898

132 South Turner Street, James Bay

Lowe was an early Victoria photographer, although the house was first rented by C. R. King, a manufacturer's agent. It is an unusual house, aggressively Gothic Revival in character, with its gable porch and skirting verandah. The detailing is also very fine.

House for John Tiarks
1898

657 Lampson Street, Esquimalt
Archt. John Gerhard Tiarks

Victoria alderman, developor and architect, Tiarks probably built this house as a speculative or investment property. The dominant feature of this large T-plan Tudoresque cottage is the half-timbered gable ends of the massive roof. The impressive interior detailed in native woods has been restored to its original splendor by the current owners.

Victoria Exhibition Building and Race Track, Willows, Oak Bay, 1904. BCARS 122446

Prospect Place, Oak Bay

In 1891 the Victoria Electric Railway Company completed streetcar lines to Windsor Park and Willows Park race track. By 1898 it had been decided to improve Willows with a large exhibition fair complex, a project completed in 1899. At this crucial moment two of Victoria's more prescient development architects purchased 15 acres of land for subdivision purposes almost midpoint between the two parks, and fronting on one of the region's popular recreational beaches. Stuart Stark in his study *Oak Bay's Heritage Buildings* has pointed out the commissioning opportunities provided to some of Victoria's most prominent architects, including the principals of the scheme Francis Mawson Rattenbury and John Gerhard Tiarks. The subdivision itself, focussing on Beach Drive, Oak Bay Avenue, Prospect Place and San Carlos Avenue, also had an impact on the nearby adjacent development of York Place to the west. Prospect Place (probably so named because its bench-like situation above Beach Drive commanded magnificent views out across Oak Bay to Mount Baker and the distant Olympic Peninsula) conveniently provided a scenic driveway directly into Rattenbury's own waterfront property. Almost immediately Tiarks and

Rattenbury were building houses. One of Tiarks' first houses, a bungalow purchased by H. F. Hewett for $1,200, was moved to Saltspring Island in 1992. Rattenbury's house and grounds, now used as a private school, remains. Eight years later, just north of the subdivision, society architect Samuel Maclure would build his own family home (since destroyed). In 1912 Rattenbury was elected a reeve of Oak Bay's municipal council. Not far away, further south on Beach Drive, stretched the manicured meadows of the Oak Bay Golf Club with its Rattenbury designed clubhouse. In recent years some of the large lots have been infilled with quite sympathetic modern residences. There have, however, been some unfortunate losses. The Hewett House, formerly at 1580 Beach Drive, was important. It was one of the first in the development, built and designed by Tiarks. The Morehead House which stood at 2425 Oak Bay Avenue was an outstanding example of the "Macluresque" by architect W. D'O. Rochfort who had apprenticed with Maclure. A stroll though this precinct today provides an interesting glimpse into the aesthetically closed and socially cloistered world in which Victoria's architectural profession practiced.

NOTE *Ref.* Stark, Stuart. "Oak Bay's Heritage Buildings: More than just Bricks and Boards." 1995.

"Annandale"
for Sir Charles Tupper
1897-1898

1587, 1595 York Place, Oak Bay
Archt. J. G. Tiarks

The two houses Tiarks designed for this site set the tone for the neighbourhood and may have provided the impetus for the Rattenbury-Tiarks real estate venture. Sir Charles, son of the famous father of confederation, had formerly been Minister of Justice. His neighbour and Victoria law partner, the Hon. Frederick Peters, had been Attorney-General and Premier of Prince Edward Island. The two adjoining properties extended through to Prospect Place and featured extensive park-like gardens. Tiarks provided the two families with 100-foot by 70-foot identical houses, quintessential examples of the Colonial Bungalow style. The family private and social spaces were on the main floor, servants were contained in the half-storey above. The drawing room and dining room could be joined across the entrance hall by throwing back wide folding doors. Gable dormers were inserted into the massive hipped roofs which sheltered skirting verandahs. Sections of verandah could be temporarily glazed to provide "a comfortable winter promenade." The Peters house was destroyed in the 1930s but the Tupper house can still be delineated from its extensive additions.

**"Sandhurst"
for Arthur and Matilda Haynes**
1898-1899

1512 Beach Drive, Oak Bay
Archt. J. G. Tiarks

One of the first houses to be built on the Rattenbury-Tiarks subdivision, "Sandhurst" is a typical example of the Colonial Bungalow housetype in which Tiarks seems to have specialized. The additive Picturesque effect is *retardetaire*, compared to the Shingle style work of other architects during this period. Gable and shed dormers have been inserted into the roof; the verandah is treated as a lean-to element and a half-timber grid has been applied over the drop-siding to achieve an effect almost like interior panelling.

"Iechninihl" for F. M. Rattenbury
1898, 1913, 1914

1701 Beach Drive, Oak Bay
Archt. F. M. Rattenbury

Whatever else may said of Francis Mawson Rattenbury, architect, town planner, capitalist, and murder victim, "Ratz's" monuments were exotic inventions within the grand romantic tradition. Like his Shingle style hotels, his own home is the ultimate evocation of this romantic potpourri of old world charm, Arts & Crafts architectural innocence, and English country rusticity. The house itself is an additive combination (built in two stages) of seventeenth century style half-timber, nineteenth century English Gothic Revivalism, and additive Picturesqueness in the manner of English Victorian architects: George Devy, William Butterfield and Norman Shaw. The southern first wing is pure Shingle style with Ratz's characteristic vaguely French blind gables. The 1913 wing gives way to the half-timbered treatment of the English Arts & Crafts as practised by Samuel Maclure. The informal garden with its creeping ivy enveloping the house unites building and grounds.

A walk through the house is an artistic experience. Each window captures a different vista of the gardens through hanging ivy and copses of trees, with every now and then a glimpse of sea through alternating sequences of shady glades and pools of sunlight. In 1935 Mr. Ian Simpson bought the estate to found a boys' preparatory school, subsequently naming it Glenlyon after his former Scottish home on the Lyon River. Although the house has remained for the most part unaltered, various additions have been made in the grounds, including the renovation of the 1914 coachhouse, which Rattenbury had built for his Cadillac, "Black Pearl" and the chauffeur.

Conrad Schwengers House
1899-1900

1660 Prospect Place, Oak Bay
Archt. J. G. Tiarks

Despite the addition of a gabled bay the original symmetrical plan bungalow

is discernible with its half-storey gable marking central entrance verandah. The building has been raised and a side sunroom was moved to the rear when the lot was further subdivided.

"Briarbrae" for A. T. Goward
1904

1605 York Place, Oak Bay
Archt. F. M. Rattenbury

Goward was the Victoria manager of British Columbia Electric who by this time ran the Victoria tramway system. In 1923 he became vice-president. Essentially an Edwardian Classical design, the hipped roof shelters a half-timbered second storey above a shingled first. On the garden front Rattenbury leavened the effect with a hint of the romantic Queen Anne using his signature Gothic blind gable to mark a two-storey bay window.

"Arran" for Thomas S. Gore
1906-1907

1580 York Place, Oak Bay
Archt. Samuel Maclure

Gore was a civil engineer and no doubt had professional contacts with both Rattenbury and Maclure. For the magnificent site on a hilly rise, Maclure oriented his Chalet design to capture the eastern views to distant Mount Baker. A southern shed dormer contains the interior staircase. The natural granite foundations rise though a massive arch to support the first storey. The landscaping was developed and extended by various owners over the years and a stone lych gate found on Oak Bay Avenue orginally led into the garden.

Judge Peter Secord Lampman House
1907, 1924, 1927-1930

1630 York Place, Oak Bay
Archts. F. M. Rattenbury
Additions: S. Maclure, P. L. James and H. Savage

Rattenbury wrote home that he was designing for his friend Judge Lampman "something extra nice" because he would have to look at it often from his own property. Into the hillside above his house Rattenbury inserted a classic chalet, the eaves defined by bracketted bargeboards, and a pair of bay windows tucked under the second storey. Maclure, an occassional collaborator with Rattenbury, skillfully added a gabled

addition in 1924, maintaining the Arts & Crafts flavour of the original design. Maclure died in 1929 so it is appropriate that James and Savage, who had been associates of Maclure, sensitively completed the scheme (1927-1930).

C. Dubois Mason House
1908, ca. 1920

1525 Prospect Place, Oak Bay
Archts. F. M. Rattenbury
Alterations: Samuel Maclure

Rattenbury provided a tight hipped-gable Chalet design, shingle with Tudor Revival detailing. Almost as a note of whimsy, for which the architect was well known, he treated the front window bay as a bracketted balcony, a fleeting reference to the Bernese Oberlander housetype which provided the original inspiration for this house form.

"Shelin"
for Mrs. Catherine Watson
1909

1535 Prospect Place, Oak Bay
Archt. D. C. Frame

Frame, who had spent time in Rattenbury's office, approached the Chalet form here more in the manner of the California Bungalows then being spec built in Fairfield and Oak Bay. The clash of textures such as the heavy granite foundationwork against the more delicate detailing of the brackets and window elements belies a fastidious attention to the craft finishes applied throughout the original house.

J. W. Morris House
1912

1558 Beach Drive, Oak Bay
Archts. James & James

P. L. James was to work with Rattenbury on the designs for the CPR's Steamship Terminal and Crystal Gardens. His brother Douglas James had been in charge of the design work in Maclure's office for the huge 1907-1908 Hatley Park project for James Dunsmuir. The massive gabled window bay and heavy granite first floor plynth out of which the structure seems to rise are almost literal quotations from Hatley Park. However, the ponderous mix of stone, half-timbering and shingle, particularly the blind dormer (now lost in subsequent renovations) with medieval embrasure was very much Rattenbury as illustrated in his own house across the street.

F. Hamilton and E. Harrison House
1923

2390 Oak Bay Avenue, Oak Bay
Archt. Samuel Maclure

Harrison became chief accountant for the Government of British Columbia in 1929. His stucco finished cottage of a few years previous represents Maclure's more restrained post-war work for a period in Victoria's history when Edwardian boom-years were fading into a distant memory. The Prospect Place gate is also a Maclure design.

"Bide-A-Wee" for Mrs. J. D. Helmcken

1538 Beach Drive, Oak Bay
Archt. Samuel Maclure

P. L. James had designed the Helmcken family house on Moss Street very much in the manner of the then popular work of F. M. Rattenbury. This site had been purchased in 1903 for a summer cottage (thus the name). The widowed Mrs. Helmcken then commissioned a new home from Maclure. Maclure's very restrained design is almost a geometrical essey in the repeated solids and voids of gable and window motifs. The richly detailed interior exhibits finely crafted cabinetry and plasterwork.

Mrs. Florence Rattenbury House
1925

1513 Prospect Place, Oak Bay
Archt. Samuel Maclure

Rattenbury and his estranged wife were not on speaking terms and the lot and house were part of an acrimonious divorce settlement. It was probably Rattenbury who asked Maclure to do the house, just as he had taken over other Rattenbury commissions. The small stucco bungalow, Chalet in form and central plan, is unique in Maclure's work for its design simplicity, sensitive scaling of details but lack of ostentation.

Robert and Sara Gibson House
1919

1590 York Place, Oak Bay
Archts. F. M. Rattenbury,
Maclure & Lort

Rattenbury prepared the original drawings for this spectacular Georgian Revival house in 1914. Maclure's office finalized the design after the war in 1919. By this time Ross Lort, who had articled with Maclure, was about to take over Maclure's Vancouver office. The house represents the finest of Maclure's work in his Classical idiom which owed much to the post-war conservative climate and the influence of English architect Edwin Lutyens. The elevated site, on a rocky promontory, dominates Oak Bay. The plan, however, with its in-line public spaces accessed from a balconied hall and grand staircase to the rear, looks back to Maclure's earlier society commissions for Robin Dunsmuir and Ross Sutherland. For lumber baron Gibson, however, Maclure was able to demonstrate his mastery of the Classical vocabulary: the exterior with its tall arched windows and round headed dormers, stucco pilaster wall treatments, and a sumptous interior setting of polished mahogany millwork against Adamesque plaster detailing.

Patio Court for C. Walden
1927

2390, 2396, 2402, 2408, 2417
San Carlos Avenue, Oak Bay
Archts. K. B. Spurgin, J. G. Johnson

An investment and development project by Mr. Walden this group of five stucco-finish houses distinguished by garden patio entrances has been noted for its "story-book fantasy" appearance. The observation is true, but what is perhaps more revealing is the observation itself in that by 1927 the Norman varient of the Queen Anne with its whimsical tower turrets, flared steep pitched roofs, and embrasured gables which had been so effectively used by Rattenbury in his Shingle style houses and Rocky Mountain resort hotels some 30 years before—now become stylistic oddities.

Capt. and Mrs. Laurence Adamson House
1928

1590 Beach Drive, Oak Bay
Archt. K. B. Spurgin

Spurgin was noted for his "Macluresque" domestic work and here the Maclure bungalow form with a stucco finish, brick and timber detailing is more reminiscent of the European variants of the Arts & Crafts aesthetic as it began to make the transition to the simple cleaner lines of the International style.

Kathleen and Seldon Humphries House
1929

1621 Prospect Place, Oak Bay
Archt. Ralph Berrill

Kathleen was a daughter of James Dunsmuir, the source of numerous commissions for Maclure—including the Humphries own country estate on Lakes Road near Duncan in 1912. Maclure died in 1929, the year Humphries commissioned this Spanish Revival style home on one of the largest lots of the Prospect Place subdivision. The park-like landscape gardens were executed by William Westby who worked with Maclure on

Patio Court

Mrs. Butchart's huge garden project at Brentwood Bay. The grounds have since been further subdivided.

J. Harman House
1931

1586 York Place, Oak Bay
Archts. P. L. James & H. Savage

This tall Chalet house was built on a rock knoll, originally part of the Gibson estate for which Rattenbury, Maclure and Lort had produced their 1919 Georgian Revival masterpiece. Mrs. Harman was a Gibson daughter. James and Savage, both of whom had worked with Maclure, produced a design very much in the late Arts & Crafts manner wherein the buildings more faithfully reference their inspirational prototypes. The Harman house would therefore fit quite happily into a rural Bernese mountainside as it is devoid of Maclure's personal and uniquely West Coast marks, particularly his rationalization of form and handling of indigenous materials.

Barwin House
1992

1574 Prospect Place
Archts. Campbell Moore

An example of creative but sympathetically scaled Post-Modern infill—continuing the tradition of design quality which began with Rattenbury and Tiarks in the first years of this development.

Residence for Lyman P. Duff
1900
1745 Rockland Avenue, Rockland
Archt. F. M. Rattenbury

Lyman P. Duff, the son of an Ontario clergyman, arrived in Victoria in 1895 to open what was to become one of British Columbia's best known law firms. Duff rounded off his long and eventful legal career as Sir Lyman Duff, Chief Justice of Canada. The house is one of Rattenbury's most interesting designs. The two upper storeys are contained within a sweeping dormered roof which rests on a low ground floor built of rough-hewn field stone. It is a highly original design which demonstrates a thorough integration of many English and American precedents. The choice of shingles (which were originally unpainted) and rough-stone lower facing shows the architect's closeness to the American Arts & Crafts idiom of Richardson, and of his contemporaries, McKim, Mead, and White. The massing and graceful linear treatment of the roofline demonstrates direct references to the English school. Butterfield's chiselled dormers were a Rattenbury monogram combined with Norman Shaw's Queen Anne treatment of the Shingle style. The lyrical sweep of the gable-wall projection over the main entrance is reminiscent of the work of C. F. A. Voysey. The expansive sweep of the roof planes is emphasized by the moulded projection of the gable which briefly accents the main entrance immediately below. The interior features a beautiful staircase finished in handcarved fir and a landing lit by a large stained glass window which looks out on the garden below. The hall is panelled in West Coast cedar and the drawing room boasts a magnificent decorated plaster ceiling. The house is in excellent condition, although the decision to paint it at some time in its history has certainly detracted from the intended natural Arts & Crafts effect of the exterior.

North Dairy Pumping Station
1900
3940 Quadra Street, Quadra, Saanich

This solidly built brick industrial structure was constructed to house steam pumps for Victoria's Elk Lake supplied water system. Since 1927 it has served as a jam factory, cooperage, winery and now a restaurant. The arched brickwork in the gable front and windowed sidebays well illustrate corbelled coursing techniques.

Rev. William Bolton House
1901
649 Admirals Road, Esquimalt
Archt. Restoration: Peter Cotton, 1970

Bolton was the founder of St. Michael University School. The house, commanding magnificient views over Esquimalt Harbour, was built in the Arts & Crafts Chalet style. It features a verandah on two sides, a gable end sleeping porch, and three large

dormers on the west (harbour) side; also a slate roof. Architect Peter Cotton restored the house in 1970 as his own residence.

"Glenday" for John Day
1901
1382 Esquimalt Road, Esquimalt

Day was the proprietor of the Esquimalt Hotel, originally located in what is now the Dockyards. The Italiantate style is here enhanced with shuttered windows and a two-sided verandah surmounted by a balcony at the second storey.

"Beckley Cottage" for Richard and Mary Jackson
1901
427 Parry Street, James Bay

Demonstrating the transition from the decorative Victorian period to the more austere Edwardian, this cottage strives for a compromise between the two. Ornamentation is elaborate but suppressed to shingle patterns and abstract sunburst designs in the gable and brackets. Particularly unusual is the hint of Art Nouveau in the gabled bargeboard profiles. Jackson was the manager of the insurance division for the B.C. Land and Investment Co. The house was moved from Simcoe Street in 1980 and restored by the Heritage Building Foundation of the Hallmark Society.

"The Chalet" for Alice Galletly
1902
1737 Rockland Avenue, Rockland
Archt. F. M. Rattenbury

A. J. C. Galletly (who lived at 1715 Rockland Avenue) built this home for his sister, who kept house for him after the accidental death of his wife and daughter. Designed as a Shingle style chalet by F. M. Rattenbury, the house type is appropriate to its rocky hillside site. It is one of Rattenbury's more successful residential commissions, sensitively detailed with decorative eave brackets, porch and verandah railings in the manner of famous Alpine archetypes.

James Muirhead House
1903

223 Robert Street, Victoria West
Archts. Hooper & Watkins

Muirhead's millwork company supplied much of interior finishes and detailing for the Parliament Buildings. It is not surprising, therefore, that some hardware items bear a striking resemblance to those in Rattenbury's monument. The house is an agglomeration of Edwardian and Victorian details. The former identified from the horizontal bungalow form and Classical detailing of the porch; the latter is seen the profusion of ornamental detail and Picturesque roof line: particularly by the corner tower and bracketted gable bay.

C. W. Newbury House
1903

131, 133 South Turner Street, James Bay

This well-preserved Queen Anne house cost $2,000 when built and contributes to the heritage streetscape of South Turner Street. The house retains its original detailing, including the roof finials, which rarely survive in the climate of the Pacific Northwest. Newbury was a post office clerk.

Residence for Alexis Martin
1904

1558 Rockland Avenue, Rockland
Archt. Samuel Maclure

This house is representative of the Arts & Crafts domestic style that took Victoria by storm during the first six or seven years of this century. At the height of it, in 1903, the Lieutenant Governor's residence was designed by the two leading architectural proponents of the movement in Victoria: Francis Mawson Rattenbury and Samuel Maclure. It is Maclure's own version of the wide-gabled, ground-hugging, Shingle style and was possibly inspired by the work of Wilson Eyre near Philadelphia where Maclure studied painting during the 1880s. The plastic use of shingles above a solid field stone base, combined with the generous half-timbered façade gables and ample windows, unite the house both texturally and spatially with the heavily treed surroundings. The skillful arrangement of the interior space allows the hall to become the spatial core of the house, functioning as a central living room. All the rooms were panelled in natural fir with matching heavy ceiling beams. Light fixtures and all the hardware were handcrafted according to original designs in an Art Nouveau flavour. The original furnishings were from the two leading craft furniture designers of the day, Gustav Stickley of Syracuse, New York, and Baillie Scott of England. The house was the subject of a feature article published in the New York magazine *The Craftsman*, in 1908, an event which gained Maclure an international reputation.

Cecil Roberts House
1904

913 Burdett Street, Fairfield
Archt. Samuel Maclure

A variation of Maclure's Chalet house-type, the original structure, and alterations made in 1920, were both designed by Samuel Maclure. The structure is well preserved and enhances the scale and character of the Cathedral Hill Precinct. Major Cecil Roberts, the original owner, moved to Victoria in 1888 and became Chief Draftsman with the Provincial Surveyor-General. He resigned in 1911 to open his own land surveying company.

"Hesket" for Joseph Wilson
1905

811 St. Charles Street, Rockland
Archt. Samuel Maclure

On the death of William Wilson, Joseph Wilson became president of the family retail clothing business, a position he retained from 1900 to 1945. His house was one of Samuel Maclure's early Edwardian Tudor Revival designs where the soon-to-become-familiar elements of Maclure's Arts & Crafts vocabulary—half timbering, brick,

shingle—have not yet achieved the masterful assured cohesion of his later work. In 1925-1926 Maclure designed alterations.

Biggerstaff Wilson Residence
1905

1770 Rockland Avenue, Rockland
Archt. Samuel Maclure

Biggerstaff Wilson was one of five sons of William Wilson, the renowned Victoria clothier and wholesale grocer. Sited among massive oaks and maples, well back from Rockland Avenue, the house remains one of the most impressive and best preserved of Maclure's work. It represents Maclure at the height of his "Medieval Revival" Arts & Crafts period. The decorative timberwork, Elizabethan chimneys, and mullioned windows all conjured up evocative romantic associations of the long-lost age of supposed feudal grandeur and rustic simplicity. This saccharine coating of old-world charm belies a structure which manifests all the rigid discipline of a centralized plan, symmetrical Neo-Georgian massing, and late Victorian convenience. For the overall effect is not that of an additive, rambling Gothic structure, but of a carefully thought-out building, designed to accommodate a range of domestic and social requirements. Maclure supplied a stately mansion fit for a country squire, complete with a grand baronial hall richly panelled in unpolished local woods and fenestrated with delicately patterned art glass. The hall features a massive fireplace beneath the second storey balcony, and a sweeping dramatic staircase. The garden plan, much influenced by the current writings of Gertrude Jekyll, survives and is also a Maclure design.

"Dalhousie Bungalow" for W. Warburton
1906

941 Meares Street, Cathedral Hill, Fairfield
Archt. Samuel Maclure

William Lorimer House
1907

122 South Turner Street, James Bay

This well-designed Edwardian bungalow makes a distinctive feature of the verandah and sleeping porch by accenting the columns in a Classical manner. The pedimented eaves and half-timbered gable demonstrate a concern with textured effects so characteristic of James Bay architecture in all its periods.

Bill Lorimer was a bookkeeper for R. Porter & Sons, a large wholesale and retail butcher business. The house cost $3,500 when built.

"Illahie" for Charles Fox Todd
1907

1041 St. Charles Street, Rockland
Archt. Samuel Maclure

One of the most Elizabethan of Maclure's designs, this house for Brampton-born C. F. Todd features a Picturesque gabled roof line, a complex symmetrical plan and large entrance porch. The half-timbered upper storey rests on a random ashlar ground storey and the building is capped by a series of stately Queen Anne chimneys. The interior entrance hall is one of Maclure's finest spaces and the landscape design is probably also by Maclure. Todd became a partner in his

This house and garden won a Residential Award of Merit in 1985 from the Hallmark Society for "the meticulous restoration and preservation." The small Chalet style cottage brings together the low profile of the colonial bungalow, half timbering in the Tudor Revival style, and Picturesque qualities of the Alpine chalet. It was built for W. Warburton, an accountant with Windsor Groceries.

father's canning firm, J. H. Todd & Sons (Horseshoe Brand Salmon), in 1877.

Frederick Jones House
1907
1759 Rockland Avenue, Rockland

F. W. Jones moved to Victoria from Montreal, leaving behind a career that saw him rise from CPR telegraph boy to manager of Producer's Rock & Gravel Co. and founding president of the B.C. Red Cross Society. His house in Rockland is a large Tudor Revival structure with extensive verandahs to take advantage of the superb views from its advantageous siting. The garden, driveway and *porte-cochere* were designed by Maclure for a later owner, Lieutenant-Governor W. C. Nichol (1927). The granite banked driveway, rising from the hillside below, cleverly controls a 180-degree vista as one approaches the house.

Residence for Dr. C. F. Newcombe
ca. 1907
1381 Dallas Road, James Bay

More reminiscent of British India than anything else, this rather fine Georgian revival structure was built for Dr. Charles F. Newcombe, prominent anthropologist, historian, biologist and medical man. He moved to Victoria from Oregon with his family in 1885 and very soon became active in the Victoria Natural History Society, collecting specimens which were later incorporated into the collections of the Provincial Museum. After Dr. Newcombe's death in 1924 his son, William Arnold Newcombe, continued to reside here. William specialized in the history, customs, and material culture of the Haida nation. Between 1928 and 1932 William was curator of biology at the Provincial Museum. The two-storey red brick structure features an imposing ground floor verandah and second-floor balcony. The Georgian Revival flavour is suggested by a number of obvious references: the horizontal windows in the verandah, the Doric portico balcony, and the balustraded roofline.

Arthur M. Coles House
1907

851 Wollaston Street, Esquimalt
Archt. F. M. Rattenbury
Restoration and Infill: W. Patterson, 1995

Shingled walls rise into a complex hipped and gabled roof from a rubble granite foundation course; on the garden side this course defines the entrance stair and first floor and to the east side is attached a heavy timbered balcony. The hip roof contains a half-timbered second floor and the tall Queen Anne chimney compliments the Rattenbury signature element on both fronts, a shingled Gothic gable. The house is a masterful melange of the architect's own personal response to the historicist Arts & Crafts vein which Maclure and others also mined so well. The colourful restoration was financed by duplexing the house and bracketing it on each side (in what was an extensive rock garden) with a range of new residences finished as more restrained versions of the Picturesque Queen Anne.

Wollaston Street view.

Uplands Residential District

Planned 1908; Developed 1909-1996
Architects: Olmsted Bros., Seattle

Originally a Hudson Bay Co. farm, the 465 acres now comprising Uplands were purchased in 1907 by a consortium headed by W. W. Gardner, and prepared for subdivision. An idyllic site, even as a farm, the area covered an expanse of gently sloping landscape interspersed with copses of Garry Oak, Maple, Douglas Fir, rock outcropping and grassland along three miles of ocean frontage. One of the best known firms of American landscape architects, Olmsted Bros., probably working from their Seattle office, planned the subdivision. The garden city concept, based on such European precedents as Letchworth in England, the work of Edwin Lutyens, E. W. Godwin, and others, was just peaking in America and England. Ebenezer Howard's book, *Garden Cities Tomorrow* published in 1902, was a strong influence in contemporary planning. The Uplands plan, as conceived by the Olmsteds and for the most part executed, combines a number of fashionable aesthetic and ideological predilections. It acknowledges the Edwardian Classical concern with the processional, while tempering it with Arts & Crafts concessions to the integrity of environment and unmolested landscape. The plan was oriented about a central axis, Midland Way, a broad, straight avenue sited between two crescents. Following the contours of the land, tree-lined boulevards web outward in a series of carefully modulated and graceful curves. Whatever the viewpoint, houses and lanes melt quietly away through a series of informal tree-fringed glades. At the same time, the lay of the lots, on five benches sloping gently toward the sea, maximized access to ocean and mountain vistas. All utilities were underground; street lighting utilized ornamental cast iron standards; small greens and parterres were designated open spaces; monumental gate posts marked the principal entrances; and a streetcar link was provided with downtown.

Following the firm's suggestions, sale contracts included a number of stipulations: residences should be built within a specified time and be equal in value to at least half the price of the lot and in any case not cost under $5,000; lots ranged from .26 acre to 3.5 acres; no commercial buildings or multiple dwellings; no livestock except horses; house plans subject to approval by Uplands Ltd.'s own architectural consultant (for many years F. M. Rattenbury); and no fences within 25 feet of the street line. Also on the Olmsteds' recommendation that a club be established

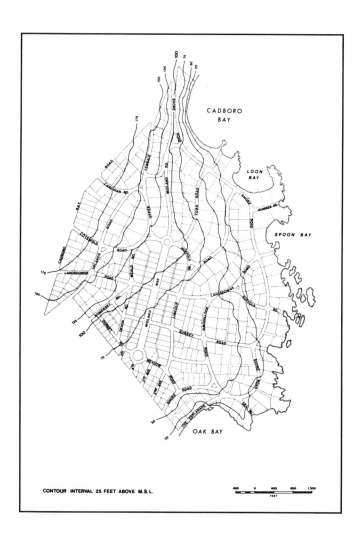

in the area, the Royal Victoria Yacht Club was given its present location and a golf course was established. The results belied the promotional expectations.

Pre-1914 only 83 lots out of the 424 total were sold. By 1914 only nine houses had been constructed; by 1930, 34 houses; by 1945, 235. In 1946 the Uplands Company traded, in lieu of back taxes, a 65-acre parcel of land stretching from Midland Avenue to the waterfront in the southern sector of the development which is now Uplands Park. While this manoeuvre may have kept the Company afloat, it seems difficult to justify the open space in terms of necessity, since the development is itself generous with park amenities at everyone's front door. It also had the effect of slicing through the symmetry of the Olmsted plan, choking the logic of the plan in the southern sector. As a consequence, the grand Edwardian axial set-piece, Midland Avenue, has never been executed.

View north, Midland Way, Uplands.

University School Limited
1908, 1911, 1924
3400 Richmond Avenue, Mount Tolmie, Saanich
Archt. Thomas Hooper

Founded in 1906 by Rev. William Washington Bolton, rector of St. Paul's Esquimalt, the school was a shareholder-owned enterprise which amalgamated a number of earlier Victoria private schools. The 15-acre site was purchased in 1908. Hooper established the style and ambiance of what has since become a large educational complex with a substantial red brick Queen Anne central block "School House." Symmetrical in plan and elevation the formal front is dominated by a pedimented entrance bay and the dormered hip roof dominated by a peaked bell tower. Other buildings have followed in simplified versions of the Queen Anne. Among the earlier ones are the Chalnor block by Hooper the same year, the east dormitory in 1911, and the gambrel roof headmaster's house in 1924.

"Wilmar" for William Todd
1908
944 St. Charles Street, Rockland
Archts. Samuel Maclure
Restoration and Infill: Jordon Mills, 1994

W. C. Todd was a principal, with his father and brother, in the very successful J. H. Todd & Sons, West Coast salmon processors and commission agents. This was one of Maclure's few residential commissions to show the marked influence of the Californian Mission style. After falling into serious disrepair the house was saved by inclusion in a very sympathetic condominium infill project to the rear of the property. This won a Victoria Real Estate Award for both restoration and townhouse design the following year.

"Chapola" for F. Landsberg
ca. 1908
106 Medana Street, James Bay

An imposing Edwardian bungalow, the dominating feature of this house is the high-quality stained glass. The glass, rustic brick foundations and boulder column bases are Arts & Crafts features and introduce a series of residences on Medana which are all good period examples in this idiom. Landsberg moved to Canada from the Ukraine in 1879, moving to BC in 1884 to establish a business.

Pemberton Memorial Chapel
1909
Royal Jubilee Hospital
1900 Fort Street, Victoria
Archt. J. C. M. Keith

Mrs. J. D. Pemberton donated the chapel. It is a simple round arched nave with a slate saddle roof nave to which is added a five-sided apse. The interior, however, shows how competently Keith could handle the Arts & Crafts decorative vocabulary. The bracketted heavy timber roof is revealed and decorated with stencil work. Stained glass, v-joint wainscotting, wood panelling and matching furnishings complete the scheme.

"Rosemead" for T. H. Slater
1909

429 Lampson Street, Esquimalt
Archt. Samuel Maclure

Slater, a successful realtor and Arts & Crafts enthusiast, commissioned from Maclure one of his largest, if most ponderous, half-timber Chalet style houses. The heavy stonework of porch and *porte-cochere* plays against the rich textured mix of leaded casement windows, shingle and half-timber treatment surfaces all enclosed within the sweeping gable bargeboards of the massive roof. The interior is organized about an impressive two-storey hall dominated by a large tiled fireplace and staircase.

"Rappahannock" for Herbert Bowen
1910

1595 Rockland Avenue, Rockland
Archt. Samuel Maclure

A large, shingle and half-timbered design by Samuel Maclure, this house was intended to make the most of its magnificent siting with the marvelous view out across Fairfield and Juan de Fuca Strait. The granite wall on Rockland features Arts & Crafts style ironwork also from Maclure's designs. Herbert Bowen was a prominent realtor.

Canadian Bank of Commerce
1910

2420 Douglas at Bay Street, Victoria
Archts. Darling and Pearson, Toronto

This is one of the few remaining prefabricated banks which were once a common sight in western Canadian communities. The design for this prefab bank, like that of its many duplicates, was adapted to patented sectional construction units which were mass produced in Vancouver by

manufacturers such as the B.C. Mills, Timber and Trading Company. The sections arrived complete with window frames, doors, and decorative detailing, ready to assemble on site. Its Classical style, then the hallmark of respectable banking institutions, is supplied by the symmetrical façade composed of wood-trim pilasters, an entablature, and the gable with an occulus window. The interior of the banking room is essentially unaltered with much of the early oak furnishings still evident. The building form originated in Ontario, where the compact simplicity of the design with its austere Classical proportions was a common domestic idiom. The shingle treatment of the second storey reflects the regional influence of British Columbia Arts & Crafts taste.

"Bannavern" for William Galliher
ca. 1910

914 St. Charles Street, Rockland
Archt. P. L. James

The Honourable Justice W. A. Galliher, known in his youth as "Wild Bill" Galliher, joined Sir Garnet Wolseley's "Canadian Voyagers" in a Nile expedition for the relief of General Gordon. The imposing Georgian Revival residence was designed by society architect P. L. James, a sometime associate of F. M. Rattenbury. Elements of both Rattenbury and Maclure can be found in the design which features a cross-axial plan, balconied central hall, and the fashional mix of half-timbered and Shingle style exterior finish.

Simon Leiser House
1911

1005 St. Charles Street, Rockland
Archt. Samuel Maclure

German-born Simon Leiser arrived in Victoria in 1873 and developed a thriving coffee and spice retail business which expanded into one of the largest BC grocery companies. His house is a large, although unpretentious, Arts & Crafts style building featuring a shingle and half-timbered façade. One curious detail is the manner in which Maclure brings down the vertical timber elements into the sill course.

George Sangster House
1911

161 South Turner, James Bay

This very well-preserved residence is a good example of Edwardian Classical

style. The design is severely geometric but not unornamented. Narrow drop siding creates densely textured wall surfaces, relieved only by the granite foundation and entrance porch columns.

The enclosed porch is balanced by a shallow window bay and the second-storey windows are tucked against the eaves. The sills, linked by a single moulding, skirt the house. The proportions, so delineated, are repeated in the arrangement of the window lights.

Victoria High School
1911
1260 Grant Street, Fernwood
Archt. C. Elwood Watkins

An imposing Edwardian Classical monument, two three-storey wings flank the main south facing façade block. The Ionic portico dominates an extensive park-like setting and an arched version of this feature is repeated in east and west wings. The very fine brick detailing articulates a decorative system of corner quoins, pilasters and panels relieved by strong horizontal bands of terracotta and a dominant cornice entablature at the roofline. When built, newspapers of the day boasted that construction costs per square foot exceeded those of the Parliament Buildings. Vic High introduced a new design formula to Victoria wherein the Classical superseded the Queen Anne. This new style was illustrated in subsequent Watkin's commissions: Oaklands (1912-1913), Burnside (1913), Monterey (1914) and also Tolmie (1912, architect H. J. R. Cullin).

Andrew Bechtal House
1911
1385 Rockland Avenue, Rockland
Archt. William D'O. Rochfort

Bechtel, an American who came to Victoria in 1873, was an early local hotelier. His house combines elements of both the Tudor and Georgian Revival. The generous proportions, splayed hipped roof and symmetrical façade designed around the central entrance porch and granite stair are typical of the Edwardian Classical Revival.

solicitor, who became solicitor for the Grand Trunk Railroad in 1910. The house is a very fine example of the California Bungalow, built on a solid granite foundation which reaches up into the verandah piers. The dormered sleeping balcony and entrance porch are marked by elaborately detailed gables, a feature of the California Arts & Crafts style.

James T. Reid House
1912
1393 Rockland Avenue, Rockland
Archt. P. L. James

Charles M. Lamb House
1912
2450 Windsor Road, Oak Bay
Archt. Samuel Maclure

A more elaborate version of its immediate neighbour, the house features a similar half-timbered second storey but the projecting hipped bays flanking the recessed entrance give the form a bolder profile. This is another variant on the Edwardian Georgian-Tudor house type.

Situated in what was originally a "country" residential district developed by B.C. Electric this central plan bungalow features a steep commodious roof with generous eaves, protecting the board-and-batten siding walls. It is contemporary with similar brick and stucco cottages of C. F. A. Voysey in England at this time. A commodious porch in its southern side demonstrates the concern of both architect and client that the surrounding garden be integrated with the body of the house. In all these informal bungalows, most of them actually serving as summer cottages, Maclure shows a deep appreciation for the utility of the Arts & Crafts approach to house construction. In its proper place this provides a pleasant and welcome relief to the more formal designs demanded by urban public lifestyle where social image was paramount.

Eric and Harriet Ulwin House
1912
1442 Rockland Avenue, Rockland
Archt. E. E. Green, Seattle

Eric Ulwin owned the house for one year. It was then purchased by D'Arcy Tate, an Irish-educated barrister and

Mount Edward's Apartments
1912
1002 Vancouver Street, Fairfield

Mount Edward's was one of Victoria's earliest apartment blocks. The three-storey pressed red brick structure exemplifies the Edwardian Classical style. The square-columned entrance way, the frieze detailing in brick below the heavy tin cornice, delineation of the attic storey with banded brick courses, and the symmetry of façade design are elements which recall the great family palazzos of Renaissance Rome and Florence. The original windows were all double-hung sash.

The scheme is a symmetrical plan with enough variety to render the finished product both neat and attractive. The commodious hipped roof which snuggly shelters the cedar board-and-batten walls contains a roomy second floor with ample sleeping accommodation. The south elevation is almost perfectly symmetrical with the generous overhang of the roof protecting the front porch. The porch opens into the dining room and living room through two sets of French doors. Under protecting gables on the east and west sides are housed a garden verandah and a small *porte-cochere*. The interior arrangement consists basically of four rooms grouped around the central entrance porch and stairwell. An indication that the setting was as important as the dwelling is that Maclure felt it necessary to also plan the landscaping.

Residence for Arthur Gore
1912

1502 Belmont Avenue, Rockland
Archt. Samuel Maclure

The Gore House represents Maclure's innovative solution to the problem of low cost but individualized housing through the use of local, durable materials. Arthur Gore was a partner in the firm Gore and MacGregor, which specialized in blueprinting, draughting and survey instruments. As Mr. Gore was Maclure's blueprinter, the house was perhaps more personally supervised than most.

Residence for George Richardson
1912

1005 Moss Street, Rockland
Archt. Samuel Maclure

For the Richardson family Maclure designed a version of a typical Victoria upper middle-class home. This hipped roof, rectangular and symmetrical house type, with only slight variations in detail, can still be found in amazing numbers in the older but better residential districts in Victoria. In other examples of this type, the black timberwork set against the white plaster tantalizes the eye from behind a variegated screen of foliage. This camouflages the real source of the design, as from any angle the elevations are symmetrical and formal: the balanced façade fenestration pattern, the paired chimneys rising from the roof hips, the squared bay window projections on either side, the horizontal division of the elevations into equal parts, and the vertical bipartite division of the side elevations by projecting bay windows reveal the inspiration of English Georgian. As in elevation, so in plan, the house is thoroughly eighteenth century, with four first-storey rooms grouped symmetrically around a central stairwell.

Residence for H. Goulding Wilson
1912

608 St. Charles Avenue, Rockland
Archt. Charles King, San Francisco

Sombre brown colouring, frank expression of materials and construction elements, broad overhanging gabled roofs, beams extended into trellisses, horizontal masses merging with the garden; these are stylistic elements of the western Arts & Crafts architecture which reached its peak of quality with the Greene brothers and Bernard Maybeck in California during the early 1900s. The Wilson residence is Victoria's most eloquent statement in this style. King was himself a California architect working in the shadow of Maybeck,

Green & Green, and the followers of Frank Lloyd Wright. The house was designed for the Wilsons while they were on honeymoon in California. It is an excellent example of an idiom which drew together Japanese approaches to wood architecture, Wright's Arts & Crafts sympathy for native materials and his suppression of the vertical in Prairie School residences, and H. H. Richardson's Shingle style plastic manipulation of surfaces. Through the use of rough and stained timbering, textured brick courses at regular intervals to emphasize the horizontal and protuding beams, and rambling trelliage which blurs the transition from interior to exterior space, the structure merges with its arboreal setting.

Residence of Thomas Hooper
1912

243 Kingston Street, James Bay
Archt. Thomas Hooper

By 1912 Thomas Hooper had become one of British Columbia's foremost public architects vying even with F. M. Rattenbury for top honours. This residence is one of the few remaining examples of his domestic work, although it has been moved from its original location at the southwest corner of Belleville and Menzies (see page 126). The gables, columns, and round headed windows carry obvious Classical references, but the generous eaves, commodious massing of the gable and roof elements and the plastic handling of the clapboard and shingle siding demonstrate that he was still very much under the spell of contemporary Eastern American Shingle style fashion mongers.

Residence for H. S. Griffith
1912
2906 Cook Street, Hillside/Quadra, Victoria
Archt. Henry Sandham Griffith

Now known as "Spencer's Castle," this residence perched on top of a rock outcrop overlooking the city of Victoria was designed by one of its fashionable early twentieth century architects for himself. Working within the half-timber idiom already firmly established in this region by such architects as Trimen, Maclure, and Rattenbury, the house is a combination of miniature castle (which is suitable to its site) and English Gothic Revival vernacular (in accordance with its domestic function). These evocations are limited to its decorative motifs, the tower, and timberwork. In the handling of the materials, the general massing, and the regularity of the plan, the structure betrays heavy Georgian-revival influence. Griffith was noted for the many stone residences he designed for a large clientele in the Victoria region. The building now serves as a community centre for the nearby condominium development.

Lewis Finch House
ca. 1912
1069 Joan Crescent, Rockland

L. A. Finch, with his brother Perry Finch, were proprietors of Finch & Finch, "men's furnishings" on Government Street. The house is

Rockland's best example of the California Bungalow style. The mix of rough "natural" materials such as random ashlar and shingle used to highlight the joinery of the porch and gable timberwork is typical of the style.

James Helmcken House
1912
1015 Moss Street, Rockland
Archts. James and James

The architectural firm of James & James designed this house for Dr. J. D. Helmcken, the Edinburgh-trained son of the famous Honourable J. S. Helmcken. This imposing Arts & Crafts style house, with obvious references to the domestic work of P. L. James' sometimes better known associate, F. M. Rattenbury, combines elements of the Tudor Revival and the American Shingle styles. The grounds are a good example of informal Edwardian landscaping.

Jim Woods House
1913
2667 Empire Street, Hillside/Quadra, Victoria

Commanding a wide prospect southward over Victoria, this California Mission style residence reinforces Victoria's long-standing north-south connections. The adobe-like white stucco structure is detailed with baroque profile parapets. The round arched windows and pantile roof verandahs were distinguishing marks of the style.

Frederick Nation Residence
1913
1320 Rockland Avenue, Rockland
Archt. Samuel Maclure

The house was designed by Samuel Maclure for F. Nation, a Manitoba department store magnate and director of The Great West Life Assurance Co. This huge building, with its half-timbered gable, large hipped roof

and towering chimneys, granite ground storey and balconied second floor verandahs, is still a major monument on The Rockland escarpment.

Lampson Street School
1913

670 Lampson Street, Esquimalt
Archt. Thomas Hooper
Restoration: Campbell Moore

Dominating its magnificent hilltop site, the school is a landmark for the Viewfield valley. When built, it was acclaimed for its modernity: reinforced concrete construction finished in redbrick, limestone and terracotta detailing to announce the Edwardian Classical Revival style. A central block is flanked by two wings (for boys and girls). A formal entrance defined by paired stone columns and crenelated parapet is approached by a stone double staircase which supports an impressive terracotta balustrade. After nearly two decades of dereliction, the building was recently completely upgraded and restored for educational use.

Ross Anthony Lort House
1913

811 Linkleas Avenue, Oak Bay
Archt. Ross A. Lort

Although Lort was articling in Maclure's office at this time, we can presume he designed this Chalet style home for himself. It is markedly non-Maclure in its direct English Arts & Crafts references, mainly M. H. Bailey Scott in the stucco finish, strong verticality of design, flush gable treatment and manner of the side eaves returns. Quite unique is the extended peak gable under which is tucked a projecting central window bay and porch, these elements treated as an additive feature and united by heavy timber details and wide shiplap cladding.

Harry Beasley House
1913

943 St. Charles Street, Rockland
Archt. Samuel Maclure

Harry Exeter Beasley made an early career in railways: 1898-1900 first CPR superintendent of the Kootenay District, ultimately becoming managing director of the E&N Railway. The shallow hipped floating roof planes and severe geometry of the detailing reveal the influences of Frank Lloyd Wright's Prairie style houses of this period.

Victoria Normal School
1913

Camosun College
1950 Lansdowne at Richmond,
Mt. Tolmie, Saanich
Archt. W. C. F. Gillam, Vancouver

This magnificently sited building was the product of Victoria's ambitions and efforts to obtain an institutional match to the University of British Columbia in Vancouver. The site was acquired in 1911, seven-and-one-half acres in what was then rural countryside on Mount Tolmie, overlooking both the city and Juan de Fuca Strait. The final set of plans allowed a contract price slightly in excess of the $300,000 limit for buildings and equipment but was thought to justify the extra cost because this scheme would enable more extensive use of local labour and materials. The revision included the replacement of terracotta ornament with sandstone, the results of which are sadly evident today in the corrosion of the decorative details. The contract was let to a Victoria firm, Luney Bros., and practically all the materials were locally procured, except for the slate from a Welsh quarry. The building was to accommodate about 150 student teachers enrolled in a one-year elementary program. The basic teaching areas around which the layout was designed were two model schools complete with classroom, cloakrooms, washrooms, and furnishings. Apart from this there were nine lecture rooms, two laboratories, a music room, and two complete housekeeping suites. An auditorium with a seating capacity of 400 was centrally located in the rear of the building. The clock tower housed a water tank for the fire alarm sprinkler system. The two-and-one-half storey structure, 76 by 313 feet, is symmetrically oriented about the 95-foot clock tower. The Renaissance Revival style is detailed with quarry-cut sandstone and red-clay brick. The ornament is concentrated on the entrance block which is defined by the central clock tower. Above the entrance is a Classical pediment which is constructed of smooth rusticated sandstone blocks. The general massing emphasized a palatial horizontality which, along with its spacious formal Italian garden landscape scheme, was intended to convey the Victorian idea of a Renaissance Villa. Gillam finished the building with an ornately decorated auditorium which today is the high point of the interior. The School served its original function until 1942 when it

Learning Resource Centre, Camosun College. Arthitects Wade Williams, 1991.

was converted into a Military Hospital. In 1946 the Normal School and Victoria College (the two had shared Craigdarroch Castle during the war) moved back. In 1967 both moved to the Gordon Head campus at the University of Victoria. Since that time the buildings have housed the Institute of Adult Studies later incorporated as Camosun College. These include the Paul Building (1961) from the Victoria College period, and more recently the Fisher Building (1981), Lazere Building (1989), Learning Resource Centre (1991) by architects Wade Williams as part of the Camosun campus. On the west side of the grounds on Richmond Avenue can be found an original VER streetcar shelter.

"Glenlyon" for John Ross
1914
908 St. Charles Street, Rockland

John Ross lived in the house only one year. Thereafter, it was occupied by the widow of James S. C. Frazer, who had been a manager of the Bank of Montreal. By 1914 "Tudor Revival" was the requisite style for a fashionable Victorian home and the half-timbering was literally applied to almost any house type—in this case, a Georgian Revival design, set firmly on a rustic granite plynth.

R. D. Finlayson House
1914
2391 Beach Drive, Oak Bay
Archt. Samuel Maclure

In 1914 Maclure was approached to design a house for R. D. Finlayson, Jr.

The location was choice: a gently sloping bench a few metres from the seashore. The Finlaysons were one of Victoria's founding families, scions of the Hudson's Bay Company establishment. R. D. Finlayson, Sr. had been chief factor at Fort Victoria. Roderick, Jr., who had qualified as a surveyor, inherited the vast family real estate holdings of his father and married the daughter of an HBC chief commissioner.

The Finlayson home is one of Samuel Maclure's finest and most personal architectural statements. It combines, in subtle harmony and with quiet understatement, most of the stylistic themes he had pursued over the preceding 14 years. The building features massive bungalow-roof forms, hipped and with extensive spreading eaves under which walls and windows nestle. The capacious closed gable of the Bernese Oberland chalet shelters the grey stuccoed walls. These are broken in the subtle play of solid and void: real in the projecting porch-bays, banks of leaded window casements and recessed porches; imaginary in the rectilinear patterns created by bracketted gables dressed in half-timber patterns. Even the tall elegant chimney flues tantalizingly evade historical analysis, only a suggestion of the Queen Anne expressed perhaps in abstract Arts & Crafts detailing. The same brick provides a foundation course which is carried to the lintel height on the seaward gabled bay. A hint of the English influence of C. F. A.

Voysey is perhaps traceable in the general massing, play of gable and roof forms, and the treatment of the low-slung eave brackets to carry down the soffits with a slightly lyrical gesture. Fastidious detailing completes the Finlayson design: the complex profile of the lip mouldings which protect the window openings in the stucco walls, the alignment of the rooftop gable windows with architectural elements below, the insertion of trellis-work into the verandahs and *porte-cochere*, all encourage the blending of garden and building.

The Finlayson house was completed in 1915 and Canada was at war. Cecil Croker Fox, Maclure's Voysey-trained Vancouver partner, had left for the front and was killed in action the following year. With uncanny prescience Maclure produced a memorial more fitting than any granite monument to his close friend and collaborator.

William and Gertrude Mercer House
1916

4366 Blenkinsop Road,
Blenkinsop Valley, Saanich
Design. W. F. Drysdale

Drysdale was a well-known Victoria builder/contractor. Here he designed and built a very trim California (or Craftsman) style bungalow farmhouse for the Mercers, an English emigrant family who ran an extensive mixed farm on valley floor. The fieldstone foundations reach into the battered piers and balustrades of the wide open-gabled entrance porch, shingled above the bevelled siding main floor.

Gordon Copeman House
1915

2346 Brighton Avenue, Oak Bay
Archt. Fred J. Henson

Unique in that it is one of the early houses built completely of hydro-stone (concrete block using a mix formula and pressed form to resemble stone). Six different products are used including sills, caps and coping mouldings. The form is similar to that of the shingled California bungalows common to the neighbourhood.

Walter Luney House
1916

1566 Hampshire Road, Oak Bay
Archt. C. Elwood Watkins

Luney Bros. were major contractors to architects such as Maclure, Rattenbury, Hooper and, in particular, schools of which Watkins was often architect. Watkins designed houses for both William (530 Foul Bay Road) and Walter. It seems both brothers required homes in manner of Samuel Maclure, here delivered as an open gable half-timbered chalet featuring a granite faced first storey.

Mrs. A. H. Brownlie House
1918
1061 St. Patrick Street, Oak Bay

At the end of the war Victoria clung to its Edwardian aesthetic predelictions for the Arts & Crafts, here in a multi-gabled California style bungalow. One of a group of houses, similar in style and date, the automobile is now accommodated within the garden, parked adjacent to the house.

East Wing
1921
Royal Jubilee Hospital
1900 Fort Street, Victoria
Archts. P. L. James, K. B. Spurgin

The East Wing provides a glimpse of how the hospital appeared in the 1920s. The design continued the Edwardian Classical style of prewar Victoria, a brick building using a chamfered corner motif above a stone foundation course. An additional storey was later added above the cornice line.

Winnifred and Geoffrey Vantreight House
1922
4423 Tyndall Avenue, Gordon Head, Saanich

At 4417 Tyndall stands the couple's first 1914 farmhouse, a verandah front, and side gable with a lean-to addition at the rear. The 1922 house marks their success with the daffodil and apple growing business. A particular feature of this California style two-storey bungalow is the extensive use of verandah features, including a *porte-couchere* which provides a deck for the second floor central porch, semi-enclosed sleeping porches off the second-floor bedrooms, and a verandah which extends the length of the south and east sides. Tyndall was the focus of the Gordon Head farming community; numerous farm houses survive, and the Community Hall (1898) of the Gordon Head Improvement Society survives at 4146 Tyndall where it was moved to in 1932.

Avard and Eleanor Pineo House
1924
339 Foul Bay Road, Oak Bay
Archt. L. W. Hargreaves

Pineo was Legislative Counsel in the Provincial Attorney-General's

Department. The Shingle style house is delicately detailed, the eaves lifted to a slight curve to mark the entrance and the window bays slightly extended below the second-storey shingle course.

Cecil and Verna Branson House
1927

2901 Seaview Road, Cadboro Bay, Saanich
Archt. Percy Leonard James

Steep pitched roofs, snug treatment of the gables and eaves, the vertical emphasis of the half-timber detailing and towering Queen Anne chimney stacks are all hallmarks of James' work in the English variant of the Arts & Crafts aesthetic. Only the fieldstone foundation and terrace on the gardenfront hint at the early West Coast precedents of Samuel Maclure.

B.C. Electric
Bay Street Substation
1928

Government at Bay Street, Victoria
Archt. Theo Korner

This is one of the finest examples of Art Deco in the Northwest. Drawing on the forms and motifs of the great "elemental" arts of the past, in particular Egyptian, Mesopotamian and Mayan, the terms "Deco" and "Moderne" were both derived from the very successful and much publicized 1925 Paris exhibition, *L'Exposition Internationale des Arts Décoratifs et Industriels Modernes*. "Deco" usually describes that school of artistic and architectural production popular during the 1920s and 1930s which attempted to beautify industrial and

functional products through applied abstract decoration.

One of the new building modes of early 1920s was reinforced concrete construction. Because it utilized a kind of cribbing and cast technique, there was ample opportunity to build in decorative detail by means of the form work. The Bay Street Substation is a particularly fine example of this. The architect has used Deco Egyptoid motifs (including the BCE winged crest on the east façade). Abstracted columns with decorated capitals and a plain entablature are applied as single units to the four façades, thus evoking a Nile Valley Pharaonic palace. The substation has been recycled as an office block.

The Dunlop commission demonstrates how Maclure had returned to Classical forms for his inspiration and here we see the George Richardson house of 1912 recast in more obvious Classical garb including the bracketted cornice line and a formal balustraded entrance.

E. F. Pooley House
1928

1337 Rockland Avenue, Rockland
Archts. Berrill and Parker

This substantial Tudor Revival home was one of the last to be built in Rockland to the scale and style of the earlier mansions. Designed by Victoria architect Ralph Berrill, with architect Jameson Parker from Portland, Oregon, the house was built on the foundations of a former house "Robleda" after which Robleda Crescent is named.

James and Annie Dunlop House
1928

1960 Lansdowne Road, Saanich
Archt. Samuel Maclure

This was one of Maclure's last commissions before his death in 1929.

Begbie Hall
1929-1930

Royal Jubilee Hospital
1900 Fort Street, Victoria
Archt. C. Elwood Watkins

Watkins continued the building program in the Edwardian Classical manner of the earlier James and Spurgin East Wing. Begbie Hall was built as a nurses' home and accommodation for the Royal Jubilee School of Nursing. The symmetrical plan brick structure is sparingly detailed but with some ornament concentrated on the entrance pavilion: swag motifs in the balustrade spandrels and composite order pilasters flanking the windows and doorway.

Esquimalt Municipal Hall
1929

1229 Esquimalt Road, Esquimalt
Archt. Ralph Berrill

Enough Classical elements can be discerned in the façade of this much-altered building to more than hint at the original architectural concept in the manner of a Renaissance Classical palazzo. There is a strict symmetry to organization of building elements: three bays of windows and two storeys framed by a Classical cornice and corner Doric pilasters. A sensitive and inexpensive restoration would boost the architectural morale of the municipality.

Tweedsmuir Mansions Apartments
1936

900 Park Boulevard, Fairfield
Archt. W. J. Semeyn

This stridently Moderne building commanded a major vista through Beacon Hill Park at its corner from Heywood and Park Boulevard. It also contained Victoria's first "penthouse." The white stucco butterfly-plan building is a slightly asymmetrical composition of geometrical elements, the clean abstract arrangement of horizontal and vertical planes only briefly ornamented to accent the main entrance. The interior plan is cleverly arranged so that each suite had its own private entrance.

Castle Block
1936

2184, 2194 Oak Bay Avenue, Oak Bay
Archt. Eric C. Clarkson

Containing the Oak Bay Theatre, this late version of the Tudor Revival anchored the "English" flavour of Oak Bay Village—so assiduously cultivated ever since. That the original concept was otherwise can be discerned from the fact that James & James Oak Bay Grocery (at 2250) was a gambrel-roofed Shingle style building, as was the 1908 house, The Oaks, a large Arts & Crafts Chalet style house at the entrance to the Village. The Bell

Block (1913, architect Archie Bunting) at 2201 is a competent essay in Edwardian Commercial Classicism.

Waldermar and Margo Bowdon House
1939

2511 Sinclair Road, Cadboro Bay, Saanich
Archts. McCulloch & Harvey

The rambling additive form, detailed with rolled eaves, hipped gables and window shutters are hallmarks of a late Arts & Crafts variant, called the Cotswold Cottage. Ross Lort and Hubert Savage also produced designs in this manner.

Bishop's Chapel
1939

912 Vancouver Street, Cathedral Hill, Fairfield
Archt. P. L. James

The chapel was built as an addition to the Bishop's residence in 1939 (now demolished). It was designed by P. L. James and was the gift of Lady Stewart Taylor in memory of her son who had died in 1936 while studying at Cambridge. The chapel was James' only venture into the ecclesiastical field. It is in the French Romanesque Revival

style, with round beaded windows and doors, stuccoed exterior walls and a barrel vaulted ceiling. In 1979 the building was restored under the direction of architect Nicholas Bawlf and now serves as a chapel and as a reading room for the adjacent Archives of the Anglican Synod of Diocese of British Columbia.

Frederick and Amy Speed House
1939-1940

1578 Ash Road, Gordon Head, Saanich

A curiosity, or architectural folly, Speed was a carpenter fascinated with the writings of Charles Dickens. During World War II he constructed the house with its bold half-timbering and multiplicity of bracketted oriel windows (even the garage has one)—a story-book evocation of Victorian Englishness by means of a Tudoresque fantasy.

J. H. Johns House
1939-1943

2753 Somass Drive, Oak Bay
Archt. P. L. James

James' Moderne style work was apparently inspired by an exhibition of Bauhaus work that he had seen on a visit to England in the 1930s. This is one his most sophisticated designs in the style. The asymmetrical composition features an inset S-curved entrance porch detailed with glass blocks. Plate glass windows on the garden side are oriented for seaward views.

"Mount St. Mary" Hospital
1940

999 Burdett Street, Cathedral Hill, Fairfield
Archt. H. Whittaker, Dept. Public Works

This Art Deco style poured-concrete building was designed in 1942 by H. Whittaker, Department of Public Works. During World War II it answered the need for hospitals for wounded returning veterans.

G. R. Flemming House
1941-1942

200 King George Terrace, Gonzales, Oak Bay
Archt. J. Hanzlik

One of a series of Moderne style houses which distinguish the rise to the peak of Gonzales Hill and also command the magnificent ocean vistas from this vantage point. A pedimental tower marks the entrance and anchors this asymmetrical composition of the two-storey white stucco design.

Richmond Pavilion
1944-1946

Royal Jubilee Hospital
1900 Fort Street, Victoria

Memorial Pavilion
1947

Royal Jubilee Hospital
2355 Richmond Avenue, Victoria
Archt. H. Whittaker, Chief Archictect, B.C. Dept. Public Works

These two large-scale Moderne structures bear the hallmarks of the Whittaker era design formula: palazzo forms, stepped and symmetrical in organization and plan, with traces of Deco detail. The Richmond Pavilion was to have been finished in brick, although this was never carried out. The Memorial Pavilion was built for returning vets.

Mr. and Mrs. F. E. Smith House
1945-1946

230 King George Terrace, Gonzales, Oak Bay
Designer F. E. Smith

A prominent rounded window bay, a wide horizontal cornice below an exaggerated parapet, these are the distiguishing features of this house in the Gonzales group. The siting is dramatic and landscaping respects the minimalist style.

Western Match Company
1945

154 Fairview Road, Esquimalt
Archts. McCarter & Nairne, Vancouver

There is almost a nautical quality to the design of this low-slung streamlined building, a classic example in Victoria of the stripped-down Moderne style. It is interesting that the architects were better known for their Vancouver work in the much more elaborate Deco style, in particular the Marine Building some 15 years earlier.

John and Clare M. Walker House
1948

3491 Mayfair Drive, Mount Tolmie, Saanich
Designer John Walker

Designed by the owner for himself, there is an ocean liner feel to this Streamlined Moderne superstructure. Indeed the house steams out into its own dramatic views from the hillside perch between two roads winding up Tolmie. The marine effect is supported by the metal eave copings and wire mesh balustrades.

William and Dorothy Woods House
1948-1949

2537 Killarney Place, Cadboro Bay, Saanich

There is an almost Moderne jazz feeling to the receding Z-plan which modulates the generously fenestrated blocks. The effect is dramatically emphasized by the generous horizontal cornice and extended parapet at the

roofline. The white stucco finish provides a striking contrast with the natural treed backdrop.

Logan Mayhew House
1950-1951

3515 Beach Drive, Uplands, Oak Bay
Archts. Sharp Thompson Berwick & Pratt

One of Victoria's earliest wood post-and-beam construction, the house is essentially two distinct wings, integral to its garden setting and shoreline view front. A dominant feature is the butterfly roof form of the major wing.

R. & H. Denny House
1952

3130 Midland Road, Uplands, Oak Bay
Archt. John Di Castri

Post-and-beam construction is exploited to open up the envelope for bands of windows sheltered under the extended eaves of the low-pitched roof. The flat-capped chimneys are a major feature; boad-and-batten vertical siding is relieved at the front by a balustrade demonstrating a creative sculptural use of concrete block.

Central School
1952

1280 Fort Street, Rockland
Archts. Birley Wade Stockdill

Central itself is a further development of their earlier pioneering Expressionist work for the Greater Victoria School Board, the monumental S. J. Willis School (1950, 923 Topaz Street). The site carries historic importance in Victoria's educational history. This was the original colonial school reserve, the school itself a wood-frame single-storey version of Craigflower. John Teague designed the first Provincial school, a brick Mansardic structure very reminiscent both of the Inner Harbour Customs House under construction at the same time and Teague's City Hall two years later. In 1882 a single-storey wing was added to the rear, replacing the old Colonial School building, to accommodate the Victoria High School. F. M. Rattenbury designed the red-brick twin-gable Queen Anne structure with its stone Tudor arched entrance which replaced Teague's building in 1902. The BWS 1952 concrete four-storey range dominates the crest of the Fort/Pandora Hill overlooking the City. The T-plan is organized about a central stair tower. The front elevation balances a gymnasium with a window-grid classroom wing. The entrance is marked by the curved clerestory wall of a foward projecting single-storey office block. The Rationalist geometry of the design and clear articulation of functional units provides a distinctly European flavour which is the hallmark of much of BSW's early Expressionist work in Victoria. It would inspire an entire generation of the British Columbia school design.

"Trend House"
for Gwendoline Cash
1954

3516 Richmond Avenue,
Mount Tolmie, Saanich
Arcvh. John Di Castri

On behalf of the western Canadian lumber industry the B.C. Coast Woods Trade Extension Bureau sponsored the

construction of ten houses across Canada to promote softwood lumber as a building material. John Di Castri was selected to design the Victoria house. It was the smallest of ten but pushed the technology and the material to its limits. The polygon plan supports diamond form roof trusses as if inspired by wooden airframe technology. A massive masonry chimney block slices diagonally into the body of the house as if to pinion the complex roof forms in flight. The building elements made extensive use of Western Hemlock and plate glass.

on which it is built. The forward open car-port has been filled in but the 1950s garden has been sensitively cultivated and envelops the house on this large set-back site.

Dr. Ralph Pronger Residence
1957
2780 Dover Road, Willows, Oak Bay
Archts. Clack & Clayton

The geometric expression of building elements, both functional and decorative, was the hallmark of Progressive post-and-beam construction. Here the forms and elements such as windows and panel screens are articulated by alternating materials such as fascia boards, vertical wood siding and plywood sheets.

Spooran Singh and Chanchil Sundher House
1954
3210 Bellevue Road, Quadra, Saanich

One of two towering Moderne style houses which dominate a hilltop in the north lee of High Quadra. These were obviously built for the multi-directional views on all sides. The sparkling white finish and smooth surfaces prove a dramatic contrast to the rocky outcrop on which they are perched and to the leafy treetop canopy which shrouds the western side of the hill.

"Windhurst" for the Brown Family
1954
3045 Beach Drive, Oak Bay
Archts. Polson and Siddall

The expressive functionalism of post-and-beam construction is revealed both in form and materials; the main body of the house is slightly raised to accommodate the large rock outcrop

Government House for Lieutenant-Governor of British Columbia
1957
1401 Rockland Avenue, Rockland
Archts. F. W. Green (1860), John Wright (1865), Maclure & Rattenbury (1903), British Columbia Dept. Public Works (1957)

Beneath the present house are the foundations of two previous structures, both of which have served as the official residence for the

Cary Castle, Rockland, *ca.* 1866.   BCARS 8197

Lieutenant-Governors of British Columbia. Cary Castle, as it was then known, was built in 1860 for the Colony's Attorney-General, John

Hunter Cary and was sold to the Colonial Government in 1865 for $19,000. Commanding a magnificent view of lower Vancouver Island and the Strait of Juan de Fuca, the stone castellated residence with its curious round tower and *porte-cochere* was vaguely reminiscent of a semi-ruined Scottish border castle. The additions of 1865 by John Wright did nothing to destroy the original scheme, but added a dormered roof to the central block, filled in the *porte-cochere,* and extended the east and west wings. The result was a mansion befitting the Crown Colony's Governor, Sir Arthur Kennedy, with its various regal-cum-martial trappings. Cary Castle was the residence of the Lieutenant-Governor after British Columbia entered Confederation. Its successor, completed in 1903 at a cost of $44,000, was designed by Samuel Maclure and F. M. Rattenbury in partnership. The new design reconstructed the distinguishing features of the old house, although very much altered to sympathize with the

Government House (1957), south front.

Government House, north elevation, drawing, 1901.
Maclure and Rattenbury.

new scheme. Thus a stone-castellated central block and Tudor-arched *porte-cochere* were set in a symmetrically planned building which was distinguished by Rattenbury's own eccentric combination of English Shavian and American Richardsonian Shingle style exterior. The extensive wings rambled gracefully along the brow of the hill, the brown shingles blending with the foliage of copses of oak, maple and fir. The interior was finished in a combination of Tudor, Jacobean, and Georgian Revival styles, the latter being emphasized in the more formal public spaces.

The high point of the interior design was the magnificent ballroom, whose decorations were designed and executed by James Bloomfield of the art glass firm in New Westminster. The ceiling was frescoed with pictorial scenes inspired by the totemic legends of British Columbian Indian tribes. The most impressive feature was a huge stained glass oriel window in the south end of the hall, produced in Bloomfield's glass studios at New Westminster. The Maclure-Rattenbury building was destroyed by fire in 1957. Over the objections of the local architectural fraternity the Provincial Government determined to rebuild in the traditional manner. Architects Peter Cotton and Alan Hodgson worked on designs for the new version incorporating the original *porte-cochere*, following the basic outline of the Maclure/Rattenbury plan, and actually replicating some of the main social spaces at a cost of $1,600,000. The landscaped grounds were laid out by Robert Savery generally following the earlier plan of Samuel Maclure in 1927.

The house is now managed by the Goverment House Foundation. A magnificient heraldic stained glass window has been installed in the entrance façade. Under their Honours Dorothy and David Lam (and the Friends of Government House Gardens), extensive garden improvements were undertaken. This included restoration of the original stable complex as a garden interpretation centre and the creation of a new Elizabethan-style rose garden. Open to the public at all times, they provide a beautiful and peaceful setting for a pleasant stroll.

Surf Motel
1959

290 Dallas Road, James Bay
Archt. R. W. Siddall

Built near the Ogden Point Breakwater, this is one of Victoria's best preserved modern buildings in the International style, combining Mies Van der Rohe's minimalist design aesthetic with a studied rational use of industrial building technologies. Rooms look out on the breakwater, built over many years (1913-1918) from 20-ton blocks of granite, the construction of which had been a passion of architect and Victoria booster, T. C. Sorby, for many years.

Apartment Building
1961

550 Quadra at Humboldt, Fairfield
Archt. A. Lionel

The walk-up apartment with its multi-storey galleried street front, first floor slightly below grade (to get the extra density) and cantilevered over the rear open parking, was a popular two- or three-lot residential design solution as the old large houses gave way to gradual densification of Victoria's downtown edge in the 1950s and 1960s.

Shamrock Motel
1961

675 Superior Street at Douglas, Victoria
Archt. F. A. Schultze

One of the few surviving early walk-up motels, the Shamrock is well preserved and well placed in proximity to Victoria's major tourist attractions: parks, museums, and downtown retail. The formula, which saw a balconied front and business rear, reduced the usable ground floor by providing for parking, tucked in under the rear elevation.

Macdonald House
1961-1962

1961 Crescent Road, Gonzales, Oak Bay
Archt. Alan Hodgson

Scale and materials respect the streetscape in this beach-front enclave which was originally developed as summer cottages for Victoria residents. The post-and-beam open-plan construction is decidedly modern, giving a formal expression to interior spaces, in particular from the front with its bold box-canopy entrance.

Oak Bay Marina
1962
1327 Marine Drive, Oak Bay
Archt. Wagg & Hambleton

Casual shaping and massing, whimsical forms, yet a certain airy weightlessness, these were the hallmarks of what came to be known in post World War II England as "Festival of Britain Architecture"—after the exhibition building on Thames South Bank site in London which in 1951 hosted the Festival of Britain. All these elements can be read from this complex which features a polygon pavilion that clings to the water's edge at the Oak Bay Marina.

Alan Hodgson Residence
1964
404 Henry Street, Victoria West
Archt. Alan J. Hodgson

The house forms an L, stepping down a steep rock escarpment on the north side. The main living areas open onto a natural rock courtyard on the interior of the corner lot location. From the street sides one catches glimpses through the landscaping of the skylights and minimal glazing which articulate the geometry of the envelope, uniquely composed of creosoted marine ply panelling.

Beckley Manor
1964
548 Dallas Road, James Bay
Archts. Buttjes & Rapske

At this time a bold insertion into the James Bay waterfront, this multi-storey apartment block was the harbinger of more to come. Corbusier's rationalism is masked by the brick balcony detailing, but undisputed was the intention at this time that James Bay could could follow the lead of West Vancouver with dramatic highrise densification. The fact that the balconies have not been glazed, as with other city projects of this period, makes this exemplary of its time and style.

Achtem House
1965

3225 Beach Drive, Uplands, Oak Bay
Archt. John Di Castri

Di Castri at his most Wrightian, from a clerestory central hall the house reaches out horizontally through subsidiary wings and the period landscape. Trellises and fences are designed with meticulous care. Building materials reinforce the plane lines, bold fascia boards skirt the roof edges above the coursed flat brickwork.

Saanich Municipal Hall
1965

770 Vernon Avenue, Saanich
Archts. Wade, Stockdill Armour & Partners

Saanich's 1911 Shingle style bungalow located in Royal Oak village was appropriate to a rural agricultural community. For the rapidly expanding suburban Saanich of the early 1960s it was not, and so design partner John Armour supplied the most overtly Progressive building Victoria had witnessed to that time. Drawing his inspiration quite openly from the work of the leading architectural theorist of the twentieth century, the Franco-Swiss Charles-Edouard Le Corbusier (1887-1965), one can identify various form-cast concrete elements from Corbu's work in 1950s at Chandigarh, India or the chapel of Ronchamp. As with much of the Swiss architect's work the building combines lyrical freeform elements which reinforced concrete allows, along with the heavy Brutalism of unrelieved wall slabs. Le Corbusier's planning theories, which in part focus on the preservation of rural green space for an increasingly industrialized urban society, reinforced the topicality of the image. The hall turns its back on the urban sprawl of Victoria and faces Swan Lake reclaimed nature sanctuary (the rustic modern Visitor Centre by architects Marshall Goldsworthy, 1988).

Hillside Shopping Centre
1969

1644 Hillside Avenue, Hillside/Quadra, Victoria
Archts. Musson Cattell Architects

Hillside followed the development of Town & Country, and Mayfair, as urban shopping malls were positioned on Victoria's municipal boundaries to serve the auto-oriented suburbs. One effect was to threaten the retail viability of Victoria's traditional civic core. Hillside was strategically positioned adjacent to the early CMHC post-war "affordable housing" subdivision in the area of Doncaster and Oakland Streets. Sears, the main retail anchor of Hillside, was given feature architectural treatment by means of a curious geometric grid applied to the wide expanses of windowless walls. This manifests as abstract crenelations at the roofline. The mall has been subject to continuous changes and additions over the years although Sears has remained substantially unaltered.

Orchard House
1969
647 Michigan Street, James Bay
Archts. Eng & Wright, Vancouver

This soaring slab, one of the tallest ever to be built in the city, set the formula for the balconied tower block in Victoria. It also spurred public debate which ultimately led to the downzoning of much of the neighbourhood. The lack of planning and viewscape analysis at the time of its construction has unfortunately resulted in the degradation of numerous harbour views of the Parliament Buildings where it seems to transfix Rattenbury's brooding domed edifice.

Jawl Industries Ltd.
1972
470 Ardersier Road, North Douglas, Saanich
Archt. Arthur Erickson, Vancouver

Built for the Home Lumber and Building Supplies division of Jawl Industries, this is probably one of the most successful of Erickson's small commissions. It combines the elemental form of an ancient temple with the dramatic simplicity of primeval treeforms. From a shallow stepped podium rise the massive timber supports of the splayed truss system, these bracketing the wide floating roof plane, centre inset with a glazed pyramidial skylight. The inset curtain walls and truss level clerestory provide a light, airy and efficient office space—replete with associative

references for the nature of the trade at hand.

Elizabeth and Terence Williams House
1973

315 King George Terrace, Gonzales, Oak Bay
Archt. Wade Williams

The steep rocky site falling away from the road snaking round the outer edge of Gonzales Hill required a creative solution. The 24-foot wide house steps down the cliff face in five cantilevered levels, each by means of skylights or full length windows affording stunning views across Shoal Bay. The spare expression of wall surfaces and structural details, and generous lighting, reveals Williams' earlier English and Scandinavian training.

Apartments for Bayview Properties
1973

1211 Beach Drive, Oak Bay
Archt. Claude Maurice

This range of two-storey townhouses hugs the Satellite Street frontage illustrating a sensitive but modern Arts & Crafts approach to materials. Vertical siding, shingled mansard roof, and split-stone walls and garden trellises lend the building a landscape texture.

Polson House
1978

1020 Joan Crescent, Rockland
Archt. Roger Smeeth

One solution to infill design in a sensitive urban context, as here, is to create a no-house. There is, however, a cool rationalism to this "stucco box" which folds itelf into the steep bank that drops away from the street on the rising curve to Craigdarroch Castle.

Huntingdon Manor Inn
1980

330 Quebec Street, James Bay
Archts. Bawlf Cooper Associates

Inspired by the Shingle style Edwardian hotels that F. M. Rattenbury built for the Western Division of the CPR, this three-storey wood-frame building rises from a rubble stone base and features a dominant shingled and gabled roof. The ground floor Quebec Street entrance is marked by Classical columned *porte-cochere*, opening into a lobby finished in wood panelling and reproduction turn-of-the-century furnishings.

Dunelm Village
1981
416 Dallas Road, James Bay
Archts. Campbell Moore

Designed as an infill housing project, these attached townhouses face the ocean front one side, but open onto an access road and communal space on the interior of the block. The frame construction repeats a range of Italianate and Queen Anne forms traditional to nineteenth century built heritage of James Bay.

Friedman House
1981
166 Dennison Road, Gonzales, Oak Bay
Archt. Wade Williams

The north skylight is the dominant feature of this Modernist post-and-beam design, inserted into the hillside near the peak of the Gonzales rise. Decks and verandahs are inserted into the cascading shingle roof-plane as the levels drop down with steep escarpment.

Canadian Broadcasting Corporation
1982
780 Kings Road, Victoria
Archts. Bastion Group, L. Holovsky

Intended to satisfy Victoria's long frustrated dream of a CBC television production capability in the province's capital, the building was finally never occupied by the Corporation. It was instead sold to a private network rival. However, like its Vancouver production centre (architect Thompson, Berwick, Pratt & Partners, 1974-1975), the design is Brutalist, softened only somewhat by the colourful expression of High-Tech structural elements.

From "Policy Plan and Songhees Design Guidelines for the Songhees Area of Victoria West," City of Victoria, 1986.

Songhees Development Victoria West

In 1983 City Council approved the *Songhees Area Concept Plan,* the largest single comprehensive development of city lands since the subdivision of the Fairfield Estates at the turn of the century. Under the plan the Provincial Government and city would cooperate in the planning and development of 170 acres of reclaimed industrial sites comprising most of the eastern half of the Victoria West Peninsula. In particular it comprises some of the city core's highest profile waterfront, lining the Outer and Inner Harbours as well as Selkirk Narrows, the entrance to the Gorge Waterway. The 1984 *Concept Plan* envisaged a zoned mix of residential, clean industrial, commericial and recreational uses with reserves for a community school and "village centre." The 1986 *Policy Plan and Design Guidelines* called for a kind of Sausalito North, a fringe of waterfront marina and a network of parks giving way to low-rise attached housing, stepping up to terraced street-friendly walk-ups and medium density highrises blending with the street retail, commercial and High-Tech industrial. The design vocabulary was to be vaguely historicist, particularly inspired by Edwardian variants of the Queen Anne.

Reality has proven somewhat shy of the expectations. The waters' edge pedestrian parkway (West Song Way) has been accomplished in co-operation with the Provincial Capital Commission; a Marine Technology

Sitkum Lodge

Tyee Housing Co-op

Queen's Port

Songhees Point Condominiums

Ocean Pointe Hotel

A developing skyline, Songhees.

Park and Ocean Towers, Songhees.

Royal Quays, Songhees.

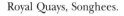

Mariner's Landing, Songhees.

Payless Gas Station, Songhees.

Park still awaits public and corporate investment. However, most criticism has been aimed at the setback highrise densification devoid of street-level interest, development which has been more concerned with "warehousing views" than creating a viable community. Songhees is still less than 50% built out and the city continues to apply "correction measures" in an attempt to recapture the original concept.

The last remaining industrial monument awaits a creative adaptive reuse. The Esquimalt and Nanaimo Railway Roundhouse complex (1912) is one of the last remaining complete structures of its kind in Canada. It comprises a ten-stall roundhouse, a functioning turntable, heavy repair pit and machine shop, and car shop—all red brick and timber-truss structures.

The first two projects, a social housing development consisting of highrise seniors accommodation and a lower density attached housing co-op, occupy the Songhees hilltop and predate the publication of *Concept Plan and Design Guidelines*. (Sitkum Lodge [1983], 411 Sitkum Road: architect Arthur Erickson and Tyee Housing Co-operative [1983] 300 Tyee Road, 420 Sitkum Road: architect Arthur Erickson.) The frank Brutalist Expressionism of the scheme, re-inforced by the grey unrelieved concrete finishes, was unpopular and played a role in prompting calls for greater formal City involvement, particularly in the production of a comprehesive development master plan. Five years later the second project (Queen's Port and Pebble Beach Condominiums [1988], 55, 65 Songhees Road: architects Wagg & Hambleton) was the most literal interpretation of the planning guidelines. The low range waterfront condominiums loosely interpret the turret, gable and rich palette of materials which connote the Victorian Queen Anne style. Oddly enough it is a Payless Gas Station ([1988] Esquimalt Roat at Tyee: architects also Wagg & Hambleton) whose abstract Gothicism marks the entrance to the Picturesque Eclecticism of Post-Modern Songhees. Songhees Point Condominiums ([1988], 50 Songhees Road: architects Downs Archambault), a condominium development of medium density, was intended as a background building, the visual interest attracted to the Picturesque gabled roofline.

Early take-up by the private sector concentrated on the waterfront and the quickly adopted formula was to reduce site coverage in favour of massing the density to favour the southward seaviews. The phased development Royal Quays West (1988), 11 Cooperage Place: architects Wagg & Hambleton and Royal Quays East (1995), 10 Paul Kane Place: architects Wagg & Hambleton, illustrates this approach. The two large-scale mirror blocks are planned around interior galleried atriums, adopting an external form which might be termed Queen Anne Modern. The wall surfaces contain an interplay of oriel bays and inset balconies rising into the mansard roof as dormer gables.

Two large-scale identical condominium blocks (Ocean Tower, 205 Kimta and Park Tower, 203 Kimta: architects Wagg & Hambleton) display a more abstract treatment of Queen Anne gable and tower and turrent elements.

Ocean Pointe Resort Hotel ([1990], 45 Songhees Road: architect Downs Archambault), is intended as an anchor design feature for southern zone, occupying a prime location on the Point and directly facing the Old Town, the Empress and the Parliament Buildings. The scheme for the 250-room hotel exhibits a controlled eclecticism, drawing on the various architectural motifs of the Inner Harbour landscape: its cupola from the those of the Parliament Buildings, and the simplified Chateau-esque roofline from the Empress. At grade the hotel opens out through a pavilion into a terraced garden landscape at the edge of the waterfront public walkway. Mariner's Landing ([1996] 75 Songhees Road: architect Herbert Kwan) steps back from the waterfront with a series of attached two-storey townhouses using a simplified Edwardian Classical vocabulary to articulate the entrance porticoes. These front a nine-storey monolithic galleried block which is overpowering at the Songhees street front despite a bold Classical pediment which tries to set some scale and unity to the elements.

The Peninsula Condominiums ([1995], Songhees Road: architect Eric Barker Inc.) is a lower profile condominium development. Attached cottage-style townhouses with garden fronts provide a screen to a landscaped courtyard and access to the larger condominium block behind.

The prominence of Songhees in Victoria's urban landscape ensures an ongoing intense level of critical debate from a population which constantly exhibits an unusually high degreee of visual literacy.

Peninsula condominiums.

E&N Round House Complex, Songhees.

NOTE

Ref. "Concept Plan for the Songhees Peninsula." n.d. "Policy Plan and Design Guidelines for the Songhees Area of Victoria West." 1986.

Appleton House
1986

940 Royal Terrace, Rockland
Archts. Patkau Architects

Having since confirmed their reputation among the more adventurist of British Columbia's Post-Modernists with recent award-winning projects such as the Seabird Island Salish school (1992) and the Strawberry Vale School in Victoria (1996), the husband and wife team here demonstrated an early interest in the European Minimalist forms combined with High-Tech structural elements. The severe cubical architectural forms here are relieved by the cantilevered constructivist entrance canopy.

The fanciful Queen Anne treatment given these two structures, a retirement and extended care complex, illustrates the historicist vein in contemporary Post-Modernism—the return to readable architecture. The brick, stucco and timber detailing is well executed, the whole constitutes an obvious link to Victoria's own architectural legacy.

BCGEU Headquarters
1988

2994 Douglas Street, North Douglas, Victoria
Archts. Campbell Moore Group Architects

The design of this brick-faced office building responds to a constricted site and the desire for staff to access natural light and fresh air. Three storeys of offices surround three sides of an internal skylit atrium; the fourth "open" side contains 1200 square feet of slightly

Parkwood Manor
1987-1989

3051 Shelbourne, Jubilee, Victoria
3000 Shelbourne, Victoria
Archts. Waisman Dewar Grout

curved glass block light bay; offices open out at each level into atrium galleries. The architects claim the solution was driven by engaging the client in a democratic interactive design process.

Somerset House
1988
540 Dallas Road, James Bay
Archts. Hulbert Group

Post-Modern historicism comes full-blown in this evocation of an Edwardian Montreux Sanitorium. The pediments, cornices, and columns are overscaled in the symmetric design which follows the Palladian formula of a portico entrance block flanked by pavilions.

Harbourside
1989
636, 630 Montreal Street, James Bay

Harbourside Coast Hotel
146 Kingston Street, James Bay
Archts. Eric Barker Architects

Two condominium tower blocks and a hotel comprise this development which reclaimed a large section of formerly derelict James Bay industrial waterfront. Particular attention has been paid to the water's edge with the dedication of a public walkway and the creation of a commercial float community on the water itelf. The towers are large scale but the traditional brick detailing and Picturesque rooflines attempt a relationship with James Bay's traditional residential fabric, but also for the waterborne visitor, introduce the monumental architectural setting of Victoria's Inner Harbour.

On The Park
1990
188 Douglas Street, James Bay
Archts. Campbell Moore Group Architects

A Post-Modern fascination with the purity of rational minimalism, compromised occasionally by brief hints of structural tension (stilted first floor, cantilevered balconies, segmented gables, the suspensed entrance canopy) make this one of the most successful residential blocks of the many which crowd Beacon Hill's periphery. While nearly mirror images, the note of tension is reinforced by the lack of balance; the north tower is taller by one storey.

Selkirk Waterfront Project
1991
Gorge Road at Dunedin Street, Gorge, Victoria
Archts. de Hoog D'Ambrosio Rowe Architects

The Jawl Group has undertaken the reclamation of this 24-acre industrial site on the Gorge Waterway, formerly the historic Cameron Bros. Sawmill. After an extensive public planning process the developers have committed to the gradual development of a mixed use live-work community utilizing the

Rogers Elementary School
1991

765 Rogers Road, North Quadra, Saanich
Archt. Hughes Baldwin, Architects

This design was winner in a competition specifically intended to raise the level of new school design for the Greater Victoria School District. The building is a major attraction on the Pat Bay Highway viewscape at the entry to Victoria. The location is a hillside site which provides natural landscape foil for the sweeping cantilevered roof decks which shelter the richly articulated building envelope, an Expressionist amalgam of red brick, concrete, steel struts and glass curtain wall.

waterfront amenities and part of the infrastructure of the old mill. The residential-commercial-industrial-and-recreational mix will be pedestrian-oriented. It will be developed according to design guidelines formulated within a Comprehensive Zoning package. Two structures, both exhibiting a High-Tech design approach with a distinctly European feel, have been built so far (Centra Gas Operations Centre 1992, architects: de Hoog, d'Ambrosio, Rowe and a British Columbia Buildings Corporation Office Complex 1996, architects Campbell Moore).

Tuller Residence
1993

376 Beach Drive, Oak Bay
Archts. Chow & Fleischauer

Rogers Elementary School

There are hints of the Moderne in the expressive functionalism of the road-front façade. Living spaces focus on a European "first floor" to exploit the majestic prospect out to Trial Island. A gabled bow window offsets an open deck. A carport instead of a front door addresses the street.

Petro-Canada Service Station
1995

1600 Fairfield Road, Fairfield
Archts. Charles E. Broudy & Associates, Philadelphia (logo and image concept)

The strident, Post-Modern packaged plastic decor, Petro-Can's image for the 1990s, is no doubt a conscious attempt to declare a popular retail presence for the products and services. The effect, however, can be jarring in traditional neighbourhoods such as Fairfield where the built fabric is finely detailed, and fragile.

University of Victoria view, 1994.

University of Victoria: The Gordon Head Campus

The 125 acres of Gordon Head military camp were acquired by Victoria College from the federal government in 1959. Victoria College, not to become a university until 1963, was then located at Lansdowne, now the location of Camosun College. Victoria Mayor Richard Biggerstaff Wilson, coincidentally active in revitalizing downtown Victoria, headed the fund drive. He and the college's consulting architect Robert Siddall were instrumental in obtaining the services of the San Francisco firm of architectural planners, Wurster, Bernardi and Emmons. Siddall was to act locally for WBE in the planning exercise. WBE brought in two San Francisco allies to work on the plan: Alfred W. Baxter Jr. university planning consultants, and Lawrence Halprin & Associates, landscape architects. Emmons immediately devised the scheme for a "garden campus." The most striking feature of the plan that emerged was a circular central campus circumscribed by a ring road. No academic unit within the pedestrian oriented ring would be more than ten-minute stroll to another. The academic buildings would be grouped around a central quadrangle of open meadow. There were further land acquisitions so that by

1988 the campus had grown to 385 acres (156 hectares). In 1961 Muirhead and Justice were engaged as landscape consultants, and in 1963 John Lantzius (who had been at Muirhead and Justice, and an apprentice in Halprin's office) was brought on as "executive landscape consultant," this still working under Halprin's overall guidance. A 1968 document *Landscape Concept—University of Victoria* articulates the guiding principles:

> It has been our intent from the beginning to reflect the native plant material of Vancouver Island on the campus, and to create an imaginative environment using such plants as Garry Oak, Arbutus, Dogwood and numerous other conifers. The major tree framework—which binds the buildings and open areas into a unified composition—is the most important and must receive the most emphasis. This tree framework of evergreen (broadleaf and conifer) trees will be used primarily in mass, to frame vistas, soften the architectural elements, as backgrounds, and as extensions of the forest areas. . . . The open areas will be contoured lawns which merge into the native forest.

Emmons insisted that no building should attempt to dominate another, or its landscape setting. Structures, roads, pathways should be landscaped in; the West Coast flora should prevail.

In 1967 Erickson Massey Architects replaced WBE as UVic's prime consultants for a three-year period. However, under their direction the extensive use of unrelieved slabs of grey concrete dominant in the design of the Commons Block and residences was not well received. In particular Erickson's disregard of the Emmons plan in his recommendation to close in the academic quadrangle with contiguous buildings was found unacceptable.

By 1972 WBE had been re-appointed and the firm was represented by Don Emmons until 1991 when the responsibility was passed to the Canon Design Group, Larry Canon having been in the office of WBE. Also by this time Don Vaughn & Associates (Vaughn formerly of Lantzius' office) had been appointed landscape consultants.

Two particular donations have reinforced the garden landscape of the university campus which, by 1975, had been transformed into verdant lawns and playing fields, bermed roads and pathways, treed boulevards and wooded glades. That year the university received by way of bequest over 100 species of rhododendrons from the Lake Cowichan estate of Jeanne Simpson. These laid the foundations of University Gardens on the main approach to campus at the juncture of Henderson and Ring roads. In 1990 Lieutenant-Governor Dr. David C. Lam donated funds to construct a major water feature, a fountain and reflecting pool in honour of outgoing university president Dr. Howard Petch. Don Vaughn was the designer.

Part of the orginal concept was to enliven the campus with public art. In addition to George Norris's monumental library panels and Di Castri's architectural sculpture, the campus features ceremonial poles by aboriginal artists such as Henry and Tony Hunt, Floyd Joseph and Charles Elliot; also free-standing bronze works by Victoria sculptor Elza Mayhew and benefactor Katharine Emma Maltwood. The University Art Collection, founded by Victoria College principal Harry Hickman, has grown to some 7,000 works, many of which enhance public spaces in campus buildings.

The Gordon Head Campus documents the development of modern architecture in Victoria over a period of some 40 years. As the scheme evolved we can discern the strands of an early debate between the international rationalists with their admiration for the legacy of Le Corbusier, his doctrine of mechanistic architecture and the formal expression of materials for their own sake—(Don Siddall, John Wade, Don Wagg, Alan Hodgson, David Hambleton, Terry Williams) on the one hand, and on the other the romantic traditionalists in the manner of Prairie School practice, Frank Lloyd Wright and Bruce Goff who were more inspired by the site itself, local craft and design tradition, and the decorative possibilities of texture—(John Di Castri, Barry Downs, Don Marshall, Allan Lester). However, in all cases pure principle was always compromised in favour of landscape aesthetics or demands of client departments or faculties. Local stone smoothed the transition through native groundcovers to exposed aggregate wall surfaces. Large multi-storey buildings were lifted above ground level, then opened up on the main floor for public use or blended with the adjacent landscape. Large building complexes provide for pedestrian interpenetration by way of pergola breezeways, intimate courtyards, glazed galleries or skylit concourses. And the habit of recessing or hooding windows creates shadow patterns on the wall surfaces much as the maturing arboreal leafy canopy treats the surface ground cover below. It remains to be seen if further additions to the built heritage at the Gordon Head Campus will continue to find this a useful design vocabulary.

NOTE

Ref. "The Development of the Gordon Head Campus." 1988. Smith, Peter L. "A Multitude of the Wise: UVic Remembered." 1993. Jupp, Ursula. "From Cordwood to Campus in Gordon Head 1852-1959." 1975.

Hamsterley Farm Water Tower
ca. 1911
For the Letitia and Algernon Pease Farm
3815 Haro Road, UVic

This Shingle style water tower and adjacent stable building are the last reminders that this was farming country at the turn of the century. Architect P. L. James' name has been connected with the tower design; he designed the Pease's house. The tower was originally a tank on a timber structure. In 1933 it was enclosed, roofed, and the tower shingled to incorporate it into the adjacent stables.

Communications Building
1941-1942
2260 McCoy Road, UVic
Archts. Department of Defence

With the gradual disappearance of Gordon Head Camp barrack structures, this communications centre may well be the only reminder of the campus's military history. Originally it contained power generation and radio equipment linked to a pylon type transmitter/receiver system. The rounded corners, smooth pebble-dash finish, and wrap-around corner windows make this a striking example of the Moderne style.

Clearihue Building
1962-1979
Archts. Wade Stockdill & Armour
Additions: Wagg & Hambleton

The first permanent new structure on the Gordon Head campus, this three-storey reinforced concrete building was designed as a general-purpose classroom block. The original exterior was exposed concrete and pre-cast concrete panels that were finished with marble aggregate set in coloured cement. The northwest part of the concourse was modified upon the completion of stage IV (Clearihue "B" Wing) in 1979; the entire configuration of the main floor was changed by major modifications in 1987. In the two original stairwells are mobile and stabile sculptures by Victoria artist and former faculty member, Prof. William D. West. Architects Wagg & Hambleton carried out additions 1971, 1976, and 1979, which resulted in a large, ponderously detailed complex of classrooms and faculty offices around an open courtyard. This stage also established the overall exterior finish of stucco and exposed concrete into which the original Clearihue has all but disappeared.

Student Union Building
1963, 1975, 1985
Archt. John A. Di Castri
Additions: Siddall Dennis Warner

The second new building on the Gordon Head campus was the "SUB." A reinforced concrete building with masonry infill, it was to represent

are, however, freestanding cast-concrete sculptures, and the basement light wells are finished with precast abstract relief sculpture panels.

In 1975, there was a major two-storey addition to the north for a cinema, and in 1995 a substantial eastern wing was added which substantially compromised the architectural integrity of the Di Castri original design. The SDW design uses a Post-Modern urban mall "festival" vocabulary to enclose a shopping and services concourse.

Elliott Building
1963 and 1964

Archt. W. R. H. Curtis, Provincial Department of Public Works

Di Castri at his most original. Eschewing progressive principles of the day, Di Castri chose to reference the Classical roots of monumental architecture by utilizing freestanding columns and a beam-end frieze at the roof line. The textured columns

The main structure is a reinforced concrete building, with pre-cast concrete panels on the exterior. The building was actually planned and designed for the Lansdowne Campus of Victoria College. Public Works architects were slow to abandon the late Moderne style with Deco touches which had been the hallmark of the Whittaker era of the 1940s. Abstract crenelations at the roofline are perhaps intended as subtle Medievalisms. The original occupants were the Departments of Biology, Chemistry and Physics. Astronomy is noted by the rooftop observatory. The adjoining "Elliott Lecture Theatre" is a one-storey reinforced concrete building with a

folded concrete plate roof that provides a clerestory for the interior central concourse.

McPherson Library
1964 and 1974

Archts. R. W. Siddall Associates
Second Stage Archt.: Siddall Dennis Warner

This is a four-storey reinforced concrete building, the first storey being below grade and an office penthouse on the roof. It is no symbolic accident that this temple-like form dominates the academic quadrangle. The library is the functional core of academe. The most impressive feature is a series of bas-relief pre-cast concrete panels designed by BC sculptor George A. Norris.

These are hung forward of the building allowing the otherwise Rationalist International style glass and aluminum curtain wall to skirt the functional structure. The attic storey is given a sculpted frieze, also by Norris. At ground level the building rests solidly on a rough granite ground floor podium. There is a glass mosaic panel in the main lobby, the work of Margaret Peterson. A major addition finished in 1974 on the north side doubled the size of the Library and further replica Norris panels were applied to preserve the design integrity.

Craigdarroch Residences
1964-1967

Archts. R. W. Siddall Associates

These residences consist of four four-storey buildings, which together house about 300 students. The buildings are of reinforced concrete with stucco and stone exterior finish. Although incorporating design elements to transmit a West Coast feel, particularly the stonework foundation and form-cast window transoms to emulate split timber, this group of buildings really documents the drift toward New Brutalism in American and European Expressionist design. At this time Paul Rudolph was finishing his ponderously scaled Art and Architecture Building at Yale. The effect of Craigdarroch's overpowering hung concrete panels is similar to Rudolph's heavy Constructivist forms. However, the interior garden courtyard, formed by the blocks and their linking pergola ramps and walkways, which are humanly scaled and inviting, provides a new world interpretation of the old-world Oxbridge cloister.

Campus Services Building
1965, 1986, 1996

Archts. Wagg & Hambleton
Addition: Jensen Group, 1996

A two-storey reinforced concrete building with masonry infill walls, Campus Services was financed by prepaid rentals from the Bank of Montreal, principal tenant of the building until 1982. Although a fairly

formal essay in Modern Rationalist design, the final effect is dominated by a floating roof form of massive prestressed concrete T-beams. Various alterations over the years, including a south facing addition in 1986, respected the original scheme. A further extension (1996) to the north with a dramatic entrance canopy feature, distinguished stylistically from the original, is the work of the Jensen Group.

link four distinct architectural elements around a small and intimate inner quadrangle. From the outset, the complex has housed the Social Science departments. For over 15 years, the interior courtyard was graced by two majestic totem poles that were carved by native artists Henry and Tony Hunt; in May 1982 these replicas of original Tsimshian poles were removed to a more visible location in the main quadrangle.

Cornett Building
1966
Archt. John A. Di Castri

A three-storey reinforced concrete multi-block structure, the design expresses Di Castri's rich textural search for a distinctive West Coast architectural idiom. The exterior is a sculptural composition in a variety of materials: expanded shale aggregate block, marble-type stucco, concrete blocks, rubbed concrete beams and columns, and local metamorphic rock. Covered breezeways marked by freestanding form-sculpted columns

MacLaurin Building
1966, 1978
Archt. Alan J. Hodgson

This building consists of several wings of offices, classrooms, and laboratories, rising to a maximum height of five storeys. Built of reinforced concrete, it has an exterior finish of concrete and coloured brick facings, but is distinguished by wooden window hoods that are both decorative and functional. MacLaurin was the university's most bold piece of

Expressionist architecture. It utilized Corbusier's concrete stilts to lift up the massive structure from its site, providing open people spaces within its glazed concourses. The Music Wing added in 1978, also by Hodgson, has respected and extended the original design vocabulary which is marked by a precise attention to design and craft detail. Originally planned as an "Education-Arts" facility, the building at first accommodated the Faculties of Education along with some humanities and Fine Arts although today it houses only the Education Faculty.

Centennial Stadium
1967

Archts. Siddall, Dennis & Associates

In cooperation with the Greater Victoria Centennial Society and municipalities of the region, the university planned and built this community stadium to celebrate the hundredth anniversary of Canadian Confederation. The cantilever roof shelters some 3,000 seats. Viewers look out on a running track and a playing field. As a frank expression of engineering principles the stadium symbolized the university's early commitment to the design principles of the modern Progressive movement.

Sedgewick Building
1968 and 1969

Arcgt. Barry V. Downs, Vancouver

The "Sedgewick Building" consists in fact of three separate but closely

grouped units built to accommodate a number of humanities and administrative departments. Downs provided a series of one-storey buildings of wood frame construction. The exterior finish is green stained cedar siding; the extended roof eaves drop down to break the fenestration courses, and like the end-wall extensions bring the building elements into the informal landscape of native Salal and conifers. Called by some "nuts-and-berry" architecture it remains the campus's most expressive and sensitive piece of West Coast design: informal and domestic rather than monumental and institutional.

Cadboro Commons
1969

Archts. Siddall, Dennis & Associates

This project consisted of two separate buildings. The major section, a dining facility, is a two-storey reinforced concrete building, with exterior of exposed concrete and stone. This is connected via a bridge and breezeway to a building originally intended as administrative offices for Craigdarroch College. The massive floating planes of reinforced form-textured concrete elements mostly comprising cantilevered roofs, balconies and windowless walls compress even the robust rock dressed understorey. The design carried Neo-Brutal Expressionism one step further than the earlier Craigdarroch Residence blocks. This can be compared to the more restrained Rationalism of the Lansdowne Residences also by Siddall Dennis and built in the same year.

University House
1970

Archts. Siddall Dennis Warner

Located at the corner of Haro and Sinclair Roads, this house was constructed as an official residence for Bruce Partridge, second President of the University.

Since 1972 it has served as a guest house and then offices. Although decidedly Modern in its formal simplicity the use of traditional Victoria domestic materials, drop siding with board-and-batten, fits the house to its edge location at Mystic Vale where the campus meets the residential neighbourhood of Cadboro Bay.

Cunningham Building
1971

Archts. Erickson Massey, Vancouver

This is a three-storey reinforced concrete building, with exterior walls of exposed concrete. It was designed to accommodate classrooms, offices, laboratories, and other research facilities of the biological sciences. The wooded site with its naturalized landscaping works to good effect to soften the boldly expressive vertical and horizontal elements which are Erickson's trademark. On the interior ductwork and services are exposed, giving the structure a "high-tech" science-is-our-business feel.

Saunders Building
1974

Archts. Peterson & Lester

The Saunders Building consists of a one-storey shop and storage building for the campus planning and maintenance departments. The wood-frame design is minimalist and contemporary but the use of cedar and native planting provides an indigenous West Coast connection. In 1979 Peterson and Lester followed the same design formula in plans provided for a second set of nearby utility buildings to temporarily house the Visual Arts Department.

McKinnon Building
1975, 1980

Archts. Rhone & Iredale, Vancouver

Built to meet the academic needs of Physical Education and sports recreation, the swimming pool and gymnasium represent the first use of pre-cast tilt construction on campus. An

extension was added in 1980, and in 1981 a solar heating system was installed on the roof. An example of modern Expressionist aesthetics, the structure bespeaks the engineering principles with an honest formalism.

University Centre
1978

Archts. Wade Williams' Partnership

This is a two-storey reinforced concrete building, with a bush-hammered finish. The main office wing is surrounded, on both levels, by a colonnade of concrete pillars. Its roofline features prominent mechanical penthouses, finished in copper. Planned as the focal point of campus activity, University Centre houses Student Records and Admissions, a Board and Senate Chamber, a large lobby, cafeteria and lounge, and the Maltwood Art Museum and Gallery. The showpiece auditorium, Canada's first "surround" hall, was opened in September 1978; it seats 1,233 people on ground floor, balcony, and choir. Among the acoustical features of the auditorium are retractable sound-absorbing banners, designed by Victoria fabric artist Carol Sabiston. In the context of Wade Williams' work the building is very much a development of

their earlier Saanich Municipal Hall (1964-1965) especially in the handling of the skylit lobby. The exterior treatment includes the use of freestanding columns, from which the walls are pulled back under the eave fascia. Second-floor level plantings intended to achieve a garden terrace effect serve to soften the design formalism and accent the expansive horizontality.

Gordon Head Residences
1978
McGill Residences
1981

Archts. Siddall Dennis Warner

The three multi-storey residence buildings for students are all of wood frame construction, with exterior finish in stucco and cedar siding. That these buildings have assumed the nondescript form of commercial condominia reveals a shift of the university to market methods of construction finance in its revenue operations. The residences were financed with the assistance of the federal government through the Central Mortgage and Housing Corporation.

Begbie Building
1980

Archts. Wagg & Hambleton

Conceived as complex series of interlocking forms which step back

design offices, scene shop and costume rooms, dressing rooms, lobby areas. The result is a building which contributes little to the design aesthetic of campus, as the warehouse effect of the steel clad elements are a direct expression of the internal functional requirements.

from the Ring Road and merge with the natural forest on three sides, the building uses a warm red brick facetted finish and recessed window bands to complete this effect. It houses the university's Faculty of Law. The entrance features a rustic heavy timbered *porte-cochere* providing an effective transition from the naturalized landscaping into the formal lobby. Many of these elements, and the close attention to finishing detail can be found in Wagg & Hambleton's later Human and Social Development Building (1992) and the two wings of the Business School (1996).

Faculty Club
1982
Archts. Marshall, Goldsworthy & Associates

This facility was built to replace a Faculty Lounge that had operated for many years in hut "E," the former Officers' Mess of the Gordon Head Army Camp. Sited in what had been swampland, the head of Bowker Creek, the single-storey wood frame building "floats" on a concrete raft. The widespread hipped shingle roof elements with extended eaves, and the use of flush cedar siding fit this into both Victoria's tradition of Arts & Crafts design and the expressive West Coast domestic work of Arthur Erickson, Fred Hollingsworth and others. The main dining room features a soaring open post-and-beam structural system finished in stained fir and cedar.

Phoenix Theatre
1980
Archts. Peterson & Lester

In keeping with the academic philosophy of the teaching program, this building was designed around three intimate and diverse theatrical spaces that might best serve the combined needs of teaching and performance. The back-stage and above-stage working areas of all three theatres are interconnected, for maximum efficiency. Surrounding these performance spaces are faculty offices, classrooms, seminar rooms, studios,

Interfaith Chapel
1985
Archt. John A. Di Castri

The chapel is a single-storey building of wood frame construction, with cedar siding finish and a hipped roof covered with cedar shingles. Following a design program that insisted the final building

be reference neutral in terms of any particular faith, the architect used Victoria's traditional but internationally ancient bungalow form to create a sacred house. The influence of Wright's Prairie School aesthetic can be felt throughout. Constructed on the edge of the University Gardens, floor to ceiling windows in the main assembly space literally bring the landscaping into the structure.

Petch Building
1986, 1990, 1995

Science and Engineering
1986

Archts. Wade Williams Partnership

Engineering Office Building
1990

Archts. Wade Williams Partnership

Engineering Laboratory Wing
1995

Archts. Wade Williams Partnership with Young Wright, Toronto

This building was planned to accommodate the university's new expanding Engineering and Science departments. The Science and Engineering Complex is a three-storey building of reinforced concrete construction. It shares a number of design features with University Centre, including the use of mechanical penthouses finished in copper and horizontal registers of concrete panels from which the functional façade is pulled back. In sharp contrast is the International style office building linked via an enclosed sky walk to the Laboratory Wing. The structure is treated as a grid glazed block, seen as a sort of Rubic's Cube of glinting mirror glass through the wooded glade in which it is sited. The Engineering Laboratory Wing provides teaching and research laboratories. Here the design vocabulary changes again to "High-Tech" utilizing an industrial modular panel finish and louvered window strips to provide indirect lighting to the computer labs.

The Fine Arts Building
1991

Archts. Marshall Goldsworthy Garyali

The cool off-white facetted concrete finish, spare lines and articulation of wall roof and base elements on a geometric grid gives this building a Classical feel. A classroom block steps down toward the Fine Arts piazza onto which the building faces along with Pheonix Theatre and Visual Arts buildings. A particular feature is the two-storey entrance hall which also serves as an exhibition space.

The Commonwealth Housing Villages
1993

The decision to the use the University of Victoria as the main venue for the 1993 Commonwealth Games provided the impetus and financial subsidies for a substantial increase in student housing and an upgrade of the sports facilities. A southern bank of seats was

Halpern Graduate Students Centre
1991

Archt. Carl Peterson

Di Castri's chapel may have inspired the Graduate Students Centre. A small building but very sophisticated design, the large hipped roof shelters a central meeting room with peripheral meeting rooms and cafeteria. The decorative trusswork, a feature of the main room, reinforces the structural expression of the timber elements and finishes, central to traditional West Coast design as originally inspired by earlier Arts & Crafts practitioners.

Also by Peterson, the Daycare Complex (1993) pursues similar design principles, even more appropriate to the woodland setting on Finnerty Road.

added to the stadium; tracks and playing fields were upgraded, consulting architects being Wade Williams with Young Wright. Six new housing complexes were constructed. A green field site on the northeast corner of Finnerty and Sinclair roads was

zoned for five villages to house students with families. Each village would contain a mix of self-contained family housing types, sharing some common spaces and facilities. A traditional Victoria design vernacular drawn from its distinctive Arts & Crafts and Victorian Queen Anne neighbourhoods was utilized throughout.

Village Five (1993: architects Campbell Moore Group) designed as an apartment complex recalls Rattenbury's Rocky Mountain Edwardian hotels for the Canadian Pacific Railway. Village Four (1993: Architects Holovsky Mansfield; Design P. Chang) adopted the local Victorian Queen Anne vernacular. Village One (1994: Architects Bas Smith) is also a variation in this Wood, Shingle and Stick style. Village Two (1994: Architect Eric Barker). Village Three (1994: Architects Bawlf Keay Associates; Design J. Keay and J. Stark) at the centre of the radial scheme, provided three floor plans including split-level and three-bedroom variations, the units drawn together around a central secure courtyard. The Commonwealth Village, Cluster Housing Complex (1994: Architect Bas Smith) was apparently more closely supervised by Larry Cannon; it adopts a more literal landscape approach with the extensive use of trelliage motifs, even utilizing a "village green" as part of the ground plan. Campus Security Building (1996) is also the work of Bas Smith.

The Visual Arts Building
1993

Archts. Chow & Fleischauer

Part of the Fine Arts enclave, the restrained Post Modernism of the design makes a striking contrast with the university's previous design tradition. An open galleried skylit entrance hall introduces the sophisticated spatial treatment of the various design and painting studios. The cool green and grey colour scheme subtly highlights the geometric fragments which form the basis of the architecural composition.

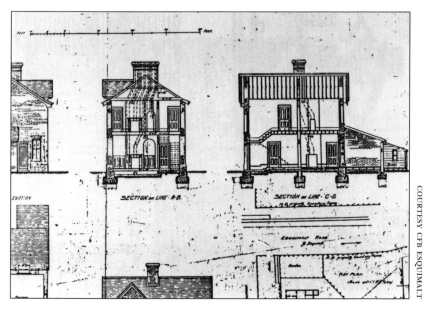

Sergeant's Mess, Work Point, Record Plan, 1903.

Esquimalt: The Military Mind

The protective presence of the Royal Navy at Victoria began in 1846 when the British transferred their Pacific Squadron headquarters from Valparaiso, Chile to Esquimalt, Vancouver Island. The Navy took over buildings at Constance Cove that the Hudson's Bay Company had constructed in 1856 for a detachment of Royal Engineers surveying the International Boundary. The Navy fitted these out for Crimean War casualties. This was to become the site of the Naden military hospital. Over the years Naden gradually expanded into the old town-site of Esquimalt. Thereafter, the military presence in Victoria fluctuated with the machinations of international diplomacy. As steam replaced sail, Esquimalt became a major coaling station. In 1867 the establishment of a graving dock was mooted and Wright and Sanders provided a set of specifications. Deteriorating Anglo-Russian relations in 1878 caused defensive batteries to be established at the entrance to Esquimalt Harbour on Macaulay Point and Brothers Island, also below Beacon Hill and Ross Bay to protect Victoria. In 1883 a Canadian artillery battery was raised and Work Point Barracks was established for it in 1887. In 1893, further Russian problems prompted a cost-sharing agreement between Britain and Canada allowing for British troops to be stationed at Work Point. New defensive batteries were built at Macaulay Point and Rodd Hill. In 1898 work started to plan and install defensive electric submarine minefields at Esquimalt Harbour entrance. Signal Hill was built to house the army corps sent for this task. The red brick complex has the feel and scale of an English village. It was built as a piece so there is remarkable homogeneity to the design and detailing of these unadorned turn-of-the-century brick buildings, many with verandah fronts. When British troops left Esquimalt in 1906, the base was mothballed until 1914. After experiencing increased activity during World War I, military activity all but ceased until 1938. By the end of World War II, gun batteries had been built at Christopher Point, May Hill, Albert Head, Belmont, Duntze Head, Black Rock, Macaulay Point, Golf Hill and Ogden Point. Observation and command posts were built on Triangle Mountain, Church Hill, Mary Hill, Gonzales Hill and Mount Tolmie. The Dockyard and Naden were administered as separate units until 1969 when they were combined under the Canadian Armed Forces "Base Concept." Work Point has operated under separate administration as a base for defensive land forces.

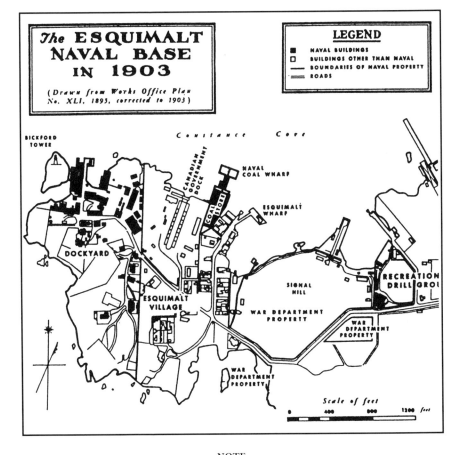

NOTE

Ref. Oliver, Nancy "CFB Esquimalt: Military Heritage." n.d.

Dockyard, Naden and Cole Island

Guard House
1864
Cole Island, Esquimalt

One-acre Cole Island at the head of Esquimalt Harbour became the storage site for Royal Naval explosives in 1860.

By the time of its decommissioning in 1937 numerous buildings had been constructed. In 1974 Parks Canada took over administration of Cole Island as part of Fort Rodd Hill historic site. The guardhouse, a two-storey structure built of brick and stone, commands a good view down the harbour toward the dockyard.

St. Paul's Garrison Church
1866
Dockyard, Esquimalt
Archt. Thomas Trounce

St. Paul's is one of finest, and largest, Gothic Revival wooden churches in the Victoria area. The stained glass in particular is notable, along with carved oak furniture dating from 1930, and an ornately decorated pipe organ. In 1903 the church was moved eastward from its original site to avoid vibration damage from the constant gunnery practice on nearby Signal Hill. The nave features a crossing and the sanctuary is treated as a separate extension of the nave area; entrance is via a side porch at the west end.

Chief Engineer's Quarters
1879
Dockyard, Esquimalt

The house was originally a two-storey L-plan cottage with a one-and-a-half storey kitchen extension to the rear. This has since had a second floor addition and a two-storey covered porch and balcony has replaced the simple front entrance verandah (ca. 1931). Early photos reveal extensive and luxurious gardens. Construction is timber frame with drop siding and sash windows.

House for the Naval Stores Officer
1885
Dockyard, Esquimalt
Archt. John Teague

As the main function of Esquimalt was that of a provisioning depot it is not surprising that the stores officer would be supplied with a substantial house.

Teague produced an Italianate style brick building using a vaguely Georgian form. The hipped roof is supported by bracketted eaves. Corner quoins set off the brick walls, the windows marked by substantial hood mouldings on the main façades. The entrance hall and stairwell are expressed at the front by a deep arched window and off-centre doorway sheltered by a balustraded portico. Two bay windows dominate the rear garden side. A gable-dormered service wing adjoins the house on the east side. The house is now known as "Admiral's House," the official residence of the Commanding Officer.

90-foot dock, 33-feet-6-inches deep, is built of granite blocks. The dock was decommissioned in 1927 but refurbished for use by Yarrows in 1945. The pump house, a low Romanesque Revival style building constructed of rusticated sandstone, featured a matching 90-foot stone tower chimney. In 1968 the height was reduced by 15 feet. On the other hand the wall heights have been raised substantially, destroying the original proportions.

Graving Dock and Pump House
1880, 1887

Dockyard, Esquimalt

Construction of the graving dock was made part of the terms of Confederation for British Columbia. Plans were drawn up by British civil engineers Knipple & Morris of London in 1874. Construction began in 1876 but problems with tendering and contract completions delayed the opening until 1887. (Total cost $1,172,664.74.) The 481-foot by

Munitions Magazines
ca. 1890

Cole Island, Esquimalt

Three such buildings on the Island, extended on masonry piers out into the waters of the harbour, allowed for loading directly from small boats. These are gable-end utilitarian structures. Similar wooden buildings were originally clad in zinc and utilized

237

brass nails in their construction to mitigate any danger of sparks. These latter have since been demolished.

Factory
1891
Dockyard, Esquimalt
Archt. John Teague

Similar in form and detail to the Admiral's house, this is probably from designs by John Teague. The main two-storey brick building with attached range of gable-ended structures housed design, drafting and machine shop functions. The English-bond brickwork is relieved by quoined corners and heavy window hoods.

Warehouse
1898
Dockyard, Esquimalt

Although constructed for use as a provisioning facility the building is a sophisticated piece of design work, technically and aesthetically. Built from land out into the harbour, the various floors can load from water at bays recessed under the piers or from the second and third storeys waterside. The land end loads into both upper storeys through heavily quoined receiving bays. Each end gable is marked by a dressed granite oculus ventilator flanked by two chimneys rising through a corbelled cornice.

Large basket arch windows light the interior, the floors and roof supported by heavy timber framing.

Prison and Warders' Residence
1899
Dockyard, Esquimalt
Archt. T. Woodgate, Eng.

A well detailed brick block, its function noted by the barred windows, the gable ends are finished with corbelled eaves, the windows set off with lug sills and the doorways with stone quoin frames. The prison wall was part of the original dockyard boundary wall. Across the street a plain stucco block contains within it the structure of what was originally the warder's residence.

PMQs, Artificers' and Warrant Officers' Quarters
1900
Signal Hill, Esquimalt

The Signal Hill area adjacent to the dockyard was developed to accommodate the extra army troops brought to install the submarine

minefields and set up defensive search lights. Of the numerous historic buildings surviving in the Signal Hill complex, among the most interesting are the permanent married quarters (PMQ). Of all the military buildings in the Esquimalt area, these are the most overtly English in character and local tradition has it that millwork and fitting, brick and roofslate were brought from England along with the designs. The Privates' Quarters are located in a row of four semi-detached units, each unit marked by a gable dormer which drops through the eaves and a shed roof entrance. Four massive brick chimneys mark the party walls as they rise through the long saddle roof. The Armament Artificers' Quarters is a mirror image two-storey duplex with triple sash windows opening up the forward gable bays. At the base of Signal Hill the two-storey Warrant Officers' residence is distinguished by its low hipped roof, projecting bay window, and the use of moulded brick on the door and window surrounds.

Naden Naval Hospital
Men's Wards and Administration
1888-1889

Hospital Stores Building
1890

Officers' Ward
1891

Naden, Esquimalt
Archt. John Teague

The south Men's Ward was built in 1888, the North Ward and Administration Block in 1889. Each

ward has two projecting rear pavilions which share an open porch. A balustraded balcony traversed the front and this was later (ca. 1900) transformed into a roofed verandah. The buildings are one storey with hipped roofs. The brick walls are detailed with heavy quoining at the corners, equally heavy window hood mouldings and sills, and generous eaves with bracketted soffits. The complex includes a stores building added in 1890, a long low Bungalow style structure distinguished by its lean-to verandah with elaborate millwork detailing. The Officers' Ward is a classic Victorian Colonial bungalow. The low rise hipped roof extends over two projecting window bays which flank the central entrance doorway. The verandah front projects out from under the bracketted eaves and is supported by ornate supporting millwork.

Bickford Tower
1901

Dockyard, Esquimalt

This octagonal brick structure functioned as a signaling station and is located on a promontory at the entrance to the harbour. The tower itself provided accommodation for the

Victualling Office
1902

Dockyard, Esquimalt
Archt. T. Woodgate Eng.

One of a series of brick structures constructed during the turn-of-the-century base expansion, the office is a no-nonsense utilitarian design but constructed to what are obviously exacting standards for finish and detail. Numerous structures similar in style and detail survive at the dockyard from the extensive building program of 1895 to 1905. Examples are the Works Office (1902), and the Stone Frigate (1904). This was built as a sailors' barracks for ships under repair. The structure could house 74 men, 8 petty officers and one warrant officer. The long saddle-roofed structure is constructed of random rubble with brick detailing for all window and door openings.

signals crew. Corbelled brickwork at the top supports a lookout platform and glazed octagonal signal room.

Administration Building
1936

Naden, Esquimalt

The military chevron motif on the pilasters distinguish this Moderne style building. Although only two storeys, the formal symmetry of the design, the landscaping and siting lend a commanding presence in the base complex.

Administration Building
1937

Dockyard, Esquimalt

The brick building traditions of the dockyard were respected in this structure

in the shadow of extended eaves and view decks, the main public spaces overlook views across Royal Roads to the Metchosin Hills.

although the design is far from utilitarian. Certainly an air of dignity, if not pretense, is added to the base by the Georgian Revival style indicated by the symmetrical façade, generous multi-pane windows, and pilastered bays reaching up to the parapet which masks a recessed fourth floor.

Warfare Training Facility
1986

Black Rock, Dockyard
Archts. Wade Williams

Junior Ranks Club
1976

Dockyard, Esquimalt
Archts. Wade Williams

Built into the side of a rocky promontory, the grey concrete building is anchored by heavy angular stair towers; deep roof-edge fascias reinforce the horizontal lines. On the water side

There is more than a hint of Rationalist 1920s Bauhaus in the compact design of this three-storey structure. But there is also a playful treatment of solids and voids as the building envelope advances or retreats from the reinforced concrete grid to comprise an overall effect that might be termed Modern Picturesque Rationalism.

PHOTO R. D'ESRUBE

Junior Ranks Club, Dockyard.

Work Point, Esquimalt

Barracks
1888

While the British Army and Navy at the Dockyards and Naden felt the need to build in low maintenance by using brick, Canadian Artillary C Battery, perhaps for speed as well as economy, built in wood. The barracks, the last surviving of three similar ranges, is a long hipped roof frame structure. The hipped roof central entry porch is flanked by gables, the only concession to ornament in the design.

Guardhouse
1889

This Bungalow style gatehouse guarded the entrance to the barracks. The steep hipped roof is caped by a brick chimney, the verandah is contained within an extended hip. The walls are finished in drop siding as original but the supporting

pillars of the verandah roof have been simplified by later modifications.

Officers' Quarters
1892

This range of officers' housing was the last structure to be built by Canadian C Battery before Work Point was turned over to the Imperial Government in 1893. The long two-storey wood frame building is clad in bevelled siding. Each unit is marked by a half-storey dormer, the gable breaking the eaves of the long saddle roof and gabled entrance porches.

Sergeants' Mess
1902

Also a Royal Engineers design, the mess is a one-storey brick building with a slate gable-end roof and clerestory at

the peak to light the mess hall. It is built over a partial cellar and also included a billiard room, kitchen, and storeroom. The dining hall became a Chapel in 1954 dedicated to St. Barbara, the patron saint of artillerymen, armorers, gunsmiths and miners.

Detention Barracks
1904

The red brick detention barracks opens onto a walled recreation yard. The design is simpler and more spare than that built earlier for similar purposes at the Dockyard. The first floor contained a guard room and kitchen, the cells were on the second floor.

Administration Building
1918, ca. 1942

The first administration building was destroyed by fire in 1917. The second structure was also wood frame with a drop siding finish. However, continuing the martial imagery of Victoria's newly constructed Armories this building was also given a castellated treatment including a crenellated parapet with protruding turrets and a central tower providing an arched entrance porch.

Signals Building
1938

This Moderne style two-storey structure housed the "telephone and radio" component of the Royal Canadian Corps of Signals from 1939. A brick foundation acts as a plinth; the brick course rises into the Deco style entrance surround of the extended portico bay.

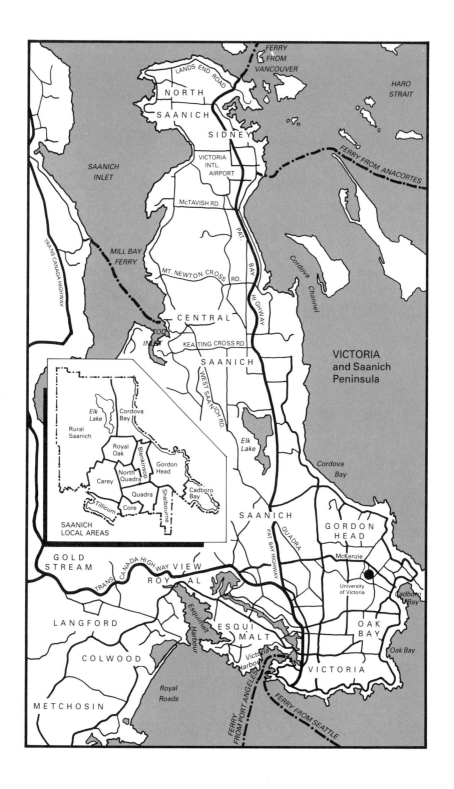

Saanich Peninsula: Rural Landscape

The mainland watersheds of the Columbia and Fraser Rivers, the expanse of saltwater we now call the Georgia Basin, and lower Vancouver Island, constitute the territory of the Coast Salish aboriginal people. The Salish wintered on Saanich Peninsula villages near Saanichton, Coles Bay and Patricia Bay from which they directed their food gathering activities. Today these bands maintain reserve villages at Tsartlip, Pauquachin, Tseycum, and Tsawout.

During the 1850s, as the Hudson's Bay Company opened its own farms closer to Fort Victoria. The company encouraged private farmers to also establish on the peninsula. Dairy, grain and produce farming was supplemented with logging. However, the peninsula really had to await the Victoria land boom of the 1890s, particularly the railways, to experience marked development. Saanich and North Saanich were finally incorporated in 1906. North Saanich, however, collapsed in 1911. In 1908 Saanich was divided into six wards. Central Saanich originally comprised Wards 5 and 6; both agitated over many years for seccesion and in 1951 this was granted by the province to Ward 6 which became the Municipality of Central Saanich. The following year Sidney was incorporated as a municipality. It represents a microcosmic view of the Peninsula's development.

NOTE

Ref. Barr, Jennifer, Nell. "Saanich Heritage Structures: An Inventory." 1991. Lillard, Charles. "Paths our Ancestors Walked: Father Vullinghs & the Saanich Peninsula 1893-1909." 1977. Luxton, Donald. "C.R.D. Art Deco and Moderne." n.d. "A Registry of Accessible Buildings of Heritage Merit." 1983. Virgin, Victor E. "History of North and South Saanich Pioneers and District." 1978.

Sidney-by-the-Sea

The first land purchases from the Hudson's Bay Company in the area now incorporated by Sidney occurred in 1859. Farming developed and in 1887 a flour mill was operational. However, real prosperity dates from 1890 when fishing, lumbering and sawmilling began to supplement farming. Beacon Avenue, with its general store, post office, hotel and boat building operation, marked the start of a concentrated settlement. In 1891, 500 acres owned by the four Brethour brothers were registered as the Township of Sidney. In 1895 the Victoria and Sidney Railway was inaugurated to serve the need to transport lumber and produce to Victoria, and holiday seekers out to Sidney. To enhance the attraction value a concert and dance pavilion was erected. By 1900 the railway linked to a mainland ferry at Sidney and in 1903 a car ferry service was available. Manufacturing underpinned the Sidney economy: Sidney Roofing Co. established in 1914 and a number of brickworks exploited good silica clay deposits (supplying for instance brick for the Empress Hotel). In 1922 Sidney became a port of entry as the Sidney-Anacortes ferry linked Vancouver Island with the Olympic Peninsula, Washington State. Even World War II saw boom years for the town as Patricia Bay "aerodrome" was established for air command coastal defence purposes. In 1967 Sidney became a town under the terms of the Provincial Municipal Act.

NOTE
Ref. "Sidney British Columbia Canada Heritage Walking Tour." n.d.

Levi Wilson House
ca. 1900
2445 Amelia Street, Sidney

Wilson's seasonal work was fishing and timber falling, skills required of the two main industries of early Sidney. This two-storey vertical Victorian house with its inset corner entrance at the gable end is typical of pioneer building types of the period.

Sea Point House for Captain L. Adamson
1909
1021 Surfside Place, Sidney

Captain Lindsay Adamson commissioned this house, along with extensive gardens and tennis court, at a time when Sidney was starting to become a leisure and retirement resort. Essentially a Shingle style Arts & Crafts house featuring a shallow hipped roof with generous eaves, the columned entrance porch provides an overt hint of the fashionable Edwardian Classical influence.

St. Andrew's Anglican Church
1910
9686 Third Street, Sidney
Archt. J. C. M. Keith

Keith, the architect of Victoria's Anglican Cathedral, also provided the Vancouver Island diocese with a number of small Shingle style parish churches. This is a good example of his work which includes others at Port Alberni, Duncan and the Gulf Islands.

The original shingle finish has been unfortunately lost; however, the interior utilizing stained glass to good effect is well preserved. At the south side entrance, outside, hangs an octave set of Harrington's tubular bells presented to St. Andrew's in 1936.

R. Oldfield House
1912
10162 Resthaven Drive, Sidney

Supposedly constructed from a set of mail-order plans, this is nevertheless an imposing structure. It is constructed of formed concrete block, sometimes called "hydro-stone" at this time. The

Classical two-storey design features a hipped roof surmounting a symmetrical façade which is dominated by the paired ionic columns of the entrance verandah.

"Orchard House" for Roy Brethour
1914
9646 Sixth Street, Sidney

The Brethour family were pioneer Sidney landowners and developers. This house, named after the area in which this subdivision was laid out, was built by Wilson Contracting and is typical of the California Bungalow residences which line Fifth and Sixth streets. Distinguishing details are the extended gable roofs, open timber work verandahs, and generous staircases to the deep porch entrances.

C. C. Cochrane House
1915
2562 Beaufort Road, Sidney

Built by developer S. Brethour for $3,500, this Arts & Crafts bungalow is sited to maximize the various sea views from what was a naturally forested lot. The inset verandah entrance is sheltered within the low-rise dormered hip roof; walls are shingle clad to sill level, then sheathed in drop siding. Such details were popularized in Victoria by the "Maclure Bungalow" of the early 1900s.

"Miraloma" for Hon. W. C. Nichol
1925
2328 Harbour Road, Sidney
Archt. Samuel Maclure
Restoration: Bawlf Cooper, 1976

Maclure contributed two major buildings to early Sidney. The first, built as Resthaven Country Club in 1912 for an unsuccessful exclusive subdivision development, was demolished in 1978 after years of use as convalescent hospital. "Miraloma," the most powerful Rustic style design of his career, was a summer holiday retreat for newspaperman and Lieutenant-Governor William C. Nichol. Maclure had experimented with unbarked slab finish in an early 1915 cottage for Moresby White near Swartz Bay. "Miraloma," built using natural fieldstone, unbarked slab and timbers, was set in an open woodland glade of native fir, cedar, arbutus and camas lily.

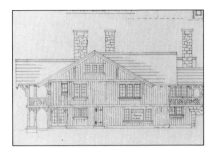

Balconies and verandahs at both levels were designed to feature the seaviews and garden vistas. Retractable windows opened onto the balconies. The interior featured natural woods, carved detailing by sculptor George Gibson and impressionistic stain paintings by artist R. Sheldon Williams worked into the panels. In 1976 architects Bawlf Cooper undertook a masterful restoration and conversion of "Miraloma" to restaurant use.

ICL Works Manager's House
1927

2340 Weiler Avenue, Sidney

This house was moved from the offshore James Island ICL explosives manufacturing plant when the plant closed in 1963. A degree of pretention is introduced by four massive Doric pillars which punctuate the inset front porch. The influence is American and rather typical of the Colonial Revival style catalogue house plans obtainable throughout North America in the 1920s.

ICL Plant Cottages
1927

2296, 2316, 2312 Mills Road, Sidney

These Craftsman style cottages (so named after the popular American magazine which popularized the idiom) were moved to Sidney when the ICL James Island explosives plant closed in 1963. These one-storey bungalows are distinguished by their shingle cladding, gabled porches and extended roof overhangs.

Satellite Fish Co. Building
1927

2550 Beacon Avenue, Sidney

This industrial building type is fast disappearing from the British Columbia

249

coastline as ports, harbours and company docks rationalize and transportation patterns change. The galvanized iron clad structure, and many others like it, acted as a goods exchange and storage depot for the coastal steamer trade which was Vancouver Island's economic and social lifeline until the massive ferry construction and road building programs of late 1950s and early 1960s overtook the CPR's coastal steamship system.

extends to the garden. The gardens have been restored to the original English Gertrude Jekyll Arts & Crafts style utilizing naturalized bulbs and native flora by garden restoration expert Cyril Hume whose clientele in Victoria included Point Ellice House and Craigflower Manor.

Finlayson House
ca. 1935
10130 Fifth Street, Sidney

A lyrical example of the English Arts & Crafts style, much in the manner of its pioneering architect C. F. A. Voysey. The steep roof planes of the double gable, the oriel window, white rough-cast finish, and sweep of one gable end to enclose a garden gate are all hallmarks of the style as introduced to Victoria by such architects as Ross Lort and Harry Day.

Mrs. Stuart House
1936
2525 Beaufort Road, Sidney
Archt. Hubert Savage

A unique blend of Arts & Crafts landscape with similar cottage residence, the design features a bay window which

Sidney Post Office
1936
2423 Beacon Avenue, Sidney

One of the Department of Public Works' standard town designs, the gabled entrance and dormers, red brick with diaper patterns and stone copings give a Picturesque Collegiate Gothic feel. The modern addition to the east side has not compromised the dominating presence of the building in the town centre streetscape.

Vancouver Island Regional Library, Sidney-North Saanich Branch
1982
10091 Resthaven Drive, Sidney
Archts. Marshall Goldsworthy Assoc.

West Coast Modern Expressionism as an architectural statement is well represented by this structure, set off by its maturing rhododendrons and generously open landscape setting. The horizontality of the bungalow form is articulated here as three semi-detached units marked by the hipped shingle roofs. The interior spaces are open and airy, revealing the trusswork of the ceiling lofts. Not surprising the overall design approach bears marked resemblances to the MGA's University of Victoria Faculty Club of the same date.

Brenher Lane
1995

10140 Fifth Street, Sidney
Archt. Zebra Designitects

This six-unit range of townhouses owes much to contemporary influence of "new age" architecture represented by the architects Andres Duany's and Elizabeth Plater-Zyberk's Romantic vernacular revivals at Seaside, Florida (1981). However, here the built form draws very literally on the Victorian era pioneer farmstead architecture of the Saanich Peninsula and perhaps points a direction to those wishing to preserve the rural village charm and character of Sidney while admitting further densification.

Saanich Peninsula

"South Saanich Hotel" for Peter Lind
1862
7778 West Saanich Road,
Central Saanich

This one-storey gable-end cottage was originally built as a two-storey road house serving as a hotel, "watering hole," and post office under the proprietorship of Peter Lind. Original construction was probably heavy timber frame with clap board cladding. From surviving photographs the overall look was Frontier Georgian, much in the manner of the early Hudson's Bay Company farmhouses such as Craigflower.

Saint Stephen's Church
1862, 1877
1921 St. Stephen's Road at Mount Newton Cross Road
Central Saanich
Archts. Wright and Sanders

One of oldest surviving Church of England small parish missions in British Columbia, the original design bears a remarkable similarity to St. John the Divine constructed at Yale in the Fraser Canyon to plans by Victoria architects Wright and Sanders. No doubt the same set of plans was used here. Construction was by a ship's carpenter, William Thompson, and this perhaps explains the high quality of the natural wood interior finish. A good example of Carpenter Gothic with its lancet windows, steep scissor truss roof and panelled ship-lap siding, the church was enlarged in 1887 in the same year as the Picturesque cemetary was dedicated. The distinctive battered side buttresses were added later.

Church of the Assumption
1869
7742 West Saanich Road, Central Saanich

Although of seemingly simple and rustic design, Our Lady of the Assumption demonstrates a more Classical feeling, both in form and detail, when compared to the Anglican churches of Saanich during this period. The tower end is oriented toward the water. The nave windows are pointed, but the roof and porch gable-ends

return suggesting a pediment, the pitch of the roof is less severe, and the ventilation window in the peak is circular. During the early years of the twentieth century a Dutch pastor, Fr. Adrian Vullinghs, developed a formal garden landscape setting for the church. This is gone, but Fr. Adrian's later work at St. Ann's Academy in the heart of Victoria is undergoing restoration.

John Dyer House
ca. 1880

5930 Patricia Bay Highway, Saanich

Dyer farmed the 100 acres on which he built this house. The spare gabled building with its wraparound verandah and lean-to additions is clad in drop siding. It is a good example of a pioneer vernacular farmhouse of these early years.

St. Michael and All Angels' Church
1883, 1953

4733 West Saanich Road, Saanich
Archts. Edward Mallandaine
Addition: Patrick Birley

Founded as a mission parish of Christ Church Cathedral in 1865, the church as built in 1883 was a simple gable-end building with four bays of double Gothic lancet windows with an entrance porch let into the fourth bay at the west end. The west-end addition designed by Birley in 1953 preserved the rural Carpenter Gothic style and scissor-beam roof trusses, a feature of the natural wood finished interior, while doubling its size to include a narthex, gallery, and baptistry. Also reinserted into the new entrance façade were the original tri-partite Gothic windows beneath the replaced spire.

John Dyer House.

Abraham Pope House
1893
7696 West Saanich Road at Mount Newton Cross Road, Central Saanich

It is believed the core of this house is an earlier cottage built about 1873. The current external character, meticulously restored in 1990, dates from 1893. The cottage presents a charming essay of late Victorian design eclecticism with numerous features. These include the ornate verandah linked to the extended gabled window bay, and extensive use of gingerbread decorative detail which rises to a crescendo in the rooftop cresting treated as a "widows walk."

Royal Oak School House
ca. 1885
4525 West Saanich Road, Royal Oak, Saanich

The original school house on this site dates from 1865; this building replaced it in 1885 and was in use until 1951. The building was moved and raised in 1922. This is a standard one-room gable-end school house design, sash windows opening up the side walls, bevelled drop-siding, and hipped-roof entrance porch. A gable end design feature is the round ventilator to provide air circulation for the school room.

Richard Layritz House
1889, 1906
4354 Wilkinson Road, Saanich

German horticulturalist Richard Layritz was to achieve worldwide fame for his nurseries which supplied fruit trees to the Okanagan, roses to the Far East, and rhododendrons throughout the Pacific Northwest. This was the site of the nursery from 1889 and many exotic tree species can be recognized in the adjacent properties today. The one-and-a-half-storey cross-gable Queen Anne cottage was built over a number of years and has recently been carefully restored. The gable front features a hip-roofed verandah supported by turned posts with ornamental brackets; the body of the house is clad with drop siding and shingled gables.

James and Amelia Barker House
1893
1330 Hastings Road, Carey, Saanich

Part of this farmhouse is of earlier construction as, interestingly enough, it was moved in 1893 from a site near the original Christ Church Cathedral on Church Hill in Victoria. It is a frame

construction L-plan gable-end house with various shed additions. The verandah still features turned posts, a spindle balustrade and fretted brackets.

gable, first-storey hip roofed verandahs and bay windows. Such houses were usually sited on knolls to command an overview of the owners' farmland and livestock as much to scenic vistas, which they do indeed still afford today.

Strawberry Vale School House
1893-1894

4100 Rosedale Avenue, Carey, Saanich

E. H. Linaker House
ca. 1893

4094 Glanford Avenue, Carey, Saanich

This early Saanich farmhouse is a good example of the type of vernacular Victorian architecture which first dotted Victoria's rural landscape. The two-storey frame building, a T-plan with gable ends and dormers, was probably built over a period of time. The verandah skirting two sides is probably a fairly late addition.

This simple frame "one-room" school house was built for $800 on nearby Hastings Street. It was moved in 1951 to make way for the new school. This is a classic example of the Canadian one-room school with vertical sash windows, and simple hipped roof, clad with economical drop siding.

A. M. Daniels House
ca. 1893

1240 Glyn Road, Carey, Saanich

Prairie Inn
1893

7806 East Saanich Road, Central Saanich

A pioneer vernacular farmhouse, the wood frame design features a cross

This pioneer hotel was built to take advantage of trade developed by the building of the Victoria and Sidney Railway. The two-storey hipped roof building is distinguished by the two-level verandah which serves both storeys on the two road fronts. Like so many of Victoria's saloons, it has a corner entrance. In recent years the hotel has undergone a complete restoration and a replica has been constructed at the rear to serve as a brewery and retail outlet.

storey and balcony atop the double gable-end verandah.

Shady Creek Church
1893

7180 East Saanich Road, Central Saanich

This Picturesque very simple wood-frame church adjoins a pioneer cemetery, itself on the bank of Shady Creek. The church was a Methodist establishment and the core congregation were black farmers. Many of their names are identifiable on the wooden cemetery headboards, among them the Alexander and Shakespeare families.

John Stevens House
ca. 1893

4794 West Saanich Road, Saanich
Stephens acquired this site in 1859 and constructed his first hotel, the "Half-Way House." This is probably the third hotel building, by this time known as the "Stephens Hotel." The two-and-one-half-storey Queen Anne style building has been slightly altered over the years with the addition of half-timbering to the clap-board second

John Piercy House
ca. 1903

5140 Santa Clara Avenue, Cordova Bay, Saanich

This side verandah gable-end cottage was used as a hunting lodge by Piercy. Piercy was married to the daughter of

George Mesher, the well-known Victoria contractor, and this might explain the general design and construction neatness of this otherwise vernacular cabin in the woods. It is also reminiscent of a time when pheasant and quail shooting was done by casually dropping off the V&S train according to mood or impulse.

Durrance's father purchased the 400-acre "Spring Valley Farm" in 1860; John inherited it in 1904. The house is a good example of the Colonial Bungalow type sheathed with drop siding, its bell-cast hipped roof sheltering the wrap-around verandah (glazed in during 1960s). The roof is opened up by a dormer and end-gable over an extended window bay.

"Norfolk Lodge" for John and Emma Oldfield
1908, 1911, 1914

5789 Brookhill Road, Saanich
Archt. Samuel Maclure

The Oldfields owned and farmed 300 acres of rural Saanich and the house served two generations of the family. Their home evolved through a series of additions designed by Maclure with the assistance of his colleague Ross Lort. The house, built atop a steep rise, affords probably the most impressive set of viewscapes of the Saanich Peninsula. The original design as built in 1908 was typical of Maclure's early Arts & Crafts Tudor Revival work. However over the next six years alterations added to the house substantially. Granite foundation work was extended, the verandah enlarged and made more substantial, and a belvedere was added to the roof. The house today commands a major prospect from almost any point in the Elk Lake Valley.

"Vallena" for Agnes and John Durrance
ca. 1910-1912

155 Durrance Road, Saanich

Royal Oak Municipal Hall
1911, 1915, 1948, 1958

4512 West Saanich Road, Royal Oak, Saanich
Archt. John Charles Malcom Keith

Saanich Municipality was incorporated in 1906 and Royal Oak was then identified as the site for the new municipal hall. Keith, who had designed numerous rural Shingle style

257

Arts & Craft churches for the Anglicans, here supplied a Shingle style central-plan bungalow with a shallow bellcast roof, generous entrance porch (now gone) and rooftop cupola. Significant additions over the years included western extensions which respected the original style and in 1958 the addition of two army huts moved from Gordon Head Camp. In 1965 the municipal administration moved to its new hall and the building was sold.

Royal Oak Community Hall
1911

4516 West Saanich Road, Royal Oak, Saanich

Beside Keith's Shingle style Municipal Hall the Community Hall seems vaguely Victorian with its shingle half-storey above the horizontal siding, vertical Tudor-arched windows, and hipped bays flanking the centre entrance. The ultimate source, however, is still the Arts & Crafts bungalow as seen under construction in various guises throughout Victoria at this time.

Butchart Gardens
1911-1925

Tod Inlet, Central Saanich
Archts. Samuel Maclure,
William Westerby, Raoul Robillard

Robert Pim Butchart started the limestone quarry and cement works in 1904 and the idea for extensive gardens to envelope the worked out portions of the quarry was the idea of his artistic wife, Jenney Foster Kennedy. Maclure became involved at least by 1911 although he may have been responsible for the Colonial bungalow house as early as 1905. The project drew on Maclure's considerable experience as a landscape architect in Victoria, and also his work during these years with international firms such as Englishman Thomas Mawson in Vancouver and Bostonians Brett & Hall at Hatley Park, Sooke. By 1912 the now-famous sunken gardens had begun to take shape and the theme gardens, Italian, Rose and Japanese, followed thereafter. Over a period of 14 years Maclure worked with landscape gardeners Westerby and Robilliard, supplying successive additions to the house: roof gardens, billiard room, saltwater swimming pool (1913), extensions to the roof gardens and conservatories (1917), sunroom (1919). Also, a series of designs for garden structures were from Maclure's office: a "Chinaman's cottage" (1917), a classical-style boathouse on the Inlet (1919), plans for the private garden and summerhouse (1920), seedstore and greenhouses for the Benvenuto

Seed Company (1920, 1925), various arbours and a "duckhouse" (1925). Butchart Gardens was the quintessential expression of Victoria, and remains so today, as Victoria throughout this early period sought to generate tourism as a "City of Gardens."

Kennedy House
ca. 1912
4040 Wilkinson Road, Carey, Saanich

This rambling English Arts & Crafts country house was built for Ernest Kennedy, managing director of the British Canadian Home Builders Company and perhaps was intended to show what they might do for you! Unfortunately by 1914 the company was bankrupt. The source of the design is unknown, but the influences are certainly English Edwardian in the manner of the designs such us those by C. F. A. Voysey and Edwin Lutyens being published in the pages of *Country Life* magazine during those years.

Caleb Payne House
1912
2847 Dysart Road, Tillicum, Saanich

Payne purchased this house new from a phenomenally successful Victoria development group, the Bungalow Construction Company Ltd. Their projects dot the landscape particularly in Fairfield and Oak Bay. The target market was five- and six-room California or Colonial style Craftsman bungalows, 10% down on occupation and the balance at a 7% or 8% mortgage payable by monthly installments. This is a good example of their work in the California variant. The house rises from a solid concrete foundation, the double-course shingled basement skirt defined at the corners ewith battered piers which support the verandah posts. The bracketted gables with cut-end bargeboards form deep overhangs and the entrance porch extends into an open verandah pergola. Casement windows are generous in size, flooding the interior with a maximum of light. These house designs, although repeated with little variation throughout the city, were well built, comparatively economical, and popular.

Joshua and Louisa Priestly House
ca. 1912-1915
3871 High Street, View Royal, Saanich

Priestly was a partner in a Victoria real estate firm. The house is an unusual piece of Shingle style design work. Details such as repeating a version of the inset front verandah as a second floor sleeping porch, the bracketted freeboard half-timbering in the gable and the tight symmetry of the overall design suggest that an architect might have been involved.

columns and slats of the balustrade are detailed in a manner reminiscent of the famous Scottish Art Nouveau designer, Charles Rennie MacIntosh, with the yin-yang or rolling S design fretted into the slats.

Wilkinson Road Methodist Church
1913

4274 Wilkinson Road, Carey, Saanich
Archts. Butler and Harrison

The Saanich Methodist mission was established in 1889 and that in Strawberry Vale came into its own in 1911. The cross-axial design, using a clapboard finish and strong bracketted bargeboard gable ends with half-timbering in the peak fits the overall effect with Edwardian Arts & Crafts design popular in Victoria during these years.

Herbert Whitehead House
ca. 1913

1318 Prillaman Avenue, Saanich
Archt. H. T. Whitehead

Victoria architect H. T. Whitehead designed this house for himself. It is a California style bungalow with fastidious attention to detail in the applied decoration. Above a shingled foundation the first storey is finished in double bevel siding; the inset gable end is half-timbered. The double verandah

James and Margaret Kellie House
1913

516 Gorge Road West, Tillicum, Saanich

A landmark residence overlooking the Gorge Waterway, it was built for James Kellie who represented West Kootenay in the Legislature and had substantial mining and lumber interests throughout the province. This imposing Edwardian Classical two-and-one-half-storey house with a substantial road-front fence is distinguished by the two-storey square-pillared verandah and balcony—no doubt designed to afford access to the beautiful views up and down the Gorge Waterway.

Bertha and Oscar Fagerberg House
1913-1921

588 Ridgegrove Avenue, Carey, Saanich

Although the main floor is delineated by a dropsiding treatment, this is really a Shingle style house in the best tradition of American Eastern Seaboard. The Chalet form is appropriate to the hillside site and the treatment of the casement windows, inset porch, and even half-timbering in the gable demonstrates a geometric discipline to the design. George Fagerberg, who finished the house after the death of his father, was manager of famed Layritz Nurseries nearby. The house was sited to take advantage of the extensive landscaped gardens.

Hubert and Alys Savage House
1914

3862 Grange Road, Carey, Saanich
Archt. Hubert Savage

It is presumed that well-known Victoria architect Hubert Savage designed their Saanich home. Certainly it commands fine prospects across the valley floor but the detailing and overall California style were not common to Savage's own work which as in the "Royal Oak Inn" favoured the Tudor Revival of the English Arts & Crafts.

Arthur and Ethel Povey House
1914

811 Jasmine Avenue, Carey, Saanich

Povey was a clerk with Hickman Tye Hardware and probably bought this house as built. These small California Bungalow style residences were popular with spec builders, many of the components delivered to site precut. Typical elements are the central

hall plan, the generous eaves for the side and gable ends. Slightly less usual are the battered wooden columns supporting the entrance verandah.

Colquitz Jail and Prison Farm
1914
4216 Wilkinson Road, Carey, Saanich
Archt. W. R. Wilson

This institution has known various names and uses: until 1916 a jail and prison farm, from 1916-1954 the Colquitz Centre of the Criminally Insane, then for two years the Vancouver Island Unit of the Oakalla Prison Farm, and from 1971 the Vancouver Island Regional Correctional Centre. To most Victoria residents it has, however, been popularly called just the Wilkinson Road Jail. In 1982 the British Columbia Building Corporation undertook a major revitalization of the building which conserved the castellated brick veneer, but replaced the interior with a modern reinforced concrete facility. Wilson's late Victorian castle scheme, in materials, detail and massing, remarkably resembles his Bay Street Armories under construction at the same time.

Captain R. N. Walker House
1915
1100 Burnside Road West, Carey, Saanich
Archt. Elmer E. Green

Originally sited to command extensive landscaped grounds, this is one of Saanich's best examples of the California Bungalow. The gabled roof encompasses a full-length verandah and the dormer above opens out onto balustraded porch. The generous eaves, gables, and verandah feature exposed stick-style decorative millwork and end-notched bargeboards; the detailing is fastidious. The shingle-clad building rises from a granite plinth and piers which support the verandah columns.

Dominion Astrophysical Observatory
1915-1918
5071 West Saanich Road, Saanich
Archt. William Henderson, Dominion Dept. Public Works

When built on Little Saanich Mountain in 1915 the observatory contained the largest reflecting mirror telescope in the world.

The 72-inch mirror disk weighing 1,960 pounds was manufactured at the St. Gobain Glassworks, Belgium, and shipped in the dying days of peace as Europe erupted into war. The 66-foot swivel dome was prefabricated by Warner and Swasey Co. in Cleveland, Ohio. Eight hundred tons of concrete were required to secure the footings, foundations and support piers. The round barrel-like structure is treated, perhaps slightly tongue-in-cheek, as a

Neo-Georgian folly with its triumphal arch entrance and brief suggestions of the Classical orders in the circular façade. The complex included residences for the chief astronomer, Dr. Plaskett, and his assistants, also an office building.

"Babacombe Farm"
for Harriet and Herbert Burbidge
ca. 1916
6187 Hunt Road, Cordova Bay, Saanich
Archt. Henry H. Gillingham

Burbidge was the son of Sir Richard Burbidge, manager of Harrods in London. Herbert came to Canada as a stores commissioner for the Hudson's Bay Company and while in Victoria was responsible for the construction of the new HBC department Store on Douglas Street. In 1921 he retired to breed Jersey Cattle and his (then Dooley

Road) home was no doubt built to fit his image of a country gentleman. The cross-axial house, added to an earlier summer cottage, was built in the popular Tudor Revival idiom following the then-prevailing style pioneered by Samuel Maclure.

Harold and Myra Thompson Farm
1920
5271 Old West Saanich Road, Saanich

Thompson was an English cabinet-maker and the farm buildings were erected over a number of years as they were required or affordable. The dominant feature of this group of buildings arranged about a traditional old country farmyard is the four-storey shingle water tower. It was actually built of timbers from a previous tower which Thompson re-erected. He inserted living accommodations into the upper floors. The water-tank itself was functional until the early 1950s. The rest of the buildings, a garage, cottage, barn and ancilliary structures, have been left unpainted in the natural state: shingle, shakes and weatherboard sheathing.

Johns' General Store Cottages
1931
4920, 4922 Cordova Bay Road,
Cordova Bay, Saanich
Archt. Percy Fox

Clarence Johns ran the first year-round general store at Cordova Bay and so had an interest in providing accommodation to holiday makers. The simple utilitarian structures are much in the manner of the cottage motels just then coming into vogue throughout

North America to serve the motoring public. The handling of materials, shingle and clapboard, and the generous balconies inset from the front gable demonstrate some thought to the design beyond strict functionalism.

Royal Oak Crematorium Chapel and Retort
1937
4673 Falaise Drive, Royal Oak, Saanich
Archt. C. Elwood Watkins

This Deco style chapel pronounced its non-sectarianism by the Modern style, although the use of vertical columns and narrow windows give the smooth stucco wall surfaces, broken only by the briefest of ornamentation, a vaguely Gothic aesthetic. Royal Oak Burial Park was developed as a public institution by the municipalities of Saanich and Victoria in 1923. Watkins, better known for architectural historicism in his schools and houses throughout Victoria, here demonstrated design facility in the more contemporary Art Deco.

"The Royal Oak Inn"
for Colin and Florence Forrest, Vera Levy and David Burnett
1939
4509 West Saanich Road, Royal Oak, Saanich
Archt. Hubert Savage

The Forrests, recently arrived from Shanghai, believed this location at the intersection of roads to Butchart Gardens and the airport would make a good location for an English style tea room. Savage supplied the designs for an Arts & Crafts style "Cotswold" cottage. He specified a patented manufactured thatched reed roof with eyebrow dormers. The parged black-and-white half-timbered walls (applied to standard frame construction) and tall brick chimneys surmounted a dry-stone terraced rock garden. The high point of the interior is a large balconied hall built using cruck timbers in the manner of a medieval barn. In 1940 the restaurant was bought by John and Katharine Maltwood, who renamed it "The Thatch" and installed their collection of antiques and Katharine's own works as sculptor. In her will Mrs. Maltwood left the museum to the University of Victoria who operated it for a number of years as a public museum. At that time a shake roof was installed. The collection was moved to a new museum on campus in 1980, the building again assumed a restaurant use.

This cubical stucco two-storey Moderne style house, with hints of Deco in the detailing, is perhaps a stylistic precursor to the substantial building activity that was to take place five years later at the hospital by W. F. K. Gardiner, H. Whittaker, and others. The entrance porch and bay window unit with its extended elliptical balcony roof it treated as a secondary box, partially inserted into the main block.

Richard and Constance Harrison House
1941
1099 Jasmine Avenue, Carey, Saanich

As the street names of this area might suggest, the Marigold area was first called "Garden City." R. E. Harrison and his father were both contractor/developers in this area. This Moderne style house with its corner wrap-around staircase, corner windows and inset corner entrance porch also features arched porch and garage openings, a reference perhaps to the Mission style family home nearby but dating from some 25 years earlier.

John and Kathleen Barraclough House
1946
5465 Alderly Road, Cordova Bay, Saanich

Owner-designed and built, this is a British Columbia Ranch style log house as found throughout the province from the 1920s. Fireplaces and chimneys are built from found fieldstone, the interior walls are sheathed in

Irene and Joseph Casey House
1940
900 Gorge Road West, Tillicum, Saanich

Casey, a line superintendent for the BCER, served numerous times on Saanich Municipal Council and also on the Board of the Royal Jubilee Hospital.

bevelled knotty pine and the living room features a second-storey balcony.

"Orchard Gate"
for Ada and Norman Yarrows
ca. 1949

5720 Patricia Bay Highway, Saanich
Archt. P. L. James

Norman Yarrows, son of British shipbuilding magnate Sir Alfred Yarrows, came to Victoria in 1914 to run the newly purchased Yarrows Limited shipbuilding subsidiary in Esquimalt. The couple built the "Orchard Gate" for their retirement years. The rambling Cottage style house is well within the English Arts & Crafts tradition. A series of gable ended units, joined in a butterfly plan, focus on the vista through extensive landscaped gardens.

Grace and Pierre Timp House
1950

5454 Fowler Road, Cordova Bay, Saanich

This Rustic style house with its dark-brown cedar siding, shake roof, and white trim boards, is actually built around the core of an old holiday cabin. However, these design elements integrate the house with its woodland garden setting, the so-called "Pierre Timp's Dutch Gardens," once a popular destination on Victoria's tourist route.

Margaret and Romeo Desjardins House
1955

2887 Colquitz Avenue, Tillicum, Saanich
Archt. John Di Castri

Orchard House.

Sited on a sloping lot, the geometric planes and volumes are nevertheless adapted to the site. Window and porch roofs extend out of the imaginary grids, defined by horizontal and vertical fascia boards in sharp colour contrast to the white stucco wall surfaces. With such houses Di Castri introduces a new, but still indigenous, design vocabulary to his Victoria clientele.

Freda and John Moran House
1955-1962
863 Royal Oak Avenue, Royal Oak, Saanich
Archt. John Di Castri

The Morans built and lived in their house over a period of seven years and it is a good example of the striking new brand of abstract expressionism that Di Castri brought to Victoria from his American training. There are hints of F. L. Wright and Prairie School in the free-floating complex gable forms, the massive fieldstone chimney that stabilizes the design, floor to ceiling plate glass windows, and the use of native woods, particularly bands of wide dimension drop siding. And the overall massing and detailing respond to the native oak meadow site.

Victoria Airport Terminal Buildings
1963, 1993
Willingdon Road, Sidney
Archts. Wade Stockdill Armour & Blewett
Extensions: Peterson and Lester, 1993

The 1963 scheme for Victoria's new international terminal should be seen in the context of WSAB's concurrent work at the University of Victoria and Saanich Municipal Hall. In all these commissions the firm was demonstrating a strident international interpretation of modern expressionism. The terminal was therefore a low horizontal minimalist building, the spare reductivist geometry broken only slightly by the use of split granite panels for the ground floor walls. The structure expressed its steel skeleton, reinforced slab floors and precast concrete cladding systems. The interior circulation was organized around a two-storey central concourse lit from tall glazed clerestory. Numerous renovations have expanded the building, the most recent in 1993. (Also visible from the terminal building is the control tower [architect Irvin Kew, 1988].)

267

Broadmead Estates
1965-1994

Display Homes, Edgewood Avenue, Saanich
Design: Mike Nixon

The 712 acres that now comprise the Broadmead Subdivision was the first post-War planned community to be developed in the Victoria area. In order to control the quality and "feel" of the treed hillside site Broadmead Farms Ltd. imposed strict design guidelines and developed Edgewood Avenue with a series of demonstration display homes. The naturalistic landscaping, and "West Coast Modern" design approach relied on expressive uses of timber construction along with fieldstone, shingle and cedar siding finishes and textures.

when Mr. and Mrs. George Poole donated 100 acres of Mount Newton's northern slope and with it Gillain Manor, recently built as an alchoholic rehabilitation centre. The university renovated the building as a residential conference centre. The rustic granite, cedar and shingle-roof structure stretches across the brow of the magificient bench site. The rooms and conference spaces command spectacular views over Victoria airport to the Gulf Islands and mainland mountain fringe beyond. The building elements, although evocative of Wright's Prairie style work, seem admirably suited to the site and building traditions of the Saanich Peninsula.

Dunsmuir Lodge
1973

1515 McTavish Road, North Saanich
Archts. Siddall, Dennis Warner

In 1985 the University of Victoria received the largest gift in its history

Barbara and Gary Winter House
1974

4739 Treetop Heights, Cordova Bay, Saanich
Archt. Claude Maurice

Perched on this hilltop site overlooking Cordova Bay, a Shingle style essay seems appropriate. The single-storey house is treated almost as a pavilion, or belvedere, open to the views but protected within the traditional cladding, a material long common to the canneries, logging camps and suburban bungalows of the Pacific Northwest. A freestanding garage has been added.

Leau,-Wel-New School
1989

7449 West Saanich Road, Central Saanich
Archts. Lubor & Trupka, Vancouver

Built for the Saanich Indian School Board this building established a reference point for the culturally based native education curriculum to be pursued in the new provincial educational initiative for tribal schools. The T-form plan, featuring a central open plan community space, expresses the traditional materials and form of the old Salish big houses of the Saanich Peninsula. Integral to the design is the artistic program directed and to a large degree executed by senior Salish artist, Charles Elliott. Elliott's entrance portal with hovering Eagle figure, the façade Thunderbird mural, and the Raven, Orca, Wolf, and Thunderbird 26-foot pole provide a formal approach to the school.

Wall-mural subsidiary themes carried throughout the school are executed in the manner of serigraph print designs.

Mount Newton Community Care Facility
1990

2158 Mount Newton Cross Road, Central Saanich
Archt. Darrel Jensen

This complex received a Premier's Award for Excellence in Accessible Design. The commission was for a purpose-built "wellness" centre for health care and rehabilitation. The building, sited in a pastoral setting, adopts its form and detail from traditional vernacular architecture of the region. The dormered gable-ended bungalow is surrounded by a wide hip-roofed verandah with slatted balustrades. Wood finishes and details are expressed clearly and honestly, yet the overall effect is new and fresh.

Saanich Agricultural Fair Grounds
1991
1528 Stelly's Cross Road, Central Saanich
Archt. John Di Castri

This new complex of structures on a agricultural green-field site was designed to replace the former Saanichton Fair Grounds and continue the over-100-year tradition of Saanich Peninsula agricultural fairs. The concept plan calls for a series of structures grouped around a larger exhibition complex. The design criteria, as demonstrated in the central pavilion (Phase 1), recalls an agricultural vernacular illustrating strong Wrightian influences and rendered with the colourful detail of a festival character.

Strawberry Vale Elementary School
1996
Rosedale Park, Strawberry Vale
Archts. Patkau Architects

Drawing on the design elements established earlier at their Sea Island School (1991) in the lower mainland, the architects claim their design is a "geometricized form of site." Certainly the building program reflects an enviornmental sensitivity for the location, an arborial edge where an Oak woodland park meets a natural marsh. The building volumes directly express the interior spatial arrangements. The multi-plane walls and roofs emphasize natural lighting and air circulation; they also collect rainwater to feed into the swamp for natural filtering.

Strawberry Vale Elementary School.

Western Communities

Northwest of Victoria the development pattern was much the same as the Saanich Peninsula. Salish territory extended as far north as present-day Sooke, itself named after the T'sou-ke people. The area was rich in salmon and shellfish for harvesting. Company farms extended out to Colwood and Langford. Sooke was established as an independent colony by Captain Walter Colquhoun Grant in 1849 with the building of a fort, waterpower sawmill and land cultivation. By 1853 Grant had sold his Sooke holding to John Muir, who came to stay, establishing Woodside and Burnside farms. Further settlement developed after 1860 by pre-emption or Crown grants. Sealing (until the protection treaty of 1911), logging, fish trapping, some mining were the mainstays of the economy. Colwood began as a waterpowered sawmill location established for the Hudson's Bay Company by Roderick Finlayson in 1847. By 1849 sawn lumber was being exported to Fort Langley on the Fraser River and California. In 1850 a hotel was operational at Parson's Bridge at the head of Esquimalt Harbour near Six Mile House today. The HBC's 600-acre Langford Farm was established as an experimental sheep farm in 1851 between the Esquimalt Harbour and Millstream Creek. Dozens of small homes were built for the native and Kanaka farm hands. Metchosin was settled as a 200-acre private farming enterprise by partners James Cooper and Thomas Blinkhorn in 1851 on a stretch of shoreland near Albert Head. (With outbreak of smallpox in 1892 this became the site of the Quarantine Station, and since 1960 a federal corrections centre.) Governor Douglas himself purchased another 320-acre section and thereafter it became fashionable for successful entrepreneurs such as Dr. O. M. Jones to own "ranches" in Metchosin. During this same period Langford and the Highlands were opening up to independent farmers and became even more accessible as the Esquimalt and Nanaimo Railway wound its way northward through the Millstream Valley in 1886. By 1910 the region had become a summer resort retreat, numerous Victoria residents building small vacation cottages. This no doubt prepared the area to become Victoria's first suburban motel strip in the 1930s as motoring caught on and the Island Highway was improved.

Sooke sparked development activity for the western communities when in 1910 the Vancouver Island Power Company established a hydroelectric facility at Jordon River to supply Victoria with electricity. In 1911 the City of Victoria Waterworks let the contract for a 27-mile concrete flowline to supply the city with water from Sooke Lake. Coincidentally, piped domestic water became available along the route. The same year the Canadian Northern Pacific Railway began building a line from Victoria through Cowichan Lake to Port Alberni; it had reached Sooke by 1918 and never made it Port Alberni. The formalization of municipal boundaries has been a long process, as has incorporation itself. Esquimalt formally became a municipality in 1912, but the Western Communities are much younger: Colwood and Metchosin 1985, View Royal 1988, Langford 1992, and Highlands 1993.

NOTE

Ref. Castle, Geoffrey. "Hatley Park An Illustrated Anthology." 1995. "101 Historical Buildings of the Sooke Region." 1985. "Our Heritage, Selections from an Inventory of Older Buildings in Colwood, Langford & View Royal." 1982.

Colwood Farm Dairy
1851-1852
Goldstream Avenue, Colwood

This is the last remaining building of the Hudson's Bay Company's Colwood Farm. Like the other four farms in the region this was owned by the Bay's subsidiary, the Puget Sound Agricultural Company. Captain Edward E. Langford, ex-officer of the Black Watch, was hired in London and sent out to develop the farm as a cattle and sheep ranch. Although by this time building timber would have been available from the HBC's nearby sawmill, field stone was no doubt chosen for its cooling properties in this low-rise utilitarian building.

Craigflower Manor
1856
110 Island Highway at Craigflower, View Royal
Archt. Restoration: Peter Cotton, 1968

Craigflower House was one of several houses built by a subsidiary of the Hudson's Bay Company, "Puget's Sound Agricultural Company," as managers' residences for extensive farms in Oregon, Washington, and Vancouver Island. Three of these still stand in Oregon. Craigflower Farm originally consisted of about 1,000 acres and included, apart from the Manor House, a sawmill, brickyard, bakery, and ancillary farm buildings. The farm was intended to make Fort Victoria self-supporting. Kenneth McKenzie was brought out from Scotland in 1843 to oversee the construction and organization of the farm and to act as bailiff for the Hudson's Bay Company. It was under his direction that the Manor was built in 1856. The name was appropriate. "Craig" means "neck" in Gaelic and the site, on a neck in the Gorge Waterway, was probably chosen to provide a sheltered inlet for boats. Historically, however, it was named after a farm in England owned by Andrew Colville, then Governor of the Hudson's Bay Company.

Now restored, Craigflower is an example of a building form derived from the eighteenth century Laird's House. The Laird's House is one of many variations on the Georgian vernacular house type, which in the American colonies enjoyed an extensive popularity in wooden frame and brick versions. The style is characterized by balanced symmetrical proportions both in elevation and plan. The symmetrical window arrangement features a second-storey band of five rectangular sash windows, with four similar windows flanking a central door on the ground floor. The floor plan is centrally divided by the stairwell and entrance porch, on each side of which are arranged parlours, kitchens, and on the upper floor, bedrooms. Fireplaces and chimneys are located midpoint at each end of the building. A familiar characteristic of the Georgian house type is its design symmetry, often complemented by Classical details such as pediments over windows and columns flanking the entrance. Craigflower is an interesting provincial variation adapted to locally available materials. The lower floor is typical Hudson's Bay Company construction: squared logs fitted into vertical grooved posts. The second storey is a mortised stud and plate frame. The fireplaces are built inside the outer walls so the chimneys rise through the roof, slightly indented at each end. What is distinctive about Craigflower, and might have been an innovation by McKenzie, is the Gothic arch motif found in the front door fanlight and repeated in the small fireplaces throughout the house. This is at extreme variance to the Georgian flavour of the building but not out of context if one remembers the popularity of Gothic in Britain at this time.

In 1968 Craigflower and some surrounding land were acquired by the Provincial and Federal Governments as a National Historic Site. It has been meticulously restored under the direction of architect Peter Cotton, even to such details as paper reproductions, inclusion of McKenzie's furniture and possessions, and sympathetic kitchen furnishings. In more recent times the landscape has been restored as a more authentic farm-like setting for the house. It is open to the public year-round.

Craigflower School House
1854-1855

2755 Admirals Road, Tillicum, Saanich

In 1854 a schoolmaster was retained by the Hudson's Bay Company to undertake the education of local children. Craigflower School was finished in February 1855 at a cost of $4,300. The two-storey structure consisted of one school room and six other rooms which were used by the teacher, his family, and the children from Colwood and Langford Farms who boarded there. The school opened with an enrollment of eight boys and six girls and constituted a significant step in the attempt to create a permanent colony on Vancouver Island. McKenzie, known locally as "The Laird," discovered limestone nearby and had a kiln constructed to make mortar and plaster which eventually simplified construction methods. A sawmill, thresher, flour mill, bakery, slaughterhouse, blacksmith's shop, and ship chandlery were subsequently constructed, and by the end of 1854, 21 houses had been erected to house a population of 76. The school house is a simple, provincial Georgian style building with chimneys at either end of its rectangular plan. The timber for its construction was sawn at Craigflower mill and rafted across the Arm. From earliest times it sported a red roof and whitewashed clapboard siding. The small entrance porch on the west side was a later addition. In 1925 the B.C. Historical Society started a campaign to save the school house, and in 1927 the Native Sons and Native Daughters of British Columbia leased the school to preserve it as an historic monument. In 1931 it was dedicated as a Museum and was operated as such until 1968 when it was confirmed a National Historic Site. Operated by the province, it is open to the public throughout the year.

Fisgard Lighthouse

Fisgard Lighthouse
1859

Fort Rodd, Esquimalt Harbour, Colwood

Archts. John Wright, Herman Otto Tiedemann
Restoration: Peter Cotton

Wright as architect, and Tiedemann as colonial engineer were responsible for the design and construction of the Fisgard and Race Rocks lights. Fisgard, built on a small rock promontory just off Rodd Point survives along with the original keeper's house. The light was automated in 1960 and Fisgard Island linked to the point in the early 1940s. The simple gable-end block house with its low-rise roof featured tall shuttered windows. Those on the first floor comprise the only stylistically readable ornamentation as they are Gothic arched. Apparently Wright patented the cast-iron spiral case which he designed for the brick light tower. Restoration work was carried out during the 1960s under the direction of Victoria architect, Peter Cotton. The tower is now a National Historic Site, open to the public.

"Moss Cottage"
for James and Mary Walsh
ca. 1865, 1977

Sooke District Museum, 2070 Phillips Road, Sooke

Reputedly Sooke's oldest surviving house, Moss Cottage was built for James and Mary Welsh and originally stood near the Muir farm on West Coast Road. In 1977 the cottage was carefully dismantled and reassembled as a period restoration at the Sooke Museum. Construction technique is unique; it is essentially a plank house, the exterior wall made from rough 2-inch by 16-inch cedar planks sheathed over with clapboard. The building is a simple gable-end house, the roof shelters a verandah along the entrance side. Today the house operates as an animated museum display, restored and furnished to illustrate life in Sooke during the pioneer period.

"Woodside Farm"
for Ann and John Muir
ca. 1869

7117 West Coast Road, Sooke

This house was one of three large houses built for the influential Muir family farms: Woodside, Burnside and Springside. John Muir, a Scot, came to Vancouver Island in 1849 to manage coal mines for the Hudson's Bay Company. Muir purchased the Grant farm holdings in 1853. The prosperity of the farms is indicated by this house, essentially a vernacular Georgian form in the manner of the Puget Sound Agricultural Company houses erected on their farms nearer Victoria in the 1850s. The two-storey central-plan timber frame house supports a hipped roof pierced by two chimneys on either side of a rooftop "widows walk." The arrangement of the six-light sash windows on the front façade is symmetrical. The verandah extends across the entire front elevation. A large one-storey lean-to kitchen abuts the rear.

"Burnside Farm"
for Matilda and Michael Muir
ca. 1870

1890 Maple Avenue, Sooke

"Burnside," as can be seen from its Georgian Vernacular style, is almost identical to the slightly earlier "Woodside" farm house. The plan was likewise identical with a one-storey kitchen lean-to at the back. Many of the large 12-light sash windows are intact, the house having undergone a complete restoration in recent years.

Metchosin School House
1871

4475 Happy Valley Road, Metchosin

When constructed, this one-room school cost $300. The colonial government

paid half, the rest was raised by the local settlers. Three large windows flood the classroom with light. An entrance porch is attached to the front gable end. The school operated until 1954. It is a designated Provincial heritage site and now operates seasonally as a museum.

Caleb Pike Homestead
ca. 1872

1589 Millstream Road, Highlands

Pike was one of the western communities' first settlers, acquiring the 286-acre farm in 1861. The cabin, however, dates from a later period, perhaps just after it was acquired by William Wale in 1872. The farm site is now owned by the Municipality of the Highlands, restored and is open to the public as an historic site. The cabin itself is a very good example of squared timber construction utilizing dovetail notching at the corner joints.

achieved present form gradually. Mariner and sealer Oscar Scarf added a second storey and operated it as a boarding house and stage-stop on the Sooke Way. In the 1920s a subsequent owner removed the upper floor and built the present gable-end half-storey and verandah modifications. The house was shingled in the 1930s.

Church of Saint Mary the Virgin
1873-1876

4125 Metchosin Road, Metchosin
Archt. Edward Mallandaine

This small rural church is one of the best preserved in the Victoria area, even the original cedar furnishing—pews, lectern, pulpit, and baptismal font—remain in use. The roof is a scissor truss construction, the interior walls are plaster with fir wainscotting. The exterior, marked by simple double-light vertical windows in the nave, an attached side entrance, and triple tall Gothic windows at the east end sanctuary, is finished in plain vertical siding. During springtime the church becomes a local attraction as the Garry Oak meadow of the graveyard is transformed into a sea of Dogtooth Violets.

Oscar Scarf House
1887, 1912, 1920s

3642 Otter Point Road, Sooke

The core of the house is a one-storey log cabin built in 1887. The house

Emerson House
1895

2666 Kemp Lake Road, Sooke

An early pre-emptor's home, this log cabin with flat notched timber construction was built by M. Emerson who pre-empted land at the junction of Otter Point and Kemp Lake roads. The simple plan is read easily from the exterior and gabled-roof sweeps down to shelter the side-entrance verandah. Although it is a later addition, this is a formula traditional to Sooke from the time of Moss Cottage.

Fort Rodd Hill, Colwood
1895

Belmont Road, Colwood

Victoria's coastal defences date from the 1878 Crimean Russian scare, a

set into the shingled walls complete the rustic Arts & Crafts effect.

result of which the British Admiralty installed guns at Finlayson Point, Macauley Point and Brothers Island. In 1897 earthworks and redoubts for disappearing guns were constructed at Duntz Head (Naval Dockyard), Black Rock and Belmont (Rodd Hill). The artillery batteries were first constructed at Rodd Hill in 1895. Operated since 1962 as a National Historic Park the entire complex consists of a number of restored and interpretive buildings which in style, and design origin, can be compared to other Victoria military establishments such as Work Point Barracks in Esquimalt. Restored structures at the Fort include the Warrant Officers' Quarters (1897).

Also operated by the Fort are Fisgard Lighthouse and Cole Island in the upper reaches of Esquimalt Harbour. The Island contains a number of unique brick munitions storage buildings established by the British Navy in the 1860s.

Lizzie and Mary Powers House
1904

1135 Goldstream Avenue, Goldstream/Langford

This Arts & Crafts bungalow overlooks Langford Lake. The inset verandah runs the full length of one side, the roof and dormers are hip-roofed with wide protective eaves and a major feature is the massive fieldstone fireplace chimney. Casement windows

Twin Creek Farm House for Alma and Nels Wiggs
1908

5000 Sooke Road, Sooke

In this very compact design, there is evidence of skill in both planning and construction. The two storeys are balloon-framed; that is the vertical studs rise through the height of the second floor, floor and roof rafters are then hung within this skeleton. The side dormer caps the central entrance below and the hip-roofed verandah with its turned posts is a major feature of the front. The design is conservative for the period and may reflect what the Wiggs were used to in their native Minnesota.

"Hatley Park"
for James and Laura Dunsmuir
1907-1908

2005 Sooke Road, Colwood
Archt. Samuel Maclure
Landscape: Brett and Hall, Boston

James Dunsmuir, coal baron and millionaire industrialist, commissioned Samuel Maclure to design Hatley Park as a suitable residence for the vast 650-acre country estate he purchased while serving as Lieutenant-Governor of British Columbia. The "castle" was magnificently sited overlooking Esquimalt Lagoon where the family yacht, *Dolaura*, could anchor. The estate, densely wooded, contained natural streams and waterfalls to provide a recreational paradise that would accommodate shooting, fishing, golf, and a model dairy. Closer to the house, extensive space was given over to the elaborate landscaping scheme designed by the Boston firm of Brett and Hall. Maclure's design is equal to the siting. It consists basically of a central castellated block flanked by two symmetrically balanced Tudoresque wings. A hint of the Picturesque is lent by the corner turret of the central tower but the wings on either side, though laced with fretted gables, dormers, bay windows, and battlements, are carefully proportioned to effect a Georgian approach to the planning and massing. The Tudor motif is carried through the arches and doorways; the handling of the *porte-cochere* in this fashion is reminiscent of the Rattenbury-Maclure treatment of the Lieutenant-Governor's residence on Rockland some five years earlier. The focal point of the interior is the grand entrance hall, a massive space designed on a grandiose scale with its twin staircases, brilliant stained glass windows by Morris & Co. of London, and large baronial fireplace.

Library, Hatley Park

Italian Garden, Hatley Park

Millword Dormitory, Hatley Park

Except for the drawing room (which is finished in Georgian decor), the house is decorated in Maclure's typical Arts & Crafts fashion. Oak beams, fir and oak panelling, Gothic Revival and Art Nouveau fittings and leaded casement windows abound, creating a surprisingly sympathetic domestic atmosphere in what otherwise would be a building of monumental proportions. At the insistence of the Dunsmuirs, the design was based on Compton Wynyates, one of the great country palaces of Tudor England. In plan Maclure has utilized his distinctive cross-axial scheme on a grand scale. Entrance through the main door under the *porte-cochere* leads into the hall space which flows past the fireplace into the drawing room which has a commanding view of the lagoon. A long transverse corridor unites the tower block to the domestic apartments. In the east or "male" wing are located the living room, beamed and panelled in mahogany, a library finished in cedar, a smoking room panelled in yaka wood, and a fir-beamed and panelled billiard room. The west or "female" wing was mainly devoted to the servants' accommodation, kitchens and pantries, but features the richly finished dining room with its built-in sideboard and carved fireplace with Art Nouveau tiles. The entrance hall itself is panelled in golden oak. The second floor opens off the central hall and contains the master bedrooms, dressing rooms and domestic apartments. The third was devoted to numerous guest rooms and the fourth floor of the tower housed the ballroom which overlooked the spacious grounds and lagoon. Approaching Hatley Park today one passes the fairways of the Royal Colwood Golf Course. This was another Dunsmuir enterprise, built in 1913, and designed by A. V. Maclean. Royal Warrant was granted in 1931. James Dunsmuir died in 1920, ten years after relinquishing his role as Lieutenant-Governor. Mrs. Dunsmuir, *née* Laura Surles of Fayetteville, a descendant of the famous Byrd family of old Southern aristocracy, remained at Hatley Park until her death in 1937. In 1940 the estate was purchased by the Dominion Government for $75,000 as a Royal Canadian Navy training centre. In 1948 it became a tri-service Cadet College. Various buildings were added. At the head of terrace stairs the Grant Block 1942; then to the west the Nixon Block dormitory, 1955. In 1973 architects Siddall, Dennis Warner were charged to develop a masterplan. As a result the modern library extending over the stream was added (1974: architects Harrison Associates); also the Post-Modern Millword Dormitory Wing (1991: architects Waisman Dewar Grout Carter). In 1995 Royal Roads became an independent university under provincial statute. The extensive grounds, still retaining their original landscaping and including the noted sunken Japanese Gardens, are open to the public every day.

"Armathwaite" for Mr. Skelton
1908-1914

694 Taylor Road, Metchosin

Skelton was a local contractor and he built this California Arts & Crafts bungalow for himself. The dormered saddle roof exends into a bracketted gable end, then extends further into the gable-ended porch entrance. This is supported on battered fieldstone columns. The house, well preserved, is a perfect match to its wooded rural setting.

Colwood Community Hall
1909-1910

2219 Sooke Road, Colwood

The Colwood Women's Institute raised the money to build the hall on donated lands. The entrance gable end giving a public face to Sooke Road features a strange assembly of eclectic ornament although the building itself is a simple saddle roof structure. A large Classical cornice has been inserted into the gable and below it the entrance is sheltered by a bracketted round-arched hood. Two windows flank the central entry, a dentilated string course marks the sill height, and below that slats have been applied over the drop siding to suggest half-timbering.

"Solheim" for Christian and Haldis Helgesen
1910

6698 Helgesen Road, Sooke

Settling 180 acres of uncleared land, this Norwegian couple developed a prosperous farm consisting of a rambling cottage-style house and large log barn. The neatly trimmed gabled units of the house are finished with drop siding, the larger section contains a substantial dormered saddle roof above the deep attached verandah. The barn was later expanded with lean-to additions, the lumber recycled from the old Victoria Public Market at what is now Centennial Square.

"Glinz Lake Cabin"
1911

Camp Thunderbird, Glinz Road, Sooke

Leonard Glinz and his brother Arnold came to Canada from Switzerland and the two built the shake-roofed cabin as a hunting lodge. In the 1930s the Glinz's made the lake property

available for the use of the YMCA and it eventually became Camp Thunderbird, its present use. The cabin is designed and built with some sophistication. The gable-ended roof originally overhung all four walls in the manner of a Swiss chalet. The front verandah is a later addition.

St. John the Baptist Church and Pioneer Cemetery
1911-1913

2050 Sooke Road, Colwood

A church was first built on this site in the 1890s. This closed and then renewed interest led to the Women's Institute raising the funds to construct a new church. They were assisted in their efforts by Mrs. Dunsmuir who felt such a church would benefit the staff and employees of Hatley Park. The church, somewhat unusual for the Anglicans, has a "Roman" appearance, caused by the use of round-headed windows. However, the overall design is simple wood frame with a drop siding finish and a bell tower built into the side gable at the entrance. The cemetery adjacent to the church is the resting place of many of the region's early pioneers.

Holy Trinity Church
1912

1962 Murray Road, Sooke

This rural shingle-style Gothic-revival church was typical of the Anglican rural missions throughout Vancouver Island during these years. The gable roof encompasses a four-bay nave and pronounced end apse. The bell-tower above the shed entrance was added in 1919. The tri-part Gothic window in the apse introduces a motif repeated in the sash windows of the nave. Changing the colour to white in recent years has significantly compromised the original rustic shingle effect.

Quarantine Station Chapel
1912

Williams Head Road, Metchosin

Now a federal penitentiary, Williams Head was established as a Dominion Government quarantine station in

response to the polio epidemic of 1892 and opererated as such until 1958. The chapel was constructed in 1912. A spare brick building set in a pictureque Garry Oak meadow, the eave returns on at the gable end and the single feature round arched window nevertheless give this stucture enough of a Classical feel so as not to be devoid of style. Four other buildings remain from the Quarantine Station Period (two ranges of gabled brick storage structures, 1880 and 1912, a residential bungalow, 1900, and the half-timbered Macluresque Superintendent's House, 1915). William Head Correctional Centre is noted today for the pioneering residential "neighbourhood" cluster units. Five neighbourhood groupings of buildings (each comprising a commons facility and four two-storey duplexes providing for six persons per unit in a home-like setting) were considered a breakthrough in Canadian penal reform. The units themselves, designed in a modern West Coast interpretation of the vernacular Queen Anne, are the work of Wagg & Hambleton (1992) and illustrate a good fit with the built history of the site.

Sheringham Light and Keeper's House
1912

Sheringham Point Road, Sooke

The distinctive, tapered 70-foot concrete tower with its deep pilaster buttresses culminates in a flaired cap on which is surmounted the light itself. The original fresnel lens can be seen today at the Sooke Museum. The tower housed the chains and weights of a wind-up chain-drive motor that rotated the light at night. This mechanism was electrified in 1955. The keeper's house was built the same year on the bluff overlooking the light. The

hipped-gable front, snug eaves and glazed shed porch attached to the front present a very trim appearance on the exposed windy site.

The Danny and Julia George House
ca. 1915

2189 Lazzar Road, Sooke

Standing on traditional native territory near the mouth of the Sooke River (Indian Reserve No. 1), the house is a good example of a small Arts & Crafts bungalow. The eave returns in the gable front suggest a Classical pediment; the corner indented entrance porch is balanced by an extruded bay window on the opposite side. The shingle roof and gable above the drop-siding main floor are secured at ground-level by a shingle skirt.

Goodall House
ca. 1925

592 Ledsham Road, Colwood

Goodall ran the first general store and post office in the area. This Craftsman style bungalow with its multiple bracketted gables, generous eave overhangs, and deep shed-roof entrance balcony demonstrates the delight in carpentry-work, almost for its own sake, that made this style so popular.

Four Mile House
1931

199 Old Island Highway, View Royal
Archt. Hubert Savage

The core of this building is actually a heavy timber structure built by Peter Calvert, a former employee of Craigflower Farm. Operated as a road house through a succession of owners and numerous alterations and additions, the building owes its current form to renovations undertaken by Hubert Savage in 1931. Subsequently, the half-timber style hotel was known as the "Lantern Inn." After numerous other uses in the 1960s and 1970s, the building has been renovated again for use as a neighbourhood pub.

Ranger Station
1937

697 Goldstream Avenue, Langford
Archts. Provincial Department of Public Works

The station house is actually part of a complex including outbuildings and a gambrel-dormered barn. These institutional rural office buildings, clapboard finished with saddle shingle roofs, were very common throughout British Columbia during the 1940s and 1950s, but are rapidly disappearing today. The large 12-light (six-over-six) sash windows flood the office interior with good task lighting.

"Windy Oak"
for Rt. Hon. Mark Kearly
1941

534 Taylor Road, Metchosin

Kearly, a British ex-military gentleman, was a well-known artist and founder of the Vancouver Island branch of the Canadian Federation of Artists in 1944. The Classical feel to this American Cape Cod Revival design is not imaginary, as the garden side of this saddle-roof house is essentially symmetrical, the second storey marked by a slight overhang. The artist's studio, added to one gable end, was accessible only from the exterior via a flight of steps.

Grace Mansion
1944

3816 Duke Road, Metchosin

The Grace family built this Georgian Revival style house during World War II in the manner of a southern plantation mansion. The dominant feature of the gable end building is the two-storey pillared porch supporting a third-storey balcony. On the main floor multi-pane vertical casement windows open on the rooms and flank a Georgian style entrance with a fan light above and flanking side lights.

Lester B. Pearson College of the Pacific
1970-1977

Pearson College Drive, Metchosin
Archts. Downs-Archambault
& Partners in association with
R. J. Thom

Pearson College was established in 1970 as part of the United World Colleges organization which is dedicated to bringing together gifted students from many countries so they can live and work together while completing the International Baccalaureate.

The campus was planned as a village of simple buildings, at the water's edge of the West Coast rain forest. The structures themselves, finished in natural cedar and generously lighted by large wall windows, skylights and clerestories, also feature expressive roofscapes and extended eaves—attempting to achieve a unity between warm human interiors and luxurious natural environment. Four students' residences with in-house teaching facilities, faculty residences, an academic block, arts building, administrative and dining structures comprise a forest campus linked by automobile-free pathways. In 1977 Downs-Archambault completed the multi-purpose Max Bell Theatre, sustaining the design tradition of the earlier work.

Colwood Municipal Hall
1989

3300 Wishart Road, Colwood
Archts. Marshall Goldsworthy

Reinforced concrete used in a post-and-plate modular plan, the building comprises two wings adjoining a central administrative hall. The

construction technique with its interior dividers and exterior curtain walls, while simple and articulate of the plan, allows for easy internal reconfigurations and external additions.

Journey Middle School
1993

6522 Throup Road, Sooke
Archts. John Neilson, Ruth Imrie

Stridently Post-Modern and expressively High-Tech, the school is a colourful inset to the rugged terrain of Sooke.

The building expresses its "four neighbourhoods," or groups of classrooms—each like a village having its own bench-lined alcove to encourage casual interaction.

Designer Ruth Imrie used a bold and rich palette for the interior surfaces. A creative landscape design integrates the structure into its natural treed and creekside setting. The exterior floorscape features a mini-amphitheatre and conversation nooks. Neilson has used grey stucco geometric wall surfaces that playfully contrast with the bright green structural elements.

Green Ways and Green Spaces

The conservation of Victoria's scenic setting has seen a gradual evolution. Starting in the 1950s provincial, regional and municipal governments began to acquire the tools to plan for the protection of natural, aesthetic and recreational values. Nowhere better is this process illustrated than in the recent history of the Provincial Capital Commission.

Victoria's PCC was founded by act of the Provincial Government in 1956 as the Capital Improvement District Commission. Its object was to preserve and enhance the beauty of the Capital Region for all British Columbians.

To achieve its ends the commission has a statutory advisory and approval role in the development of government-owned properties in the district—including buildings, lands and highways. The commission may also award grants, purchase or lease lands, own and operate attraction businesses, enter into partnerships. Over the years it has done all these things. In support of its activities the commission has received annual grants from the province. It also relies on revenues from its property holdings.

One of the first projects of the PCC was the creation of a 69-mile scenic marine drive, encircling the peninsula from Victoria to Sidney. A second project was Waterway Improvements. Beginning in the early 1960s public access has been reclaimed, and through land acquisitions a linear park system created, which brings the pedestrian once again to the shores of the Gorge Inlet, the beachfronts of Songhees, the banks of Bowker and Colquitz creeks, the waterside of Victoria's Inner Harbour.

An early program of the PCC has been securing the scenic amenities of the "Capital Ways," that is the arterial approaches to and through Victoria. In the 1960s major tracts of undeveloped land along the Trans-Canada Highway were acquired to ensure adequate natural landscape buffers along these routes. Recently the PCC has turned to land swaps with private and public agencies, along with the acquisition of protective covenants and easements. The Capital Ways strategy also provided funds for roadside beautification: extensive median and curb greening, tree planting, with particular emphasis on native shrub ground covers.

It was the success of this particular effort by the commission which led to first the formation of the Greenbelt Policy and then in 1982 to the Comprehensive Plan with a broader scope. The overall objective of the

Former E&N Railway Cut, Selkirk Narrows, Gorge.

plan was to consolidate the various scenic beautification initiatives of the PCC and other government agencies within a strategic plan. One particular result would be linking this legacy of parks, green spaces and other heritage assets with a system of public-access trails and viewscapes. In 1993 this became the Capital Greenways Program and in 1994 a special advisory committee of concerned and expert citizens was created to oversee its development through the application of funding programs of public works partnerships and advisory services.

A greenway may constitute a natural feature such as an escarpment or waterway, the margins of a roadway or an abandoned railway track. Conceptualized as a "green corridor" it should connect open spaces such as parks, natural areas, cultural features or historic sites. These latter constitute the "nodes," areas of heightened interest or attractions which generate the connections.

An important function of the Greenways program has been to identify these nodes, then to devise linkages. These linkages may be physically accessible as trackways; or they may be merely visual through protected vegetation or habitat on private or institutional land. However, an equally important criterion is sustainability: assurance that infrastructure systems—legal, financial, scientific, organizational—will provide ongoing maintenance.

The greenways are multi-purpose: recreational as in hiking trails or bikeways, water management (flood control, fish enhancement), wildlife and habitat conservation—"amenity corridors." Linear open spaces can be used to buffer and separate conflicting land uses, such as at the margins of highways next to residential uses. Greenways along watercourses provide an environmental buffer filtering runoff, absorbing floodwaters, assisting in the uptake and transpiration of water from the soil. As urban development displaces and reduces wildlife populations, linear green spaces can protect botanical communities and provide conservation corridors, wildlife runs between habitats.

In 1990 the Commission developed a View Protection Strategy based on the landscape articulation methodologies of geographers, D. Linton, E. H. Zube, R. B. Linton and others. A sophisticated analysis of the arterial approaches to Victoria identified and priorized key landscape features and lands, essential for the maintenance of characteristic view corridors. For instance, the Patricia Bay Highway approach to Victoria reveals a series of panoramas, enclosed and focal arboreal screens, and portal features. These elements exemplify unique indigenous ecosystems, particularly those of the Garry Oak and Camas Lily Community, the Douglas Fir, Western Red Hemlock and Salal association, and the Western Red Cedar, Red Alder and Skunk Cabbage peat bogs. The identification of elements such as these allowed for the design of a multi-faceted acquisition and conservation strategy.

GIS computerized mapping has allowed for sophisticated resource inventorying of land features, resources and habitats. A combination of habitat type, location, and availability was analyzed for a series of major additions to the Greater Victoria Parks system in 1994. The provincial government, the Capital Regional District (the largest parks operator in the region), the Municipalities and the Provincial Capital Commission cooperated in this major acquisition program. These additions represented the most threatened habitats of the region: coastal parkland, stream beds, coniferous forest, and peat bog.

The success of such programs will always to some degree remain dependent on their public amenity values. A greenways linkage project, the Galloping Goose Park Corridor, illustrates this in the use of an abandoned Canadian National Railroad right-of-way from downtown Victoria through the Saanich Peninsula and Western Communities. Working with the PCC, local governments have acquired ownership of a network of railway cuts and trestle bridges. These are now being developed as green recreational transportation corridors designed for use by pedestrians, bicyclists, and equestrians. The Galloping Goose Corridor, with its attendant spurs, will link the Western Communities and Saanich Peninsula with the promenades of the Inner Harbour, Songhees and the Gorge Waterway.

NOTES

Ref. Chaster, G. D. & Ross, D. W. & Warren, W. H. "Trees of Greater Victoria: A Heritage." 1988. "Comprehensive Plan." Provincial Capital Commission. 1988. "Trees and Towns." 1983. "Community Greenways Linking Communities to Country, and People to Nature." 1995.

Selected Biographies

BARKER, Eric J.

A graduate of the School of Architecture, University of Winnipeg (1989), Barker worked as a research associate for CMHC. He came to Victoria in 1981 working in the office of Bawlf Cooper. Barker established his own Victoria firm in 1983. Major projects include Harbourside Hotel and condominium complex, the Regent, Family Student Housing, University of Victoria, Royal Oak Golf Clubhouse, a housing complex, Royal Links & Park Royal, Saanich; Broad Street Square, and Sterling Mews.

BAWLF, Nicholas R.

Nick Bawlf graduated from the University of British Columbia School of Architecture in 1963 with a thesis on the rejuvenation of Bastion Square, Victoria, for which he was awarded a Pilkington Scholarship for architectural studies abroad. He worked in London, England (the Civic Trust), Denmark and Ireland before returning to Canada to work with a number of Vancouver firms such as Thompson, Berwick and Pratt, and Erickson Massey. While with Erickson he was senior designer on the Bank of Canada building, Ottawa. In 1972 he established the practice in Victoria in association Cooper, Tanner Associates, Vancouver; in 1978 this became Bawlf Cooper Associates. Major projects have included numerous restorations such as Market Square and St. Andrew's Cathedral, Jewish Synagogue, heritage rehabilitation (Belmont Building), contemporary contextual work (Victoria Conference Centre, Huntington Manor Hotel), and historical restoration work at Barkerville, Cottonwood, Hat Creek and Yale. His Conference Centre design won a Lieutenant-Governor of British Columbia Medal for Excellence.

BAXTER, Robert

Baxter completed a B.Arch. at the University of British Columbia in 1960 and since then has pursued a dual specialty in institutional design and heritage restoration. Restoration work has included the Legislative Building, Fort Steele Historic Park, St. Andrew's Presbyterian Church, Craigdarroch Castle, Point Ellice House, Lampson Street and Victoria High Schools. In Victoria he has worked on numerous institutional projects: renovations to Royal Jubilee Hospital, Victoria General Hospital, completion of Christ Church Cathedral, and St. Andrew's High School. His work on the Pacific Forestry Centre with Wade Williams earned a Governor-General's Medal. Before locating in Victoria in 1973 he worked in Richmond, Calgary and Vancouver. From 1973 to 1978 he was associated with Alan J. Hodgson, then until 1983 was an associate of Wagg and Hambleton; then followed three years as partner and project architect with Wade Williams and from

1986-1990 was a member of the firm Holovsky, Baxter and Mansfield. In 1990 he became an associate partner of the Campbell Moore Group and in 1995 joined Paul Merrick Architects as partner and director of the Victoria office.

BAYNE, Richard Roskill   1827-1901

It is not clear that Bayne actually built anything in Victoria although he opened an office in 1891 and played an active role in the formation of the British Columbia Institute of Architects. He was born in Warwickshire, trained with his father and then in the office of Charles Barry. While studying at the South Kensington School of Design he won the Queen's Prize, then in 1864 was awarded the prestigious R.I.B.A. Soan Medal. From 1866 to 1890 he served as engineer to the East Indian Railway in Calcutta. He was responsible for numerous large commissions in British India but is now noted for the large collection of architectural sketches and paintings documenting his travels throughout Europe (1864-1865) and India (1870-1883). These are held by the University of Victoria.

BLOOMFIELD, James   1871-1951

The firm of "H. Bloomfield, Stained and Leaded Glass Manufacturer" was established in New Westminster in 1891. It quickly gained prominence as the leading art-glass supplier to the Victoria-Vancouver region, receiving among various commissions part of the painted-glass contact for the new Legislative Buildings and later, commemorative windows for the Maclure-Rattenbury Lieutenant-Governor's residence on Rockland. During a visit to B.C. the Governor-General, the Earl of Aberdeen, was presented with an illuminated address, executed by Henry Bloomfield's son, James. The Earl was so impressed with the workmanship of the scroll that he sent for James and offered to finance the boy's further education. Thus at the Earl's expense, which was apparently quite liberal, the young Bloomfield went first to Chicago where he worked as an assistant designer in an art-glass firm, then toured Europe looking at glass and visiting firms in Antwerp, Brussels, London and Manchester. James then returned to take over his father's firm in New Westminster. Among his most famous pieces that have been credited to this firm was the commemorative Jubilee Window which, until the library was added to the Legislative Buildings, was inserted in the south wall behind the chamber. During recent renovations this window has come to light again, been restored, and replaced in its original building. Other Victoria projects included windows for Christ Church Cathedral and Government House. After World War I Bloomfield moved to Toronto where he worked as an architectural decorator and artist until his death in 1951.

CAMPBELL, Douglas

Graduating from the University of British Columbia in 1972, Campbell worked in Vancouver until moving to Victoria in 1976. In 1977 he joined Doug Campbell to establish Moore & Campbell Designer/Builders Co. Campbell became principal of the firm Campbell Moore Group Architects Ltd. 1983. This firm has been responsible for numerous Victoria commissions including the Commonwealth Place Aquatic Centre, Hotel Grand Pacific, the British Columbia Employees Union Building, the IBM Building Douglas Street, Olympic View Golf Club,

Metchosin, Wedgewood Point Condominiums, and design guidelines for large-scale residential developments such as Christmas Hill, Saanich and Bamberton, New Town. Campbell has served on the City of Victoria Advisory Planning Commission, the Advisory Design Panel, and also on the Board of the Commonwealth Games Society.

CHOW, Sid

A partnership with Gary Fleischauer established in 1984. Representative Victoria projects of the firm are the Visual Arts Building, University of Victoria, Berwick House Congregate Care Facility and the Canadian Imperial Bank of Commerce Building, Oak Bay. Chow graduated with a B.Arch. (Hons.) from UBC in 1979; he holds an R.A.I.C. Gold Medal and has served on the Victoria Advisory Design Panel.

CISEK, Albert Franz   1866-1943

A Viennese by birth, Cisek resided in Victoria for two years during the construction of the Parliament Buildings (ca. 1895). He was a highly skilled cornice maker with the firm of Perry and Turner. The large copper domes, much of the decorative tin in the Parliament Buildings, and the famous statue of Captain Vancouver atop the central dome are products of his craft. When the Parliament Buildings contract was finished Cisek returned to Tacoma where he was responsible for much of the decorative work on the Union Station.

D'AMBROSIO, Frank M.

D'Ambrosio holds architectural degrees from Ryerson and UBC that included an urban design study term in the UK. Before forming de Hoog D'Ambrosio Rowe Architects, he worked with the firms of Hotson Bakker and Bruno Freschi in Vancouver. Subsequently he was a consultant to the Campbell Moore Group in Victoria. Main projects with these firms were CN Lands Urban Design Study, Calgary; Bayshore Lands Competition, Vancouver (winning scheme); Cameron Island Master Plan, Nanaimo; Wharf Street Waterfront Project, Victoria and the Bamberton Town Centre Plan. Since the founding of the partnership, projects have included Comprehensive Plans for the Selkirk Waterfront and Mattick's Farm, Victoria; Channel Ridge Village, Saltspring Island; and Island Hall Resort, Parksville. Buildings include 1990 Fort Street Medical/Dental and the new View Royal Town Hall.

de HOOG, Peter

A principal of de Hoog D'Ambrosio Rowe Architects, de Hoog graduated from the Technical University of Nova Scotia in 1981. He worked for the Government of the Northwest Territories for two years in Iqualuit before returning to B.C. where he worked with several firms, eventually becoming an associate with the Campbell Moore Group. During that time he designed the BCGEU Headquarters Building and the Hotel Grand Pacific. Since the formation of dDRA in 1991 his responsibilities have included the Centra Gas Operations Building, the Traffic Control Tower at Swartz Bay, Cottonwood Close Townhouses in Ganges and the new Blanshard Community Centre.

DI CASTRI, John A.

Born in Victoria, Di Castri articled with the B.C. Department of Public Works in 1942, then in 1948 worked briefly in the office of Birley Wade and Stockdill. In 1949 Di Castri left Victoria for three years at the University of Oklahoma where he studied under Bruce Goff. Returning in 1951 he opened a practice in partnership with F. W. Nichols; then in 1952 started his own practice. Di Castri has played a seminal role establishing modern architecture in Victoria during the early post-war years. His Canadian Trend House design still stands as built. From 1976 to 1980 he chaired the Canadian Housing Design Council, and also the Community Planning Association of Canada (1958-1968). Major work in Victoria includes the Institute for the Blind, Centennial Square and View Street Parkades, the Student's Union Building, Cornett Building, and Chapel at the University of Victoria, St. Patrick's Church Oak Bay, St. Joseph's Church, Strawberry Vale, Queens Wood Hosue of Studies, and the entrance foyer addition to the Royal British Columbia Museum. One of Di Castri's largest projects was planning and building designs for Notre Dame University at Nelson, British Columbia.

DONOVAN, J. P.   d. 1896

J. P. Donovan came to Victoria in 1894 but practised architecture for only two years. He died of consumption in May of 1896. During that time he designed a number of residences and commercial blocks but was remembered mainly for his supervision of the construction of St. Andrew's Cathedral for the architects Messrs. Perrault & Messiard of Montreal.

ERICKSON, Arthur

Trained at McGill School of Architecture, Erickson made his name in partnership with Geof Massey winning the design competition for Simon Fraser University, from there developing his worldwide practice and cosmopolitan reputation. Work in Victoria includes his plans for the Inner Harbour, McKinnon Biological Sciences Building at the University of Victoria, Songhees housing projects, Jawl Industries Building and British Columbia Buildings Corporation Headquarters.

EWART, A. C.   active 1890s

A. C. Ewart practised in Victoria briefly from 1889 to 1900. During that time he designed and supervised the construction of the British American Paint Company's factory on Humboldt Street, the Leiser Building, and a number of residences. On subsequently moving to Nelson he designed many commercial and residential structures in Nelson and other centres then opening up the interior of British Columbia.

FISHER, Elmer. H.

E. H. Fisher was a native of Edinburgh. At 17 he emigrated to Worcester, Massachusetts, where he worked in an architectural office. The architect arrived in Victoria in 1883 and designed a number of commercial structures for both Victoria and Vancouver. He was briefly in partnership with Ridgeway Wilson. In 1888 Fisher moved to Seattle where he was immediately very successful.

FLEISCHAUER, Gary

Fleischauer holds degrees from Ryerson Polytechnical Institute (Cert. Arch. Tech. 1967), University of Michigan (B.Arch. 1971) and University of Michigan/Massachusetts Institute of Technology (M.Arch. 1972). He registered in British Columbia in 1974. The Chow Fleischauer partnership specializes in institutional and residential work of which the following are examples: Berwick House congregate care facility; Canadian Imperial Bank of Commerce, Oak Bay, Shelbourne and McKenzie, and Saanichton branches; Keating Elementary School, Central Saanich; Cordova Village Homes and Swan Lake Estates Townhouses.

GARYALI, Shiv K.

Awarded a Diploma of Architecture in Delhi (1963), Garyali joined Marshall, Goldsworthy & Associates, Victoria in 1979. In the Victoria area Garyali has been design architect for numerous commissions, among them the Youth Detention Centre, Fine Arts Building and Faculty Club at the University of Victoria, Swan Lake Nature Sanctuary, Colwood City Hall, Esquimalt Library and the Urban Plan for Songhees, and Gulf Islands Secondary School.

GIBSON, George S. 1867-1942

Along with Charles Marega, George Gibson was one of British Columbia's major architectural sculptors during the period 1910-1940. Born in Edinburgh, Scotland, Gibson apprenticed with a firm specializing in ecclesiastical decoration. In the early 1890s he immigrated to New York where he practised briefly before returning to Edinburgh to marry and continue in the trade with his brother. In 1908 the family came to Canada, settled in Nelson, then moved to Vancouver in 1909, and finally to Shawnigan Lake in 1910. It seems he was immediately employed by both Maclure and Rattenbury. For Maclure's clients Gibson was to provide high-quality carving: fireplaces, newel posts, plaster and wood decorative detailing. Among the major commissions over the years were Hatley Park, the Robert Dunsmuir house, Miraloma for W. C. Nichol and the P. J. Angus home. Under Rattenbury he supplied carved ornament for the Legislative Library, the Speaker's chair, and the heads of Neptune in cast stone for the CPR marine terminal. Throughout his career Gibson continued his special interest in ecclesiastical work and was responsible for most of the sculptural program (in cast stone and wood) for Christ Church Cathedral, as well as various reredos, choir stalls, lecterns, and other ornaments for the small Anglican mission churches throughout British Columbia. George Gibson died at Shawnigan Lake in 1942.

GOLDSWORTHY, Ray

A graduate of UBC School of Architecture (1961), Goldsworthy founded his own firm in 1971; from 1978 to 1990 he partnered with Donovan Marshall (Marshall Goldsworthy) and since that time has practised as Raymond Goldsworthy Architect Ltd. Work in partnership included the Victoria Conference Centre with Bawlf Cooper. Raymond Goldsworthy Architect Ltd. completed The Lodge at Broadmead, Beckley Farm Lodge, Tillicum Lodge and Resthaven Lodge (Sidney), the CBC Building and Esquimalt Branch Library.

GREEN, Frederick Walter   d. 1877

Green was in partnership with Lammot and Freeman "Surveyors, Engineers, and Draftsmen." The stone "castle," which later was converted by John Wright into the official residence for Governor Kennedy, was designed by Green for George Hunter Cary. When the architect died in 1877 he was City Surveyor and Water Commissioner.

GRIFFITH, Henry Sandham   1865-1944

H. S. Griffith operated one of the quality practices in Victoria during the boom years 1900-1912. The firm expanded rapidly, opened a Vancouver office, and was involved in many of the larger commercial commissions in both cities. Griffith was born in 1865 at Aston Vicarage, Oxfordshire, and educated at Royse's School, Abingdon, Birkshire, then Christ Church College, Oxford. In 1882 he was articled to the firm of Webb & Tubb at Reading. Coming to Canada in the early 1890s, Griffith worked first in Winnipeg, then Saskatoon, before arriving in Victoria. Among the most impressive work of his Victoria years were the Times Building and Stobart-Peas Building in Victoria, and the Mining Building in Vancouver. The commercial work exhibited Griffith's fine sense of proportion combined with a sensitive handling of Edwardian classical decoration. Griffith's domestic commissions were heavily influenced by Maclure and showed a preference for random rubble stonework and heavy massing. One of the most impressive of these works was his own house, "Spencer's Castle," dominating Cook Street in Victoria. With the collapse of his firm in 1918 and closure of the Victoria office, the "Castle" was sold to the Spencer family of Department Store renown. Griffith died in Vancouver in 1944.

HAMBLETON, David H.

Hambleton trained at the Regent Street Polytechnic where he was awarded the Sir Bannister Fletcher Scholarship. In London he worked in the offices of Sir Louis de Soissons and Sir Albert Richardson on the restoration and reconstruction of war-damaged historic buildings, then on redevelopment projects with Trehearne Norman Preston & Partners. In 1958 Hambleton emigrated to Canada joining the Birley & Wagg partnership in Victoria. From 1966 the practice has been known as Wagg & Hambleton. Hambleton has chaired the Victoria Heritage Advisory Committee, the Advisory Design Panel and the Craigdarroch Castle Historical Museum Society. He was president of the AIBC in 1975 and the RAIC in 1980.

HARRISON, Eli

Eli Harrison, an Englishman, had learned the craft of mural painting in Italy. Harrison moved on to the United States where in 1853 he joined a Mormon Caravan going west. In Salt Lake City he used his talents painting religious symbols for their temples. Passing through San Francisco on the way, Harrison moved to Victoria where he established a decorating business. In 1860 he joined the local Masonic fraternity and passed through the various offices in both the subordinate lodge and Grand Lodge. Harrison, his son Eli Jr., and Thomas Trounce comprised the board of trustees who instigated the plan to build a new Masonic Temple in

1877. He held the office of Grand Master of British Columbia for an unprecedented three years. Little is remembered about Harrison's decorative interior designs of later years. We do know, however, that his youthful republican and Sectarian leanings were abandoned and, like so many other successful Victorians of his day, Harrison was formally known as an Anglican and a Conservative. Harrison's son, Eli Harrison Jr., became a well-known British Columbia lawyer and later Chief Justice.

HODGSON, Alan

Hodgson started out in the B.C. Department of Public Works in 1952, then completed the UBC architectural diploma in 1958. From 1967 to 1970 he taught at UBC as Associate Professor of Design and was involved in the Venice Project. Major work in Victoria has included the McPherson Playhouse and Parliament Buildings restorations, St. John's Anglican Church Seniors Housing infill, the Education and Music buildings at the University of Victoria, the Island Dairies Plant, the Odd Fellows Hall restoration, the Mayhew Sculpture Studio, James Bay, the Foster House, Sooke, and his own residence/studio at 404 Henry Street, Victoria West. In 1981 Heritage Canada awarded him a National Heritage Conservation award.

HOLOVSKY, Ladislav

Graduating from the University of Victoria, Holovsky gained work experience in Germany and Switzerland (1965-1968) and Toronto before joining the Bastion Group in Victoria in 1975, then Associated Architects in 1978. He formed his own firm in 1981. Various partnerships followed: Holovsky Whitfield (1984-1985), Holovsky Whitfield Piets (1986-1989), and Holovsky Baxter Mansfield (1989-1990); from 1990 Holovsky Mansfield. Representative projects include the Western Community Courthouse, Claremont Secondary School additions, Stelly's Secondary School additions, the W. & J. Wilson restoration and renovations, Blanshard Centre, the CBC Broadcasting Facility, Royal Colwood Golf and Country Club and as part of the Commonwealth Group Architects, the Saanich Commonwealth Place pool and recreation centre.

HOOPER, Thomas   1857-1935

Thomas Hooper was born in Devonshire, England and emigrated to London, Ontario in 1871 where he worked as a joiner and apprenticed as an architect to J. H. Dod and Son. By 1878 he was working in Emerson, Manitoba, as an architect and contractor and by 1883 was working in Winnipeg. Some three years later he moved to Vancouver where he worked as a supervisory architect for the provincial government (Hooper's brother Samuel served in a similar capacity to the Province of Manitoba). In 1889 he moved to Victoria. During the 1890s his firm was briefly known as Hooper and Goddard. In the early 1900s Hooper took C. E. Watkins, a former apprentice, into partnership. Hooper's earlier work, represented by the two Methodist churches and the Protestant Orphanage, shows him very much under the influence of the American Richardsonian school of architecture. Yet only his Orphanage achieved any semblance of the ample robust spatial dimensions of Richardson—the two churches in their somewhat pinched proportioning and attenuated Picturesque rooflines are still very much part of the High Victorian tradition. It was Hooper, together with John Teague, who was responsible for the majority of commercial buildings which were constructed during the boom years of the late nineteenth and early twentieth century. Many of them still line lower Johnson, Yates and Wharf Streets today. Hooper operated offices in both Victoria and Vancouver and also briefly in Edmonton. By 1907 these practices were responsible for a large percentage of British Columbia's public architecture. The Carnegie Library in Victoria and the civic buildings in Revelstoke and Vernon were among the products of this era during which the predominant style progressed from a rugged Arts & Crafts blend of Richardsonian and Art Nouveau to a severe Edwardian classical revival. During World War I Hooper moved his practice to New York though he later returned to Vancouver to retire. He died in 1935 at the age of 77. In Vancouver some of his more notable buildings are the Winch Building adjoining the Post Office, the Spencer Building on Cordova, and the rear addition to the Vancouver Court House. In addition, a number of significant architects apprenticed in his office, among them Watkins and also J. Y. McCarter, architect of Vancouver's Marine Building.

JAMES, Antoni

James received degrees from the University of Manitoba (B.Arch. 1970) and the University of British Columbia (MA Planning, 1989). From 1968 he worked in Toronto with Ron Thom, from 1970 in Winnipeg with Etienne Gaboury, from 1976 in Calgary (with Clark James Coupland), then from 1988 to 1992 with Wagg & Hambleton in Victoria. From 1992 he was principal of Antoni James Architecture Urban Design Planning which has now merged with SDW Architecture. He is now a principal of Warner James Architects.

JAMES, Percy Leonard   1878-1970

P. L. James, of the well-known Victoria firm, James and James, was born in London in 1878. His father, Samuel James, was a well-known London artist. Percy was educated at the International College at Hampstead in London and in 1893 articled with his uncle, John Elford MSA, borough architect and engineer to the city of Poole, England. In 1896 James returned to London and worked in a number of offices; most notable is that of Saxon & Snell FRIBA. In 1906 James emigrated to Canada, settling first in Edmonton and opening a partnership with M. A. Magoon and E. C. Hopkins. In 1908 James moved to Victoria and was joined there in 1910 by his brother, Douglas James, also a London-trained architect. P. L. James is notable for his close associations with F. M. Rattenbury in a number of projects, in particular the CPR Steamship Terminal and Crystal Gardens. James's early domestic commissions show a very marked influence by Rattenbury and for many years the firm of James & James was second only to Sam Maclure for the quality and prestige of their residential work. Examples include houses for J. W. Morris (Prospect Place), C. S. Baxter (Beach Drive), R. T. Reid (Rockland), Capt. W. Hobart Molson (Rockland), C. L. Branson (Ten Mile Point), A. B. Cotton (Rockland) and P. W. De P. Taylor (Sooke). James worked with K. B. Spurgin on the Jubilee Hospital commission in 1919, and entered a partnership with Hubert Savage (1929-1934).

JENSEN, Darrel L.

Trained at the École des Beaux Arts, Paris (1971) and the UBC School of Architecture (1972) Jensen worked in Victoria during the 1970s first with Alan Hodgson, then with Siddall Dennis Warner, and from 1976 to 1979 as CMHC architect for Vancouver Island. Victoria work includes Sara Spencer House, Mount Newton Centre Society building, Saanichton, Constance Court Esquimalt and the Youth Hostel rehabilitation project for which he won a B.C. Heritage award.

KEITH, John Charles Malcom 1858-1940

Born in Nairn, Scotland in 1858, son of a clergyman, Keith was educated in grammar schools at Lincoln, Claremont, Surrey, and Wallasey, Cheshire. He entered the architectural practice of Scottish architect Alexander Ross (designer of Inverness Cathedral) in 1874, in 1883 continuing studies in London. Keith emigrated to California in 1887 and practised there for two years before moving to Seattle. In 1891 Keith arrived in Victoria specifically to compete in the competition for the design of Christ Church Cathedral. Although winning the competition in 1892, which earned him fellowship in the Royal Institute of British Architects, Memorial Hall was not built until 1923 and the Cathedral itself was only started in 1926. It is still unfinished. Keith held memberships in Rotary, the Pacific and Arion Clubs and in 1912 was president of the Victoria chapter of the British Columbia Architects Association. Among the many buildings deriving from his 50-year Victoria career are the Moss Street School, the Seaman's Institute (James Bay), the City Police Court, Anglican churches at Nanaimo and Port Alberni, and the Chapel of Jubilee Hospital. Keith died on his birthday, December 19, 1940.

KEW, Irvin H.

A graduate of the Thames Polytechnic, London, Kew established his Victoria firm in 1981. From 1968 he practised in London, UK, then joined firm of Wagg & Hambleton Architects, Victoria in 1978. From 1986 to 1989 Kew was in partnership with Darrel Jensen. Victoria projects include the Canada Customs House and P. L. James Place renovations, Bordon Mercantile and CEIC offices, B.C. Assessment Authority office and the Via Rail Canada station.

KWAN, Herbert H.

From 1976 to 1987 Kwan was a design partner with Wagg & Hambleton. In 1987 he opened his own firm.

LEVINSON, Benjamin Bryce

A graduate of the University of Manitoba School of Architecture (1966), Levinson opened his Victoria architectural practice in 1970. Representative of Levinson's Victoria work are the restored Gibson House, the University of Victoria Fire Hall, #3, Hillcrest Elementary School Addition and Beacon Hill Villa Intermediate Care Home.

LEWIS, Richard   active 1860s

Trained as an architect in London Lewis arrived in Victoria via Chile and San Francisco. Active in civic affairs, he was three times a city alderman and once Mayor of Victoria. The first Masonic Temple and the Lascelles Building (extant) at Fort and Government were designed by him.

MACLURE, Samuel   1860-1929

Maclure is probably the most notable of Victoria's architects for both the quality and originality of the work that stemmed from his 40-year practice in British Columbia. The first white child to be born in the pioneer community of New Westminster, he was the eldest son of John Maclure, a Scottish emigrant who came west with the Royal Engineers, then served as a surveyor and telegraph operator. Following an early ambition to study art, Sam attended the Spring Garden Institute in Philadelphia from 1884 to 1885. It was during this time that he discovered his interest in architecture. Financial difficulties cut short his stay, however, and Maclure returned to British Columbia. While supporting himself as a telegraph operator for the Esquimalt and Nanaimo Railroad, he studied architecture at home. In 1887 he joined C. H. Clow in New Westminster, then in 1891 he established a brief practice with G. L. T. Sharpe. The buildings surviving from those years exhibit the prevailing High Victorian eclectic tastes of the day. In 1892 Maclure opened his own architectural practice in Victoria. Maclure's first commissions were small Shingle style bungalows, a distinctive feature of which was rather rigid symmetrical planning. His first major project, the Temple Building for Robert Ward, demonstrated Maclure's memories of the mid-west commercial styles of the 1880s. Commercial work, however, was not to be the core of Maclure's later successful practice. During the 1890s Maclure worked in the Shingle style bungalow idiom, achieving his most successful results in the Munn house of 1899 and the Martin house of 1904. The Robin Dunsmuir house of 1900 (destroyed) was his successful breakthrough to the continued patronage of Victoria's commercial and political "aristocracy." It later brought him the lucrative commission for Robert Dunsmuir's Hatley Park. In 1903 Maclure was joined by Cecil Croker Fox who had previously been a student with Charles F. Annesley Voysey in England. Fox ran the Vancouver office of the firm which closed when he was killed in the early days of World War I. It was during these years that many Voysey elements appear in Maclure's commissions, particularly in the smaller houses. After the war the Vancouver office was re-opened with Ross Lort as the partner in charge. Maclure then turned increasingly toward the Neo-Georgian idiom and away from the robust vernacular styles of the pre-war years. The period 1900 to 1914 represented the high point of his practice. It was during these years that he popularized the English half-timber idiom which, along with the contributions of his many imitators, now forms an essential component of the character of present-day Victoria. For smaller cottages he utilized the board-and-batten style. Maclure's larger houses were characterized by their superb, dramatic staircases and magnificent halls which provided a fit setting for the extremely active social life of these years. His plans were noted for their meticulous detail. Maclure's difficulty in retaining contractors to execute his designs was an indication of his insistence on a high quality of materials and workmanship as well as the thoroughness of his supervision. While in his early work Maclure was obviously under the spell of Arts & Crafts and Shingle style promoters (his use of materials and strong axial planning show a marked affinity to the work of Wilson Eyre whose circle he may have known in Philadelphia) Maclure worked increasingly toward a compromise with the more markedly English tastes of his clientele. Though a native son of B.C., not given to extensive travel, Maclure was always cognizant of the outside world. He was renowned during his life as an extremely kind and cultured man. He was an avid water-colourist; he was knowledgeable in literature and music (his wife was an accomplished pianist); and he boasted a very fine library. His work was published in *The Canadian Builder, The Craftsman, The Studio*, and *Country Life*. Particularly interesting is his correspondence with Frank Lloyd Wright which is reputed to have extended over several years. One of the gems of his library was the 1910 Berlin publication of Wright's work. There is much evidence of Wright in the extensive roof-overhangs of his houses and in the treatment of exterior wall surfaces. Among other architects outside Victoria probably his closest friend was K. K. Cutter of Cutter and Malgrem of Spokane. During his post-war practice a few notable works stand out. Among these is his Rustic style Nichol house "Miraloma" (latterly "The Latch") in Sidney, but in the main these are years of decline in the wealth and status of Victoria and, consequently, in social life. The great halls and staircases hardly ever occur after 1920; large commissions were fewer and farther between. Samuel Maclure died in 1929. His practice in Victoria was liquidated though the Vancouver branch was continued by Ross Lort very much on Maclure's early Arts & Crafts principles.

MALLANDAINE, Edward   1827-1905

Edward Mallandaine was born in Singapore in 1827, received his primary education in France, and attended a business school in London. He received architectural training while articled in the London area's District Surveyors Office and during this time was admitted as a student at the Royal Institute of British Architects. He then worked in England at the architectural offices of J. C. Robinson and later W. Tress of the I.E. Railway. Mallandaine passed through Victoria with the gold rush in 1858 and later returned to teach Hebrew and French in a private boys school. In 1869, with another schoolmaster, Mr. Silversmith, he compiled the first directory of Victoria and British Columbia. In 1866 he opened his first architectural practice on Yates Street. His major commission was the old Victoria Customs House and Post Office on the site of the present Federal Building on Government Street. Apart from that, he did many churches and hotels—St. Luke's on Cedar Hill and St. John's at Cowichan Bay still stand. The Colonial Hotel at New Westminster, various commercial blocks in Vancouver, Victoria and Nanaimo, and many residences, like that of Bishop Cridge, were from his designs. He died in 1905, leaving for posterity his colourful and critically opinionated memoirs which record nearly 50 years of Victoria's social, commercial, and political life. (These are now preserved in the Provincial Archives.)

MAREGA, Charles   d. 1939

Marega arrived in Vancouver in 1910. A Genoese by birth he had studied at Zurich and Vienna and then worked in South Africa. During an active career specializing in monumental and private sculptural commissions, he also taught at the Vancouver School of Art. Among his better known works are the 14 famous personalities for the Provincial Library sculptural program; the Lions guarding the Stanley Park entrance to Lions Gate Bridge; the Harding Memorial and bust of David Oppenheimer in Stanley Park; and the King Edward Fountain at the Vancouver Court House. Marega died in 1939.

MARSHALL, Donovan

A UBC School of Architecture graduate of 1961, Marshall began practice in 1964 in partnership with Gerald Sager. He practised on his own from 1971 to 1978 when he formed a Victoria partnership with Ray Goldsworthy and Shiv Garyali (associate partner). The firm was restructured as Marshall & Garyali Architects in 1990. Victoria area commissions include numerous schools: Bayside Middle School, Sir James Douglas, Parklands, Spencer, and the Faculty Club and Fine Arts Building at the University of Victoria.

MAURICE, Claude

Maurice completed a University of Manitoba B.Arch. in 1962 with a thesis on the redevelopment of Bastion Square. He practised for three years in Charlottetown, PEI, then in Vancouver. His Victoria office was established in 1971. In 1990 he received a Hallmark Society Award for the restoration of 1525 Amelia, in 1983 a Canadian Housing Design Council Award for the Malleson Residence, Saanich, and in 1982 a Heritage Canada Honour Award for his Capital Iron project. Other projects include three branches for the Canadian Imperial Bank of Commerce; the Lawn Bowling Clubhouse, Victoria West; Monterey Mews, Oak Bay. He has served on the Victoria Advisory Planning Commission and Advisory Design Panels in Comox, Nanaimo, Sidney and Victoria.

MESHER, George Charles   1860-1938

A noted Victoria contractor and architect, Mesher was born in Weybourne, Surrey, England. He was responsible for numerous large office buildings during the Edwardian boom years including the Pemberton and Sayward Buildings, Bank of Commerce buildings in Victoria and Nanaimo; also a number of early apartment buildings such as Hampton Court on Cook Street and October Mansions. Mesher retired to his "ranch" at Port Alberni in 1928 although he continued to maintain his large Dallas Road home.

MORETTI, Victor   active 1890s

Moretti, a fresco artist and decorator, collaborated with F. M. Rattenbury to design and oversee the decorative detailing for the Parliament Buildings. It is disappointing that, as yet, so little else is known about him.

MUIR, Alexander Maxwell   active 1890s

Andrew Maxwell Muir was born in Glasgow, Scotland, and received his architectural training there. In 1885 he emigrated to the United States where he worked some two-and-a-half years in Troy, New York. Before moving west he accepted a position with Wm. Parsons & Sons of Topeka, Kansas, who were then engaged in the construction of many public schools and civic buildings throughout the state. After going to San Diego to work on designs for the Hotel del Coronado, he came to Victoria and in 1889 worked as a draughtsman for John Teague during the planning of Jubilee Hospital, the additions to the City Hall, and extensions to First Presbyterian Church. His own designs won competitions for the City Market (now destroyed) and, in 1891, for the Board of Trade Building on Bastion Square. Muir's specialty, however, was heavy brick and stone structures as evidenced by his commercial blocks and bridging work. Some of his perspective plans for a Clyde dock scheme were exhibited in the Inter Colonial Exhibition at Edinburgh, Scotland.

MUSSON, Frank

Musson is the founding partner of Musson Cattell Mackey Partnership, Vancouver, which dates from 1968. He graduated from the Architectural Association School of Architecture, London, England in 1955. Among his better known buildings in Vancouver are the Bentall Centre, the B.C. Hydro Building, Dunsmuir Street, and Park Place, Canada Place (with Downs Archambault), the Pan Pacific Hotel (with Downs Archambault and Zeidler Roberts) and Chateau Whistler. In Victoria the firm was responsible for the Hillside Shopping Centre, the Bentall Building and the Centra Gas Building. The Daon Centre, Vancouver, won a Governor-General's Gold Medal for Architecture in 1982.

PEARSE, J. B.   1832-1902

Born in Devonshire, England in 1832, Pearse arrived in Victoria in 1851 and was soon after appointed Surveyor to the Crown Colony. Among his many tasks was surveying the townsite of Victoria, overseeing the erection of government buildings, and under Colonial Surveyor J. D. Pemberton, laying out most of the first roads on Vancouver Island. Pearse was also active in British Columbia politics and, after the union of the colonies, served as a member of the executive council which voted the Colony of British Columbia into confederation with the Dominion of Canada. In 1872 he was appointed Provincial Engineer of the Dominion Works Department. Among the buildings he superintended during those years were the Customs House and Post Office in Victoria. Pearse also held a seat on Victoria City Council and served for some years on the Victoria Sewage Commission which introduced piped sewers to the city in the early 1890s. In 1860 Pearse built for himself the famous mansion "Fernwood" (since destroyed); its estate later became the prestigious residential district still bearing that name. Pearse died in 1902.

PETERSON, Carl E.

After completing a Master of Engineering at Boston University, Peterson then went on to do a B.Arch. at Montana State. In Victoria from 1975 to 1978 he was design and project architect with the Bastion Group, then a principal with Marshall Goldsworthy and Associates until 1987. Since 1987 he has maintained his own firm, Carl Peterson Architect, and from 1989 a joint venture with the Wade Williams Corporation. A number of Victoria projects are Peterson's authorship including the Canadian Forces Recruitment Centre; the Victoria Conference

Centre (in association with Bawlf Cooper); 3 Point Motors; Victoria Police Headquarters; and at Camosun College Interurban Campus, the Campus Centre, Technologies Building, and Centre for Business Access.

RATTENBURY, Francis Mawson 1867-1937

F. M. Rattenbury was British Columbia's premier institutional architect from the time he won the competition for the Parliament Buildings in 1892 to the collapse of the pre-war expansion in 1918. He designed court houses, bank buildings, shipping terminals, hotels, and railway stations throughout the province. Born in Leeds in 1867, Rattenbury was educated at Leeds Grammar School and then articled for five years in his uncle's firm, Lockwood and Mawson. He arrived in Canada at the age of 23 having already won an "honourable mention" for a housing scheme and club building at Bradford in England. In 1891 he was an exhibitor at the Royal Academy. Architecture was only one of his many interests. Today he might be accused of what we call in business "vertical integration," operating companies which fed into and benefitted from his practice. Rattenbury & Co., Estates, purchased thousands of acres of farm land in the Nechaco and Bulkley valleys along the planned route of the Grand Trunk Pacific Railroad for which the architect designed a chain of luxury hotels and of which he was also a director. In Victoria Rattenbury was the founder of the well-known Melrose Paint and Decorating Co., consultant architect to the Uplands Ltd., and member of the Union Club and Royal Victoria Yacht Club. In 1911 he was president of the B.C. Architects Association. In 1913 he served as Reeve of Oak Bay. Among his various other projects was the founding of a Company (the Lake Bennett & Klondyke Transportation Co.) which financed and designed three knockdown steamboats which were delivered to Skagway and carried to Lake Bennett, there to act as transportation and supply vessels for gold rush miners. He also had interests in a scheme for shipping portable unitized housing to the Canary Islands, in the founding of Edmonton Breweries Ltd., and in a project involving shipping frozen salmon to Europe. Through a series of commissions, Rattenbury developed a keen interest in the Chateau style. This is illustrated in his Empress Hotel, Victoria (1901-1908), the court houses at Nanaimo (1895) and Nelson (1899), and in his finest piece, the Bank of Montreal Building in Victoria (1896). Most impressive of schemes in this idiom was a chain of luxury hotels for the Grand Trunk Pacific Railroad from Prince Rupert to Mount Robson. In other and later works such as the CPR shipping terminal and Crystal Gardens, he follows the classical Edwardian tradition which carries through a Beaux Arts flavour found earlier in the Parliament Buildings and Vancouver Court House. Rattenbury's few domestic commissions illustrate the architect's impatience with details. His interiors lack the feeling for space and proportion so obvious in those of Samuel Maclure, his friend and contemporary. The best of these houses, however, demonstrate a two-fold interest in the American Shingle style of McKim, Mead, and White and the Vernacular Revival styles of Norman Shaw and others in Britain. The Lieutenant-Governor's Residence (designed in partnership with Maclure, 1901) and his own house on Beach Drive (1908) illustrate these interests. During the post-war years, many of the commissions were carried out in partnership with P. L. James. Rattenbury, known familiarly to friends as

"Ratz," left Victoria for Bournemouth, England in 1928. He died in 1937 much in style of his colourful and varied life, the victim of murder at the hands of a domestic servant.

ROWE, Christopher

A principal of the firm de Hoog D'Ambrosio Rowe Architects, founded in 1991, Rowe is a graduate in art history, University of Victoria, the UBC School of Architecture and recipient of the RAIC Medal. Before forming the partnership Rowe worked with Patkau Architects, Vancouver and the Campbell Moore Group, Victoria. Design projects include the proposed Maritime Museum of B.C., Victoria; the Olympic View Golf Club, Metchosin; the Centra Gas Operations Centre and The Arc office building, Victoria.

SIDDALL, Bob

Siddall is a graduate of the University of Manitoba, 1948, and worked two years in Vancouver with C. B. K. Norman, a firm well known for its pioneering residential work in the West Coast style. Siddall worked briefly with Richard Neutra in California. He opened his Victoria office in 1951 as Polson & Siddall, taking over the partnership of P. Leonard James and Hubert Savage. In 1910 James had associated with Francis Mawson Rattenbury, and over the years with his brother, Douglas James and Savage. (Savage himself had associated with Samuel Maclure, completing the work at hand after Maclure's death in 1929.) In 1957 the firm operated as R. W. Siddall, from 1965 as Siddall Dennis and Associates. In 1970 David Warner became an associate and from 1986 the firm was known as SDW Architects. In 1995 a new association was formed with Antoni James and Kenneth B. Johson, who had previously worked together in Winnipeg, Calgary and Victoria.

SMITH, Barry (Bas)

Completing diplomas in architecture (Leeds, 1964) and town planning (1966), Smith served as senior architect for the City of Bath (1967-1972) before emigrating to Canada in 1974. From 1974 to 1978 he was Senior Architect at Armour Blewett and Partners, Vancouver, and from 1980 to 1986 partnered with Vic Davies. As the principal of Bas Smith Architects, he has directed the firm's work particularly in the housing sector: The Caledonia on Gladstone, The Birches on Hillside, two student housing villages for the University of Victoria, and the Security Services Building also for the University.

SORBY, Thomas C.   1836-1924

Thomas C. Sorby was an accomplished architect before he arrived in Victoria in 1887 and was one of the most industrious and ingenious architects to practise in Victoria and Vancouver during the boom decades at the turn of the century. He was born at Wakefield, Yorkshire, in England and educated in London where he practised as a civil engineer and architect for 25 years. For ten years he served as County Court Surveyor for England and Wales, later as district surveyor, and Consultant Architect to the Home Office and Treasury. He was a Fellow of the Royal Institute of British Architects, a Fellow of the Royal Geological Society, and a member of the Royal Society of Arts. In 1883 he emigrated to Montreal where he designed a number of stations and hotels for the Canadian Pacific Railway. Three years later he came west to Vancouver and participated in the post-fire building boom. He designed the early Hotel Vancouver, St. James Church, the first CPR terminal buildings at the foot of Cordova, and a residence for Mr. Abbot, Superintendent of the CPR's Lower Mainland operations. In Victoria Sorby designed such significant residences as that of Robert Ward on Rockland and the Parsonage for Christ Church Cathedral. Neither his domestic nor his commercial architecture is notable for stylistic innovation but he handled stylistic elements competently. What is significant about Sorby is the technical brilliance of his designs, illustrated in houses by gimmicky features such as disappearing sash windows and in his commercial buildings by basic structural and planning innovations such as those discussed in the Weiler Building. Throughout his life in Victoria Sorby remained fascinated with a scheme to redevelop the Inner Harbour and make Victoria the "Super-port" for the West Coast. Though this never materialized, Sorby continued to promote the plan into which he put years of work, producing studies from economic, technological and aesthetic points of view. As a spinoff from these interests he won a competition design for a new Johnson Street Bridge which was never built and for which he was never paid the prize money. The filling in of James Bay, the building of large graving docks for marine repairs, development of waterfront recreation parks, dredging of the Inner Harbour—all part of Sorby's 1896 plans compiled at his own expense—have since become part of Victoria's development history. The Dominion Government appreciated Sorby's efforts and utilized his services in the designing of the Ogden Point Shipping Terminal; the city, however, never officially acknowledged its debt to him though many of the ideas he promoted until his death in 1924 have since been executed.

SYME, James 1832-1881

James Syme was born in Edinburgh, Scotland, in 1832 and came through Victoria in 1862 on his way from San Francisco to the Cariboo gold rush. As a gifted but peripatetic individual with a wide variety of talents and interests he variously turned his hand to fish-curing and canning at New Westminster in 1868, interior decorating and ornamental plastering in San Francisco in 1869, landscape oil painting at Victoria again in 1872, and then architecture until his death in 1881, at the age of 49. Among the buildings constructed from his designs were the original St. Joseph's Hospital, a house for Chief Justice Gordon Hunter at Belleville and Oswego, and the Grayham residence at 441 Simcoe.

TEAGUE, John 1833-1902

Born in Cornwall, England, in 1833, John Teague was a contractor and architect who became one of Victoria's pre-eminent builders in the late 1800s. Little is known about Teague's training. Lured to the New World by the promise of finding gold, Teague erected mine buildings during the California gold rush and, in 1859, ventured into the Cariboo. Disillusioned with the gold rush, Teague settled in Victoria and began constructing buildings for the Royal Navy at Esquimalt. Among his surviving buildings there is the very handsome Admiral's House (later, residence of the Base Commander). A short time later, Teague established his architectural office in Trounce Alley. Plans for numerous commercial buildings and shop fronts came out of his office in the 1870s, but 1874 proved to be an important year in his practice. That year, he obtained the commission for the Church of Our Lord, a congregation of the Reformed Episcopal Church, which counted among its members many of Victoria's character civic leaders. Teague's rise as Victoria's first notable institutional architect was significant. Central School (1875-1876) and High School (1882, 1885, 1888), Victoria Masonic Temple (1878), Victoria City Hall (1878) and Royal Jubilee Hospital (1889-1890) were all executed in the Mansardic style, Teague's institutional signature, complementing variations on the Italianate style for his residential and commercial buildings. Teague's distinctive Mansardic roofline and entrance towers contributed greatly to Victoria's late nineteenth century cityscape. The Driard Hotel (1892) in the Richardson vocabulary was Teague's last major commission. The Depression of the mid-1890s effectively put an end to what would have been the final, exuberant phase of his career. Unbuilt commissions of that era included the magnificent headquarters for the Garesche Green & Co. Bank, an eclectic building of imposing scale capped with a picturesque roof. This was the Victorian builder's dream unfulfilled. Teague died a respected architect in October 1902.

TIARKS, John G.   active 1890s

John G. Tiarks came to Victoria from Weston-Super-Mare, England in 1888. During the following ten years he not only established himself as a popular local domestic architect but also handled business investments for English clients with an eye to some profitable land speculation. He served as a city alderman for the Fourth Ward from 1891. The Weiler brothers' bungalow on Dallas Road from the early 1890s and the residence for the Hon. G. Dewdney on Rockland were representative examples of Tiarks' work which evolved from Downing Picturesque to the popular Tudor Revival according to the change in local prevailing tastes.

TIEDEMANN, Hermann Otto   1821-1891

Tiedemann was born in Berlin, Germany in 1821 and trained in Germany as a civil engineer. Arriving in Victoria in 1858, he first worked as a surveyor and architect under the James Douglas regime. During this early period in the colony's life Tiedemann was charged with designing the Colonial Administration Buildings (familiarly known as the "Birdcages") and superintending work on a number of public projects including lighthouses, court, and customs buildings. As a surveyor Tiedemann worked briefly for the CPR and was employed on a number of mapping projects for private companies and the provincial government. (Tiedemann Glacier at the head of Bute Inlet still bears his name.) Between 1863 and his death in 1891 Tiedemann accepted a large number of private commissions, including both domestic and commercial work.

TRIMEN, Leonard Buttress   d. 1891

Leonard Buttress Trimen came to Victoria from England in the early 1880s and during a relatively brief architectural career in Victoria designed many of Victoria's most prestigious residences. However, the most significant feature of his practice was the introduction and popularization of the Gothic Vernacular Revival styles which were later picked up and developed by Maclure, Rattenbury, and

James to such an extent that they became the dominant feature of the Victoria landscape. The most magnificent of Trimen's creations was "Ashnola" (later Gorge Road Hospital and destroyed in the early 1970s), a red brick Jacobean revival residence for one of the Dunsmuir daughters. The G. H. Burns home which stood on Fairfield, the William Russell residence on Boyd, and the Angus home still standing on Rockland were good examples of this typically Victorian eclectic combination of Queen Anne shingle decorations, Tudor arches and entrances, half-timbered detailing, crenellated stone parapets, and attenuated towering chimneys grouped and massed in a Picturesque fashion. To judge by his popularity, this melange thoroughly pleased his upper-class clientele. After a very successful career, L. B. Trimen died in 1891.

VAUGHAN, Don W.

Trained at the University of Oregon in landscape architecture Vaughn worked first with the Vancouver firm of John Lantzius where he was responsibile for projects such as Simon Fraser University Campus, the University of Victoria and projects at the University of British Columbia. Don Vaughan & Associates was formed in 1965. Various of the firm's projects include ongoing work at the University of Victoria, the Dr. Sun Yat-Sen Garden, Vancouver and other Vancouver work including the Daon Plaza, Bentall Centre and Burrard Street ALRT Station (Discovery Square).

WADE, John H.

Immediately following World War II, Wade returned to practise in partnership with S. P. Birley and C. D. Stockdill. Terry Williams joined the firm in 1969. In its early years the firm was responsible for numerous institutional buildings including the planning of Centennial Square, buildings for the University of Victoria, Saanich Municipal Hall, the Victoria Airport Terminal Building and a number of schools for the Greater Victoria School District and Sooke School District. His Pacific Forestry Centre received a Governor-General's Award for Excellence in 1986.

WAGG, Donald

Don Wagg was articled to Ernest A. Newton A.R.I.B.A. in Manchester, England, and trained at the School of Art, and the Technical College in that city. He qualified as a chartered architect, A.R.I.B.A. and after several years' experience in offices in various towns in England, became city architect of Peterborough. He served in the Royal Engineers during World War II, and emigrated to Canada in 1948, locating in Nelson, B.C., where he completed the design of Mount St. Francis Hospital. In 1950 he moved to Victoria, setting up a partnership with retired Provincial Architect, W. H. Whittaker. The firm specialized in hospital design, carrying out extensive additions to the Jubilee and St. Joseph hospitals in Victoria, and also designed many hospitals for rural communities throughout the province. Whittaker retired in 1954, and Wagg formed a partership with Patrick Birley, who died prematurely in 1961. Birley had articled with John Teague. Numerous architects now in private practice in Victoria worked in his office, notably David Hambleton (1958) and Brian Bartle (1965) who became partners in the firm of Wagg &

Hambleton in 1966 and 1976 respectively. This list also includes Bob Baxter, Sid Chow, Gary Fleischauer, Herb Kwan, Irvin Kew, Ben Levinson, Alan Lowe and David Warner. Wagg retired in 1979, but the firm retained his name, and continues to specialize in hospitals, as well as a range of university, commercial, domestic and institutional buildings.

WARNER, David

A graduate of the London Northern Polytechnic in 1954, Warner practised in London before coming to Canada. He worked briefly for Birley and Simpson in Victoria; then in 1958 joined Polson & Siddall architects. From 1960 to 1968 he maintained a private practice in Calgary, then returned to Victoria to join Siddall Dennis as an associate. In 1970 this became Siddall Dennis Warner Architects. The link with Siddall who assumed the practice of P. L. James can thereby also trace its local roots to F. M. Rattenbury. On the retirement of the other principals in 1986 Warner assumed leadership of the firm. He has chaired the Vancouver Island chapter of the AIBC. Representative works of the firm include the Richard Blanshard Building; the City Centre Plaza retail and office complex, Dunsmuir Lodge; B.C. Hydro Administrative Centre, Royal Oak; the Worker's Compensation Centre and numerous buildings at the University of Victoria. In 1995 the firm evolved to Warner, James, Johnson Architects and Planners.

WARREN, Jesse   d. 1953

Warren began his architectural practice in San Francisco after the fire in 1906 and then went to New York for further training. He later settled in Seattle before coming to Victoria in 1911. His stay in Victoria was brief, but during that time he designed some notable structures, among them the Central Building and Pantages Theatre. He later settled in Santa Barbara where he died in 1953.

WHITE, John   d. 1907

John White, artist and draughtsman with the Royal Engineers, came to the colony with the contingent under Captain R. M. Parsons in 1858. He worked on designs to convert Colonel Moody's house into Government House in New Westminster for Governor Seymour in 1864. He designed St. Mary's Church there in 1865. After the disbanding of the Engineers he became a surveyor and artist with the Collins Overland Telegraph. From 1864 he worked as a draughtsman with the Lands and Works Department of the Colonial Government and later the Provincial Government. During his lifetime he was well known for his watercolours, oils, and scene paintings for the local theatres. As yet there is no evidence that he designed any buildings in Victoria although he may have worked closely with John Wright and H. O. Tiedemann. White died in 1907.

WHITEWAY, William Tuff   1856-1940

Born in Newfoundland and educated at the Wesleyan Academy, St. John's, Whiteway arrived in Victoria in 1882. Listed as a carpenter, he apprenticed with S. M. Goddard (who was briefly associated with Thomas Hooper), moving to Vancouver in 1886. By 1888 he was practising in Port Townsend, Wash. with J. C. Schroeder. In 1893 he designed a Court House for St. John's and from 1896 to 1898 practised in Halifax as Whiteway and Horton. In 1900 he returned to Vancouver where he ran a lucrative practice which included such commissions as the Sun Tower and the Duncan Elementary School (1913). In Victoria he designed the Simeon Duck Block.

WILLIAMS, Terence J.

Principal of the Wade Williams Corporation, Williams graduated from the Bath University of Science and Technology, then went on to work in Bristol, London, Helsinki and New York where he worked on the BOAC terminal at Kennedy Airport. He joined the firm of Rhone Iredale, Architects, Vancouver in 1967 moving to Victoria in 1971 as a partner in Wade Stockdill Armour & Blewett. In 1987 he became president of the Wade Williams Corporation. Williams has served as President of the Architectural Institute of British Columbia and President of the Royal Architectural Institute of Canada. William's work has influenced the urban landscape of Victoria through his campus plans for Camosun College Lansdowne Campus, Glenlyon School and Norfolk schools. His Bank of Hongkong, Fort Street, received an AIBC award.

WILLIAMS, Warren Heywood   1844-1888

Born in 1844, Williams trained as an architect in the San Francisco practice which his father, Stephen Hiddon Williams, started in 1850. He entered this firm in about 1862, and by 1868 he was a partner. In 1869 he designed the Odd Fellows Hall in Portland, Oregon, moving permanently to Portland in 1872 in time to take part in the rebuilding of the town after a disastrous fire that year. He first formed a partnership with E. M. Barton, and together they squeezed out the established prominent local architect W. W. Piper, who had been responsible for the majority of large public and private commissions up to that time. Williams popularized what was then called the "modern Italianate style," a bracketted decorative style which utilized Italian Renaissance motifs within the Victorian Picturesque tradition. Williams maintained a healthy practice even during the business recession of the middle 1870s designing among others for Portland the H. W. Corbet Mansion and the Good Samaritan Hospital in 1874, and during the 1880s some 50 buildings of note, among them the Union Block, Allen and Levi's Blocks, the First National Bank, the Portland Savings Bank, the Temple Beth Israel, and several other churches and residences. His domestic styles included the Italianate Villa and French Mansardic. The buildings are noted for his uniform decorative technique of plaster — cementing over the exterior brick surfaces, then moulding the stone courses and rustication; he also made extensive use of applied iron ornament. In Eugene, Oregon Williams was responsible for the Masonic Temple and the Dan Block, both in 1887, and one of his largest commissions, the Eugene Deady Hall for the University of Oregon. Victoria boasts at least two Williams buildings, the first Bank of British Columbia (1886) on Government Street and Dunsmuir's Craigdarroch Castle on Joan Crescent. Williams died in 1888.

WILSON, William Ridgeway   1863-1957

William Ridgeway Wilson was born in Hong-Gow, China in 1863. Later, having moved to England, he was articled for four years to an architectural firm in

Liverpool and then worked in the office of Sir Horace Jones, City Architect of London. While in London he sat for the examinations of the Kensington Science and Art Department, the successful results of which entitled him to lecture on building construction and gave him the rank of student at the Royal Academy. Wilson came to Victoria in 1887, and opened his offices in Spencer's Arcade, forming a partnership with E. H. Fisher in 1888. The team of Fisher & Wilson subsequently built many residential and commercial structures both in Victoria and Vancouver. Wilson maintained his practice until the early 1940s and during that time designed many generations of Victoria's buildings. He remained, however, one of the most conservative of the local practitioners—at his best in the High Victorian Picturesque styles. These are best represented by the ornate "Gypyswyck," now the Art Gallery of Greater Victoria on Moss Street. The Bay Street Armory and Wilkinson Road Mental Home allowed him to produce variations on the Late Victorian castellated manse. From 1902 Ridgeway Wilson received various commissions with the militia reserve, finally achieving the rank of colonel and commanding a prisoner of war camp at Vernon during World War I. He died at the age of 94 in 1957 and was buried from St. John's Anglican Church which was also one of his commissions.

WRIGHT, John   1830-1915

John Wright was born in Killearn, Scotland in 1830. He came to Victoria in 1859 from San Francisco. As an architect with the Colonial Government he is reputed to have been the first professional to practise in Victoria. In cooperation with Herman Otto Tiedemann, Wright's first commissions were lighthouses and towers for the east coast of the Island. One of these, Fisgard Lighthouse and keeper's residence, was made a historic site. As an architect he was thoroughly imbued with the Victorian spirit. An innovative engineer, he introduced steam heating to Victoria in 1859 with his design for the Pandora Street Methodist Church; as a High Victorian architect he understood and practised the Gothic Revival style, well exemplified by Angela College. In 1861 Wright was joined in practice by his brother-in-law, George Sanders. Amongst other commissions were "Woodlands" (1861) for James Bissett, a prominent HBC official, and "Fairfield" (1861), a private residence for the later first Lieutenant-Governor of B.C., Joseph William Trutch and "Pentrelew" (1875) for Judge Henry Pering Pellew Crease. One of Wright's smaller domestic assignments was the Richard Carr house. His extant domestic buildings, the Carr House, "Woodlands," and "Pentrelew" demonstrate his dedication to the principles of A. J. Downing and a preference for the Italian Villa idiom—so aptly suited to early Victoria's idyllic image of itself. In 1863 the offices of Wright & Sanders were advertised at Yates and Langley. In 1867 the decision was made to move the offices to San Francisco where the firm met with considerable success and to this day is remembered for its famous Nob Hill residences. Despite the removal, Wright continued to design structures for Victoria clients and visited friends here many times. On one such visit in 1915 he was taken ill on the ferry crossing from Seattle and subsequently died in the Jubilee Hospital.

Glossary

AESTHETIC MOVEMENT The term used to describe the nineteenth century artistic circle which included, at various times, such luminaries as William Morris, William Dolman Hunt, the Rossettis, Walter Pater, Oscar Wilde and J. M. Whistler, and featured a common espousal of "arts for art's sake" along with a hypersensitivity to natural and organic forms.

ARCUATED A term used to describe a building or part of a building structurally dependent on the use of arches. (For opposite see trabeated.)

ART DECO Derives its name from the Exposition des Arts Decoratifs (Paris, 1925) and is characterized by low relief geometric ornament. Abstract or vaguely historical patterns in this clean-lined style lent themselves easily to concrete form-work methods of reproduction on buildings.

ART NOUVEAU The "new art" style which spread throughout Europe and America in the 1980s. Is identifiable especially by flat, organic patterns of writhing vegetable forms. Was applied to buildings and was particularly popular in the decorative arts.

ARTICULATE Using architectural elements such as mouldings, string courses, and crestings to delineate and emphasize the structural components in a building.

ARTS & CRAFTS MOVEMENT An English social and aesthetic movement which later spread to America 1870-1920. It encompassed an admiration for folk art and nostalgic interest in medieval craft products and society. Combining utopianism, guild practices, socialism, and craft technology the Arts & Crafts Movement was sparked by such people as William Morris, A. W. Pugin, John Ruskin and in America, Elbert Hubbard and Gustav Stickley.

ASHLAR Hewn or cut blocks of masonry finished with an even surface.

BALUSTRADE A series of balusters or short pillars supporting a rail or coping.

BAROQUE Term describing the art and architectural style of the seventeenth and early eighteen centuries. Characterized by exuberent decoration, curvaceous forms, a delight in large-scale sweeping vistas, and a preference for spatially complex compositions.

BATTERED A term describing the face of a wall inclined at angle back from the vertical.

BAY WINDOW An angular or curved wall projection containing a window: also called bow window if curved and oriel or oriel window on an upper floor.

BEAUX ARTS The name applied to derivatives of classicism taught at the École des Beaux Arts in Paris; a form of Greco-Roman revival but more complex in surface composition and decoration.

CARPENTER GOTHIC A primitive version of the "pointed" or masonry medieval Gothic style adapted to vernacular wood technology and particularly popular in America during the nineteenth century.

CHAMFERRED Describes the edge of a block of wood or stone when cut away at an angle, usually 45 degrees to the surface plane.

CLERESTORY (clearstory) The upper stage of the main walls, usually of a church, pierced by windows.

CONSOLE An ornamental bracket with a reverse-curve outline.

COPING A capping or protective upper covering for a wall.

CORBEL A projecting block on a wall face usually supporting a beam or other horizontal member.

CORNICE A projecting ornamental moulding along the top of a building or wall, usually crowning it. Classical architecture: the top, projecting section of the entablature.

CRENELLATED Treated like a battlement or parapet with alternating indentations or embrasures.

CRESTING Ornamental finish along the top of a screen, wall or roof.

CURVILINEAR Consisting of curved lines.

DENTILLATED Consisting of small squared blocks run in series, usually comprising a string course and used in classical cornices.

DIAPERWORK Facetted surface decoration composed of a small repeated pattern, i.e., Lozenges or squares. Particularly common in brick façades.

DORMER A roof projection containing a window.

EDWARDIAN CLASSICAL The generous large-form Classical Revival style common to the buildings of the period 1900-1920.

ENGLISH VERNACULAR The English "folk" styles such as half-timbered Elizabethen or brick-and-tile Queen Anne which were revived with a vengeance 1880-1935.

ENTABLATURE The upper or horizontal part of a classical order consisting of architrave, frieze, and cornice.

FENESTRATION The arrangement of windows in a building or façade of a building.

FINAL A formal ornament at the top of a canopy, gable, pinnacle, etc.

FRETWORK Perforated decorative woodwork, usually ornamental trim for buildings in the picturesque building tradition.

GABLE The triangular upper portion of a wall carrying a pitched roof.

FRIEZE A horizontal band of decoration.

HIGH VICTORIAN The period 1870-90 during the reign of Queen Victoria noted for its flamboyant decorative architectural forms and styles.

ITALIANATE A building style deriving from the Romano-Florentine building styles of the fifteenth and sixteenth centuries.

HIPPED ROOF A roof sloped on all four sides.

JOINERY A specialized branch of carpentry involving the fabrication of furniture and interior wooden fittings.

KNOT GARDEN A small formal garden composed of geometrically arranged beds or "Knots." Popular in England, sixteenth to eighteenth centuries.

LIGHTS Openings between the mullions or crossbars of a window.

LOGGIA A gallery open on one side or more, usually attached to a building and screened by pillars.

MANSARD A double slope roof, the lower slope steeper; named after the French architect Francois Mansart.

MISSION STYLE Generally, a variant of the Spanish Colonial Revival style but *ca.* 1900 became a term applied to domestic interiors and especially furniture featuring unornamented spare lines and crude construction.

MONOPOD Literally "single leg"; a column standing alone.

MOULDING A contoured decorative element, usually a horizontal band, projecting from a wall surface.

MULLION The perpendicular member which divides bays or lights of windows or screen-work.

NARTHEX An antechamber or entrance hall inside the main entrance of a church adjoining the nave.

OCULUS A round window.

ORIEL WINDOW An upper storey bay window.

PALLADIAN Related to the Classical style buildings of the sixteenth century Italian architect Andrea Palladio.

PANTILE A roofing tile of curved S-shaped section.

PEDIMENT In classical architecture, a low-pitched gable above a portico; a similar feature above doors, windows, etc.

PERISTYLE A range of columns screening a building or open court.

PIER A solid vertical masonry support.

PILASTER A shallow pier or rectangular column projecting slightly from the wall surface.

POIDIUM A continuous solid or plinth, in the classical tradition supporting columns.

PORTICO A roofed space or porch forming the entrance to a building, often with columns.

PROSTYLE A projecting portico in the Classical style.

QUEEN ANNE Refers to the period in English architecture 1792-1714, but often applied to red-brick houses *ca.* 1660-1720. In the nineteenth century this term was revived to describe red-brick and slate construction (in America wood-shingle) as applied to Picturesque domestic architecture.

QUOINED A term used to describe the corners of buildings when treated with dressed stone. From the French coin (corner).

ROMANESQUE A round arcuated style of construction predating Gothic in Europe and describing buildings *ca.* ninth to twelfth century. Under this general heading scholars variously include Carolingian, Anglo-Saxon, Norman, and Cluniac church architecture. During the late nineteenth century this style was reinterpreted and revived by H. H. Richardson in the United States. It featured round arches, heavy forms, and coarse textures.

SGAGLIOLA COLUMNS An imitation stone, sometimes marble, made of plaster mixed with glue and colouring.

SHAKES Wooden roof tiles split from blocks.

SHINGLES Wooden roof tiles sawn from blocks.

SPANDREL The surface or infill between two arches; or in particular the triangular space between the voussoirs of two adjacent arches.

STRING COURSE A continuous projecting horizontal band set in the surface of a wall, usually moulded.

TRABEATED Describes the post-and-beam principle of building construction, in contrast to Arcuated construction.

TRANSOMS A horizontal bar of stone or wood across the opening of a window or panel.

TRUNCATED The top cut off. In particular with reference to a cone, pyramid or column.

VOUSSOIR The curve of an arch as it falls away from the vertical.

WAINSCOT A wooden lining or panelling applied to walls.

Selected Bibliography

Adams, John D. "Heritage Cemeteries in British Columbia." Victoria, BC, Victoria Branch, British Columbia Historical Federation. 1985.

———. "Historic Guide to Ross Bay Cemetery: Victoria, B.C. Canada." Heritage Architectural Guides. Victoria, BC, 1983.

Barr, Jennifer Nell. "Saanich Heritage Structures: An Inventory." The Corporation of the District of Saanich. Victoria. 1991.

Barrett, Anthony A. & Liscombe, Rhodri Windsor. "Francis Rattenbury and British Columbia: Architecture and Challenge in the Imperial Age." UBC Press, Vancouver, BC, 1983.

Baskerville, Peter A. "Beyond the Island: An Illustrated History of Victoria." Windsor Publications, Ltd. Burlington, Ontario. 1986.

Bernstein, William & Cawker, Ruth. "Contemporary Canadian Architecture. The Mainstream and Beyond." Fitzhenry & Whiteside. Ontario. 1982.

Bingham, Janet. "Samuel Maclure Architect." Horsdal & Schubert, Vancouver, BC, 1985.

"A Brief History of Beacon Hill Park 1882-1982." City of Victoria Parks Department, Victoria, BC, 1981.

"British Columbia, Designated Heritage Sites Registry." Province of BC, Ministry of Municipal Affairs, Recreation and Culture. Archaeology Branch. Resource Information Services Program. 1993.

"Burnside Neighbourhood Plan." UMA Engineering Ltd., March 1991.

Cameron, Christina, "Index of Houses Featured in Canadian Homes and Gardens From 1925 to 1944." Parks Canada, 1980.

Candelaria, Fred. "West Coast Review. Architecture in British Columbia." West Coast Review Publishing Society. Volume XV/4 Spring 1981.

"Capital Region of British Columbia: Transportation Study." Traffic Research Corporation. March 1965.

Castle. Geoffrey. "Hatley Park An Illustrated Anthology." The Friends of Hatley Park Society, Victoria, BC, 1995.

"Central Area." City of Victoria, Department of Community Development, Victoria, BC, 1973.

Chaster, G. D. & Ross, D. W. & Warren, W. H. "Trees of Greater Victoria: A Heritage." Heritage Tree Book Society. 1988.

"Christ Church Cathedral Self Guide for the Convenience of Visitors." Victoria, 1967.

"City of Victoria Downtown Heritage Management Plan." Foundation Group Designs Ltd. 1989.

"City of Victoria: Official Community Plan." Municipal Council, Victoria, BC, July 21, 1986.

Clark, Cecil. "The Best of Victoria: Yesterday and Today." *Victorian Weekly*. Victoria, BC, 1976.

"Comprehensive Plan." Provincial Capital Commission, Victoria, BC 1988.

"Concept Plan for the Songhees Peninsula, Victoria." Province of BC and the City of Victoria, Victoria, BC, n.d.

Collier, Allan. "The Trend House Program." Society for the Study of Architecture in Canada: Bulletin. Volume 20. Number 2. June 1995.

"Context: OCP: Background Report Official Community Plan City of Victoria." Planning Department, Victoria, BC, September 1986.

"Community Greenways Linking Communities to Country, and People to Nature." BC Ministry of Environment, Lands and Parks, Victoria, BC, 1995.

Cotton, Peter. "A Little of What You Fancy: Some Notes on the Transport of Architectural Ideas to Victoria, British Columbia." *British Columbia Library Quarterly*, 31 (July 1967), 23-28.

———. "The Stately Capitol," *Royal Architectural Institute Journal*. 35 (April 1958). 116-18.

———. Craigflower Manor: Vol. I, "The Structure. The Rationale of Decisions Made During Restoration of the Manor in 1968." Unpublished manuscript. British Columbia Public Archives. 1970.

———. "Vice Regal Mansions of British Columbia." Elgin Publications Ltd. For the British Columbia Heritage Trust, Vancouver, BC, 1981.

315

"The Crystal Gardens: West Coast Pleasure Palace." Crystal Gardens Preservation Society, Victoria, BC, 1977.

"The Development of the Gordon Head Campus." UVic. Victoria, BC, November 26, 1988.

Downs, Barry. *Sacred Places. British Columbia's Early Churches.* Douglas & McIntyre, Vancouver, BC, 1980.

"Downtown Victoria Plan 1990." City of Victoria, Victoria, BC, April 1990.

Duffus, Maureen. *Beyond the Blue Bridge; Stories from Esquimalt: History and Reminiscences Compiled by The Esquimalt Silver Threads Writers Group.* Desktop Publishing Ltd., Victoria, BC, 1990.

Dunnett, Peter J. S. *Royal Roads Military College 1940-1990: A Pictorial Retrospective.* Royal Roads Military College, Victoria, BC, 1990.

Eaton, Leonard K. *The Architecture of Samuel Maclure.* The Art Gallery of Greater Victoria, Victoria, BC, 1971.

Edwards, Gregory. *Hidden Cities: Art & Design in Architectural Details of Vancouver & Victoria.* Talonbooks, Vancouver, BC, 1991.

Ewert, Henry. *The Story of the B.C. Electric Railway Company.* Whitecap Books, Vancouver, BC, 1986.

Field, Dorothy. *Built Heritage in Esquimalt.* Hallmark Society, Victoria, BC, 1984.

Forward, C. N. "The Immortality of a Fashionable Residential District: The Uplands." Residential & Neighbourhood Studies. *Western Geographic Series*, Vol. 5. UVic.

Foundation Group Designs. "City of Victoria Downtown Heritage Inventory." City of Victoria, Victoria, BC, 1990.

Freeman, John Crosby, "The Other Victoria." RACAR, *Canadian Art Review.* 1 (1974). 37-46.

Franklin, Douglas & Fleming, John. "Early School Architecture in British Columbia: An Architectural History and Inventory of Buildings to 1930." Heritage Conservation Branch, Victoria, BC, 1980.

Gowans, Alan. *Building Canada: An Architectural History of Canadian Life.* Toronto. Oxford U P, 1966.

———. *The Comfortable House: North American Suburban Architecture. 1890-1930.* The Massachusetts Institute of Technology, 1986.

———. *Styles and Types of North American Architecture: Social Function and Cultural Expression.* Harper Collins, NY, 1992.

Gibson, Edward & Guest, Patricia. "British Columbia Architectural Carver George Gibson." *Canadian Collector.* January, February 1980.

Gregson, Harry. *A History of Victoria 1842-1970.* The Victoria Observer Publishing Co. Ltd., Victoria, BC, 1970.

Hamilton, Margaret. "Old Houses of Victoria and District Worthy of Preservation on Account of Historical Significance or for Architectural Beauty or Both." Unpublished manuscript. Public Archives of British Columbia. 1960.

———. "A List of Some of the Oldest Business Buildings in Victoria and District and a Few Schools and Churches." Unpublished manuscript. Public Archives of British Columbia. 1960.

———. "Some Random Jottings on James Bay Houses of the Past." Unpublished manuscript. Public Archives of British Columbia. n.d.

Hamilton, William G. "Canadian Urban Landscape Examples." *The Canadian Geographer*, No. 4, 1993 365-71.

"Harris Green" City of Victoria, Department of Community Development, 1979.

Hawker, Ronald W. "Monuments in the Nineteenth-Century Public Cemeteries of Victoria, British Columbia." *Material History Bulletin*, Fall 1987.

Henderson, L. G. "Henderson's British Columbia Gazetteer and Directory." Victoria, BC, 1889.

Hora, Z. D. & Miller, L. B. "Dimension Stone in Victoria, B.C." BC Ministry of Energy, Mines and Petroleum Resources, Victoria, BC, 1994.

Iglauer, Edith. *Seven Stones: A Portrait of Arthur Erickson, Architect.* Harbour Publishing, BC, 1981.

"Inner City Neighbourhoods." City of Victoria, Department of Community Development, Victoria, BC, 1976.

Insight, Consultants. "Heritage Inventory of Industrial Buildings Victoria." Victoria, BC, 1982.

"James Bay." City of Victoria, Department of Community Development, 1973.

Jupp, Ursula. *From Cordwood to Campus in Gordon Head 1852-1959.* Ursula Jupp, Victoria, BC, 1975.

Kalman, Harold & Phillips, Ron & Ward, Robin. "Exploring Vancouver." *The Essential Arhitectural Guide*, UBC Press, Vancouver, 1993.

Kalman, Harold D. "A History of Canadian Architecture." Volume 2, Oxford U P, Toronto, 1994.

———. *The Railway Hotels and the Development of the Chateau Style in Canada*. Maltwood Museum, Victoria, BC, 1968.

"The Kirk That Faith Built: St. Andrew's on Douglas Street 1890-1990." The Session of St. Andrew's Presbyterian Church, Victoria, BC, 1989.

Kynaston, Matthew. *Edifice Complex: Poor Man's Purse: A Century of Dreams*. James Bay United Church, Victoria, BC, 1967.

Lai, David Cheunyan. *Arches of British Columbia*. UVic, British Columbia. Sono Nis Press. Victoria, BC, 1982.

———. *The Forbidden city within Victoria: Myth symbol and streetscape of Canada's Earliest Chinatown*. Orca Book Publishing, Victoria, BC, 1991.

Leung, Felicity & McConnell, David & Parent Jean-Claude. "Manufacturing Locations in Canada: The Identification and Evaluation of Significant Multiple-Industry Manufacturing Complexes." A Report prepared for the Historic Sites and Monuments Board of Canada, Department of Canadian Heritage, Ottawa, November, 1990.

Lillard, Charles. *Paths Our Ancestors Walked: Father Vullinghs & the Saanich Peninsula 1893-1909*. Victoria Indian Cultural Centre, Victoria, BC, 1977.

Lines, Kenneth. "A Bit of Old England: The Selling of Tourist Victoria." Unpublished MA Thesis, UVic, 1972.

Lort, Ross. "Samuel Maclure, MRAIC 1860-1929." *Journal of the Royal Architectural Institute of Canada*, 1958, 114-15.

Luxton, Donald. *C.R.D. Art Deco and Moderne*. The Hallmark Society & the BC Heritage Trust, Victoria, BC, n.d.

Madoff, Pamela. "The Selkirk Waterfront Project. The shape of things to come." *The Magazine of Urban Living. Boulevard*. Victoria, BC, April/May, 1994.

Ricketts, Shannon. *A Guide to Canadian Architectural Styles*. Broadview Press Ltd., Peterborough, ON, 1992.

Marshall, John. *History of the Grand Lodge of British Columbia*. Victoria, Grand Lodge of British Columbia." Victoria, Grand Lodge of Ancient, Free and Accepted Masons, Victoria, BC, 1971.

Martin, Harry & Busher, Dick. *Contemporary Homes of the Pacific Northwest*. Madrona Publishers, Seattle, WA, 1980.

Mazer, L. D. & Segger, M. "City of Victoria Central Area Heritage Conservation Report." City of Victoria, Victoria, BC, 1975.

McCurdy, Arthur W. "Factors Which Modify the Climate of Victoria." *National Geographic Magazine*, 18 (May 1907), 345-48.

McMillan, Paula. "Journey Middle School. The face of school design." *Victoria Boulevard*, Victoria, BC, February, March 1994.

Measure, Harry. "Saanich: Agrarian to Urban." Unpublished Private Paper. n.d.

Minaker, Dennis. "Early Architects of Victoria." Private Paper. Victoria BC, 1996.

Monteyne, David P. "Constructing Buildings and Histories: Hudson's Bay Company Department Stores, 1910-1930." *Society For the Study of Architecture in Canada: Bulletin*, Volume 20, Number 4, December, 1995.

Morgan, Roland & Disher, Emily. *Victoria Then and Now*. Bodima Publications. Vancouver, BC, 1977.

Murray, Peter. *Home from the Hill: Three Gentlemen Adventurers*. Horsdal & Schubart Publishers Ltd., Victoria, BC, 1994.

Nesbitt, James Knight. *Album of Victoria Homes and Families*. Hebden Print Co., Victoria, BC, 1956.

Nelson, John, "Victoria: The Picturesque Portal of the Pacific." *Victoria Daily Times* (Royal Souvenir number), 1901.

Nobles, P. E. "Some Developments in Canadian Architecture." *Country Life*, 43, January 1923.

———. "100 Years of B.C. Living." *Western Homes*, Vancouver, BC, January 1958.

"Oaklands Draft Neighbourhood Plan." Oaklands Steering Committee, City of Victoria, Victoria, BC, October 1991.

"Official Regional Plan. Victoria Metropolitan Area." Capital Regional District, Victoria, BC, 1975.

"Old Town Report." Old Town Study Group, Victoria, BC, August 1971.

"Old Cemeteries Committee. Walk Through History in Victoria's Old Cemeteries." Old Cemeteries Committee, Victoria, BC, n.d.

Oliver, Nancy "CFB Esquimalt: Military Heritage." Heritage Conservation Branch, Government of British Columbia, n.d.

"101 Historical Buildings of the Sooke Region." Sooke Region Historical Society and Sooke Region Historical Book Committee, Sooke Region Historical Society. Sooke, BC, 1985.

Ormsby, Margaret A. *British Columbia: A History*. MacMillan Company of Canada, Toronto, ON, 1958.

"Our Heritage, Selections from an Inventory of Older Buildings in Colwood, Langford & View Royal." Capital Regional District, Victoria, BC, 1982.

"Overall Plan for The City of Victoria." Capital Regional Planning Board of British Columbia, Victoria, BC, 1965.

Pallister, Carey. "The Old Cemeteries Society: Stories in Stone." Victoria, BC, The Old Cemeteries Society, Volume 1, Number 2, 1991.

Palmer, Bernard C. "Development of Domestic Architecture in British Columbia." *Journal of the Royal Architectural Institute of Canada*, 5, November 1928.

Parker, Douglas V. "No Horsecars in Paradise: A History of the Street Railways and Publick Utilities in Victoria, British Columbia before 1897."

Pethick, Derek. *Victoria: the Fort*. Vancouver, BC, Mitchell Press, 1968. Mitchell of British Columbia, Victoria, BC, Hancock House, 1975.

——. *Men of British Columbia*. Hancock House, Victoria, BC, 1975.

——. *A Summer of Promise: Victoria 1864-1914*. Sono Nis Press, Victoria, BC, 1980.

"A Plan for the Rehabilitation of Chinatown." City of Victoria, Victoria, BC, August 1979.

Plasterer, Dr. Herbert P. "Fort Victoria from Fur Trading Post to Capital City of British Columbia, Canada." Provincial Archives, Victoria, BC, n.d.

"Policy Plan and Design Guidelines for the Songhees Area of Victoria West." City of Victoria, Victoria, BC, October 1986.

"A Precinct For Victoria: Recommendations for Development Policies." Department of Public Works, Victoria, BC, April 1975.

"A Registry of Accessible Buildings of Heritage Merit." Corporation of the District of Saanich, Victoria, BC, March 1983.

Reksten, Terry. *Rattenbury*. Sono Nis Press, Victoria, BC, 1978.

——. *Craigdarroch: The Story of Dunsmuir Castle*. Orca Book Publishers, Victoria, BC, 1987.

——. *More English than the English: A Very Social History of Victoria*. Orca Book Publishers, Victoria, BC, 1942.

Ritchie, Thomas. *Canada Builds 1867-1967*. Toronto, U of Toronto P, 1967.

"Rockland." City of Victoria Planning Department, Victoria, BC, 1970.

Ronnenberg, Norman. *John Wright (1830-1915) Grandfather of West Coast Architecture*. Maltwood Art Museum and Gallery, Victoria, BC, 1990.

Ruzicka, Stanley Edward. "The Decline of Victoria as the Metropolitan Centre of B.C. 1885-1901." Unpublished MA Thesis, UVic. 1973.

"Saanich Heritage Evaluation: An OFY Project." Victoria, B.C. n.d.

Sage, Walter N., "British Columbia and Confederation." B.C. *Historical Quarterly*, 15 (1951), 71-84.

Savery, Robert. "On View at Government House." *Western Homes and Living*, Mitchell Press Limited, Vancouver, BC, July 1961.

Schaefer, Edward. "Christ Church Cathedral, Victoria, B.C. Canada." *Stained Glass*, Volume 89, Number 3, Fall 1994.

Scholefield, E. O. S. *British Columbia, From the Earliest Times to the Present*. S. J. Clarke, Vancouver, BC, 1914.

Sedgwick, Charles Peter. "The Context of Economic Change and Continuity in an Urban Overseas, Chinese Community." Unpublished MA Thesis. UVic. 1973.

Segger, Martin. Ed. "The British Columbia Parliament Buildings." North Vancouver B.C. Associated Resource Consultants Ltd. 1979.

——. *The Buildings of Samuel Maclure: In Search of Appropriate Form*. Sono Nis Press, Victoria, BC, 1986.

——. "House Beautiful: Style in Decorative and Applied Arts 1860-1920: An Exhibition." British Columbia Provincial Museum, Victoria, BC, 1974.

——. "St. Andrew's Cathedral, Victoria: A Guide." Heritage Tour Guides, CANAAP Press for the Diocese of Victoria, Victoria, BC, 1990.

Segger, Martin & Douglas Franklin. *Victoria: A Primer for Regional History in Architecture 1843-1929*. American Life Foundation, Watkins Glen, NY, 1974.

"Sidney British Columbia Canada Heritage Walking Tour." Town of Sidney Heritage Advisory Committee, Sidney Museum, Sidney, BC, n.d.

"Slicing the Circle. Rogers Elementary School, Victoria, B.C." *The Architectural Review: Architecture Design Landscape Urbanism Worldwide*, London, May 1993.

Smith, Peter L. "A Multitude of the Wise: UVic Remembered." Alumni Association of the University of Victoria, Victoria. BC, 1993.

——. *Come Give a Cheer! One Hundred Years of Victoria High School 1876-1976*. Victoria High School Centennial Celebrations Committee, Victoria, BC, 1976.

Sorby, Thomas C. "The Harbour and City of Victoria; the Part of Vancouver Island, B.C." Victoria Inner Harbour Assn., Victoria, BC, 1916.

"Springridge Neighbourhood Improvement Plan." City of Victoria Planning Department, Victoria, BC, n.d.

Stark, Stuart. *Oak Bay's Heritage Buildings: More than just Bricks and Boards.* The Hallmark Society, Victoria, BC, 1995.

"Strawberry Vale School." *The Canadian Architect,* December 1994.

Stursberg, Peter. *Those Were the Days: Victoria in the 1930s.* Horsdal and Schubart Publishers Limited, Victoria, BC, 1969.

"The Suburban Neighbourhoods." City of Victoria, Department of Community Development, Victoria, BC, 1977.

"Thirty Years of Effort 1956-1986: Recording 30 Years of Amenity Enhancement in Victoria's Capital Region." Capital Improvement District Commission, 1986.

"This Old House: An Inventory of Residential Heritage." City of Victoria, Victoria, BC, 1991.

"This Old Town: City of Victoria Central Area Heritage Conservation Report." City of Victoria, Victoria, BC, 1983.

"Trees and Towns." Technical Paper Series 5. British Columbia Heritage Trust, Heritage Conservation Branch, Province of BC, 1983.

Underhill, Stuart. *The Iron Church 1860-1985.* Braemar Books Ltd., Victoria, BC, 1984.

Virgin, Victor E. *History of North and South Saanich Pioneers and District.* Saanich Pioneer Society, Victoria, BC, 1978.

"Victoria Historical Sites." Victoria Section British Columbia Historical Association, Victoria BC, 1989.

"Victoria West." City of Victoria, Department of Community Development, Victoria, BC, 1972.

"Victoria Illustrated." Victoria: Ellis and Co., Victoria, BC, 1891.

Von Baeyer, Edwinna. "A Selected Bibliography for Garden History in Canada." Environment Canada, National Historic Parks and Sites Branch, Ministry of Supply and Services, 1987.

"Wharf Street: City of Victoria: Heritage Designation Report." City of Victoria, Heritage Advisory Committee and the Department of Community Development, January 1974.

Wolfenden, Margaret. "The Early Architects of British Columbia." *Western Homes and Living,* Vancouver, BC, September 1968.

Street and Place-Name Gazetteer

Academy Close 79, 80
Admirals Road 169, 276
Alderly Road 265
Amelia Street 33
Ardesier Road 208
Ash Road 198
Bastion Square 88-92
Battery Street 152, 154
Bay Street 72, 181, 194
Beach Drive 160, 162, 164, 165, 167, 191, 200, 202, 203, 207, 209, 219
Beacon Hill Park 145, 155
Belleville Street 49, 73, 74, 126, 144, 156
Bellevue Road 202
Belmont Avenue 185
Black Rock 241
Blanshard Street 28, 30, 43, 57, 67, 70, 72, 78, 81, 82, 105, 106
Blenkinsop Valley 192
Brighton Avenue 192
Broad Street 32, 33, 38, 42, 63, 105
Broadmead Estates 269
Brookhill Road 258
Broughton Street 33, 39, 55, 63, 70, 99
Burdett Street 142, 172, 198
Cadboro Bay 194, 197, 200
Carey 255, 256, 259, 260, 261, 262, 263, 265
Catharine Street 151
Cathedral Hill 127, 173, 197, 198
Cedar Hill Cross Road 150
Centennial Square 85-87, 121
Central Saanich 253, 254, 256, 259, 270, 271
Chinatown 109-21
Cole Island 237, 238
Colquitz Avenue 267
Colwood 275, 277, 279, 281, 283, 284, 286, 288
Cook Street 145, 187
Cordova Bay Road 264
Cordova Bay 264, 265, 266, 269
Cormorant Street 68
Courtenay Street 64
Crescent Road 205
Dallas Road 175, 205, 206, 210, 218
Dennison Road 210
Discovery Street 57
Dockyard 236, 242
Douglas Street 32, 39, 40, 41, 57, 60, 64, 65, 68, 71, 74, 78, 82, 83, 97, 98, 101, 106, 107, 108, 145, 155, 181, 205, 217, 218
Dover Road 202
Duke Road 287
Durrance Road 258

Dysart Road 259
East Saanich Road 256
Eaton Centre 102-04
Empire Street 188
Esquimalt Road 170, 196
Esquimalt 133, 155, 159, 169, 170, 176, 181, 189, 196, 235
Fairfield Road 143, 184, 220
Fairfield 129, 141, 142, 143, 145, 148, 152, 172, 173, 184, 196, 197, 198, 205, 220
Fairview Road 199
Falaise Drive 264
Fan Tan Alley 118
Fernwood 131, 153, 183
Fisgard Street 32, 69, 71, 106, 107, 111-20
Fort Street 27, 32, 36, 53, 59, 65, 68, 83, 98, 99, 103, 146, 149, 157, 180, 193, 195, 199, 201
Foul Bay Road 193
Fowler Road 267
Gillespie Place 143
Glinz Road 283
Goldstream Avenue 275
Gonzales 205, 209, 210
Gordon Head 140, 193, 198
Gordon Street 68
Gorge Road West 261, 265
Gorge Road 41, 148, 218
Government Street 26, 28, 36, 42, 44, 49, 53-58, 60, 63, 67, 69, 70, 72, 79, 81, 115, 116, 118, 119, 120, 140, 142, 145, 194
Grant Street 183
Hampshire Road 192
Happy Valley Road 278
Haro Road 223
Head Street 155
Helgesen Road 283
Henry Street 153, 206
Herald Street 112, 117, 118
Heritage Court 139
Heron Street 139
High Street 259
Hillside Avenue 207
Hillside/Quadra 153, 187, 188, 207
Humboldt Street 29, 30, 62, 67, 68, 98, 205
Hunt Road 264
Island Highway 275
Island Road 158
James Bay 126, 140, 142, 144, 145, 151, 152, 154-71, 174, 175, 180, 182, 186, 205, 209, 210, 218
Jasmine Avenue 265
Joan Crescent 147, 187, 209

320

Johnson Street 32, 36, 38, 40, 41, 56, 62, 63, 69, 70, 73, 74, 78, 94, 95, 96, 97, 99, 100, 105
Kemp Lake Road 279
Killarney Place 200
King George Terrace 198-99, 209
Kings Road 153, 210
Kingston Street 186
Lambrick Way 140
Lampson Street 159, 181, 189
Langley Street 53, 59, 64, 92
Lansdowne Road 189, 195
Lazzar Road 286
Ledsham Road 286
Linkleas Avenue 189
Maple Avenue 278
Marine Drive 206
Market Square 93-96, 123
Mayfair Drive 200
McGregor Avenue 157
McTavish Road 269
Meares Street 173
Medana Street 180
Metchosin Road 279
Metchosin 278, 279, 283, 284, 287
Michigan Street 208
Midland Road 200
Montreal Street 217
Moss Street 150, 185, 188
Mount Newton Cross Road 253, 254, 270
Mount Tolmie 180, 190, 195, 200, 201
Naden 240, 241
North Park 97, 98
North Saanich 268, 269
Oak Bay Avenue 165, 196
Oak Bay 129, 139, 158, 160-67, 184, 189, 191, 192-94, 196-200, 202, 206, 209, 219
Old Island Highway 286
Old West Saanich Road 264
Otter Point Road 229
Pandora Street 28, 33, 38, 40, 65, 70, 72, 77, 80, 82, 94, 95, 100, 107, 111, 112, 114
Park Boulevard 196
Parliamentary Precinct 45-52
Parry Street 170
Patricia Bay Highway 253, 266
Pearson College Drive 287
Pembroke Street 37
Philips Road 277
Pleasant Street 140
Prillaman Avenue 260
Prospect Place 160-68
Quadra Street 26, 28, 38, 66, 69, 75, 77, 127, 169, 202, 205
Quebec Street 105, 209
Richardson Street 152
Richmond Avenue 180, 189, 201
Robert Street 171
Rockland Avenue 141, 149, 151, 153-55, 169, 170, 171, 173, 174, 175, 180, 181, 182, 183, 184, 188, 195, 202
Rockland 27, 75, 127, 141, 143, 146, 147, 149-51, 153-55, 157, 169-75, 180-89, 191, 195, 201, 202, 210, 217

Rogers Road 219
Rosedale Park 271
Royal Oak 254, 255, 258, 259, 264, 269
Royal Terrace 216
Saanich 132, 169, 180, 195, 207, 209, 219, 254, 258, 261, 263, 264, 267, 268, 269, 271
Saanich Peninsula 245-70
Saanichton 256, 270, 271
Saint Stephen's Road 253
San Carlos Avenue 166
Seaview Road 194
Shelbourne Avenue 217
Sheringham Point Road 285
Sidney 246-51
Signal Hill 238
Sinclair Road 197
Somass Drive 198
Songhees Way 212
Songhees 211-15
Sooke Road 280, 281, 283, 284
Sooke 277, 278, 279, 280, 183, 284, 285, 286, 289
South Turner Street 151, 156-59, 171, 174, 182
Springridge 131
St. Charles Street 157, 172, 174, 180, 182, 186, 189, 191
St. Patrick Street 193
Stelly's Cross Road 271
Store Street 27, 62, 70, 95, 100
Strawberry Vale 271
Superior Street 50, 145, 158, 205
Taylor Road 283, 287
Throup Road 289
Tillicum 259, 261, 265, 268, 276
Treetop Heights 269
Trounce Alley 38, 67
Trutch Street 141
Tyndall Avenue 193
University of Victoria 221-35
Uplands 177, 178, 179, 200, 207
Vancouver Street 107, 148, 152, 184, 197
Vernon Avenue 107
Victoria West 133, 151, 153, 171, 206, 212
Victoria 26-125, 139, 140, 148, 157, 180, 181, 193, 194, 196, 199, 206, 211, 217, 218
View Royal 259, 261, 275, 286
View Street 43, 59, 64, 69, 97, 105, 108
Waddington Alley 35, 54
West Coast Road 277
West Saanich Road 253, 254, 255, 258, 259, 264, 270
Western Communities 271-92
Wharf Street 27, 31, 33, 34, 59, 72, 73, 76, 78, 89, 94, 99, 123
Wilkinson Road 259, 260
William Head Road 284
Willingdon Road 267
Windsor Road 184
Wishart Road 288
Wollaston Street 176
Work Point 242, 243
Yates Street 31, 35, 37, 39, 54-58, 60, 73, 78, 79, 80, 81, 82, 105, 107
York Place 161, 163, 166, 168

321

Index

Abkhazi, Prince and Princess, Rhodendron Gardens 138
Abstract Expressionism 25, 79
Achtem House 207
Adamson, Capt. and Mrs. Laurence 167, 247
Administration Building 18, 240, 243
Admiral's House 143, 237
Aesthetic Movement 20
Agricultural Association 146
Agricultural Exhibition 11
Agricultural Land Reserve 133
Albert Head 271
Albion Iron Works 34, 37, 39, 89, 134, 147
Alexandria Club 64, 99
All Saints Temple 112
Alsop, Owen 154
Alsop, Thomas 154
Amelia Street Houses 33
America City Beautiful movement 136
American Adamesque 66
American Queen Anne 156
American Shingle style 129
Anderson Building 32
Anderson, Elijah Howe 40
Andrews, A. H. 148
Angela College 142
Angus, James 128, 151
Annandale 161
Appleton House 216
Archives of the Anglican Synod 197
Armament Artificers' Quarters 239
Armathwaite for Mr. Skelton 281
Armour, John 207
Army and Navy Veterans Club 78
Arran 163
Art and Architecture Building at Yale 225
Art Deco 23, 24, 78, 81, 108, 131, 194, 198
Art Nouveau 20, 53, 57, 63, 170, 280
Arts & Crafts 20, 21, 22, 57, 132, 135, 136, 141, 162, 164, 167, 168, 169, 171, 172, 173, 177, 181, 182, 184, 186, 188, 189, 191, 193, 194, 197, 209, 230, 232, 258, 265, 280, 284, 301; bungalow 248, 258; Chalet style 169, 196; Tudor Revival style 257
Athlone Apartments 80
Atlas Theatre 78
Atwood-Wilson, P. 157

Babcombe Farm for Harriet and Herbert Burbridge 263
Bachus, Philip M. 90
Bacon, Percy 76
Ballantine, James 76

Ballantyne's Florists 83
Banff Springs Hotel 61
Bank of British Columbia 10, 11, 20, 36, 143
Bank of Commerce Building 97
Bank of Montreal 20, 54, 69, 191
Bank of Nova Scotia 73
Bank of Toronto 81
Bank Street School 131
Bannavern 182
Barker, Eric 25, 152, 215, 233, 291
Barker, James and Amelia, House 254
Barnard, Francis Jones 141
Barnard, Frank 137
Baroque Revival 71, 87
Barracks 242
Barraclough, John and Kathleen, House 265
Barry, Sir Charles 292
Bartle and Gibson Building 79
Barton, E. M. 310
Bastion Group 210, 303
Bastion Square 85, 88, 93, 121
Bauhaus 198
Bautenheimer, Mark 89
Bawlf Cooper Associates 28, 36, 43, 89, 100, 146, 153, 209, 249, 291, 295, 304
Bawlf Keay Associates 31, 233
Bawlf, Nicholas 25, 93, 197, 291
Bawlf, Sam 93, 123
Baxter, Alfred W. 220
Baxter, Robert 75, 76, 291, 309
Bay Company Constance Cove Farm 134
Bay Street Armories 72
Bay Street Electric Substation 17
Bay, The 11
Bayne, Richard Roskill 292
Bayview properties 209
B.C. Agricultural Society 137
B.C. Architects' Association 299
B.C. Board of Trade 91
B.C. Building Corporation 64, 262
B.C. Coast Steamships 158
B.C. Coast Woods Trade Extension Bureau 201
B.C. Dept. Public Works 199, 202, 203
B.C. Electric 163, 184; Building 82; Bay Street Substation 194
B.C. Electric Railway Co. 137, 265; Depot 57; Offices 59
B.C. Heritage Trust 124
B.C. Historical Society 274
B.C. Institute of Architects 19
B.C. Land and Investment Company 96, 154, 170
B.C. Mills, Timber and Trading Company 182
B.C. Pottery and Terra Cotta Company 56

B.C. Power Commission Building 17, 78
B.C. Protestant Orphanage 153
B.C. Public Works 89
BCER 266
BCGEU Headquarters 216
Beacon Hill 130, 135, 217, 234; Park 127, 144, 145, 196
Beasley, Harry, House 189
Beaux Arts 60, 63, 68, 69, 71, 73, 106; Classicism 100
Beaven, R. H. 136
Beaver Building 90
Beaver 140
Bechtal, Andrew, House 183
Beckley Cottage 170
Beckley Manor 206
Begbie Building 229
Begbie Hall 195
Begbie, Sir Mathew Ballie 68
Bell Block 197
Belmont (Rodd Hill) 278
Belmont Block 67
Belmont Building (1912) 16, 17, 93
Benvenuto Seed Company 136
Berrill and Parker 195
Berrill, Ralph 167, 196
Bickford Tower 239
Bide-A-Wee 165
Biggerstaff Wilson, Mayor Richard 220
Binning, B. C. 83
Birdcage Walk 145
Birdcages 47, 126
Birley & Wagg 298
Birley and Frame 79
Birley and Simpson 309
Birley Wade Stockdill 24, 80, 108, 131, 201
Birley, Patrick S. 24, 80, 108, 253, 308
Bishop's Chapel 197
Bissett, James 140
Black Rock 235, 241, 278
Blair, John 16, 135, 144, 145
Blinkhorn, Thomas 271
Bloomfield, Henry 292
Bloomfield, James 204, 292
Bloomfield, Sir Arthur 76
Board of Trade Building 91
Bolton, Rev. William Washington 180; House 169
Bossi Building 94
Bossi, Carlo 94
Bossi, Giacomo 94
Bostock, Hewitt 155
Boston, Massachusetts 41, 73
Boucherat Building 37
Bowdon, Waldermar and Margo, House 197
Bowen, Herbert 181
Branson, Cecil and Verna, House 194
Brayshaw, Dr. Chris 138
Brazilia 85
Brenher Lane 251
Brentwood Bay 167
Breseman & Durfee, Seattle 66, 69
Brett & Hall 136, 258, 279
Briarbrae 163
Bridgeman Building 28, 63

Briggs, Alfred, House 156
British Admiralty 278
British Colonist 147
British West Indies 19
Broad Street Square 105
Broadmead 25,133; Estates 268; Farms Ltd. 268
Brotchie Ledge 145, 234, 278
Broudy, Charles E., & Associates 219
Brown, P. R. 154
Browne, Irwin, Farm Houses 158
Brownlie, Mrs. A.H., House 193
Brutalism 25, 210, 214, 225
Bungalow Construction Company Ltd. 259
Bungalow style 193, 239, 242
Bunting, Archie 197
Burdett-Coutts, Baroness Angela 66, 142
Burleith 134
Burnes House 90
Burnes, Thomas J. 90
Burns, Robert 146
Burnside Elementary 131, 183
Burnside Farm for Matilda and Michael Muir 271, 275, 276
Burris, S. G. 90
Business School 230
Butchart Gardens 136, 258
Butchart, Robert Pim 258
Butler and Harrison 260
Butterfield, William 21, 162, 169
Buttjes & Rapske 206

CPR Steamship Terminal 73
Cadboro Bay 130
Cadboro Commons 227
Cadillac-Fairview 102
Caleb Payne House 260
Caleb Pike Homestead 276
Calgary 71
California 109, 136, 271
California Craftsman style 77, 192, 193, 259; Arts & Crafts 129, 281
California Bungalow style 10, 130, 164, 184, 188, 192, 193, 248, 261, 262; Mission style 77, 180
Calvert, Peter 284
Cameron Bros. Sawmill 217
Cameron Building 38
Cameron, W. G. 38
Camosun College 189, 191
Campbell & McCandless Building 56
Campbell Moore Group 105, 210, 216, 217, 218, 233, 292, 293, 305
Campbell, Clive 25, 85
Campbell, D. E. 56
Campbell, Douglas 25, 292
Campbell, Hugh 135, 147
Campus Security Building 225, 233
Canadian Artillary C Battery 242
Canadian Bank of Commerce 181
Canadian Bridge Co. 74
Canadian Broadcasting Corporation 210
Canadian Federation of Artists 285
Canadian National Institute for the Blind Building 82
Canadian National Railway 290

323

Canadian Northern Pacific Railway 272
Canadian Pacific Navigation Co. 158
Canadian Pacific Railway 9, 20, 54, 233
Canadian Pacific Steamship Co. 29
Cannon, Larry 221, 233
Cape Cod Revival 285
Capital Improvement District Commission 288
Capital Regional District 290
Capital Regional Planning Board 121
Capital Ways 288
Carey Building 94
Carey, John Hunter 203
Carey, Joseph Westrope 94
Cariboo 10
Carlton Hotel 69
Cary Castle 203
Carnegie Foundry 90
Carnegie Library 57
Carpenter Gothic style 30, 252
Carr, Emily 90
Carr, Richard 90, 140; House 135, 142
Casey, Irene and Joseph, House 265
Cash, Gwendoline 201
Castle Block 196
Cathedral Hill and Rockland 127, 172
Causeway Garage Building for Imperial Oil 76
Caveno, Joseph 83
Cecil Hotel 67
Cedar Hill School 131
Centennial Methodist Church 19, 41
Centennial Square 24, 85, 87, 107, 121
Centennial Stadium 227
Centra Gas building 106, 107
Centra Gas Operations Centre 218
Central Building 69
Central Junior High 131, 201
Central Saanich 245
CFB Esquimalt 18
Chalet style 22, 157, 168, 174, 189
Chalet, The 170
Chambers, William 116
Chan Tong Or 115
Chancer Chambers 92
Chandler, Kaston Kennedy 106
Chang, P. 233
Chapola 180
Chateau Frontenac 61
Chateau style 30, 55, 103, 129, 215
Chicago 59, 67, 148
Chicago School style 53, 64, 65, 113, 119
Chief Engineer's Quarters 236
China 136
Chinatown 109, 121, 125
Chinese Benevolent Association Building 112, 120
Chinese Canadian Friendship Association 114
Chinese Consolidated Benevolent Association School 115
Chinese Empire Reform Society 115
Chow & Fleischauer 218, 233, 295
Chow, Sid 293, 309
Christ Church Cathedral 26, 30, 75, 130, 253, 254, 299
Chung, Lee 116

Church of Saint Mary the Virgin 277
Church of St. John the Divine 66
Church of the Assumption 252
Cisek, Albert Franz 293
City Hall, Victoria 85, 202
City Market 11
City of Victoria Police Station 119
City of Victoria Waterworks 272
Clack & Clayton 202
Clack, Rod 24, 25, 85, 86, 87, 88, 146
Clarkson, Eric C. 24, 78, 196
Classical cottage 158
Classical Revival style 26, 66
Clearihue Building 223
Cloverdale School 131
Clow, C. H. 300
CMHC 208
CNIB Building 17
Coast Salish 9, 245
Cochrane, Andrew 50
Cochrane, C. C., House 248
Cole Island 236, 237, 278
Coles Bay 245
Coles, Arthur M., House 176
Collegiate Gothic style 77
Colonial Administration Building 18, 46, 126
Colonial Bungalow style 130, 158, 161, 257, 258, 259
Colonial Government 126, 203
Colonial Metropole Hotel 41
Colonial Revival style 249
Colonial School 202
Colquitz Jail and Prison Farm 262
Columbia River 245
Colville, Andrew 273
Colwood 271, 272
Colwood Community Hall 281
Colwood Farm Dairy 273
Colwood Municipal Hall 286
Colwood Women's Institute 281
Commonwealth Games 232
Commonwealth Housing Villages 232, 233
Communications Building 223
Compton Wynyates 280
Confederation Square 47, 138
Congregational Church 66
Conservation Areas 124
Constance Cove 234
Constructivist style 225
Cooper, James 271
Cooper, Tanner Associates 291
Copeman, Gordon, House 192
Corbusier, Charles-Edouard Le 132, 133, 206, 208, 227, 222
Cornett Building 226
Cotswold cottage 265
Cotton, Peter 25, 28, 33, 68, 91, 97, 142, 169, 170, 204, 273, 274
Country Gothic style 142
Coupland, Clark James 298
Cowichan 10
Cox, Arthur A. 68, 69, 73, 100
CPR 100, 128, 175, 189, 210, 250
CPR steamboat terminal 20, 123

Craftsman style 249, 259
Craftsman, The 172
Craigdarroch Castle 128, 135, 146, 191
Craigdarroch Residences 225
Craigflower Farm 284
Craigflower Manor 17, 202, 250, 252, 273
Craigflower School House 274
CRD Housing Corporation 107
Cridge Memorial Hall 31
Cridge, Reverend Edward 30, 127
Crown Colony of British Columbia 142
Crystal Gardens 16, 17, 20, 73, 74, 101
Crystal Palace 11
Cullin, H. J. R. 131, 183
Cunningham Building 228
Curtis, W. R. H. 224
Customs House 105, 202
Cutter and Malgrem 301
Cutter, K. K. 301
D'Ambrosio, Frank M. 293
Daily British Colonist 147
Dalhousie Bungalow 173
Daniels, A. M., House 255
Darling and Pearson 181
Dat, Lim 113
Davie, Dr. J. C. 149
Davie, Honourable Theodore, Chief Justice 91
Davis, A. J. 31
Day, Harry 250
Daycare Complex, UVic 232
De Cosmos, Amor 147
de Hoog D'Ambrosio Rowe Architects 25, 217, 218, 293, 305
de Hoog, Peter 25, 293
Deco style 70, 79, 83, 224, 243, 265; Egyptoid 195
Deluge Fire Company Hall 31
Demers, Bishop Modeste 29, 139
Denny, R. & H., House 200
Department of Defence 223
Dept. Public Works 198, 202
Desjardins, Margaret and Romeo, House 266
Detention Barracks 243
Devey, George 21, 162
Di Castri, John 17, 23, 25, 51, 82, 85, 200, 201, 206, 221, 222, 223, 227, 230, 267, 294
Dickens, Charles 198
Dickson Campbell & Co. Building 27
Diocese of British Columbia 198
Doane Building 40
Dockyard 236, 238
Dodd, Capt. Charles and Grace, House 140
Dodd, J. H. and Son 297
Doll, Neale Staniszkis 105
Dominion Bank 78
Dominion Custom House 31, 72
Dominion Dept. Public Works 262
Dominion Hotel 39
Domonion Astrophysical Observatory 262
Don Vaughan Associates 138, 221
Donahue, J. D. 11
Donovan, J. P. 294
Dorisy, C. E. 71

Douglas Building 47
Douglas, Sir James 9, 22, 46, 131, 141, 271, 299
Downing, Andrew Jackson 18, 30, 135, 140, 141
Downs Archambault 214, 285, 303
Downs, Barry 23, 223, 227
Driard Hotel 102
Driard, Sosthenes 103
Drysdale, W. F. 192
Duaney, Andres 251
Duck Building 42
Duff, Sir Lyman P. 129; Residence 168
Dufferin, Earl of 120
Dunelm Village 210
Dunlop, James and Annie, House 195
Dunn, Robert 158
Dunsmuir Lodge 268
Dunsmuir family 39; James 134, 135, 165; Joan 147; Robert 9, 37, 128, 135, 147; Robin 166
Duntz Head (Naval Dockyard) 278
Dyer, John, House 253
Earle Building 56
Eastern Colonial style 22
Eastern Vernacular Revival style 22
Eastlake style 37
Eaton's Centre 102
Eclectic Victorian style 107
Edwardian bungalow style 174
Edwardian Classical style 27, 58, 63, 64, 71, 92, 105, 118, 119, 163, 177, 182, 184, 185, 189, 195, 260
Edwardian Commercial Classicism 107, 197
Edwardian Italianate style 67, 70, 113
Edwardian Neoclassical style 80
Edwardian Arts & Crafts style 260
Elizabethan Vernacular Revival style 21
Elk Lake Valley 257
Ella, Capt. Henry 27
Ellesmere 151
Elliott Building 224
Elliott, Charles 43, 222, 269
Elwood, Watkins, C. 265
Emerson House 277
Emmons, Don 221
Empire Hotel and Restaurant 95
Empress Hotel 16, 17, 20, 55, 60, 73, 100, 137, 214, 246
Eng & Wright 208
Engineering Laboratory Wing 231
Engineering Office Building 231
English Arts & Crafts style 250, 260, 261, 266
English Gothic Revivalism 162
English Queen Anne style 30
Episcopalian Church 66
Eric Barker Architects 105, 108, 216, 217
Erickson Massey Architects 221, 228, 291
Erickson, Arthur 23, 208, 214, 230, 294
Esquimalt and Nanaimo Railway 96, 134, 156, 189, 271; Roundhouse 213
Esquimalt 17, 18, 25, 26, 132, 135, 234, 272; Harbour 271, 278; Lagoon 279; Municipal Hall 196
Ewart, A. C. 54, 294
Exposition Internationale des Arts 194

325

Expressionism 98
Expressionist style 150, 227, 229
Eyre, Wilson 171

Faculty of Law 229
Fagerberg, Bertha and Oscar, House 261
Fairfield Block 68
Fairfield Farm 127, 141
Fairfield 25, 129, 131, 164, 259
Fairhome 149
Fan Tan Alley 110, 112, 113,118
Farewell, M. S. 70
Fell & Co. Building 32
Fernwood 131
Festival of Britain Architecture 206
Finch & Finch 187
Finch, Lewis, House 187
Finch, Perry 187
Fine Arts Building 231
Finlayson Building 33, 111
Finlayson House 250
Finlayson, Roderick 33, 112, 271; House 191
First Baptist Church 98
First Church of Christ Scientist 72
First Island Financial Building 106
First Presbyterian Church 69
Fisgard Lighthouse 17, 275, 278
Fisher and Wilson 38
Fisher Building 191
Fisher, Elmer H. 36, 311, 294
Fiske, J. W. 46
Fleischauer, Gary 293, 295, 309
Flemming, G. R., House 198
Florence, Italy 185
Foo Hong Building 119
Foote, George, Dunhan & C. H. Wallwork 72
Forrest, Vera, Levy 265
Fort Kamloops 139
Fort Langley 271
Fort Rodd Hill 236, 277
Fort Victoria 12, 17, 126, 139, 191
Fort Victoria Properties Ltd. 123
Foul Bay Point 130
Foundation Group 124
Four Mile House 284
Fox & Berrill 114
Fox, Cecil Croker 21, 192, 300
Fox, Percy 22, 70, 263
Frame, D. C. 62, 78, 79, 81, 99, 119, 131, 164
Francis, Charles 21
Fraser Canyon 252
Fraser River 109, 245
French Baroque style 30
Freschi, Bruno 293
Friedman House 210
Friends of Government House 204
Frontier Georgian style 252

Gaboury, Etienne 298
Galletly, A. J. C. 154
Galletly, Alice 170
Gallicher, House 129
Galliher, William 182
Galloping Goose Park Corridor 290

Galpin Block 36
Garden City 265
gardens, City of 134-38
Gardiner, William Frederick K. 81, 265
Gardner, W. W. 177
Garesche, Green & Co. 150
Garyali, Shiv K. 295
Gate of Harmonious Interest 110, 120
Gee Tuck Tong Benevolent Association 114
George Jay Elementary 131
George, Danny and Julia, House 284
Georgia Basin 245
Georgian style 140, 237, 279, 274; Revival style 43, 166, 168, 175, 182, 184, 187, 204, 241, 285; Vernacular style 273, 276
Gibson, George S. 249, 295
Gibson, Robert and Sara, House 166
Gillain Manor 268
Gillam, W. C. F. 137, 189
Gillespie, George 143
Gillet & Johnson 87
Gillingham, Henry H. 263
Girls Collegiate School 142
Glenlyon 162, 191
Glinz Lake Cabin 281
Godwin, E. W. 177
Golden Gate 74
Goldsworthy, Ray 295
Gonzales Hill 235
Goodall House 284
Gordon Head 24, 131
Gordon Head Army Camp 220, 230
Gordon Head Campus 24, 191, 223, 258
Gordon Head Improvement Society 194
Gordon Head Residences 229
Gore and MacGregor 185
Gore, Arthur, Residence 185
Gore, Thomas S. 163
Gorge Waterway 132, 133, 134, 135, 217, 261, 273, 290; Park 137
Gothic Revival style 67, 70, 153, 159, 187, 236, 280
Gotter, Henri 71
Government House 129, 135, 138, 202; Foundation 204
Goward, A. T. 163
Gower, Chris 24
Grace Episcopal Cathedral 76
Grace Mansion 285
Grand Pacific Hotel 94
Grand Trunk Pacific Railroad 184, 304
Grant and Lineham 68
Grant Block 280
Grant, Walter Colquhoun 271
Graving Dock and Pump House 237
Gray, Alexander Blair 144
Gray, Andrew 151
Gray, Thomas 143
Great West Life Assurance Co. 188
Greater Victoria Centennial Society 227
Greater Victoria Public Library 99
Greater Victoria School District 156, 201, 218
Green & Green 186
Green Ways 288

Green, A. A. 38, 128, 150, 154
Green, E. E. 184
Green, Elmer 262
Green, F. W. 202
Green, Frederick Walter 298
Greenbelt Policy 288
Greene Brothers 186
Griffith, Henry Sandham 64, 65, 68, 187, 298; Residence 187
Grimm's Carriage Factory 97
Grimm, William 97
Guard House 236, 242
Gutmann, Marianne 266
Gyppeswyk 150
H. Bloomfield, Stained and Leaded Glass 292
Haddington Island 47, 55
Hafer Machine Co. Building 62
Hall Building 55
Hall, Rev. John 70
Hall, Robert 22
Hallmark Society 170, 174
Halpern Graduate Students Centre 232
Hambleton, David H. 222, 298, 308
Hamilton, F., House 165
Hamsterley Farm Water Tower 223
Hanna's Undertaking Parlour 58
Hanna, W. J. 58
Hanzlik, J. 198
Harbourside 217; Coast Hotel 217
Hargreaves, L. W. 65, 118, 193
Harman, J., House 168
Harris and Hargreaves 36
Harris Green 107
Harris, Dennis 28
Harrison Associates 280
Harrison, E., House 165
Harrison, Eli 32, 298
Harrison, R. E. 265
Harrison, Richard and Constance, House 265
Hart Building Livery Stables 112
Harvard, Mass. 154
Hatley Park for James and Laura Dunsmuir 135, 136, 137, 165, 258, 279, 282
Hawthorn, Mansfield Towers 64, 99
Hayes, Arthur and Matilda 162
Hayward, Charles 69; House 148
HBC 130, 135, 139, 140, 145
Helmcken House 129, 139
Helmcken, Dr. J. D. 188
Helmcken, Dr. J. S. 51, 139
Helmcken, James, House 188
Helmcken, Mrs. J. D. 165
Henderson, William 262
Henson, Fred J. 192
Herald Building 119
Herbert Burbridge 263
Heritage Advisory Committee 124
Heritage Building Foundation 170
Heritage Canada Foundation 93, 123
Heritage Conservation Act 123
Heritage Conservation Branch 124
Heritage Registry 124
Hesket 172

Hewett, H. F. 161; House 161
Hickman Tye Hardware 261
Hickman, Harry 222
Higgins, David W. 128, 146
High Tech style 25, 106, 210, 212, 216, 218, 228, 231, 287
High Victorian Gothic Revival 43
High Victorian 91, 135
Highlands 271, 272
Hills, Bishop George 30, 66
Hillside Shopping Centre 209
Hindley, W. J. 66
Hing, Tong Ork On 111
Hochelaga 154
Hodgson, Alan 17, 49, 23, 25, 67, 85, 87, 204, 205, 207, 222, 226, 297; Residence 206
Holabird and Roche 67
Holden, Charles 80
Holland Point 127
Hollingsworth, Fred 230
Holovsky Baxter Mansfield 292, 297
Holovsky Whitfield Piets 297
Holovsky, Ladislav 211, 297
Holy Trinity Church 282
Home Lumber and Building Supplies 208
Hong Kong 109
Hongkong Bank of Canada 99
Hook Sin Tong Building 117
Hooper & Watkins 57, 58, 59, 62, 116, 171
Hooper, Samuel 297
Hooper, Thomas 19, 28, 29, 38, 41, 42, 54, 56, 63, 67, 77, 95, 104, 113, 116, 135, 152, 153, 180, 186, 189, 192, 297; Residence 186
Horton, Hoult 67
Horwood & White 71
Hospital Stores Building 239
Hotel Douglas 65
Hotel Grand Pacific 105
Hotson Bakker 293
Howard, Ebenezer 177
Hoy Sun Ning Young Benevolent Association 111
Huang Caves 120
Hudson's Bay Company 9, 10,17, 33, 51, 65, 66, 126, 147, 177, 191, 234, 245, 246, 252, 263, 271, 274; Department Store 71, 106
Hudson's Bay Company *Colwood Farm* 273
Hughes Baldwin, Architects 218
Hulbert Group 217
Human & Social Development Building 230
Humber, Maurice 148
Hume, Cyril 250
Humphries, Kathleen and Seldon, House 167
Hunt, Henry and Tony 101, 222, 226
Hunter, Joseph 145
Huntingdon Manor Inn 209
hydro-stone 247

IBI Group 102, 105
ICL Plant Cottages 249
ICL Works Manager's House 249
Iechninihl 162
Illahie 174
Imperial Bank of Commerce 79
Imperial Oil Gas Station 17

327

Imrie, Ruth 287
Inglehurst 157
Inner Harbour 20, 121, 290
Interfaith Chapel 230
International Modernism 24
International Style 80, 205, 231
Iron Church 11
Irvin Kew Architecture Inc. 100
Island Arts & Crafts Society 137
Italianate style 94, 95, 113, 148, 158, 210, 237;
  Commercial style 28; Cottage style 141; Villa style 140

Jack Davis Building 106
Jackson, Richard and Mary 170
Jacobean style 204; Tudor Revival style 154
Jacobsen, Captain 155
James and James 24, 63, 81, 142, 164, 188, 196, 298
James and Savage 168
James and Spurgin 195
James Bay 29, 74, 121, 126, 139
James Yates Building 27
James, Antoni 298
James, Douglas 80, 81, 129, 134, 145, 165, 298, 305
James, Percy Leonard 1878-1970 20, 22, 73, 74, 129, 163, 165, 167, 182, 184, 193, 194, 197, 198, 223, 298, 304, 305, 308, 309
Japan 136
Jawl Industries Ltd. 208
Jazz Deco style 105
Jeffrey's Clothing 10
Jekyll, Gertrude 136, 250
Jenkins, Margaret, School 131
Jensen Group 225
Jensen, Darrel L. 35, 269, 299
Jervis Inlet 47
Jockey Club 145
John Neilson Associates 100
Johns General Store Cottages 263
Johns, Clarence 263
Johns, J. H., House 198
Johnson and Spurgin 24
Johnson Street Bridge 73
Johnson, J. G. 166
Jones Building 69
Jones Design Corp 106
Jones, Dr. O. M. 271
Jones, Frederick, House 175
Jones, T. J. 149
Jordan River 271
Joseph, Floyd 222
Journey Middle School 287
Joy, Allen Bruce 46
Juan de Fuca Strait 128, 130, 144, 190
Junior Ranks Club 241

Kaiserhof Hotel 67
Kaw, Lee Mong 113
Keay, John 25, 38, 149, 153, 233
Keith, J. C. M. 69, 75, 119, 131, 180, 247, 257, 299
Kellie, James and Margaret, House 260
Kennedy House 259

Kennedy, Jenny Foster 258
Kennedy, Sir Arthur 203
Kent Apartments 67
Kertland, Douglas L. 78
Kew, Irvin H. 267, 269, 299, 309
Kinemacolour Theatre 70
King, C. R. 159
King, Charles 10, 129, 186
Kishata, Isaburo 137
Knights of Pythias 42
Knipple & Morris 237
Knot Garden 85
Kobe, Japan 150
Korner, Theo 194
Kresge Department Store 23, 104
Kung Shaw Society 115
Kwagiulth 101
Kwan, Herbert H. 215, 299, 309
Kwong Lee & Co. 111

L'Exposition Internationale des Arts Decoratifs et Industriel Modernes 195
Labourchere 140
Lai, David C. 120
Lake Cowichan 221
Lam, Lieutenant-Governor Dr. David C. 221
Lam, M. 88, 120
Lamb, Charles M. 184
Lampman, Peter Secord, House 163
Lampson Street School 189
Landsberg, F. 180
Langford 17, 271, 272
Langford, Captain Edward E. 273
Lansdowne 131
Lansdowne Residences 228
Lantzius, John 138, 221
Laquechier, Jacques 140
Laritz, James 136
Laurel Point 121
Law Chambers 91, 93
Law Courts 127, 138
Lawrence Halprin & Associates 138, 220
Laycock, Rev. E. P. 76
Layritz Nurseries 261
Layritz, Richard, House 254
Lazere Building 191
Le Courbusier, Charles Edouard 132, 133, 208
Leau,-Wel-New School 269
Lee, Yan Yow 63
Lee Benevolent Association Building 117
Lee Block 116
Lee Cheong and Lee Weong Building 114
Lee Cheong Building 63
Lee, Woy 63
Lee, Yanyou 116
Leiser Building 54
Leiser, Simon 54; House 182
Lemmens, Bishop 43
Leonard Buttress 21
Leslie, H. H. 146
Lester, Allan 222
Letchworth 177
Lettice and Sears Building 103, 104
Lever House 83

328

Levinson, Benjamin Bryce 299, 309
Lew Chew Fan Building 111
Lewis & Co. 39
Lewis, Richard 300
Liberty of London 55
Light House Saloon 96
Lim and Wong Building 118
Lim Bang 65, 116, 118
Lim Dat Building 116
Lim Dat/Wong Soon Lim Building 113
Lim, Wong Soon 113
Linaker, E. H., House 255
Lindbergh, Charles A. 76
Lionel, A. 205
Lockwood and Mawson 19, 304
Lok Kwun Free School 112
London 38, 80, 206
London Block 42
London Education Authority Schools 156
London Hotel 42
London Saloon 42
Loo Tai Cho Building 113
Lord and Burnham Company 16, 74
Lorimer, William, House 174
Loring P. Rexford 10
Lort, Ross A. 22, 166, 168, 189, 197, 250, 257, 300, 301; House 189
Lowe, Alan 107, 309
Lowe, Skene, House 159
Lubor & Trupka 269
Lum Look Building 112
Luney Brothers 42, 70, 190, 193
Luney, Walter 192
Lutyens, Edwin 21, 101, 66, 177, 260
Mable Carriage Works 62
Mable, W. J. 62
Macaulay Point 234
Macaulay, William James 152
MacDonald Block 89
Macdonald House 205
MacDonald, W. J. 89
MacIntosh, Charles Rennie 63, 260
MacLaurin Building 226
Maclean, A. V. 280
Maclure & Lort 166
Maclure & Rattenbury 202, 203, 292
Maclure and Savage 23
Maclure, John 300
Maclure, Samuel 21, 53, 59,113, 129, 135, 136, 137, 155, 157, 158, 161, 163-65, 168, 171, 172-75, 180, 181, 182, 184, 185, 187, 188, 189, 191, 192-95, 203, 257, 258, 263, 279, 296, 298, 300, 304, 307
Macauley Point 278
Magoon, M. A. and Hopkins, E. C. 298
Mahon Building 60
Mahon, Edward 60
Mahon, McFarland & Proctor 60
Main Post Office and Federal Building 81
Mallandaine, Edward 18, 19, 135, 143, 150, 253, 277, 301
Maltwood Art Museum and Gallery 229
Maltwood, Katharine Emma 222, 265

Mansard style 155, 202
Mansfield, Holovsky 233
Miraloma for Hon. W. C. Nichol 248
Marech, Vernon 46
Marega, Charles 295, 301
Mariner's landing 215
Maritime Museum of British Columbia 88, 91
Market Square 93, 100, 123
Marshall Goldsworthy Garyali 231
Marshall Goldsworthy 100, 208, 230, 250, 286, 295
Marshall, Donovan 222, 295, 302
Martin, Alexis Residence 171
Martin, Mungo 51
Mason, C. Dubois 164
Masonic Temple 32
Massey, Geof 294
Maurice, Claude 27, 209, 268, 302
Mawson, Thomas 136, 258
Maybeck, Bernard 73, 186
Mayfair 208
Mayhew, Elza 222
Mayhew, Logan, House 200
Maynard Building 40
Maynard Court 97
McCandless, A. G. 56
McCarter Nairne Architects 97, 199
McCarter, J. Y. 298
McCulloch & Harvey 197
McDonald's Restaurant 107
McElroy, G. A. 23, 104
McGill Residences 229
McGregor, J. H. 92
McKenzie, Kenneth 273
McKim, Mead and White 169, 304
McKinnon Building 228
McPherson Library 85, 225
McPherson Theatre 17
McPherson, Thomas 87
McPhillips, Judge A. E. 129
Meadlands 137
Mears and Stainbank 76
Medieval Revival style 173
Melrose Paint and Decorating Co. 304
Memorial Arena 17, 81, 106
Memorial Pavillion 199
Menzies Street Drill Hall 47
Mercer, William and Gertrude 192
Merchants Bank 60
Merino, Luis 93
Merrick, Paul 24
Mesher, George Charles 64, 65, 156, 302
Metchosin 135, 271, 272; School House 276
Methodists 66
Metropolitan, The 108
Metropolitian Methodist Church 19, 38, 66, 154
Michaud, Fr. Joseph 29
Midland Way 177
Miles, Elizabeth 141
Mills, Jordon 180
Millstream Valley 271
Milne Building 95
Milne, Alexander Roland 95
Ministry of Forests building 100

Ministry of Mines 106
Mission style 265; Furniture 21
Mitchel, T. G., House 157
Modern Picturesque Rationalism 241
Modern Rationalist style 226
Moderne style 23, 24, 60, 78, 79, 80, 81, 96, 194, 196, 198, 199, 223, 224, 240, 243, 265, 267; Streamline style 80
Monterey Elementary 131, 183
Moore & Moody 71
Moore, Campbell 189
Moran, Freda and John, House 267
Morehead House 161
Moretti, Victor 302
Morley's Soda Water Factory 35
Morrell, Leon 140
Morris & Co. of London 279
Morris, E. A. Tobacconist 42
Morris, J. W., House 164
Mortimer & Reid 46
Moss Cottage for James and Mary Walsh 275
Mount Baker 160, 163
Mount Douglas 131
Mount Edward's Apartment 184
Mount Newton Community Care Facility 269
Mount St. Mary Hospital 198
Mount Tolmie 131, 235
Muir, A. Maxwell 10, 11,18, 26, 27, 35, 91, 154, 302
Muir, John 271, 275
Muirhead and Justice 138, 221
Muirhead, James, House 171
Muller & Sturn 156
Municipal Affairs Building 105
Munitions Magazines 237
Munn, A. A. 129
Musson Cattell 207; Mackay 107, 303
Musson, Frank 83, 303

Naden 234, 236, 240; Naval Hospital 239
Nairne, Charles Robert Residence 154
Nanaimo 147
Nash, John 38, 116
Nation, Frederick Residence 188
National Electric Tramway and Light Company 135
National Historic Park 278
National Historic Site 274, 275
National Trust Building 78
Native Sons and Native Daughters of British Columbia 274
Naval Cemetary 135
Naval Dockyard 143
Naval Stores Officer, House 236
Needham, Hon. Sir Joseph 141
Neilson, John 287
Nelson Island 47
Neobrutalist style 83, 228
Neoclassical style 72
Neoclasssical Revival style 73
Neoedwardian style 102
Neogeorgian style 22, 145, 173, 263
Nesbitt, Samuel 128

Neutra, Richard 305
New England Hotel 41, 44
New Westminster 36
New York 83
Newbury, C. W., House 171
Newcastle Island 60, 76
Newcombe, Dr. C. F. Residence 175
Newcombe, William Arnold 175
Newton, Ernest A. 308
Nichol, Hon. W. C. 136, 175, 248
Nichols and Di Castri 82
Nichols, F. W. 294
Niemeyer, Oscar 85
Nixon Block dormitory 280
Nixon, Mike 268
Nootka Court 98
Norfolk Lodge 257
Norman, C. B. K. 305
Norris, George A. 99, 221, 225
North Dairy Pumping Station 169
North Park Manor 97
North Saanich 245
Norwich Plan 85
Nuttgens, J. E. 76

O'Reiley, Caroline Agnes 141
O'Reilly, Hon. Peter 140; House 135
Oak Bay 25, 129, 131, 135, 136, 160, 259; Golf Club 161; Golf Course 130; Marina 206; Municipal Hall 23; Native Plant Garden 136; Secondary School 131; Municipal council 161
Oaklands 131
Ocean Pointe Resort Hotel 214
Ocean Tower 214
Odeon Theatre 80
Officers' Quarters 242
Officers' Ward 239
Official Community Plan 125
Ogden Point 93, 121, 127, 146, 235
Old Town Victoria 25, 124, 214
Oldfield, John and Emma 257
Oldfield, R., House 247
Olmsted 130; Bros. 136, 177
Olympic Coast Range Mountains 128, 130, 135, 144
Olympic Peninsula, Washington State 246
On Hing and Brothers Store 111
On Hing Company 115
On the Park 217
Orchard Gate for Ada and Norman Yarrow 266
Orchard House for Roy Brethour 248
ORCHARD HOUSE APARTMENTS 208
Oregon 273
Oriental Hotel 11, 35, 41
Orrock, J. W. 61
Our Lady of the Assumption Church 137

Pacific Club 65
Painter, W. S. 61
Palladian style 217
Palladio, Andrea 80
Palm Springs 77
Palmolive Building 76

Panama Pacific International Exhibition, San Francisco 73
Pantages Theatre 87
Parfitt Brothers 76
Park Tower 214
Parks Canada 236
Parkwood Manor 216
Parliament Buildings 19, 47, 73, 121, 138, 171, 214
Parliamentary Precinct 46, 123
Parsons, Wm. & Sons 303
Partridge, Bruce 228
Pat Bay 137
Patio Court 166
Patkau Architects 216, 270, 305
Patricia Bay 245; "Aerodrome" 246; Highway 290
Patterson, William 70, 176
Paul Building 191
Paul Merrick Architects 29, 108, 292
Pauquachin 245
Payless Gas Station 214
Payne, Caleb, House 259
Pazzi Chapel 63
Pearse, Benjamin William (B. W. Pearse) 10
Pearse, J. B. 303
Pearson, Lester B., College of the Pacific 285
Pease, Letitia and Algernon, Farm 223
Pemberton Block 65, 129
Pemberton Memorial Chapel 180; Operating Theatre 157
Pemberton, J. D. 10, 157, 303
Pemberton, Mrs. J. D. 181
Pendray's Soap Works 10
Pendray, W. J. 135; House 156
Peninsula Condominiums 215
Perrault & Mesnard 43, 294
Petch, Dr. Howard 221; Building 231
Peters, Hon. Frederick 161
Peterson & Lester 90, 91, 228, 230, 267
Peterson, Carl E. 232, 232, 303
Peterson, Margaret 83, 225
Petro-Canada Service Station 219
Philadelphia 148, 171
Phoenix Brewing Company 96
Phoenix Theatre 230
Picturesque style 24, 31, 32, 42, 43, 55, 61, 73, 135, 153, 155, 156, 162, 171, 174, 176, 217, 252, 256, 279; Collegiate Gothic style 250; Eclecticism 214; French Gothic (Chateauesque) style 147; Gothic Revival style 142; Italianate style 147
Piercy, John, House 256
Pierre Timp's *Dutch Gardens* 266
Pinchon & Lenfesty Building 40
Pinehurst 152
Pineo, Avard and Eleanor, House 193
Ping Shan Hall 120
Pioneer Square 26
Pirelli Building, Milan 98
Pither and Leiser 37; Building 56
Pitts and Hall Buildings 34
Pitts, Sidney 35
PMQs, Artificers' and Warrant Officers' Quarters 238

Point Ellice Bridge 134; House 140, 250
Pollen, Mayor Peter 122
Polson & Siddall 202, 309
Polson House 209
Ponti, Geo 98
Poole, George 268
Pooley, E. F., House 195
Poon, Billington, Gardner 60
Pope, Abraham, House 253
Porter Block 57
Porter, Arthur 17
Porter, R. & Sons 174
Porter, Robert J. 57; House 158
Portland 9, 10, 103
Poseidon 73
Post Modern style 25, 72, 78, 104, 105, 106, 107, 108, 214, 215, 216, 217, 219, 224, 233, 280, 287
Post Office 72, 79
Povey, Arthur and Ethel, House 261
Powers, Lizzie and Mary, House 278
Prairie Inn 255
Prairie School style 186, 189, 268
Presbyterians 66
Price, Bruce 61
Priestly, Joshua and Louisa, House 259
Prior, E. G. 128
Prison and Warders' Residence 238
Privates' Quarters 239
Producer's Rock & Gravel Co. 175
Progressive Movement 24, 132; style 131, 132, 202, 207, 227
Promise Block 58
Promise, Oscar 58
Pronger, Dr. Ralph 202
Prospect Place 160
Protestant Orphanage 19
Provincial Archives 50
Provincial Capital Commission 30, 74, 133, 211, 288
Provincial Department of Public Works 78, 224, 285
Provincial Museum (Royal British Columbia Museum) 121
Public Library 19
Puget Sound Agricultural Company 126, 273, 275

Quadra School 131
Quadra Street Cemetary 26
Quarantine Station Chapel 282
Quebecois Recollet churches 30
Queen Anne style 53, 59, 62, 127, 131, 154, 156, 157, 163, 166, 169, 171, 174, 176, 180, 183, 191, 194, 210, 211, 214, 216, 254, 256, 283
Queen's Port and Pebble Beach Condominiums 214

Rainbow Mansion Apartments 79
Rambusch Co., NY 43
Ranft, Eric 106
Ranger Station 285
Rappahannock 181
Rationalism 228

Rationalist International style 225
Rattenbury, Francis Mawson 14, 19, 21, 47, 54, 57, 59, 60, 69, 73, 74, 78, 90, 91, 92, 93, 100, 113, 129, 135, 160, 161, 162, 164, 166, 168, 169, 171, 176, 178, 182, 186, 187, 188, 192, 202, 203, 210, 279, 298, 302, 309, 304, 307
Rattenbury, Mrs. Florence, House 165
Redfern, C. E. 86
Reformed Episocpal Church 30
Regents Park 105, 146
Reid, James Murray 89
Reid, James T., House 184
Rennaissance Revival style 27, 87, 149, 190
Resthaven Country Club 248
Rexford, Loring P. 68
Rhone & Iredale 228
Richardson, George Residence 185, 195
Richardson, Henry Hobson 19, 38, 41, 154, 156, 169, 186
Richardsonian Romanesque style 38, 56, 57, 61, 90, 91, 95, 99
Richardsonian Shingle style 204
Richmond Pavillion 199
Ridgeway, R. 131
Rithet Building 11, 89
Rithet, Robert Patterson 37, 89
Robert Ward and Company 53
Roberts, Cecil, House 172
Robillard, Raoul 136, 258
Robson, Hon. John 145
Rochfort & Sankey 70
Rochfort, W. D'O. 161, 183
Rockland 130, 136; Avenue 10; District 126; Estates 135; Plan 129
Rococo Revival style 26
Rodd Hill 234
Roger's Chocolate Shop 19, 53, 57
Rogers Elementary School 218
Rohani Building 98
Roman Catholic Bishop's Palace 57, 59
Romanesque Revival style 28, 105, 237
Romantic Historicism 82
Rome 185
Rosemead 181
Roslyn 151
Ross Bay 146; Cemetary 26, 135, 143
Ross, John 191
Rowe, Christopher 305
Royal Bank 69; Building 63
Royal British Columbia Museum 47, 49, 138, 139
Royal Canadian Navy Training Centre 280
Royal Colwood Golf Course 280
Royal Engineers 9, 234
Royal Institute of British Architects 76
Royal Jubilee 157
Royal Jubilee Hospital 180, 193, 195, 199, 265
Royal Navy 234
Royal Oak 25, 133; Burial Park 264; Community Hall 258; Crematorium Chapel and Retort 264; Inn 261, 264; Municipal Hall 257; School House 254
Royal Quays East 214; West 214
Royal Roads 280

Royal Trust Building 83
Royal Victoria Yacht Club 179
Royal Victorian Theatre 70
Rudolph, Paul 225
Rustic style 267
S. J. Willis High School 131
Saanich 23, 132; Agricultural Fair Grounds 270; Indian School Board 269; Municipal Hall 207, 267; Municipality of 130, 132; Peninsula 150, 245, 290
Saanichton 245; Fair Grounds 270
Sabiston, Carol 229
Sage, H. 22
Saint Stephen's Church 252
Salgo, Andres 83
Salish 271; big houses 269
Saltspring Island 161
Salvation Army Citadel 80; Building 99
Sam, Lum 112
San Francisco, California 9, 10, 11, 74, 76, 89, 109, 129, 145, 148, 186
San Jose, California 58
Sand's Memorial Chapel 77
Sanders, George 311
Sandhurst 162
Sangster, George, House 182
Satellite Fish Co. Building 249
Saturna 91
Saunders Building 228
Savage, Hubert and Alys, House 261
Savage, Hubert 81, 131, 163, 167, 197, 250, 261, 264, 284, 298, 305
Savery, Robert 46, 137, 204
Saxon & Snell 74, 298
Sayward Building 64
Sayward, J. A. 64
Scarf, Oscar, House 277
Schaefer, William 148
Schnoter, Andrew 151
schools 131
Schuhuum 155
Schultze, F. A. 205
Schwengers, Conrad, House 162
Science and Engineering Building 231
Scott & Peden Building 95; Warehouse Complex 70
Scott, J. C. 88
Scott, M. H. Baillie 22, 172, 189
Scott, Sir Walter 152
Scott, Thomas Seaton 31
SDW Architects 57
Sea Point House 247
Seabird Island Salish school 216
Seaside, Florida 251
Seattle 75, 87
Second Empire style 31, 32, 86, 105, 149, 155
Sedgewick Building 227
Seibner, Herbert 51
Selkirk Waterfront Project 217
Selkirk Waters 25
Semeyn, W. J. 196
Sen, Dr. Sun Yat 117
Senior Citizens' Centre 85

Sergeants' Mess 242
Sever Hall, Harvard 19, 154
Seymen, W. J. 24
Shadbolt, Doug 23
Shady Creek Church 256
Shamrock Motel 205
Sharp Thompson Berwick & Pratt 82, 200
Sharpe, G. L. T. 300
Shaw, Richard Norman 21, 162, 169, 304
Sheldon Williams, R. 249
Shelin 164
Sheringham Light and Keeper's House 283
Shingle style 131, 158, 162, 166, 170, 186, 187, 188, 194, 207, 210, 223, 247, 261
Shon Yee Benevolent Association 117
Siddall Dennis Warner 82, 98, 223, 225, 228, 229, 268, 280
Siddall, Dennis & Associates 227
Siddall, R. W. Associates 25, 87, 225
Siddall, Robert 85, 86, 205, 220, 225, 305
Sidney 136, 245; Post office 250; Roofing Co. 246
Sidney-by-the-Sea 246
Signal Hill 235, 236, 238
Signals Building 243
Simpson, Ian 162
Simpson, Jeanne 221
Singh, Sporan and Sundher, Chancil, House 202
Sisters of St. Ann 51, 62, 143
Sitkum Lodge 214
Six Mile House 271
Skidmore Owings and Merril 83
Slater, T. H. 181
Slater, W. 66
Smeeth, Roger 209
Smith and Williams 147
Smith, Barry (Bas) 25, 107, 233, 305
Smith, F. E. 199
Smith, Mr. and Mrs. F. E., House 200
Solheim for Christian and Haldis Helgesen 281
Somerset House 217
Songhees 211, 290; Indian Reserve 134
Songhees Point Condominiums 214
Sooke 271; Lake 272
Sorby, Thomas C. 18, 21, 129, 205, 305
South Saanich 135; Hotel 252
South Ward School 155
Southgate and Lascelles Block 28
Spanish, The 9
Spanish Revival style 167
Speed, Frederick and Amy 198
Spencer's Castle 187
Sperry, Elmer A. 76
Spokane 87
Spratt, Joseph 37
Spring Ridge Emmanuel Baptist Church 153
Spring Ridge 131
Spring Valley Farm 257
Springside Farm 275
Spurgin & Semeyn 131
Spurgin, K. B. 167, 193, 298
St. Luke's Anglican Church 150
St. John's Anglican Church (Iron Church) 11, 12
St. Joseph's Hospital 30
St. Michael University School 169

St. Andrew's Presbyterian Church 39
St. Andrew's Roman Catholic Cathedral 43, 97
St. Andrew's Anglican Church 247
St. Ann's Academy 29, 123, 137, 253; Gardens 62, 253; School House 139
St. Catharine's Docks warehouses 59
St. George's Hotel 102
St. Gobain Glassworks, Belgium 262
St. James Hotel 69
St. John the Baptist Church 282
St. John the Divine, Yale 252
St. John's Iron Church 66
St. Joseph's Hospital 62
St. Louis College 77
St. Michael and All Angels' Church 253
St. Paul's Garrison Church 236
St. Saviour's Anglican Church 153
Stark, J. 233
Stark, Stuart 160
Station Hotel 95
Stephen's Hotel 256
Stevens, John, House 256
Steward Building 117
Stickley, Gustav 172
Stirling, James 99
Stockdill, C. D. 131
Stone Frigate 240
Strand Hotel 96
Strathcona Hotel 65
Strauss Bascule Bridge Co. 73
Strauss, Joseph 74
Strawberry Vale 260; Elementary School 270; School House 255
Streamlined Moderne style 79, 200
Stuart, Mrs., House 250
Student Union Building 223
Sullivan, Louis H. 53
Sullivanesque 53
Sundance Elementary 131
Sunderland, Maurice 102
Supreme Court Building 88, 90
Surf Motel 205
Sussex Building 108
Sutherland, Ross 166; House 136
Suzhou, China 120
Swan Lake 208
Swartz Bay 248
Sweeney McConnel Building 64
Syme, James 144, 306
Syracuse, New York 172

T'sou-ke people 271
Taiwan 120
Tam King Temple 118
Tate, D'Arcy 184
Taylor, John George 154
Taylor, Lady Stewart 197
Teague, John 10, 11,18, 29, 30, 31, 32, 34, 35, 40, 44, 53, 55, 86, 90, 103, 111, 112, 140, 143, 145, 148, 152, 202, 236, 238, 239, 306
Teidemann, H. O. 33
Telford, Thomas 59
Temple Building 53, 59
Temple Emanuel 28, 105

333

Texada Island 76
The Royal Oak Inn for Colin and Florence Forrest, Vera Levy and David Burnett 265
Theatre Alley 110, 111
Thom, David 105
Thom, Ron J. 82, 285
Thompson, Berwick and Pratt 210, 291
Thompson, C. J. 60
Thompson, Harold and Myra, Farm 263
Thompson, William 252
Thos. Meehan Nurseries, Philadelphia 146
Thunderbird Park 51
Tiarks, J. Gerhard 19, 158, 159, 161, 162, 307
Tiedemann, Hermann Otto 18, 39, 90, 275, 307, 309
Tiger Engine Company 31
Tillicum 131
Times Building 102, 103
Timp, Grace and Pierre, House 266
Tip, Low and Lee Building 113
Tod Inlet 135
Todd, C. F. 129
Todd, Charles 174
Todd, J. H. & Sons 175, 180
Todd, John 129; House 139
Todd, William 180
Tolmie School 131, 183
Tong, Ning Young Yee Hing 111
Toronto Dominion Bank Building 83
Town & Country 208
Townley and Matheson 23, 76
Township of Sidney 246
Trebatha 149
Trehearne Norman Preston & Partners 296
Trend House 201
Trimen, Leonard Buttress 27, 39, 128, 151, 187, 307
Trounce Alley 38
Trounce, Thomas 18, 33, 38, 236
Trutch, Sir Joseph 37, 129, 141
Tsartlip 245
Tsawout 245
Tseycum 245
Tudor Revival style 22, 26, 27, 129, 151, 164, 172, 174, 184, 198, 261, 263, 279
Tugwell, Thomas 41
Tupper, Sir Charles 161
Turner, Beeton and Company Ltd. 34
Turner, John H. 34
Tweedsmuir Mansions Apartments 196
Twin Creek Farm House for Alma and Nels Wiggs 278
Tye Chong Building 94
Tyee Housing Co-operative 214

Ulwin, Eric and Harrriet, House 184
Union Bank Building 69
Union Club of British Columbia 10, 64, 68, 304
Union Hook and Ladder Company 31
Union Iron Works 89
United Church 66
Univeristy of British Columbia 190
University Gardens 231
University Heights 133
University House 228
University of Victoria 24, 133, 191, 220, 265, 267; Faculty Club 251; Gordon Head Campus 220ff.
University School Limited 180
University Centre 229
Uplands 19, 20, 130; Estates Ltd. 23, 129, 136, 177, 179, 304
Upper Harbour 73
Urban Approaches 126

Vallena for Agnes and John Durrance 257
Valparaiso, Chile 234
Vancouver Island Agriculture and Horticulture Society 137
Vancouver Island Power Company 271
Vancouver Island Regional Correctional Centre 262
Vancouver Island Regional Library 250
Vancouver Island Rock and Alpine Garden Society 137
Vancouver, British Columbia 19, 71, 74, 110, 166, 211
Vantreight, Winnifred and Geoffrey, House 193
Vaudreuil, Quebec 29
Vaughan, Don W. 308
Vefra Building 107
Veger Hotel and Station 61
Vereydhen, Charles 29, 128, 135
Vernacular Georgian style 275
Vernon Building 56
Verrinder, Dr. Robert 157
Via Rail Station 100
Viceroy's House, Delhi 101
Vickers, Roy 43
Victoria Airport Terminal Buildings 267
Victoria and Sidney Railway 246, 255
Victoria Brick and Tile Company 17
Victoria Chamber of Commerce 91
Victoria City Hall 86
Victoria Civic Heritage Trust 124
Victoria College 148, 191, 220, 224
Victoria Conference Centre 61, 100
Victoria Conservatory of Music 148
Victoria District Church 127
Victoria Electric Lighting and Railway Company 127, 129; Electric Railway Company 160
Victoria Gas Building 37
Victoria Hallmark Society 121
Victoria Heritage Foundation 124
Victoria High School 132, 183, 202
Victoria Horticulture Society 137
Victoria Hotel 26
Victoria Machinery Depot 93
Victoria Natural History Society 175
Victoria Normal School 137, 189
Victoria Parks Board 136
Victoria Public Library 64
Victoria Roller Flour and Rice Mill 27
Victoria School Board 148
Victoria Theatre 103
Victoria Union Club 68
Victoria West 133, 211

Victorian Gothic style 27; Italianate style 33, 35, 39, 40, 127, 145, 149; Italianate Villa 146; Queen Anne style 21, 151, 152, 157, 214, 232; Romanesque Revival style 55
Victualling Office 240
View Royal 272
Villa Rotunda 73
Ville Radieuse 132
Visual Arts Building 233
Voysey, Charles F. Annesley 21, 63, 169, 184, 191, 250, 260, 300
Vullinghs, Fr. Adrian 30, 137, 253
Waddington Alley 10, 35
Waddington Building 99
Wade Stockdill Armour & Blewett 97, 98, 267
Wade Williams 47, 75, 99, 191, 209, 210, 229, 231, 241, 291
Wade Williams with Young Wright 232
Wade, John H. 23, 85, 222, 308
Wade, Stockdill and Armour 78, 207, 223
Wagg & Hambleton 25, 55, 65, 70, 74, 86, 87, 99, 206, 214, 223, 225, 229, 230, 283, 291, 298, 299, 308
Wagg, Donald 85, 222, 308
Waisman Dewar Grout 216; Carter 280
Walden, C. 166
Walker, Captain RN, House 262
Walker, John and Clare M., House 200
Warburton, W. 157, 173
Ward, Robert 37, 129
Ward, William C. 143
Warfare Training Facility 241
Warner and Swasey Co., Cleveland 262
Warner James Architects 298
Warner, David 309
Warrant Officers' Quarters 278
Warren, Jesse M. 69, 87, 95, 117, 309
Washington 273
Watkins, C. Elwood 19, 77, 116, 117, 118, 131, 132, 183, 192, 195, 264, 297, 298
Watson, Catherine 164
Weiler Bros. Department Store 20, 33, 103
Weiler Building 55
Weiler, John 33
Weiler, Otto 55
Wellington 147
Wenstob, Wayne 33, 98
Wentworth Villa 27
West Coast style 90, 98, 169, 194, 221, 225, 227, 228, 230, 232, 283; Modern Expressionism 251; Modern style 268
West Edmonton Mall 102
West, Prof. William D. 223
Westerby, William 258
Western Communities 271, 290
Western Match Company 199
White, John 309
White, Moresby 248
Whitehead, H. T. 260; House 260
Whiteway, William Tuff 42, 260, 309
Whittaker, W. H. 78, 198, 199, 224, 265, 308
Wilkerson's Jewelry 53
Wilkinson Road Methodist Church 260
Wilkinson, Jack C. S. 51, 85
William Head 282; Correctional Centre 283
Williams, Elizabeth and Terence House 209
Williams, Michael 42, 70
Williams, Terence J. 222, 310
Williams, Waren Heywood 10, 11, 36, 128, 135, 310
Willie's Bakery 36
Willie, G. D. 107
Willis, S. J. School 201
Willows 130; Park 160; School 131
Wilmar 180
Wilson Clothiers 67
Wilson, Biggerstaff Residence 173
Wilson, Goulding H. Residence 186
Wilson, H. G., House 10, 129
Wilson, Joseph 129, 172
Wilson, Levi, House 247
Wilson, Mrs. P. 157
Wilson, Richard Biggerstaff 24, 85, 121, 129, 136
Wilson, W. & J., Building 67
Wilson, William Ridgeway 57, 60, 66, 67, 72, 113, 128, 140, 155, 173, 262, 310
Winch Building 102-04
Winch, R. V. 104
Windhurst 202
Windsor Hotel 13, 26
Windsor Park 130, 135, 160
Windy Oak for Rt. Hon. Mark Kearly 285
Winnipeg 71
Winter, Barbara and Gary, House 268
Wolseley, Sir Garnet 182
Women's Institute 282
Wong, Jan Way 118
Wong, Lee 116
Woodgate, T. 238, 240
Woodlands 140
Woods, Jim, House 188
Woods, William and Dorothy, House 200
Woodside Farm for Ann and John Muir 271, 275, 276
Work Point 242; Barracks 234, 278
Works office 240
World War I 235
World War II 198, 235
Wright & Sanders 27, 28, 38, 70, 140, 141, 142, 234, 252
Wright, Frank Lloyd 21, 82, 186, 189, 267, 202
Wright, John 10, 18, 19, 41, 89, 102, 128, 140, 203, 275, 311
Wurster, Bernardi and Emmons 138, 220

Yale 142
Yangshou 120
Yarrows 237
Yarrows, Sir Alfred 266
Yates Block 34
Yee Fung Toy Tong 114
YMCA 282
Yorkshire Trust Co. 68; Building 100
Yue Shan Society 113

Zebra Designitects 251
Zeidler Roberts 303

335

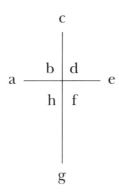

Photo Credits and Notes

Unless otherwise listed here, photos copyright the authors. Copyright reserved as follows: **Ian Baird**: 258 d, f; 192 h, f; 194 b; 197 c; 200 f. **Nick De Caro**: 236 e; 237 h, d; 238; 239 b; 240; 242; 243; 254 d; 255 b, d, f, h; 256 g; 257 b, d; 259; 260; 261; 262; 263; 264; 265; 266; 274; 275; 276; 277; 278; 281; 282 b, d, h; 283 f; 284; 285 a, b, d; 286 g; 287 g. **Al Fry**: 157 h; 159 e; 161; 163 b, d, h; 164 b; 165 d; 166 b; 167 b; 168 b; 169 e; 170 b, h, f; 172 d; 175 b; 180 e; 181 h, e; 182 h; 183 b, e; 184 b, k, d; 186 a; 187 a; 188 b; 189 b, e; 191 a; 192 d; 193 d; 194 d; 195 a; 196 b; 197 a; 198 c; 200 d; 201 e; 202 a; 208 g; 209 d; 216 c, h; 218 e; 269 g. **Ann West**: 247; 248 b, c, d, h; 249 d, e, f, h; 250; 252; 253; 255 g; 256 d; 257 f; 258 a; 267 g; 268 h.

The following are courtesy of: **Alan Hodgson Architect**: 206 g. **Archives of the Anglican Diocese of British Columbia**: 75 d (Christ Church Cathedral, elevation drawing, architect J. C. M. Keith, n.d.). **British Columbia Archives and Records Service**: 12; 13; 14; 16; 29 d (St. Ann's Academy, *ca.* 1871); 46; 47; 52 g; 102 a; 109; 122 c; 127; 128; 130 g; 134; 135; 136; 160; 204. **Butchart Gardens Ltd.**: "Butchart Gardens Residence," 258 g. **Canadian Forces Base Esquimalt**: 234; 235. **City of Victoria Archives**: 11; 87 b (Premiated Design, City Hall, Architect J. Teague, 1878). **Craigdarroch Castle Historical Museum Society**: 147 f. **Fort Rodd Hill, National Historic Site**: 236 b. **Ron Green**: 206 g. **Heritage Building Foundation/City of Victoria, Department of Community Planning**: (**Norm Spanos**) 141 e; 152 e; 156 e; 173 g; (**Frank Fish**) 59 e; 148; 157 e; 159 a; 171 h; 188 g. **University of Victoria, McPherson Library Special Collections**: 15; 31 b (Dominion Customs House, Elevation, architect T. S. Scott, n.d.); (**UVic Photo Services**) 220; 223 d; 224; 225; 226 h, f; 227; 228; 229; 230 e; (**Dane Campbell**) 248 f; 249 b ("Miraloma," elevation, architect S. Maclure, 1925). **Wade Williams Architects**: 67 e; 241 d; 207 d; 209 b; 241 g. **William Head Institution, Correction Services of Canada**: 283 c (View of William Head Quarantine Station, n.d.).

JACKET ART: Plan for the interior of Mrs. A. R. Walsh house, Victoria (1891), architect Samuel Maclure. Courtesy Special Collections, McPherson Library, University of Victoria (ref. V.A.P. 1819), with photo detail from Douglas Franklin photograph of "Pinehurst," 617 Battery Street, James Bay.